Programming in
ANSI C
Second Edition

Comprehensive and Authoritative Computer Books from Tata McGraw-Hill

BASIC

Balagurusamy	:	Programming in BASIC, Third Edition
Gottfried	:	Programming with BASIC, Third Edition
Jain	:	BASIC Programming—With Applications
Oberoi	:	BASIC Made Easy

COBOL

Roy & Ghosh Dastidar	:	COBOL Programming: Including MS-COBOL and COBOL-85, Second Edition
Roy & Ghosh Dastidar	:	COBOL Programming: Problems and Solutions

dBASE III PLUS

Taxali	:	dBASE III PLUS Made Simple: With dBASE IV and FoxBASE+

FORTRAN

Balagurusamy	:	FORTRAN For Beginners: Including FORTRAN 77
Jain & Suri	:	FORTRAN 77 with Applications to Science and Engineering
Ramkumar	:	Programming with FORTRAN 77
Rao	:	Programming in FORTRAN, Second Edition

PASCAL

Mathur	:	Introduction to PASCAL
Gottfried	:	Programming with PASCAL

UNIX

Koparkar	:	Unix for You

WORDSTAR

Taxali	:	WordStar Professional 4.0 Made Simple: With an Overview of Release 5.5

Forthcoming Titles

Das	:	UNIX System V.4: Concepts and Applications
Taxali	:	LOTUS 1-2-3 Made Simple
Kishore & Naik	:	SQL for Professionals

Programming in
ANSI C
Second Edition

E. BALAGURUSAMY
Director
PSG Institute of Management Studies
Coimbatore

Tata McGraw-Hill Publishing Company Limited
NEW DELHI

McGraw-Hill Offices

New Delhi New York St Louis San Francisco Auckland Bogotá Guatemala
Hamburg Lisbon London Madrid Mexico Milan Montreal Panama
Paris San Juan São Paulo Singapore Sydney Tokyo Toronto

Tata McGraw-Hill

*A Division of The **McGraw-Hill** Companies*

Eighteenth reprint 1998

DZ + DZDXRDLRRXDDZ

This edition can be exported from India only by the publishers,
Tata McGraw-Hill Publishing Company Limited

ISBN 0-07-460401-5

Published by Tata McGraw-Hill Publishing Company Limited,
7 West Patel Nagar, New Delhi 110 008, typeset at Quick Photocomposers,
and printed at Sheel Print-N-Pack, Babarpur, Delhi 110 032

PREFACE TO SECOND EDITION

The growth of C language during the last few years has been phenomenal. It has emerged as the language of choice for most applications due to speed, portability and compactness of code. It has now been implemented on virtually every sort of computer, from micro to mainframe.

For many years, the *de facto* standard for implementing the language has been the original *C Reference Manual* by Kernighan and Ritchie published in 1978. During these years of growth and popularity, C has undergone many changes. Numerous different features and facilities have been developed and marketed. This has resulted in minor problems in terms of portability of programs. Consequently, the American National Standard Institute (ANSI) constituted a committee to go into the language features and to produce a more comprehensive and unambiguous definition of C. The result is ANSI C. Most compilers have already adopted ANSI standards.

The second edition incorporates all the features of ANSI C that are essential for a C programmer. While retaining the overall structure and the emphasis on examples, an attempt has been made to refine some of the material and examples. Also included is a new chapter on linked lists and dynamic memory management. As before, all the programs have been tested.

Since the ANSI standard is based on the reference manual of K & R, there are not many major changes. The new standard proposes only a few additional features and therefore all the old programs would remain valid. The most important ANSI additions are:

- A new format for declaring and defining functions has been suggested.
- Facility for doing floating point computations has been introduced.
- Two new type qualifiers **const** and **volatile** and two new data types **enum** and **void** have been introduced.
- The preprocessor includes some new macros.
- A standard ANSI C library has been defined.

These and other new standards of ANSI are explained in detail in appropriate places. For the convenience of readers, these places have been noted in the text by a special mention.

The second edition also incorporates the C language curriculum of DoE 'O' level examination, CSI National Test in programming, ICCPI examination and CMC certificate examination. Since no previous knowledge of programming has been assumed, the students appearing for these examinations would find the book very useful.

Finally, I would like to thank many of my colleagues and students for their comments and suggestions on the first edition. Their suggestions have vastly improved the text of the present edition.

E BALAGURUSAMY

PREFACE TO FIRST EDITION

C is a general-purpose structured programming language that is powerful, efficient, and compact. C combines the features of a high-level language with the elements of the assembler and is, thus, close to both man and machine. Programming in C which has recently become popular can be both interesting and fun.

This book is intended to teach the reader how to program in C. It assumes no previous exposure to the language and is suited to both beginners and experienced programmers.

The concept of 'learning by example' has been stressed throughout the book. Each major feature of the language is treated in depth followed by a complete program example to illustrate its use. Case studies at the end of the chapters not only describe the common ways C features are put together but also show real-life applications. Wherever necessary, pictorial descriptions of concepts are included to facilitate better understanding. The last chapter presents guidelines for developing efficient, error-free programs in C.

The book contains more than 100 examples and programs. All the programs have been tested using compilers compatible to both UNIX and MS-DOS operating systems and, wherever appropriate, the nature of output has been discussed. These programs also demonstrate the general principles of a good programming style.

The material is largely derived from the lectures I delivered to the participants of the Post-Graduate Diploma in Computer Systems and a number of short courses on C programming. I would like to record my thanks to all the participants for their positive criticism and feedback. My special thanks are due to my colleagues, Mr M L Saikumar, Mr Thomas Jacob and Mr P Sreenivasa Rao for their invaluable assistance in preparing the manuscript. Mr P Sreenivasa Rao is mainly responsible for getting the book in the present form.

Finally, my thanks are due to my wife, Sushila, for her constant encouragement and support throughout the project.

E BALAGURUSAMY

CONTENTS

1
OVERVIEW OF C

1.1. INTRODUCTION

'C' seems a strange name for a programming language. But this strange sounding language is one of the most popular computer languages today. C was an offspring of the 'Basic Combined Programming Language' (BCPL) called B, developed in the 1960's at Cambridge University. B language was modified by Dennis Ritchie and was implemented at Bell Laboratories in 1972. The new language was named C. Since it was developed along with the UNIX operating system, it is strongly associated with UNIX. This operating system, which was also developed at Bell Laboratories, was coded almost entirely in C.

For many years, C was used mainly in academic environments, but eventually with the release of C compilers for commercial use and the increasing popularity of UNIX, it began to gain widespread support among computer professionals. Today, C is running under a number of operating systems including MS-DOS. Since MS-DOS is a dominant operating system for micro-computers, it is natural that C has begun to influence the microcomputer community at large.

This book describes the features of C that are generally supported by most compilers. It also includes all the essential features of ANSI C.

1.2 IMPORTANCE OF C

The increasing popularity of C is probably due to its many desirable qualities. It is a robust language whose rich set of built-in functions and operators can be used to write any complex program. The C compiler combines the capabilities of an assembly language with the features of a high-level language and therefore it is well suited for writing both system software and business packages. In fact, many of the C compilers available in the market are written in C.

Programs written in C are efficient and fast. This is due to its variety of data types and powerful operators. It is many times faster than BASIC. For example, a program to increment a variable from 0 to 15000 takes about one second in C while it takes more than 50 seconds in an interpreter BASIC.

There are only 32 keywords and its strength lies in its built-in functions. Several standard functions are available which can be used for developing programs.

C is highly portable. This means that C programs written for one computer can be run on another with little or no modification. Portability is important if we plan to use a new computer with a different operating system.

C language is well suited for structured programming, thus requiring the user to think of a problem in terms of function modules or blocks. A proper collection of these modules would make a complete program. This modular structure makes program debugging, testing and maintenance easier.

Another important feature of C is its ability to extend itself. A C program is basically a collection of functions that are supported by the C library. We can continuously add our own functions to the C library. With the availability of a large number of functions, the programming task becomes simple.

1.3 SAMPLE C PROGRAMS

Before discussing any specific features of C, we shall look at some sample C programs and analyse and understand how they work.

Sample Program 1: Printing a Message

Consider a very simple program given in Fig. 1.1. This program when executed, will produce the following output:

I see, I remember

```
main( )
{
/*...........printing begins...............*/

        printf("I see, I remember");

/*...........printing ends .................*/
}
```

Fig. 1.1 *A program to print one line of text*

Let us have a close look at the program. The first line informs the system that the name of the program is **main** and the execution begins at this line. The **main( )** is a special function used by the C system to tell the computer where the program starts. Every program must have *exactly one* **main** function. If we use more than one **main** function, the compiler cannot tell which one marks the beginning of the program.

The empty pair of parentheses immediately following **main** indicates that the function **main** has no *arguments* (or parameters). The concept of arguments will be discussed in detail later when we discuss functions (in Chapter 9).

The opening brace '{' in the second line marks the beginning of the function **main** and the closing brace '}' in the last line indicates the end of the function. In this case, the closing brace also marks the end of the program. All the statements between these two braces form the *function body*. The function body contains a set of instructions to perform the given task.

In this case, the function body contains three statements, out of which only the **printf** line is an executable statement. The lines beginning with /* and ending with */ are known as *comment* lines. These are used in a program to enhance its readability and understanding. Comment lines are not executable statements and therefore anything between /* and */ is ignored by the compiler. In general, a comment can be inserted anywhere blank spaces can occur—at the beginning, middle, or end of a line, but never in the middle of a word.

Because comments do not affect the execution speed and the size of a program, we should use them liberally in our programs. They help the programmers and other users in understanding the various functions and operations of a program and serve as an aid to debugging and testing. We shall see the use of comment lines more in the examples that follow.

Let us now look at the **printf( )** function, the only executable statement of the program.

printf("I see, I remember");

printf is a predefined, standard C function for printing output. *Predefined* means that it is a function that has already been written and compiled, and linked together with our program at the time of linking. The concepts of compilation and linking are explained later in this chapter (Section 1.6). The **printf** function causes everything between the starting and the ending quotation marks to be printed out. In this case, the output will be:

I see, I remember

Note that the print line ends with a semicolon. *Every statement in C should end with a semicolon* (;) mark.

Suppose we want to print the above quotation in two lines as

I see,
I remember !

This can be achieved by adding *another* **printf** function as shown below:

printf("I see, \n");
printf("I remember !");

The information contained between the parentheses is called the *argument* of the function. The argument of the first **printf** function is "I see,\n" and the second is "I remember !". These arguments are simply strings of characters to be printed out.

Notice that the argument of the first **printf** contains a combination of two characters \ and **n** at the end of the string. This combination is collectively called the *newline* character. A newline character instructs the computer to go to the next (new) line. It is similar in concept to the carriage return key on a typewriter. After printing the character comma (,) the presence of the newline character \n causes the string "I remember" to be printed on the next line. No space is allowed between \ and n.

If we omit the newline character from the first **printf** statement, then the output will again be a single line as shown below.

I see,I remember !

This is similar to the output of the program in Fig. 1.1. However, note that there is no space between , and I.

It is also possible to produce two or more lines of output by one **printf** statement with the use of newline characters at appropriate places. For example, the statement

printf("I see,\n I remember !");

will output

I see,
I remember !

while the statement

printf("I\n.see,\n.....I\n......remember !");

will print out

I
. see,
.....I
...... remember !

Before we proceed to discuss further examples, we must note one important point. C does make a distinction between *uppercase* and *lowercase* letters. For example, **printf** and **PRINTF** are not the same. In C, everything is written in lowercase letters. However, uppercase letters are used for symbolic names representing constants. We may also use uppercase letters in output strings like "I SEE" and "I REMEMBER".

The above example that printed **I see, I remember** is one of the simplest programs. Figure 1.2 highlights the general format of such simple programs. All C programs need a **main** function.

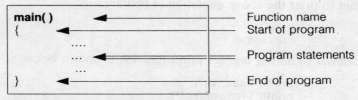

```
main( )  ◄──────────────────────── Function name
{        ◄──────────────────────── Start of program
    ....
    ...  ◄──────────────────────── Program statements
    ...
}        ◄──────────────────────── End of program
```

Fig. 1.2 *Format of simple C programs*

Sample Program 2: Adding Two Numbers

Consider another program which performs addition on two numbers and displays the result. The complete program is shown in Fig. 1.3.

```
/* Program ADDITION                       line-1   */
/* Written by EBG                          line-2   */
main( )                                     /* line-3   */
{                                           /* line-4   */
        int     number;                     /* line-5   */
        float   amount;                     /* line-6   */
                                            /* line-7   */
        number  =  100;                     /* line-8   */
                                            /* line-9   */
        amount  =  30.75  +  75.35;         /* line-10  */
        printf("%d\n", number);             /* line-11  */
        printf("%5.2f", amount);            /* line-12  */
}                                           /* line-13  */
```

Fig. 1.3 *Program to add two numbers*

This program when executed will produce the following output:

100
106.10

The first two lines of the program are comment lines. It is a good practice to use comment lines in the beginning to give information such as name of the program, author, date, etc. Comment characters are also used in other lines to indicate line numbers.

The words **number** and **amount** are *variable names* that are used to store numeric data. The numeric data may be either in *integer* form or in *real* form. In C, *all variables should be declared*, to tell the compiler what the variable names are and what *type of data* they hold. The variables must be declared before they are used. In lines 5 and 6, the declarations

int number;
float amount;

tell the compiler that **number** is an integer (**int** is the abbreviation for integer) and **amount** is a floating (**float**) point number. Declaration statements must appear at the beginning of the function as shown in Fig. 1.3. All declaration statements end with a semicolon. C supports many other data types and they are discussed in detail in Chapter 2.

The words such as **int** and **float** are called the *keywords* and cannot be used as variable names. A list of keywords is given in Chapter 2.

Data is stored in a variable by *assigning* a data value to it. This is done in lines 8 and 10. In line-8, an integer value 100 is assigned to the integer variable **number** and in line-10, the result of addition of two real numbers 30.75 and 75.35 is assigned to the floating point variable **amount**. The statements

number = 100;
amount = 30.75 + 75.35;

are called the *assignment* statements. Every assignment statement must have a semicolon at the end.

The next statement is an output statement that prints the value of **number**. The print statement

printf("%d\n", number);

contains two arguments. The first argument "%d" tells the compiler that the value of the second argument **number** should be printed as a *decimal integer*. Note that these arguments are separated by a comma. The newline character\ n causes the next output to appear on a new line.

The last statement of the program

printf("%5.2f", amount);

prints out the value of **amount** in floating point format. The format specification %5.2f tells the compiler that the output must be in floating point, with five places in all and two places to the right of the decimal point.

Sample Program 3 : Interest Calculation

The program in Fig. 1.4 calculates the value of money at the end of each year of investment, assuming an interest rate of 11 percent and prints the year and the corresponding amount, in two columns. The output is shown in Fig.1.5 for a period of 10 years with an initial investment of 5000.00. The program uses the following formula:

Value at end of year = Value at start of year (1+interest rate)

In the program, the variable **value** represents the value of money at the end of the year while **amount** represents the value of money at the start of the year. The statement

amount = value;

makes the value at the end of the *current* year as the value at the start of the *next* year.

```
/*.......................INVESTMENT PROBLEM.......................... */
#define PERIOD      10
#define PRINCIPAL   5000.00
/*.......................MAIN PROGRAM BEGINS ...................... */
main( )
{
/*.......................DECLARATION STATEMENTS ...................... */
      int    year;
      float  amount, value, inrate;
/*.......................ASSIGNMENT STATEMENTS ...................... */
      amount=   PRINCIPAL;
      inrate =  0.11;
      year   =  0;
/*.......................COMPUTATION STATEMENTS...................... */
/*.......................COMPUTATION USING while LOOP .............. */
      while(year <= PERIOD )
      {
            printf("%2d        %8.2f\n",year,amount);
            value    = amount + inrate * amount;
            year     = year + 1;
            amount   = value;
      }
/*.......................while LOOP ENDS .............................. */
}
/*.......................PROGRAM ENDS ............................. */
```

Fig. 1.4 *Program for investment problem*

Let us consider the new features introduced in this program. The second and third lines begin with **#define** instructions. A **#define** instruction defines value to a *symbolic* constant for use in the program. Whenever a symbolic name is encountered, the compiler substitutes the value associated with the name automatically. To change the value, we have to simply change the definition. In this example, we have defined two symbolic constants **PERIOD** and **PRINCIPAL** and assigned values 10 and 5000.00 respectively. These values remain constant throughout the execution of the program.

0	5000.00
1	5550.00
2	6160.50
3	6838.15
4	7590.35
5	8425.29
6	9352.07
7	10380.80
8	11522.69
9	12790.19
10	14197.11

Fig. 1.5 *Output of the investment program*

A **#define** is a compiler directive and not a statement. Therefore **#define** lines should not end with a semicolon. Symbolic constants are generally written in uppercase so that they are easily distinguished from lowercase variable names. **#define** instructions are usually placed at the beginning, before the **main( )** function. Symbolic constants are not declared in declaration section.

We must note that the defined constants are not variables. We may not change their values within the program by using an assignment statement. For example, the statement

PRINCIPAL = 10000.00;

is illegal.

The declaration section declares **year** as integer and **amount, value,** and **inrate** as floating point numbers. Note that all the floating point variables are declared in one statement. They can also be declared as

```
float  amount;
float  value;
float  inrate;
```

When two or more variables are declared in one statement, they are separated by a comma.

All computations and printing are accomplished in a **while** loop. **While** is a mechanism for evaluating repeatedly a statement or a group of statements. In this case as long as the value of **year** is less than or equal to the value of **PERIOD**, the four statements that follow **while** are executed. Note that these four statements are grouped by braces. We exit the loop when **year** becomes greater than **PERIOD**.

C supports the basic four arithmetic operators (−, +, *, /) along with several others. They are discussed in Chapter 3.

Sample Program 4: Use of Subroutines

So far, we have used only **printf** function that has been provided for us by the C system. The program shown in Fig. 1.6 uses a user-defined function. A function defined by the user is equivalent to a subroutine in FORTRAN or subprogram in BASIC.

```
/*....................... PROGRAM USING FUNCTION ......................... */
/*....................... MAIN PROGRAM BEGINS ............................. */
main( )
{
        int     a, b, c;
        a  =  5;
        b  =  10;
        c  =  mul(a,b);
        printf("Multiplication of %d and %d is %d",
               a,b,c);
}
/*..................... MAIN PROGRAM ENDS
                        MUL( ) FUNCTION STARTS ......................... */
mul  (x,y)
int  p,x,y; /* ......... ARGUMENT DECLARATIONS ......................... */
{
        p  =  x*y;
        return(p);
}
/*..................... MUL( ) FUNCTION ENDS............................... */
```

Fig. 1.6   *A program using a user-defined function.*

Figure 1.6 presents a very simple program that uses a **mul( )** function. The program will print the following output:

Multiplication of 5 and 10 is 50

The **mul(x,y)** multiplies the values of **x** and **y** and the result is returned to the **main( )** function when it is called in the statement

c = mul(a,b);

The **mul( )** has two *arguments* **x** and **y** that are declared as integers. The values of **a** and **b** are passed on to **x** and **y** respectively when the function **mul( )** is called. User-defined functions are considered in detail in Chapter 9.

Sample Program 5: Use of Math Functions

We often use standard mathematical functions such as cos, sin, exp, etc. We shall see now the use of a mathematical function in a program. The standard mathematical functions are defined and kept as a part of C **math library**. If we want to use any of these mathematical functions, we must add an **#include** instruction in the program. Like **#define**, it is also a compiler directive that instructs the compiler to link the specified mathematical functions from the library. The instruction is of the form

#include <math.h>

math.h is the filename containing the required function. Figure 1.7 illustrates the use of cosine function. The program calculates cosine values for angles 0,10,20.......,180 and prints out the results with headings.

Another **#include** instruction that is often required is

#include <stdio.h>

stdio.h refers to the *standard* I/O header file containing standard input and output functions.

```
/ ******************************************************************** /
/*                 PROGRAM USING COSINE FUNCTION                  */
/ ******************************************************************** /
#include <math.h>
#define     PI          3.1416
#define     MAX         180

main( )
{
        int    angle;
        float  x,y;

        angle = 0;
        printf("              Angle         Cos(angle)\n\n")

        while(angle <= MAX)
        {
             x = (PI/MAX)*angle;
             y = cos(x);
             printf("%15d %13.4f\n", angle, y);
             angle = angle + 10;
        }
}
Output
                Angle          Cos(angle)

                   0             1.0000
                  10             0.9848
                  20             0.9397
                  30             0.8660
                  40             0.7660
                  50             0.6428
                  60             0.5000
                  70             0.3420
                  80             0.1736
                  90            -0.0000
                 100            -0.1737
                 110            -0.3420
                 120            -0.5000
                 130            -0.6428
                 140            -0.7660
                 150            -0.8660
                 160            -0.9397
                 170            -0.9848
                 180            -1.0000
```

Fig. 1.7 *Program using a math function*

1.4 BASIC STRUCTURE OF C PROGRAMS

The examples discussed so far illustrate that a C program can be viewed as a group of building blocks called *functions*. A function is a subroutine that may include one or more *statements* designed to perform a *specific task*. To write a C program, we first create functions and then put them together. A C program may contain one or more sections shown in Fig. 1.8.

Documentation Section
Link Section
Definition Section
Global Declaration Section
main( ) Function Section   {
Declaration Part
Executable Part
}
Subprogram section
Function**1**
Function**2**   (User-defined functions)
Function**n**

Fig. 1.8 *An overview of a C program*

The documentation section consists of a set of comment lines giving the name of the program, the author and other details which the programmer would like to use later. The link section provides instructions to the compiler to link functions from the system library. The definition section defines all symbolic constants.

There are some variables that are used in more than one function. Such variables are called *global* variables and are declared in the global declaration section that is outside of all the functions.

Every C program must have one **main( )** function section. This section contains two parts, declaration part and executable part. The declaration part declares all the variables used in the executable part. There is at least one statement in the executable part. These two parts must appear between the opening and the closing braces. The program execution begins at the opening brace and ends at the closing brace. The closing brace of the main function section is the logical end of the program. All statements in the declaration and executable parts end with a semicolon.

The subprogram section contains all the user-defined functions that are called in the **main** function. User-defined functions are generally placed immediately after the **main** function, although they may appear in any order.

All sections, except the **main** function section may be absent when they are not required.

1.5 PROGRAMMING STYLE

Unlike some other programming languages (COBOL, FORTRAN, etc.), C is a *free-form* language. That is, the C compiler does not care, where on the line we begin typing. While this may be a license for bad programming, we should try to use this fact to our advantage in developing readable programs. Although several alternative styles are possible, we should select one style and use it with total consistency.

First of all, we must develop the habit of writing programs in lowercase letters. C program statements are written in lowercase letters. Uppercase letters are used only for symbolic constants.

Braces group program statements together and mark the beginning and the end of functions. A proper indentation of braces and statements would make a program easier to read and debug. Note how the braces are aligned and the statements are indented in the program of Fig. 1.4.

Since C is a free-form language, we can group statements together on one line. The statements

```
a = b;
x = y+1;
z = a+x;
```

can be written in one line as

```
a = b; x = y+1; z = a+x;
```

In this book, each statement is written on a separate line.

The generous use of comments inside a program cannot be overemphasized. Judiciously inserted comments not only increase the readability but also help to understand the program logic. This is very important for debugging and testing the program.

1.6 EXECUTING A 'C' PROGRAM

Executing a program written in C involves a series of steps. These are:

1. Creating the program.
2. Compiling the program.
3. Linking the program with functions that are needed from the C library.
4. Executing the program.

Figure 1.9 illustrates the process of creating, compiling and executing a C program. Although these steps remain the same irrespective of the *operating system*, system commands for implementing the steps and conventions for naming *files* may differ on different systems.

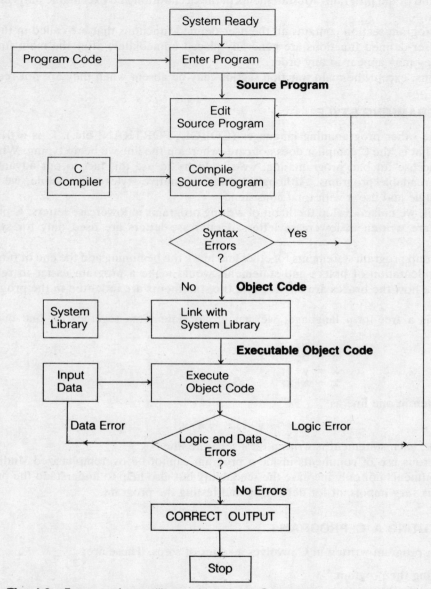

Fig. 1.9 *Process of compiling and running a C program*

An operating system is a program that controls the entire operation of a computer system. All input/output operations are channelled through the operating system. The operating system, which is an interface between the hardware and the user, handles the execution of user programs.

The two most popular operating systems today are UNIX (for minicomputers) and MS-DOS (for microcomputers). We shall discuss briefly the procedure to be followed in executing C programs under both these operating systems.

UNIX System

Creating the program

Once we load the UNIX Operating system into the memory, the computer is ready to receive the program. The program must be entered into a *file*. The file name can consist of letters, digits and special characters, followed by a *dot* and a letter **c**. Examples of valid file names are:

> *hello.c*
>
> *program.c*
>
> *ebg1.c*

The file is created with the help of a text *editor*, either **ed** or **vi**. The command for calling the editor and creating the file is

> **ed** *filename*

If the file existed before, it is loaded. If it does not yet exist, the file has to be created so that it is ready to receive the new program. Any corrections in the program are done under the editor. (The name of your system's editor may be different. Check your system manual.)

When the editing is over, the file is saved on disk. It can than be referenced any time later by its file name. The program that is entered into the file is known as the *source program*, since it represents the original form of the program.

Compiling and Linking

Let us assume that the program has been created in a file named *ebg1.c*. Now the program is ready for compilation. The compilation command to achieve this task under UNIX is

> **cc** *ebg1.c*

The source program instructions are now translated into a form that is suitable for execution by the computer. The translation is done after examining each instruction for its correctness. If everything is alright, the compilation proceeds silently and the translated program is stored on another file with the name *ebg1.o*. This program is known as *object code*.

Linking is the process of putting together other program files and functions that are required by the program. For example, if the program is using **exp()** function, then the object code of this function should be brought from the **math library** of the system and linked to the main program. Under UNIX, the linking is automatically done (if no errors are detected) when the **cc** command is used.

If mistakes in the *syntax* and *semantics* of the language are discovered, they are listed out and the compilation process ends right there. The errors should be corrected in the source program with the help of the editor and the compilation is done again.

The compiled and linked program is called the *executable object code* and is stored automatically in another file named **a.out**.

Note that some systems use different compilation command for linking mathematical functions.

cc *filename* **-lm**

is the command under UNIPLUS SYSTEM V operating system.

Executing the Program

Execution is a simple task. The command

a.out

would load the executable object code into the computer memory and execute the instructions. During execution, the program may request for some data to be entered through the keyboard. Sometimes the program does not produced the desired results. Perhaps, something is wrong with the program *logic* or *data*. Then it would be necessary to correct the source program or the data. In case the source program is modified, the entire process of compiling, linking and executing the program should be repeated.

Creating Your Own Executable File

Note that the linker always assigns the same name **a.out**. When we compile another program, this file will be over written by the executable object code of the new program. If we want to prevent from happening, we should rename the file immediately by using the command

mv a.out *name*

We may also achieve this by specifying an option in the **cc** command as follows:

cc -o *name source-file*

This will store the executable object code in the file name and prevent the old file **a.out** from being destroyed.

Multiple Source Files

To compile and link multiple source program files, we must append all the file names to the **cc** command.

cc *filename-1.c ..... filename-n.c*

These files will be separately compiled into object files called

filename-i.o

and then linked to produce an executable program file **a.out** as shown in Fig. 1.10.

It is also possible to compile each file separately and link them later. For example, the commands

cc -c mod1.c
cc -c mod2.c

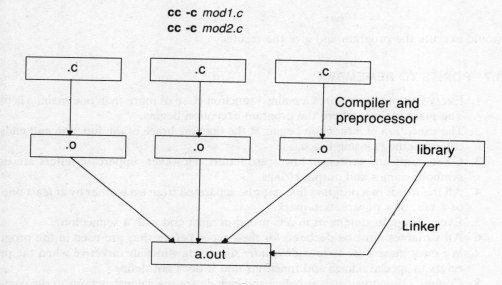

Fig. 1.10 *Compilation of multiple files*

will compile the source files *mod1.c* and *mod2.c* into object files *mod1.o* and *mod2.o*. They can be linked together by the command

cc mod1.o mod2.o

We may also combine the source files and object files as follows:

cc mod1.c mod2.o

Only *mod1.c* is compiled and then linked with the object file *mod2.o*. This approach is **useful** when one of the multiple source files need to be changed and recompiled or an already existing object file is to be used along with the program to be compiled.

MS-DOS System

The program can be created using any word processing software in non-document mode. The file name should end with the characters ".c", like **program.c, pay.c**, etc. Then the command

MSC pay.c

under MS-DOS operating system would load the program stored in the file **pay.c** and generate the **object code**. This code is stored in another file under the name **pay.obj**. In case any language errors are found, the compilation is not completed. The program should then be corrected and compiled again.

The linking is done by the command

LINK pay.obj

which generates the **executable code** with the filename **pay.exe**. Now the command

pay

would execute the program and give the results.

1.7 POINTS TO REMEMBER

1. Every C program requires a **main( )** function (Use of more than one **main( )** is illegal.). The place **main** is where the program execution begins.
2. The execution of a function begins at the opening brace of the function and ends at the corresponding closing brace.
3. C programs are written in lowercase letters. However, uppercase letters are used for symbolic names and output strings.
4. All the words in a program line must be separated from each other by at least one space, or a tab, or a punctuation mark.
5. Every program statement in a C program must end with a semicolon.
6. All variables must be declared for their types before they are used in the program.
7. We must make sure to include *header files* using **#include** directive when the program refers to special names and functions that it does not define.
8. Compiler directives such as **define** and **include** are special instructions to the compiler to help it compile a program. They do not end with a semicolon.
9. The sign # of compiler directives must appear in the first column of the line.
10. When braces are used to group statements, make sure that the opening brace has a corresponding closing brace.
11. C is a free-form language and therefore a proper form of indentation of various sections would improve legibility of the program.
12. A comment can be inserted almost anywhere a space can apperar. Use of appropriate comments in proper places increases readability and understandability of the program and helps users in debugging and testing. Remember to match the symbols /* and*/ appropriately.

REVIEW QUESTIONS AND EXERCISES

1.1 If you have access to a computer system with the C compiler, find out the details of the operating system and special features of the compiler.

1.2 Compile and run all the programs discussed in this chapter. Compare the outputs with those presented with the programs.

1.3 Remove the semicolon at the end of the **printf** statement in the program of Fig. 1.1 and try to execute it. What is the output of the program?

1.4 In the Sample Program 2, delete line-5 and execute the program. How helpful is the error message?

1.5 Modify the Sample Program 3 to print the following output:

Year	Amount
1	5550.00
2	6160.00
.	.
.	.
.	.
10	14197.11

Note that the modified output contains only 10 values (for Year = 1,...,10).

1.6 Identify syntax errors in the following program:

```
Include < math.h>
main{ }
(
    FLOAT X;
/*** ASSIGNMENT SECTION***
    X = 2.5,
    Y = exp (x);
/*** PRINTING SECTION***/
    print(x, y)
)
```

1.7 Write a progam that will print your mailing address in the following form:

First line: Name
Second line: Door No, Street
Third line: City, Pin code

1.8 Write a program to output the following multiplication table:

$5 \times 1 = 5$
$5 \times 2 = 10$
$5 \times 3 = 15$
.
.
.
$5 \times 20 = 100$

1.9 Write a program that will print the following figure:

1.10 State whether the following statements are TRUE or FALSE:

(a) Every line in a C program should end with a semicolon.
(b) In C language, lowercase letters are significant.
(c) Every C program ends with an END word.
(d) main( ) is where the program begins its execution.
(e) A line in a C program may have more than one statement.
(f) A printf( ) statement can generate *only one* line of output.
(g) The closing brace of the main( ) in a program is the logical end of the program.
(h) Syntax errors will be detected by the compiler.

CONSTANTS, VARIABLES, AND DATA TYPES

2.1 INTRODUCTION

A programming language is designed to help process certain kinds of *data* consisting of numbers, characters and strings and to provide useful output known as *information*. The task of processing of data is accomplished by executing a sequence of precise instructions called a *program*. These instructions are formed using certain symbols and words according to some rigid rules known as *syntax rules*(or *grammar*). Every program instruction must confirm precisely to the syntax rules of the language.

Like any other language, C has its own vocabulary and grammar. In this chapter, we will discuss the concepts of constants and variables and their types as they relate to C programming language.

2.2 CHARACTER SET

The characters that can be used to form words, numbers and expressions depend upon the computer on which the program is run. However, a subset of characters is available that can be used on most personal, micro, mini and mainframe computers. The characters in C are grouped into the following categories:

1. Letters
2. Digits
3. Special characters
4. White spaces

The complete character set is given in Table 2.1.

The compiler ignores white spaces unless they are a part of a string constant. White spaces may be used to separate words, but are prohibited between the characters of keywords and identifiers.

Trigraph Characters

Many non-English keyboards do not support all the characters mentioned in the Table 2.1. ANSI C introduces the concept of "trigraph" sequences to provide a way to enter certain characters that are not available on some keyboards. Each trigraph sequence consists of three characters (two

Table 2.1 C Character Set

Letters	Digits
Uppercase A.....Z	All decimal digits 0 9
Lowercase a.....z	

Special Characters

,	comma	&	ampersand
.	period	^	caret
;	semicolon	*	asterisk
:	colon	–	minus sign
?	question mark	+	plus sign
'	apostrophe	<	opening angle bracket (or less than sign)
"	quotation mark	>	closing angle bracket (or greater than sign)
!	exclamation mark	(	left paranthesis
|	vertical bar	)	right paranthesis
/	slash	[	left bracket
\	backslash	]	right bracket
~	tilde	{	left brace
_	under score	}	right brace
$	dollar sign		
%	per cent sign		
#	number sign		

White Spaces

Blank space
Horizontal tab
Carriage return
New line
Form feed

question marks followed by another character) as shown in Table 2.2. For example, if a keyboard does not support square brackets, we can still use them in a program using the trigraphs **??(** and **??)**.

Table 2.2 ANSI C Trigraph Sequences

Trigraph sequence		Translation
??=	#	number sign
??(	[	left bracket
??)	]	right bracket
??<	{	left brace
??>	}	right brace
??!	|	vertical bar
??/	\	back slash
??'	^	caret
??–	~	tilde

2.3 C TOKENS

In a passage of text, individual words and punctuation marks are called *tokens*. Similarly, in a C program the smallest individual units are known as C tokens. C has six types of tokens as shown in Fig. 2.1. C programs are written using these tokens and the syntax of the language.

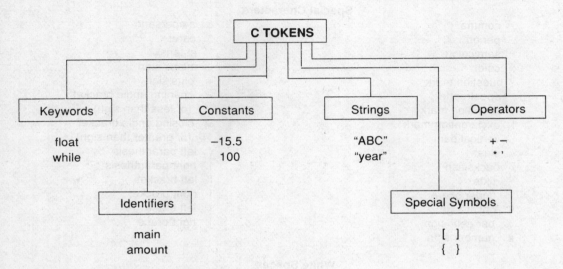

Fig. 2.1 *C tokens and examples*

2.4 KEYWORDS AND IDENTIFIERS

Every C word is classified as either a *keyword* or an *identifier*. All keywords have fixed meanings and these meanings cannot be changed. Keywords serve as basic building blocks for program statements. The list of all keywords in ANSI C are listed in Table 2.3. All keywords must be written in lowercase. Some compilers may use additional keywords that must be identified from the C manual.

Table 2.3 ANSI C Keywords

auto	double	int	struct
break	else	long	switch
case	enum	register	typedef
char	extern	return	union
const	float	short	unsigned
continue	for	signed	void
default	goto	sizeof	volatile
do	if	static	while

Identifiers refer to the names of variables, functions and arrays. These are user-defined names and consist of a sequence of letters and digits, with a letter as a first character. Both uppercase and lowercase letters are permitted, although lowercase letters are commonly used. The underscore character is also permitted in identifiers. It is usually used as a link between two words in long identifiers.

2.5 CONSTANTS

Constants in C refer to fixed values that do not change during the execution of a program. C supports several types of constants as illustrated in Fig. 2.2.

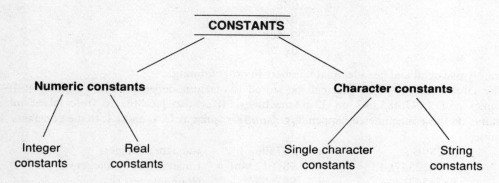

Fig. 2.2   *Basic types of C constants*

Integer Constants

An *integer* constant refers to a sequence of digits. There are three types of integers, namely, *decimal*, *octal* and *hexadecimal*.

Decimal integers consist of a set of digits, 0 through 9, preceded by an optional – or + sign. Valid examples of decimal integer constants are :

123
–321
0
654321
+78

Embedded spaces, commas, and non-digit characters are not permitted between digits. For example,

15 750
20,000
$1000

are illegal numbers. Note that ANSI C supports *unary plus* which was not defined earlier.

An *octal* integer constant consists of any combination of digits from the set 0 through 7, with a leading 0. Some examples of octal integers are:

037

0

0435

0551

A sequence of digits preceded by 0x or 0X is considered as *hexadecimal* integer. They may also include alphabets A through F or a through f. The letters A through F represent the numbers 10 through 15. Following are the examples of valid hex integers.

0X2

0x9F

0Xbcd

0x

We rarely use octal and hexadecimal numbers in programming.

The largest integer value that can be stored is machine-dependent. It is 32767 on 16-bit machines and 2,147,483,647 on 32-bit machines. It is also possible to store larger integer constants on these machines by appending *qualifiers* such as U, L and UL to the constants. For example:

56789U	or	56789u	(unsigned integer)
987612347UL	or	98761234ul	(unsigned long integer)
9876543L	or	9876543l	(long integer)

The concept of unsigned and long integers are discussed in detail in Section 2.7.

Example 2.1

Representation of integer constants on a 16-bit computer.

The output in Fig. 2.3 shows that the integer values larger than 32767 are not properly stored on a 16-bit machine. However, when they are qualified as long integer (by appending L), the values are correctly stored.

```
    Program

/******************************************************************/
/*        INTEGER NUMBERS ON 16-BIT MACHINE              */
/******************************************************************/

main()
{
   printf("Integer values\n\n");
   printf("%d %d %d\n", 32767,32767+1,32767+10);
    printf("\n");
   printf("Long integer values\n\n");
```

```
        printf("%ld %ld %ld\n", 32767L,32767L+1L,32767L+10L);
    }


    Output

    Integer values

    32767 −32768 −32759

    Long integer values

    32767 32768 32777
```

Fig. 2.3   *Representation of integer constants*

Real Constants

Integer numbers are inadequate to represent quantities that vary continuously, such as distances, heights, temperatures, prices, and so on. These quantities are represented by numbers containing fractional parts like 17.548. Such numbers are called *real* (or *floating point*) constants. Further examples of real constants are:

$$0.0083$$
$$-0.75$$
$$435.36$$
$$+247.0$$

These numbers are shown in *decimal notation*, having a whole number followed by a decimal point and the fractional part. It is possible to omit digits before the decimal point, or digits after the decimal point. That is,

$$215.$$
$$.95$$
$$-.71$$
$$+.5$$

are all valid real numbers.

A real number may also be expressed in *exponential* (or *scientific*) *notation*. For example, the value 215.65 may be written as 2.1565e2 in exponential notation. e2 means multiply by 102. The general form is:

$$\boxed{\text{mantissa } \mathbf{e} \text{ exponent}}$$

The *mantissa* is either a real number expressed in *decimal notation* or an integer. The *exponent* is an integer number with an optional *plus* or *minus* sign. The letter **e** separating the mantissa and the exponent can be written in either lowercase or uppercase. Since the exponent causes the decimal point to "float", this notation is said to represent a real number in *floating point form*. Examples of legal floating point constants are:

$$0.65e4$$
$$12e-2$$
$$1.5e+5$$
$$3.18E3$$
$$-1.2E-1$$

Embedded white space is not allowed.

Exponential notation is useful for representing numbers that are either very large or very small in magnitude. For example, 7500000000 may be written as 7.5E9 or 75E8. Similarly, −0.000000368 is equivalent to −3.68E−7.

Floating point constants are normally represented as double-precision quantities. However, the suffixes f or F may be used to force single-precision and l or L to extend double-precision further.

Some examples of valid and invalid numeric constants are given in Table 2.4

Table 2.4   Examples of Numeric Constants

Constant	Valid ?	Remarks
698354L	Yes	Represents long integer
25,000	No	Comma is not allowed
+5.0E3	Yes	(ANSI C supports unary plus)
3.5e−5	Yes	
7.1e 4	No	No white space is permitted
−4.5e−2	Yes	
1.5E+2.5	No	Exponent must be an integer
$255	No	$ symbol is not permitted
0X7B	Yes	Hexadecimal integer

Single Character Constants

A single character constant (or simply character constant) contains a single character enclosed within a pair of *single* quote marks. Examples of character constants are:

'5'   'X'   ';'   ' '

Note that the character constant '5' is not the same as the *number* 5. The last constant is a blank space.

Character constants have integer values known as ASCII values. For example, the statement

printf("%d", 'a');

would print the number 97, the ASCII value of the letter a. Similarly, the statement

printf("%c", 97);

would output the letter 'a'. ASCII values for all characters are given in Appendix II.

Since each character constant represent an integer value it is also possible to perform arithmetic operations on character constants. These are discussed in Chapter 8.

String Constants

A string constant is a sequence of characters enclosed in *double* quotes. The characters may be letters, numbers, special characters and blank space. Examples are:

> "Hello!"
> "1987"
> "WELL DONE"
> "?...!"
> "5+3"
> "X"

Remember that a character constant (e.g., 'X') is not equivalent to the single character string constant (e.g., "X"). Further, a single character string constant does not have an equivalent integer value while a character constant has an integer value. Character strings are often used in programs to build meaningful programs. Manipulation of character strings are considered in detail in Chapter 8.

Backslash Character Constants

C supports some special backslash character constants that are used in output functions. For example, the symbol '\n' stands for newline character. A list of such backslash character constants is given in Table 2.5. Note that each one of them represents one character, although they consist of two characters. These character combinations are known as *escape sequences*.

Table 2.5 Backslash Character Constants

Constant	Meaning
'\a'	audible alert (bell)
'\b'	back space
'\f'	form feed
'\n'	new line
'\r'	carriage return
'\t'	horizontal tab
'\v'	vertical tab
'\''	single quote
'\"'	double quote
'\?'	question mark
'\\'	backslash
'\0'	null

2.6 VARIABLES

A *variable* is a data name that may be used to store a data value. Unlike constants that remain unchanged during the execution of a program, a variable may take different values at different times during execution. In Chapter 1, we used several variables. For instance, we used the variable **amount** in Sample Program 3 to store the value of money at the end of each year (after adding the interest earned during that year).

A variable name can be chosen by the programmer in a meaningful way so as to reflect its function or nature in the program. Some examples of such names are:

Average
height
Total
Counter_1
class_strength

As mentioned earlier, variable names may consist of letters, digits, and the underscore(_) character, subject to the following conditions:

1. They must begin with a letter. Some systems permit underscore as the first character.
2. ANSI standard recognizes a length of 31 characters. However, the length should not be normally more than eight characters, since only the first eight characters are treated as significant by many compilers.
3. Uppercase and lowercase are significant. That is, the varible **Total** is not the same as **total** or **TOTAL**.
4. The variable name should not be a keyword.
5. White space is not allowed.

Some examples of valid variable names are:

John	Value	T_raise
Delhi	x1	ph_value
mark	sum1	distance

Invalid examples include:

123	(area)
%	25th

Further examples of variable names and their correctness are given in Table 2.6.

Table 2.6   Examples of Variable Names

Variable name	Valid ?	Remark
First_tag	Valid	
char	Not valid	char is a keyword
Price$	Not valid	Dollar sign is illegal
group one	Not valid	Blank space is not permitted
average_number	Valid	First eight characters are significant
int_type	Valid	Keyword may be part of a name

If only the first eight characters are recognized by a compiler, then the two names

average_height
average_weight

mean the same thing to the computer. Such names can be rewritten as

avg_height and **avg_weight**

or

ht_average and **wt_average**

without changing their meanings.

2.7 DATA TYPES

C language is rich in its *data types*. Storage representations and machine instructions to handle constants differ from machine to machine. The variety of data types available allow the programmer to select the type appropriate to the needs of the application as well as the machine.

ANSI C supports four classes of data types :

1. Primary (or fundamental) data types
2. User-defined data types
3. Derived data types
4. Empty data set

The primary data types and their extensions are discussed in this section. The user-defined data types are defined in the next section while the derived data types such as arrays, functions, structures and pointers are discussed as and when they are encountered. The empty data set is discussed in the chapter on functions.

All C compilers support four fundamental data types, namely integer (**int**), character (**char**), floating point (**float**), and double-precision floating point (**double**). Many of them also offer extended data types such as **long int** and **long double.** Various data types and the terminology used to describe them are given in Fig. 2.4. The range of the basic four types are given in Table 2.7. We discuss briefly each one of them in this section.

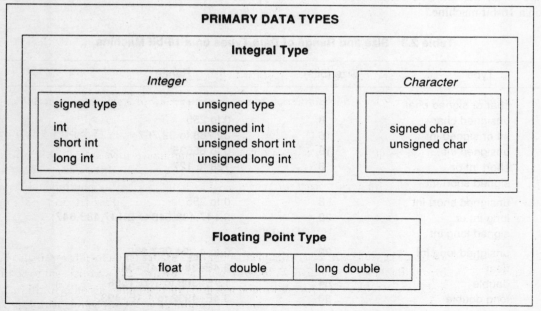

Fig. 2.4 *Primary data types in C*

Table 2.7 Size and Range of Basic Data Types

Data type	Range of values
char	−128 to 127
int	−32,768 to 32,767
float	3.4e−38 to 3.4e+38
double	1.7e−308 to 1.7e+308

Integer Types

Integers are whole numbers with a range of values supported by a particular machine. Generally, integers occupy one word of storage, and since the word sizes of machines vary (typically, 16 or 32 bits) the size of an integer that can be stored depends on the computer. If we use a 16 bit word length, the size of the integer value is limited to the range −32768 to +32767 (that is, -2^{15} to $+2^{15}-1$). A signed integer uses one bit for sign and 15 bits for the magnitude of the number. Similarly, a 32 bit word length can store an integer ranging from −2, 147, 483, 648 to 2,147,483, 647.

In order to provide some control over the range of numbers and storage space, C has three classes of integer storage, namely **short int**, **int**, and **long int**, in both **signed** and **unsigned** forms. For example, **short int** represents fairly small integer values and requires half the amount of storage as a regular **int** number uses. Unlike signed integers, unsigned integers use all the bits for the magnitude of the number and are always positive. Therefore, for a 16 bit machine, the range of unsigned integer numbers will be from 0 to 65,535.

We declare **long** and **unsigned** integers to increase the range of values. The use of qualifier **signed** on integers is optional because the default declaration assumes a signed number. Table 2.8 shows all the allowed combinations of basic types and qualifiers and their size and range on a 16-bit machine.

Table 2.8 Size and Range of Data Types on a 16-bit Machine

Type	Size (bits)	Range
char or signed char	8	−128 to 127
unsigned char	8	0 to 255
int or signed int	16	−32,768 to 32,767
unsigned int	16	0 to 65535
short int or signed short int	8	−128 to 127
unsigned short int	8	0 to 255
long int or signed long int	32	−2,147,483,648 to 2,147,483,647
unsigned long int	32	0 to 4,294,967,295
float	32	3.4E−38 to 3.4E+38
double	64	1.7E−308 to 1.7E+308
long double	80	3.4E−4932 to 1.1E+4932

Floating Point Types

Floating point (or real) numbers are stored in 32 bits (on all 16 bit and 32 bit machines), with 6 digits of precision. Floating point numbers are defined in C by the keyword **float.** When the accuracy provided by a **float** number is not sufficient, the type **double** can be used to define the number. A **double** data type number uses 64 bits giving a precision of 14 digits. These are known as *double precision* numbers. Remember that **double** type represents the same data type that **float** represents, but with a greater precision. To extend the precision further, we may use **long double** which uses 80 bits.

Character Types

A single character can be defined as a character(**char**) type data. Characters are usually stored in 8 bits (one byte) of internal storage. The qualifier **signed** or **unsigned** may be explicitly applied to **char**. While **unsigned char**s have values between 0 and 255, **signed char**s have values from -128 to 127.

2.8 DECLARATION OF VARIABLES

After designing suitable variable names, we must declare them to the compiler. Declaration does two things:
1. It tells the compiler what the variable name is.
2. It specifies what type of data the variable will hold.
The declaration of variables must be done before they are used in the program.

Primary Type Declaration

A variable can be used to store a value of any data type. That is, the name has nothing to do with its type. The syntax for declaring a variable is as follows:

> **data-type** v1,v2,....vn ;

v1, v2, ...vn are the names of variables. Variables are separated by commas. A declaration statement must end with a semicolon. For example, valid declarations are:

> **int** count;
> **int** number, total;
> **double** ratio;

int and **double** are the keywords to represent integer type and real type data values respectively. Table 2.9 shows various data types and their keyword equivalents.

Table 2.9 Data Types and Their Keywords

Data type	Keyword equivalent
Character	char
Unsigned character	unsigned char

Signed character	signed char
Signed integer	signed int (or int)
Signed short integer	signed short int (or short int or short)
Signed long integer	signed long int (or long int or long)
Unsigned integer	unsigned int (or unsigned)
Unsigned short integer	unsigned short int (or unsigned short)
Unsigned long integer	unsigned long int (or unsigned long)
Floating point	float
Double-precision floating point	double
Extended double-precision floating point	long double

The program segment given in Fig. 2.5 illustrates declaration of variables. **main()** is the beginning of the program. The opening brace { signals the execution of the program. Declaration of variables is usually done immediately after the opening brace of the program. The variables can also be declared outside (either before or after) the **main** function. The importance of place of declaration will be dealt in detail later while discussing functions.

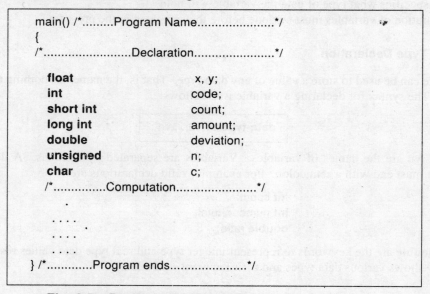

```
    main() /*.........Program Name.....................*/
    {
    /*.........................Declaration.......................*/

    float           x, y;
    int             code;
    short int       count;
    long int        amount;
    double          deviation;
    unsigned        n;
    char            c;
    /*...............Computation.......................*/
        .
    . . . .  .
    . . . .
    . . . .
    } /*.............Program ends.....................*/
```

Fig. 2.5 *Declaration of variables*

When an adjective (qualifier) **short, long, or unsigned** is used without a basic data type specifier, C compilers treat the data type as an **int.** If we want to declare a character variable as unsigned, then we must do so using both the terms like **unsigned char**.

User-Defined Type Declaration

C supports a feature known as "type definition" that allows users to define an identifier that would represent an existing data type. The user-defined data type identifier can later be used to declare variables . It takes the general form:

> **typedef** *type* identifier;

Where *type* refers to an existing data type and "identifier" refers to the "new" name given to the data type. The existing data type may belong to any class of type, including the user-defined ones. Remember that the new type is 'new' only in name, but not the data type. **typedef** cannot create a new type. Some examples of type definition are:

> **typedef int** units;
> **typedef float** marks;

Here, **units** symbolizes **int** and **marks** symbolizes **float**. They can be later used to declare variables as follows:

> **units** batch1, batch2;
> **marks** name1[50], name2[50];

batch1 and batch2 are declared as **int** variable and name1[50] and name2[50] are declared as 50 element floating point array variables. The main advantage of **typedef** is that we can create meaningful data type names for increasing the readability of the program.

Another user-defined data type is enumerated data type provided by ANSI standard. It is defined as follows:

> **enum** identifier {*value1, value2, ... valuen*};

The "identifier" is a user-defined enumerated data type which can be used to declare variables that can have one of the values enclosed within the braces (known as *enumeration constants*). After this definition, we can declare variables to be of this 'new' type as below:

> **enum** identifier v1, v2, ... vn;

The enumerated variables v1, v2, ... vn can only have one of the values *value1, value2, ... valuen*. The assignments of the following types are valid:

> v1 = value3;
> v5 = value1;

An example:

> **enum day** {Monday,Tuesday, ... Sunday};
> **enum day** week_st, week_end;
>
> week_st = Monday;
> week_end = Friday;
> if(week_st == Tuesday)
> week_end = Saturday;

The compiler automatically assigns integer digits beginning with 0 to all the enumeration constants. That is, the enumeration constant *value1* is assigned 0, *value2* is assigned 1, and so on. However, the automatic assignments can be overridden by assigning values explicitly to the enumeration constants. For example:

enum day {Monday = 1, Tuesday, ... Sunday};

Here, the constant Monday is assigned the value of 1. The remaining constants are assigned values that increase successively by 1.

The definition and declaration of enumerated variables can be combined in one statement. Example:

enum day {Monday, ... Sunday} week_st, week_end;

Declaration of Storage Class

Variables in C can have not only *data type* but also *storage class* that provides information about their location and visibility. The storage class decides the portion of the program within which the variables are recognized. Consider the following example:

```
/* Example of storage classes */

int  m;
main()
{
    int i;
    float balance;
    ....
    ....
    function1();
}

function1()
{
    int i;
    float sum;
    ....
    ....
}
```

The variable **m** which has been declared before the **main** is called *global* variable. It can be used in all the functions in the program. It need not be declared in other functins. A global variable is also known as an *external* variable.

The variables **i**, **balance** and **sum** are called *local* variables because they are declared inside a function. Local variables are visible and meaningful only inside the functions in which they are declared. They are not known to other functions. Note that the variable **i** has been declared in both the functions. Any change in the value of **i** in one function does not affect its value in the other.

C provides a variety of storage class specifiers that can be used to declare explicitly the scope and lifetime of variables. The concepts of scope and lifetime are important only in multifunction and multiple file programs and therefore the storage classes are considered in detail later when functions are discussed. For now, remember that there are four storage class specifiers (**auto**, **register**, **static**, and **extern**) whose meanings are given in Table 2.10.

Table 2.10   Storage Classes and Their Meaning

Storage class	Meaning
auto	Local variable known to only to the function in which it is declared. *Default is auto.*
static	Local variable which exists and retains its value even after the control is transferred to the calling function.
extern	Global variable known to all functions in the file.
register	Local variable which is stored in the register.

The storage class is another qualifier (like **long** or **unsigned**) that can be added to a variable declaration as shown below:

```
auto int count;
register char ch;
static int x;
extern long total;
```

Static and external (**extern**) variables are automatically initialized to zero. Automatic (**auto**) variables contain undefined values (known as 'garbage') unless they are initialized explicitly.

2.9   ASSIGNING VALUES TO VARIABLES

Variables are created for use in program statements such as

```
value = amount + inrate * amount;
while (year <= PERIOD)
{
    ....
    ....
    year = year + 1;
}
```

In the first statement, the numeric value stored in the variable **inrate** is multiplied by the value stored in **amount** and the product is added to **amount.** The result is stored in the variable **value.** This process is possible only if the variables **amount** and **inrate** have already been given values. The variable **value** is called the *target variable*. While all the variables are declared for their type, the variables that are used in expressions (on the right side of equal (=) sign of a computational statement) *must* be assigned values before they are encountered in the program. Similarly, the variable **year** and the symbolic constant **PERIOD** in the **while** statement must be assigned values before this statement is encountered.

Assignment Statement

Values can be assigned to variables using the assignment operator = as follows:

$$\boxed{\text{variable\_name = constant;}}$$

We have already used such statements in Chapter 1. Further examples are:

```
initial_value    =       0;
final_value      =     100;
balance          =   75.84;
yes              =     'x';
```

C permits multiple assignments in one line. For example

initial_value = 0; final_value = 100;

are valid statements.

    An assignment statement implies that the value of the variable on the left of the 'equal sign' is set equal to the value of the quantity (or the expression) on the right. The statement

year = year + 1;

means that the 'new value' of **year** is equal to the 'old value' of **year** plus 1.

    During assignment operation, C converts the type of value on the right-hand side to the type on the left. This may involve truncation when real value is converted to an integer.

    It is also possible to assign a value to a variable at the time the variable is declared. This takes the following form:

$$\boxed{\textbf{data-type}\ \text{variable\_name = constant;}}$$

Some examples are:

```
int final_value = 100;
char yes       = 'x';
double balance = 75.84;
```

The process of giving initial values to variables is called *initialization*. C permits the initialization of more than one variables in one statement using multiple assignment operators. For example the statements

```
p = q  = s = 0;
x = y  = z = MAX;
```

are valid. The first statement initializes the variables **p**, **q**, and **s** to zero while the second initializes **x**, **y**, and **z** with **MAX**. Note that **MAX** is a symbolic constant defined at the begining.

    Remember that external and static variables are initialized to zero by *default*. Automatic variables that are not initialized explicitly will contain garbage.

Example 2.2

Program in Fig. 2.6 shows typical declarations, assignments and values stored in various types of variables.

The variables **x** and **p** have been declared as floating-point variables. Note that the way the value

Program

```
/********************************************************************/
/*               EXAMPLES OF ASSIGNMENTS                          */
/********************************************************************/

main()
{
/*.........DECLARATIONS...............................*/

   float    x, p ;
   double   y, q ;
   unsigned  k ;

/*.........DECLARATIONS AND ASSIGNMENTS............*/

   int       m = 54321 ;
   long int  n = 1234567890 ;

/*.........ASSIGNMENTS...............................*/

   x = 1.234567890000 ;
   y = 9.87654321 ;
   k = 54321 ;
   p = q = 1.0 ;

/*.........PRINTING.................................*/

   printf("m = %d\n", m) ;
   printf("n = %ld\n", n) ;
   printf("x = %.12lf\n", x) ;
   printf("x = %f\n", x) ;
   printf("y = %.12lf\n",y) ;
   printf("y = %lf\n", y) ;
   printf("k = %u  p = %f  q = %.12lf\n", k, p, q) ;
}
```

Output

```
m = –11215
n = 1234567890
x = 1.234567880630
x = 1.234568
y = 9.876543210000
y = 9.876543
k = 54321  p = 1.000000  q = 1.000000000000
```

Fig. 2.6 *Examples of assignments*

of 1.234567890000 that we assigned to **x** is displayed under different output formats. The value of **x** is displayed as 1.234567880630 under %. 12 lf format, while the actual value assigned is 1.234567890000. This is because the variable **x** has been declared as a **float** that can store values only upto six decimal places.

The variable **m** that has been declared as **int** is not able to store the value 54321 correctly. Instead, it contains some garbage. Since this program was run on a 16-bit machine, the maximum value that an **int** variable can store is only 32767. However, the variable **k** (declared as **unsigned**) has stored the value 54321 correctly. Similarly, the **long int** variable **n** has stored the value 1234567890 correctly.

The value 9.87654321 assigned to **y** declared as double has been stored correctly but the value is printed as 9.876543 under %lf format. Note that unless specified otherwise, the **printf** function will always display a **float** or **double** value to six decimal places. We will discuss later the output formats for displaying numbers.

Declaring a Variable as Constant

We may like the value of certain variables to remain constant during the execution of a program. We can achieve this by declaring the variable with the qualifier **const** at the time of initialization. Example:

const int class_size = 40;

const is a new data type qualifier defined by ANSI standard. This tells the compiler that the value of the **int** variable **class_size** must not be modified by the program. However, it can be used on the right_hand side of an assignment statement like any other variable.

Declaring a Variable as Volatile

ANSI standard defines another qualifier **volatile** that could be used to tell explicitly the compiler that a variable's value may be changed at any time by some external sources (from outside the program). For example:

volatile int date;

The value of **date** may be altered by some external factors even if it does not appear on the left-hand side of an assignment statement. When we declare a variable as **volatile**, the compiler will exmaine the value of the variable each time it is encountered to see whether any external alteration has changed the value.

Remember that the value of a variable declared as **volatile** can be modified by its own program as well. If we wish that the value must not be modified by the program while it may be altered by some other process, then we may declare the variable as both **const** and **volatile** as shown below:

volatile const int location = 100;

Overflow and Underflow of Data

Problem of data overflow accurs when the value of a variable is either too big or too small for the data type to hold. The largest value that a variable can hold also depends on the machine. Since floating point values are rounded off to the number of significant digits allowed (or specified), an overflow normally results in the largest possible real value, whereas an underflow results in zero.

Integers are always exact within the limits of the range of the integral data types used. However, an overflow which is a serious problem may occur if the data type does not match the value of the constant. C does not provide any warning or indication of integer overflow. It simply gives incorrect results. (Overflow normally produces a negative number.) We should therefore exercise a greater care to define correct data types for handling the input/output values.

Reading Data from Keyboard

Another way of giving values to variables is to input data through keyboard using the **scanf** function. It is a general input function available in C and is very similar in concept to the **printf** function. It works much like an INPUT statement in BASIC. The general format of **scanf** is as follows:

> **scanf**("control string", &variable1, &variable2,....);

The control string contains the format of data being received. The ampersand symbol **&** before each variable name is an operator that specifies the variable name's *address*. We must always use this operator, otherwise unexpected results may occur. Let us look at an example:

scanf("%d", &number);

When this statement is encountered by the computer, the execution stops and waits for the value of the variable **number** to be typed in. Since the control string "%d" specifies that an integer value is to be read from the terminal, we have to type in the value in integer form. Once the number is typed in and the `Return' Key is pressed, the computer then proceeds to the next statement. Thus, the use of **scanf** provides an interactive feature and makes the program `user friendly'.

Example 2.3

The program in Fig. 2.7 illustrates the use of **scanf** function.

The first executable statement in the program is a **printf**, requesting the user to enter an integer number. This is known as "prompt message" and appears on the screen like

Enter an integer number

As soon as the user types in an integer number, the computer proceeds to compare the value with 100. If the value typed in is less than 100, then a message

Your number is smaller than 100

is printed on the screen. Otherwise, the message

Your number contains more than two digits

is printed. Outputs of the program, run for two different inputs are also shown in Fig. 2.7.

```
/*************************************************************************/
/*          INTERACTIVE COMPUTING USING scanf FUNCTION        */
/*************************************************************************/

main()
{
    int  number;

    printf("Enter an integer number\n");
    scanf ("%d", &number);

    if ( number < 100 )
      printf("Your number is smaller than 100\n\n");
    else
      printf("Your number contains more than two digits\n");
}
```

Program

Output

```
Enter an integer number
54
Your number is smaller than 100

Enter an integer number
108
Your number contains more than two digits
```

Fig. 2.7 *Use of scanf function*

Some compilers permit the use of the 'prompt message' as a part of the control string in **scanf**, like

> **scanf("Enter a number %d",&number);**

We discuss more about **scanf** in Chapter 4.

In Fig. 2.7 we have used a decision statement **if...else** to decide whether the number is less than 100. Decision statements are discussed in depth in Chapter 5.

Example 2.4

Sample Program 3 discussed in Chapter 1 can be converted into a more flexible interactive program using **scanf** as shown in Fig. 2.8.

In this case, computer requests the user to input the values of the amount to be invested, interest rate

rate and period of investment by printing a prompt message

Input amount, interest rate, and period

and then waits for input values. As soon as we finish entering the three values

```
Program

/*********************************************************************/
/*           INTERACTIVE INVESTMENT PROGRAM                  */
/*********************************************************************/

main()
{

    int   year, period ;
    float  amount, inrate, value ;

    printf("Input amount, interest rate, and period\n\n") ;
    scanf ("%f %f %d", &amount, &inrate, &period) ;
    printf("\n") ;
    year = 1 ;

    while( year <= period )
    {
        value = amount + inrate * amount ;
        printf("%2d  Rs %8.2f\n", year, value) ;
        amount = value ;
        year = year + 1 ;
    }
}

Output

Input amount, interest rate, and period

10000  0.14  5

1    Rs 11400.00
2    Rs 12996.00
3    Rs 14815.44
4    Rs 16889.60
5    Rs 19254.15

Input amount, interest rate, and period
```

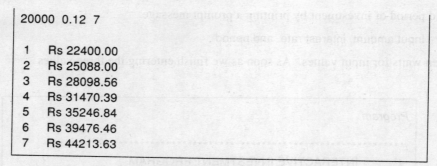

```
20000  0.12  7

     1    Rs 22400.00
     2    Rs 25088.00
     3    Rs 28098.56
     4    Rs 31470.39
     5    Rs 35246.84
     6    Rs 39476.46
     7    Rs 44213.63
```

Fig. 2.8 *Interactive investment program*

corresponding to the three variables **amount, inrate,** and **period,** the computer begins to calculate the amount at the end of each year, upto 'period' and produces output as shown in Fig. 2.8.

Note that the **scanf** function contains three variables. In such cases, care should be exercised to see that the values entered match the *order* and *type* of the variables in the list. Any mismatch might lead to unexpected results. The compiler may not detect such errors.

2.10 DEFINING SYMBOLIC CONSTANTS

We often use certain unique constants in a program. These constants may appear repeatedly in a number of places in the program. One example of such a constant is 3.142, representing the value of the mathematical constant **"pi"**. Another example is the total number of students whose mark-sheets are analysed by a 'test analysis program'. The number of students, say 50, may be used for calculating the class total, class average, standard deviation, etc. We face two problems in the subsequent use of such programs.

1. Problem in modification of the program.
2. Problem in understanding the program.

Modifiability

We may like to change the value of "pi" from 3.142 to 3.14159 to improve the accuracy of calculations or the number 50 to 100 to process the test results of another class. In both the cases, we will have to search throughout the program and explicitly change the value of the constant wherever it has been used. If any value is left unchanged, the program may produce disastrous outputs.

Understandability

When a numeric value appears in a program, its use is not always clear, especially when the same value means different things in different places. For example, the number 50 may mean the number of students at one place and the 'pass marks' at another place of the same program. We may forget what a certain number meant, when we read the program some days later.

Assignment of such constants to a *symbolic name* frees us from these problems. For example, we may use the name **STRENGTH** to define the number of students and **PASS_MARK** to define the pass marks required in a subject. Constant values are assigned to these names at the beginning of the program. Subsequent use of the names **STRENGTH** and **PASS_MARK** in the program has the effect of causing their defined values to be automatically substituted at the appropriate points. A constant is defined as follows:

> **#define** *symbolic-name*   *value of constant*

Valid examples of constant definitions are:

```
#define STRENGTH        100
#define PASS_MARK        50
#define MAX             200
#define PI             3.14159
```

Symbolic names are sometimes called *constant identifiers*. Since the symbolic names are constants (not variables), they do not appear in declarations. The following rules apply to a **#define** statement which define a symbolic constant.

1. Symbolic names have the same form as variable names. (Symbolic names are written in CAPITALS to visually distinguish them from the normal variable names which are written in lowercase letters. This is only a convention, not a rule.)
2. No blank space between the pound sign '#' and the word **define** is permitted.
3. '#' must be the first character in the line.
4. A blank space is required between **#define** and *symbolic name* and between the *symbolic name* and the *constant*.
5. **#define** statements must not end with a semicolon.
6. After definition, the *symbolic name* should not be assigned any other value within the program by using an assignment statment. For example, STRENGTH = 200; is illegal.
7. Symbolic names are NOT declared for data types. Its data type depends on the type of constant.
8. **#define** statements may appear *anywhere* in the program but before it is referenced in the program (the usual practice is to place them in the beginning of the program).

#define statement is a *preprocessor* compiler directive and is much more powerful than what has been mentioned here. More advanced types of definitions will be discussed later. Table 2.11 illustrates some invalid statements of **#define**.

Table 2.11   Examples of Invalid #define Statements

Statement	Validity	Remark
#define X = 2.5	Invalid	'=' sign is not allowed
# define MAX 10	Invalid	No white space between # and define
#define N 25;	Invalid	No semicolon at the end
#define N 5, M 10	Invalid	A statement can define only one name.
#Define ARRAY 11	Invalid	define should be in lowercase letters
#define PRICE$ 100	Invalid	$ symbol is not permitted in name

CASE STUDIES

1. Calculation of Average of Numbers

A program to calculate the average of a set of N numbers is given in Fig. 2.9.

```
Program

/*******************************************************************/
/*              AVERAGE OF n VALUES                                */
/*******************************************************************/

#define     N    10                    /* SYMBOLIC CONSTANT */

main()
{
    int    count ;                     /* DECLARATION OF */
    float  sum, average, number ;      /* VARIABLES */

    sum   = 0 ;                        /* INITIALIZATION */
    count = 0                          /* OF VARIABLES */

    while( count < N )
    {
        scanf("%f", &number) ;
        sum   = sum + number ;
        count = count + 1 ;
    }

    average = sum/N ;
    printf("N = %d  Sum = %f", N, sum);
    printf("  Average = %f", average);
}

Output

1
2.3
4.67
1.42
7
3.67
4.08
2.2
4.25
8.21
N = 10  Sum = 38.799999  Average = 3.880000
```

Fig. 2.9 *Average of N numbers*

The variable **number** is declared as **float** and therefore it can take both integer and real numbers. Since the symbolic constant **N** is assigned the value of 10 using the **#define** statement, the program accepts ten values and calculates their sum using the **while** loop. The variable **count** counts the number of values and as soon as it becomes 11, the **while** loop is exited and then the average is calculated.

Notice that the actual value of sum is 38.8 but the value displayed is 38.799999. In fact, the actual value that is displayed is quite dependent on the computer system. Such an inaccuracy is due to the way the floating point numbers are internally represented inside the computer.

2. Temperature Conversion Problem

The program presented in Fig. 2.10 converts the given temperature in fahrenheit to celsius using the following conversion formula:

$$C = \frac{F - 32}{1.8}$$

```
Program

/*************************************************************************/
/*        FAHRENHEIT - CELSIUS CONVERSION TABLE               */
/*************************************************************************/

#define  F_LOW    0           /* ***************************** */
#define  F_MAX   250          /* SYMBOLIC CONSTANTS   */
#define  STEP     25          /* ***************************** */

main()
{
    typedef float  REAL ;                  /* TYPE DEFINITION */
    REAL   fahrenheit, celsius ;           /* DECLARATION    */

    fahrenheit = F_LOW ;                   /* INITIALIZATION  */
    printf("Fahrenheit        Celsius\n\n") ;
    while( fahrenheit <= F_MAX )
    {
        celsius = ( fahrenheit – 32.0 ) / 1.8 ;
        printf(" %5.1f      %7.2f\n", fahrenheit, celsius);
        fahrenheit = fahrenheit + STEP ;
    }
}
```

```

   Fahrenheit              Celsius

        0.0                -17.78
       25.0                 -3.89
       50.0                 10.00
       75.0                 23.89
      100.0                 37.78
      125.0                 51.67
      150.0                 65.56
      175.0                 79.44
      200.0                 93.33
      225.0                107.22
      250.0                121.11
```

Fig. 2.10 *Temperature conversion*

The program prints a conversion table for reading temperature in celsius, given the fahrenheit values. The minimum and maximum values and step size are defined as symbolic constants. These values can be changed by redefining the **#define** statements. A user-defined data type name **REAL** is used to declare the variables **fahrenheit** and **celsius**.

The formation specifications %5.1f and %7.2 in the second **printf** statement produces two column output as shown.

REVIEW QUESTIONS AND EXERCISES

2.1 What are trigraph characters? How are they useful?

2.2 Describe the four basic data types. How could we extend the range of values they represent?

2.3 What is an unsigned integer constant? What is the significance of declaring a constant unsigned?

2.4 Describe the characteristics and purpose of escape sequence characters.

2.5 What is a variable and what is meant by the "value" of a variable?

2.6 How do variables and symbolic names differ?

2.7 State the differences between the declaration of a variable and the definition of a symbolic name.

2.8 What is initialization? Why is it important?

2.9 What are the qualifiers that an int can have at a time?

2.10 A programmer would like to use the word DPR to declare all the double-precision floating point values in his program. How could he achieve this?

2.11   What are enumeration variables? How are they declared? What is the advantage of using them in a program?

2.12   Describe the purpose of the qualifiers **const** and **volatile**.

2.13   When dealing with very small or very large numbers, what steps would you take to improve the accuracy of the calculations?

2.14   Which of the following are invalid constants and why?

0.0001	5x1.5	99999
+100	75.45 E–2	"15.75"
–45.6	–1.79 e + 4	0.00001234

2.15   Which of the following are invalid variable names and why?

Minimum	First.name	n1+n2	&name
doubles	3rd_row	n$	Row1
float	Sum Total	Row Total	Column-total

2.16   Find errors, if any, in the following declaration statements.

```
Int x;
float letter,DIGIT;
double = p,q
exponent alpha, beta;
m, n, z: INTEGER
short char c;
long int m; count;
long float temp;
```

2.17   What would be the value of x after execution of the following statements?

```
int  x, y = 10;
char z = 'a';

x = y + z;
```

2.18   Identify syntax errors in the following program. After corrections, what output would you expect when you execute it?

```
#define  PI  3.14159
main()
{
        int R,C;                          /* R-Radius of circle */
        float perimeter;                  /* Circumference of circle */
        float area;                       /* area of circle */
        C = PI
        R = 5;
        Perimeter = 2.0 * C *R;
        Area     = C*R*R;
        printf("%f", "%d",&perimeter,&area)}
```

2.19 Write a program to determine and print the sum of the following harmonic series for a given value of n:

$$1+ 1/2 +1/3 +....+ 1/n$$

The value of n should be given interactively through the terminal.

2.20 Write a program to read the price of an item in decimal form (like 15.95) and print the output in paise (like 1595 paise).

OPERATORS AND EXPRESSIONS

3.1 INTRODUCTION

C supports a rich set of operators. We have already used several of them, such as =, +. −, *, & and <. An *operator* is a symbol that tells the computer to perform certain mathematical or logical manipulations. Operators are used in programs to manipulate data and variables. They usually form a part of the mathematical of logical *expressions*.

C operators can be classified into a number of categories. They include:

1. Arithmetic operators.
2. Relational operators.
3. Logical operators.
4. Assignment operators.
5. Increment and decrement operators.
6. Conditional operators.
7. Bitwise operators.
8. Special operators.

3.2 ARITHMETIC OPERATORS

C provides all the basic arithmetic operators. They are listed in Table 3.1. The operators +, −, *, and / all work the same way as they do in other languages. These can operate on any built-in data type allowed in C. The unary minus operator, in effect, multiplies its single operand by −1. Therefore, a number preceded by a minus sign changes its sign.

Table 3.1 Arithmetic Operators

Operator	Meaning
+	Addition or unary plus
−	Subtraction or unary minus
*	Multiplication
/	Division
%	Modulo division

Integer division truncates any fractional part. The modulo division produces the remainder of an integer division. Examples of arithmetic operators are:

```
a − b       a + b
a * b       a / b
a % b      −a * b
```

Here **a** and **b** are variables and are known as operands. The modulo division operator % cannot be used on floating point data.

Note that C does not have an operator for *exponentiation*. Older versions of C does not support unary plus but ANSI C supports it.

Integer Arithmetic

When both the operands in a single arithmetic expression such as a+b are integers, the expression is called an *integer expression*, and the operation is called *integer arithmetic*. Integer arithmetic always yields an integer value. The largest integer value depends on the machine, as pointed out earlier. In the above examples, if **a** and **b** are integers, then for **a** = 14 and **b** = 4 we have the following results:

```
a − b = 10
a + b = 18
a * b = 56
a / b = 3    (decimal part truncated)
a % b = 2    (remainder of division)
```

During integer division, if both the operands are of the same sign, the result is truncated towards zero. If one of them is negative, the direction of truncation is implementation dependent. That is,

$$6/7 = 0 \text{ and } -6/-7 = 0$$

but −6/7 may be zero or −1. (Machine dependent)

Similarly, during modulo division, the sign of the result is always the sign of the first operand (the dividend.) That is

```
−14 %   3 = −2
−14 %  −3 = −2
 14 %  −3 =  2
```

Example 3.1

The program in Fig. 3.1 shows the use of integer arithmetic to convert a given number of days into months and days.

The variables **months** and **days** are declared as integers. Therefore, the statement

months = days/30;

truncates the decimal part and assigns the integer part to **months**. Similarly, the statement

days = days%30;

assigns the remainder part of the division to **days**. Thus the given number of days is converted into an equivalent number of months and days and the result is printed as shown in the output.

```
Program
/********************************************************************/
/*       PROGRAM TO CONVERT DAYS TO MONTHS AND DAYS        */
/********************************************************************/
main( )
{
      int      months, days;
      printf("Enter days\n");
      scanf("%d", &days);

      months  =  days / 30;
      days    =  days % 30;

      printf("Months = %d   Days = %d", months, days);
}

Output
Enter days
265
Months = 8    Days = 25

Enter days
364
Months = 12   Days = 4

Enter days
45
Months = 1    Days = 15
```

Fig. 3.1 *Illustration of integer arithmetic*

Real Arithmetic

An arithmetic operation involving only real operands is called *eal arithmetic*. A real operand may assume values either in decimal or exponential notation. Since floating point values are rounded to the number of significant digits permissible, the final value is an approximation of the correct result. If **x**, **y**, and **z** are **floats**, then we will have:

$$x =   6.0/7.0 =   0.857143$$
$$y =   1.0/3.0 =   0.333333$$
$$z = -2.0/3.0 = -0.666667$$

The operator % cannot be used with real operands.

Mixed-mode Arithmetic

When one of the operands is real and the other is integer, the expression is called a *mixed-mode arithmetic* expression. If either operand is of the real type, then only the real operation is performed and the result is always a real number. Thus

$$15/10.0 = 1.5$$

where as

$$15/10 = 1$$

More about mixed operations will be discussed later when we deal with the evaluation of expressions.

3.3 RELATIONAL OPERATORS

We often compare two quantities, and depending on their relation, take certain decisions. For example, we may compare the age of two persons, or the price of two items, and so on. These comparisons can be done with the help of *relational operators*. We have already used the symbol '<', meaning 'less than'. An expression such as

$$a < b \text{ or } 1 < 20$$

containing a relational operator is termed as a *relational expression*. The value of a relational expression is either *one* or *zero*. It is one if the specified relation is *true* and zero if the relation is *false*. For example

$$10 < 20 \text{ is } true$$

but

$$20 < 10 \text{ is } false$$

C supports six relational operators in all. These operators and their meanings are shown in Table 3.2.

Table 3.2   Relational Operators

Operator	Meaning
<	is less than
<=	is less than or equal to
>	is greater than
>=	is greater than or equal to
==	is equal to
!=	is not equal to

A simple relational expression contains only one relational operator and takes the following form:

ae−1 relational operator ae−2

ae−1 and *ae−2* are arithmetic expressions, which may be simple constants, variables or combination of them. Given below are some examples of simple relational expressions and their values:

4.5 <=	10	TRUE	
4.5 <	−10	FALSE	
−35 >=	0	FALSE	
10 <	7+5	TRUE	
a+b ==	c+d	TRUE	only if the sum of values of *a* and *b* is equal to the sum of values of *c* and *d*.

When arithmetic expressions are used on either side of a relational operator, the arithmetic expressions will be evaluated first and then the results compared. That is, arithmetic operators have a higher priority over relational operators.

Relational expressions are used in *decision statements* such as, **if** and **while** to decide the course of action of a running program. We have already used the **while** statement in chapter 1. Decision statements are discussed in detail in Chapters 5 and 6.

3.4 LOGICAL OPERATORS

In addition to the relational operators, C has the following three *logical operators*.

&& meaning	logical **AND**
‖ meaning	logical **OR**
! meaning	logical **NOT**

The logical operators **&&** and **‖** are used when we want to test more than one condition and make decisions. An example is:

$$a > b \ \&\& \ x == 10$$

An expression of this kind which combines two or more relational expressions is termed as a *logical expression* or a *compound relational expression*. Like the simple relational expressions, a logical expression also yields a value of *one or zero*, according to the *truth table* shown in Table 3.3. The logical expression given above is true only if **a > b** is *true* and **x == 10** is *true*. If either (or both) of them are false, the expression is *false*.

Table 3.3   Truth Table

op-1	op-2	Value of the expression	
		op-1 && op-2	op-1 ‖ op-2
Non-zero	Non-zero	1	1
Non-zero	0	0	1
0	Non-zero	0	1
0	0	0	0

Some examples of the usage of logical expressions are:

1. **if** (age > 55 && salary < 1000)
2. **if** (number < 0 ‖ number > 100)

We shall see more of them when we discuss decision statements.

3.5 ASSIGNMENT OPERATORS

Assignment operators are used to assign the result of an expression to a variable. We have seen the usual assignment operator, ' = '. In addition, C has a set of 'shorthand' assignment operators of the form

$$\boxed{v\ \mathbf{op}=\ exp;}$$

Where *v* is a variable, *exp* is an expression and *op* is a C binary arithmetic operator. The operator **op**= is known as the *shorthand* assignment operator.

The assignment statement

$$\mathbf{v\ op=\ exp;}$$

is equivalent to

$$\mathbf{v\ =\ v\ op\ (exp);}$$

with **v** evaluated only once. Consider an example

$$\mathbf{x\ +=\ y+1;}$$

This is same as the statement

$$\mathbf{x\ =\ x\ +\ (y+1);}$$

The shorthand operator += means 'add y+1 to x' or 'increment x by y+1'. For y $\neq$ 2, the above statement becomes

$$\mathbf{x\ +=\ 3;}$$

and when this statement is executed, 3 is added to x. If the old value of x is, say 5, then the new value of x is 8. Some of the commonly used shorthand assignment operators are illustrated in Table 3.4.

Table 3.4 Shorthand Assignment Operators

Statement with simple assignment operator	Statement with shorthand operator
a = a + 1	a += 1
a = a − 1	a −= 1
a = a * (n+1)	a *= n+1
a = a / (n+1)	a /= n+1
a = a % b	a %= b

The use of shorthand assignment operators has three advantages:

1. What appears on **the** left-hand side need not be repeated and therefore it becomes easier to write.
2. The statement is more concise and easier to read.
3. The statement is more efficient.

These advantages may be appreciated if we consider a slightly more involved statement, like

$$\mathbf{value(5*j-2)\ =\ value(5*j-2)\ +\ delta;}$$

With the help of the += operator, this can be written as follows:

$$\mathbf{value(5*j-2)\ +=\ delta;}$$

It is easier to read and understand, and is more efficient because the expression 5*j−2 is evaluated only once.

Example 3.2

Program of Fig. 3.2 prints a sequence of squares of numbers. Note the use of the shorthand operator *=

The program attempts to print a sequence of squares of numbers starting from 2. The statement

$$a \; *= \; a;$$

which is identical to

$$a \; = \; a*a;$$

replaces the current value of **a** by its square. When the value of **a** becomes equal or greater than N (=100) the **while** is terminated. Note that the output contains only three values 2, 4 and 16.

```
Program
/***********************************************************************/
/*      PROGRAM TO SHOW USE OF SHORTHAND OPERATORS      */
/***********************************************************************/

#define        N        100
#define        A        2

main( )
{
    int        a;
    a  =  A;
    while( a < N )
    {
        printf("%d\n", a);
        a  *=  a;
    }
}

Output
2
4
16
```

Fig. 3.2 *Use of shorthand operator *=*

3.6 INCREMENT AND DECREMENT OPERATORS

C has two very useful operators not generally found in other languages. These are the *increment* and *decrement* operators:

$$++ \text{ and } --$$

The operator $++$ adds 1 to the operand while $--$ subtracts 1. Both are unary operators and take the following form:

```
++m; or m++;
--m; or m--;
++m; is equivalent to m = m+1; (or m += 1;)
--m; is equivalent to m = m-1; (or m -= 1;)
```

We use the increment and decrement statements in **for** and **while** loops extensively.

While $++m$ and $m++$ mean the same thing when they form statements independently, they behave differently when they are used in expressions on the right-hand side of an assignment statement. Consider the following:

```
m =  5;
y =  ++m;
```

In this case, the value of y and m would be 6. Suppose, if we rewrite the above statements as

```
m =  5;
y =  m++;
```

then, the value of y would be 5 and m would be 6. A prefix operator first adds 1 to the operand and then the result is assigned to the variable on left. On the other hand, a postfix operator first assigns the value to the variable on left and then increments the operand.

Similar is the case, when we use $++$ (or $--$) in subscripted variables. That is, the statement

```
a[i++] = 10;
```

is equivalent to

```
a[i] = 10;
    i = i + 1;
```

The increment and decrement operators can be used in complex statements. Example:

```
m = n++ -j+10;
```

Old value of **n** is used in evaluating the expression. **n** is incremented after the evaluation. Some compilers require a space on either side of n++ or ++n.

3.7 CONDITIONAL OPERATOR

A ternary operator pair "? :" is available in C to construct conditional expressions of the form

```
exp1 ? exp2 : exp3;
```

where *exp1*, *exp2*, and *exp3* are expressions.

The operator ? : works as follows: *exp1* is evaluated first. If it is nonzero (true), then the expression *exp2* is evaluated and becomes the value of the expression. If *exp1* is false, *exp3* is evaluated and its value becomes the value of the expression. Note that only one of the expressions (either *exp2* or *exp3*) is evaluated. For example, consider the following statements.

```
a = 10;
b = 15;
x = (a > b) ? a : b;
```

In this example, x will be assigned the value of b. This can be achieved using the **if..else** statements as follows:

```
if (a > b)
    x = a;
else
    x = b;
```

3.8 BITWISE OPERATORS

C has a distinction of supporting special operators known as *bitwise operators* for manipulation of data at bit level. These operators are used for testing the bits, or shifting them right or left. Bitwise operators may not be applied to **float** or **double**. Table 3.5 lists the bitwise operators and their meanings. They are discussed in detail in Appendix I.

Table 3.5 Bitwise Operators

Operator	Meaning
&	bitwise AND
|	bitwise OR
^	bitwise exclusive OR
<<	shift left
>>	shift right
~	One's complement

3.9 SPECIAL OPERATORS

C supports some special operators of interest such as comma operator, **sizeof** operator, pointer operators (& and *) and member selection operators (. and –>). The comma and **sizeof** operators are discussed in this section while the pointer operators are discussed in Chapter 11. Member selection operators which are used to select members of a structure are discussed in Chapters 10 and 11. ANSI committee has introduced two preprocessor operators known as "string-izing" and "token-pasting" operators (# and ##). They will be discussed in Chapter 13.

The Comma Operator

The comma operator can be used to link the related expressions together. A comma-linked list of expressions are evaluated *left to right* and the value of *right-most* expression is the value of the combined expression. For example, the statement

$$value = (x = 10, y = 5, x+y);$$

first assigns the value 10 to **x**, then assigns 5 to **y**, and finally assigns 15 (i.e, 10+5) to **value**. Since comma operator has the lowest precedence of all operators, the parentheses are necessary. Some applications of comma operator are:

In **for** loops:

$$for (n = 1, m = 10; n <= m; n++, m++)$$

In **while** loops:

$$\text{while(c = getchar(), c != '10')}$$

Exchanging values:

$$t = x, x = y, y = t;$$

The sizeof Operator

The **sizeof** is a compile time operator and, when used with an operand, it returns the number of bytes the operand occupies. The operand may be a variable, a constant or a data type qualifier.

Examples:

$$m = \textbf{sizeof}(sum);$$
$$n = \textbf{sizeof}(\textbf{long int}):$$
$$k = \textbf{sizeof}(235L);$$

The **sizeof** operator is normally used to determine the lengths of arrays and structures when their sizes are not known to the programmer. It is also used to allocate memory space dynamically to variables during execution of a program.

Example 3.3

In Fig. 3.3, the program employs different kinds of operators. The results of their evaluation are also shown for comparison.

Notice the way the increment operator ++ works when used in an expression. In the statement

$$c = ++a - b;$$

new value of **a** (= 16) is used thus giving the value 6 to **c**. That is, **a** is incremented by 1 before it is used in the expression. However, in the statement

$$d = b++ + a;$$

the old value of **b** (=10) is used in the expression. Here, **b** is incremented by 1 after it is used in the expression.

We can print the character % by placing it immediately after another % character in the control string. This is illustrated by the statement

$$\textbf{printf("a\%\%b = \%d\textbackslash n", a\%b);}$$

The program also illustrates that the expression

$$c > d ? 1 : 0$$

assumes the value 0 when **c** is less than **d** and 1 when **c** is greater than **d**.

Program

```
/*************************************************************************/
/*                    ILLUSTRATION OF OPERATORS                        */
/*************************************************************************/
main( )
{
    int a, b, c, d;
    a = 15;
    b = 10;
    c = ++a − b;
    printf("a = %d  b = %d  c = %d\n",a, b, c);
    d = b++ +a;
    printf("a = %d  b = %d  d = %d\n",a, b, d);
    printf("a/b = %d\n", a/b);
    printf("a%%b = %d\n", a%b);
    printf("a *= b = %d\n", a*=b);
    printf("%d\n", (c>d) ? 1 : 0);
    printf("%d\n", (c<d) ? 1 : 0);
}
```

Output
```
a = 16  b = 10  c = 6
a = 16  b = 11  d = 26
a/b = 1
a%b = 5
a *= b = 176
0
1
```

Fig. 3.3 *Further illustration of arithmetic operators*

3.10 ARITHMETIC EXPRESSIONS

An arithmetic expression is a combination of variables, constants, and operators arranged as per the syntax of the language. We have used a number of simple expressions in the examples discussed so far. C can handle any complex mathematical expressions. Some of the examples of C expressions are shown in Table 3.6. Remember that C does not have an operator for exponentiation.

3.11 EVALUATION OF EXPRESSIONS

Expressions are evaluated using an assignment statement of the form

$$variable = expression;$$

Table 3.6   Expressions

Algebraic expression	C expression
a × b − c	a * b − c
(m+n) (x+y)	(m+n) * (x+y)
$\dfrac{ab}{c}$	a * b/c
$3x^2 + 2x + 1$	3 * x * x + 2 * x + 1
$\dfrac{x}{y} + c$	x/y+c

Variable is any valid C variable name. When the statement is encountered, the expression is evaluated first and the result then replaces the previous value of the variable on the left-hand side. All variables used in the expression must be assigned values before evaluation is attempted. Examples of evaluation statements are

```
x = a *b − c;
y = b / c * a;
z = a − b / c + d;
```

The blank space around an operator is optional and adds only to improve readability. When these statements are used in a program, the variables **a**, **b**, **c**, and **d** must be defined before they are used in the expressions.

Example 3.4

The program in Fig. 3.4 illustrates the use of variables in expressions and their evaluation.

Output of the program also illustrates the effect of presence of parentheses in expressions. This is discussed in the next section.

3.12 PRECEDENCE OF ARITHMETIC OPERATORS

An arithmetic expression without parentheses will be evaluated from *left to right* using the rules of precedence of operators. There are two distinct priority levels of arithmetic operators in C

High priority	* / %
Low priority	+ −

The basic evaluation procedure includes two left-to-right passes through the expression. During the first pass, the high priority operators (if any) are applied as they are encountered. During the second pass, the low priority operators (if any) are applied as they are encountered. Consider the following evaluation statement that has been used in the program of Fig. 3.4.

```
Program
/*****************************************************************/
/*                EVALUATION OF EXPRESSIONS                     */
/*****************************************************************/
main( )
{
    float   a, b, c, x, y, z;
    a = 9;
    b = 12;
    c = 3;
    x = a -  b / 3 + c * 2 - 1;
    y = a -  b / (3 + c) * (2 - 1);
    z = a - (b / (3 + c) * 2) - 1;
    printf("x = %f\n", x);
    printf("y = %f\n", y);
    printf("z = %f\n", z);
}
Output
x =  10.000000
y =  7.000000
z =  4.000000
```

Fig. 3.4 *Illustrations of evaluation of expressions*

$$x = a - b/3 + c*2 - 1$$

When a = 9, b = 12, and c = 3, the statement becomes

$$x = 9 - 12/3 + 3*2 - 1$$

and is evaluated as follows
First pass

Step1: x = 9 - 4 + 3*2 - 1
Step2: x = 9 - 4 + 6 - 1

Second pass

Step3: x = 5 + 6 - 1
Step4: x = 11 - 1
Step5: x = 10

These steps are illustrated in Fig. 3.5. The numbers inside parentheses refer to step numbers.
However, the order of evaluation can be changed by introducing parentheses into an expression. Consider the same expression with parentheses as shown below:

$$9 - 12/(3+3)*(2-1)$$

Whenever parentheses are used, the expressions within parentheses assume highest priority. If two or more sets of parentheses appear one after another as shown above, the expression contained in the left-most set is evaluated first and the right-most in the last. Given below are the new steps.

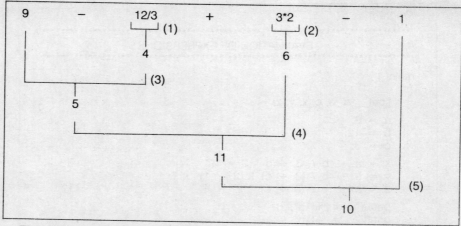

Fig. 3.5 *Illustration of hierarchy of operations*

First pass

Step1: 9−12/6 * (2−1)
Step2: 9−12/6 * 1

Second pass

Step3: 9−2 * 1
Step4: 9−2

Third pass

Step5: 7

This time, the procedure consists of three left-to-right passes. However, the number of evaluation steps remain the same as 5 (i.e equal to the number of arithmetic operators).

Parentheses may be nested, and in such cases, evaluation of the expression will proceed outward from the innermost set of parentheses. Just make sure that every opening parenthesis has a matching closing one. For example

$$9 - (12/(3+3) * 2) - 1 = 4$$

where as

$$9 - ((12/3) + 3 * 2) - 1 = -2$$

While parentheses allow us to change the order of priority, we may also use them to improve understandability of the program. When in doubt, we can always add an extra pair just to make sure that the priority assumed is the one we require.

3.13 SOME COMPUTATIONAL PROBLEMS

When expressions include real values, then it is important to take necessary precautions to guard against certain computational errors. We know that the computer gives approximate values for real numbers and the errors due to such approximations may lead to serious problems. For example, consider the following statements:

$$a = 1.0/3.0;$$
$$b = a * 3.0;$$

We know that (1.0/3.0)3.0 is equal to 1. But there is no guarantee that the value of **b** computed in a program will equal 1.

Another problem is division by zero. On most computers, any attempt to divide a number by zero will result in abnormal termination of the program. In some cases such a division may produce meaningless results. Care should be taken to test the denominator that is likely to assume zero value and avoid any division by zero.

The third problem is to avoid overflow or underflow errors. It is our responsibility to guarantee that operands are of the correct type and range, and the result may not produce any overflow or underflow.

Example 3.5

Output of the program in Fig. 3.6 shows round-off errors that can occur in computation of floating point numbers.

```
Program
/********************************************************************/
/*              PROGRAM SHOWING ROUND-OFF ERRORS                   */
/*                   Sum of n terms of 1/n                         */
/********************************************************************/
main( )
{
    float  sum, n, term;
    int    count = 1;
    sum = 0;
    printf("Enter value of n\n");
      scanf("%f", &n);
    term = 1.0/n;
    while( count <= n )
    {
        sum = sum + term;
        count++;
    }
    printf("Sum = %f\n", sum);
}
Output
Enter value of n
99
Sum = 1.000001
Enter value of n
143
Sum = 0.999999
```

Fig. 3.6 *Round-off errors in floating point computations*

We know that the sum of n terms of 1/n is 1. However, due to errors in floating point representation, the result is not always 1.

3.14 TYPE CONVERSIONS IN EXPRESSIONS

Automatic Type Conversion

C permits mixing of constants and variables of different types in an expression, but during evaluation it adheres to very strict rules of type conversion. We know that the computer. considers one operator at a time, involving two operands.

If the operands are of different types, the 'lower' type is automatically converted to the 'higher' type before the operation proceeds. The result is of the higher type. A typical type conversion process is illustrated in Fig. 3.7.

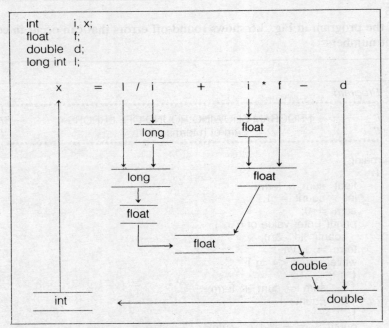

Fig. 3.7 *Process of automatic type conversion*

Given below is the sequence of rules that are applied while evaluating expressions.

All **short** and **char** are automatically converted to **int**; then

1. if one of the operands is **long double**, the other will be converted to **long double** and the result will be **long double**;
2. else, if one of the operands is **double**, the other will be converted to **double** and the result will be **double**;

3. else, if one of the operands is **float**, the other will converted to **float** and the result will be **float**;

4. else, if one of the operands is **unsigned long int**, the other will be converted to **unsigned long int** and the result will be **unsigned long int**;

5. else, if one of the operands is **long int** and the other is **unsigned int**, then:
   (a) if **unsigned int** can be converted to **long int**, the **unsigned int** operand will be converted as such and the result will be **long int**;
   (b) else, both operands will be converted to **unsigned long int** and the result will be **unsigned long int**;

6. else, if one of the operands is **long int**, the other will be converted to **long int** and the result will be **long int**;

7. else, if one of the operands is **unsigned int**, the other will be converted to **unsigned int** and the result will be **unsigned int**.

Note that some versions of C automatically convert all floating-point operands to double precision.

The final result of an expression is converted to the type of the variable on the left of the assignment sign before assigning the value to it. However, the following changes are introduced during the final assignment.

1. **float** to **int** causes truncation of the fractional part.
2. **double** to **float** causes rounding of digits.
3. **long int** to **int** causes dropping of the excess higher order bits.

Casting a Value

We have just discussed how C performs type conversion automatically. However, there are instances when we want to force a type conversion in a way that is different from the automatic conversion. Consider, for example, the calculation of ratio of females to males in a town.

ratio = female_number/male_number

Since **female_number** and **male_number** are declared as integers in the program, the decimal part of the result of the division would be lost and **ratio** would represent a wrong figure. This problem can be solved by converting *locally* one of the variables to the floating point as shown below:

ratio = **(float)** female_number/male_number

The operator **(float)** converts the **female_number** to floating point for the purpose of evaluation of the expression. Then using the rule of automatic conversion, the division is performed in floating point mode, thus retaining the fractional part of result.

Note that in no way does the operator **(float)** affect the value of the variable **female_number**. And also, the type of **female_number** remains as **int** in the other parts of the program.

The process of such a local conversion is known as *casting* a value. The general form of a cast is:

(type-name) expression

Where *type-name* is one of the standard C data types. The *expression* may be a constant, variable or an expression. Some examples of casts and their actions are shown in Table 3.7.

Table 3.7 Use of Casts

Example	Action
x = (**int**) 7.5	7.5 is converted to integer by truncation.
a = (**int**) 21.3/(**int**) 4.5	Evaluated as 21/4 and the result would be 5.
b = (**double**)sum/n	Division is done in floating point mode.
y = (**int**) (a+b)	The result of a+b is converted to integer.
z = (**int**)a+b	a is converted to integer and then added to b.
p = cos((**double**)x)	Converts x to double before using it.

```
Program
/**************************************************************************/
/*              PROGRAM SHOWING THE USE OF A CAST               */
/**************************************************************************/
main( )
{
    float   sum;
    int     n;
    sum = 0;
    for( n = 1; n <= 10; ++n )
    {
        sum = sum + 1/(float)n;
        printf ("% 2d %6.4f\n", n, sum);
    }
}
Output
    1   1.0000
    2   1.5000
    3   1.8333
    4   2.0833
    5   2.2833
    6   2.4500
    7   2.5929
    8   2.7179
    9   2.8290
   10   2.9290
```

Fig. 3.8 *Use of a cast*

Casting can be used to round-off a given value. Consider the following statement:

$$x = (\textbf{int}) \ (y+0.5);$$

If **y** is 27.6, y+0.5 is 28.1 and on casting, the result becomes 28, the value that is assigned to **x**. Of course, the expression, being cast is not changed.

Example 3.6
Figure 3.8 shows a program using a cast to evaluate the equation

$$sum = \sum_{i=1}^{n} (1/i)$$

When combining two different types of variables in an expression, never assume the rules of automatic conversion. It is always a good practice to explicitly force the conversion. It is more safer and more portable. For example, when **y** and **p** are **double** and **m** is **int**, the following two statements are equivalent.

y = p + m;
y = p + (double)m;

However, the second statement is preferable. It will work the same way on all machines and is more readable.

3.15 OPERATOR PRECEDENCE AND ASSOCIATIVITY

Each operator in C has a precedence associated with it. This precedence is used to determine how an expression involving more than one operator is evaluated. There are distinct *levels of precedence* and an operator may belong to one of the levels. The operators at the higher level of precedence are evaluated first. The operators of the same precedence are evaluated either from left to right or from right to left, depending on the level. This is known as the *associativity* property of an operator. Table 3.8 provides a complete list of operators, their precedence levels, and their rules of association. The groups are listed in the order of decreasing precedence (rank 1 indicates the highest precedence level and 15 the lowest). The list also includes those operators which we have not yet discussed.

It is very important to note carefully, the order of precedence and associativity of operators. Consider the following conditional statement:

if (x == 10 + 15 && y < 10)

The precedence rules say that the *addition* operator has a higher priority than the logical operator (&&) and the relational operators (== and <). Therefore, the addition of 10 and 15 is executed first. This is equivalent to:

if (x == 25 && y < 10)

The next step is to determine whether **x** is equal to 25 and **y** is less than 10. If we assume a value of 20 for x and 5 for y, then

x == 25 is FALSE (0)
y < 10 is TRUE (1)

Note that since the operator < enjoys a higher priority compared to ==, y < 10 is tested first and then x == 25 is tested.
Finally we get:

if (FALSE && TRUE)

Because one of the conditions is FALSE, the complex condition is FALSE.

In the case of **&&**, it is guaranteed that the second operand will not be evaluated if the first is zero and in the case of ¦¦, the second operand will not be evaluated if the first is non-zero.

3.16 MATHEMATICAL FUNCTIONS

Mathematical functions such as cos, sqrt, log, etc. are frequently used in analysis of real-life problems. Most of the C compilers support these basic math functions. However, there are systems that have a more comprehensive math library and one should consult the reference manual to find out which functions are available. Table 3.9 lists some standard math functions.

As pointed out earlier in Chapter 1, to use any of these functions in a program, we should include the line:

#include <math.h>

in the beginning of the program. In addition, the command for compilation should be:

cc filename −lm

under UNIPLUS SYSTEM 5 operating system.

Table 3.8 Summary of C Operators

OPERATOR	DESCRIPTION	ASSOCIATIVITY	RANK
( )	Function call	Left to right	1
[ ]	Array element reference		
+	Unary plus		2
−	Unary minus	Right to left	
++	Increment		
−−	Decrement		
!	Logical negation		
~	Ones complement		
*	Pointer reference (indirection)		
&	Address		
sizeof	Size of an object		
(type)	Type cast (conversion)		
*	Multiplication	Left to right	3
/	Division		
%	Modulus		
+	Addition	Left to right	4
−	Subtraction		

Table 3.8 *Contd.*

OPERATOR	DESCRIPTION	ASSOCIATIVITY	RANK
<< >>	Left shift Right shift	Left to right	5
< <= > >=	Less than Less than or equal to Greater than Greater than or equal to	Left to right	6
== !=	Equality Inequality	Left to right	7
&	Bitwise AND	Left to right	8
^	Bitwise XOR	Left to right	9
|	Bitwise OR	Left to right	10
&&	Logical AND	Left to right	11
||	Logical OR	Left to right	12
?:	Conditional expression	Right to left	13
= *= /= %= += -= &= ^= |= <<= >>=	Assignment operators	Right to left	14
,	Comma operator	Left to right	15

Table 3.9 Math Functions

Function	Meaning
Trigonometric	
acos(x)	Arc cosine of x
asin(x)	Arc sin of x
atan(x)	Arc tangent of x
atan2(x,y)	Arc tangent of x/y
cos(x)	Cosine of x
sin(x)	Sine of x
tan(x)	Tangent of x

Hyperbolic

cosh(x)	Hyperbolic cosine of x
sinh(x)	Hyperbolic sine of x
tanh(x)	Hyperbolic tangent of x

Other functions

ceil(x)	x rounded up to the nearest integer
exp(x)	e to the power x (e^x)
fabs(x)	Absolute value of x.
floor(x)	x rounded down to the nearest integer
fmod(x,y)	Remainder of x/y
log(x)	Natural log of x, x > 0
log10(x)	Base 10 log of x, x > 0
pow(x,y)	x to the power y (x^y)
sqrt(x)	Square root of x, x > = 0

Note: 1. x and y should be declared as **double**.
2. In trigonometric and hyperbolic functions, x and y are in radians.
3. All the functions return a **double**.

CASE STUDIES

1. Salesman's Salary

A computer manufacturing company has the following monthly compensation policy to their sales-persons:

Minimum base salary	: 1500.00
Bonus for every computer sold	: 200.00
Commission on the total monthly sales	: 2 per cent

Since the prices of computers are changing, the sales price of each computer is fixed at the beginning of every month. A program to compute a sales-person's gross salary is given in Fig. 3.9.

Given the base salary, bonus, and commission rate, the inputs necessary to calculate the gross salary are, the price of each computer and the number sold during the month.

The gross salary is given by the equation:

Gross salary = base salary + (quantity * bonus rate)
+ (quantity * Price) * commission

Program

```
/*****************************************************************/
/*         PROGRAM TO CALCULATE A SALESMAN'S SALARY         */
/*****************************************************************/

#define        BASE_SALARY        1500.00
#define        BONUS_RATE         200.00
#define        COMMISSION           0.02

main( )
{
    int     quantity;
    float   gross_salary, price;
    float   bonus, commission;

     printf("Input number sold and price\n");
    scanf("%d   %f", &quantity, &price);

    bonus        = BONUS_RATE * quantity;
    commission   = COMMISSION * quantity * price;
    gross_salary = BASE_SALARY + bonus + commission;

    printf("\n");
    printf("Bonus          = %6.2f\n", bonus);
    printf("Commission   = %6.2f\n", commission);
    printf("Gross salary  = %6.2f\n", gross_salary);

}
```

Output

```
Input number sold and price
5   20450.00

Bonus          = 1000.00
Commission   = 2045.00
Gross salary  = 4545.00
```

Fig. 3.9 *Program of salesman's salary*

2. Solution of the Quadratic Equation

An equation of the form

$$ax^2 + bx + c = 0$$

is known as the *quadratic equation*. The values of x that satisfy the equation are known as the *roots* of the equation. A quadratic equation has two roots which are given by the following two formulae:

$$\text{root1} = \frac{-b + sqrt(b^2 - 4ac)}{2a}$$

$$\text{root2} = \frac{-b - sqrt(b^2 - 4ac)}{2a}$$

A program to evaluate these roots is given in Fig. 3.10. The program requests the user to input the values of **a**, **b** and **c** and outputs **root1** and **root2**.

```
Program
/**************************************************************************/
/*                 SOLUTION OF QUADRATIC EQUATION                     */
/**************************************************************************/
#include <math.h>
main( )
{
    float  a, b, c, discriminant,
           root1, root2;
    printf("Input values of a, b, and c\n");
    scanf("%f %f %f", &a, &b, &c);

    discriminant = b*b − 4*a*c ;

    if(discriminant < 0)
        printf("\n\nROOTS ARE IMAGINARY\n");
    else
    {
        root1 = (−b + sqrt(discriminant))/(2.0*a);
        root2 = (−b − sqrt(discriminant))/(2.0*a);
        printf("\n\nRoot1 = %5.2f\n\nRoot2 = %5.2f\n",
                root1,root2 );
    }
}
Output
Input values of a, b, and c
2 4 −16

Root1 =    2.00

Root2 =  −4.00

Input values of a, b, and c
1 2 3

ROOTS ARE IMAGINARY
```

Fig. 3.10 *Solution of a quadratic equation*

The term $(b^2 - 4ac)$ is called the *discriminant*. If the discriminant is less than zero, its square roots cannot be evaluated. In such cases, the roots are said to be imaginary numbers and the program outputs an appropriate message.

REVIEW QUESTIONS AND EXERCISES

3.1 Which of the following arithmetic expressions are valid ? If valid, give the value of the expression; otherwise give reason.

(a) 25/3 % 2   (e) −14 % 3

(b) +9/4 + 5   (f) 15.25 + - 5.0

(c) 7.5 % 3   (g) (5/3) * 3 + 5 % 3

(d) 14 % 3 + 7 % 2   (h) 21 % (int)4.5

3.2 Write C assignment statements to evaluate the following equations:

(a)   Area   = $\pi r^2 + 2\pi rh$

(b)   Torque = $\dfrac{2m_1 m_2}{m_1 + m_2} \cdot g$

(c)   Side   = $\sqrt{a^2 + b^2 - 2ab\ \cos(x)}$

(d)   Energy   = mass $\left[\text{acceleration} \times \text{height} + \dfrac{(\text{velocity})^2}{2} \right]$

3.3 Identify unnecessary parentheses in the following arithmetic expressions.

(a) ((x−(y/5)+z)%8) + 25

(b) ((x−y) * p)+q

(c) (m*n) + (−x/y)

(d) x/(3*y)

3.4 Find errors, if any, in the following assignment statements and rectify them.

(a)   x = y = z = 0.5, 2.0. −5.75;

(b)   m = ++a * 5;

(c)   y = sqrt(100);

(d)   p * = x/y;

(e)   s = /5;

(f)   a = b++ −c * 2

3.5 Determine the value of each of the following logical expressions if a = 5, b = 10 and c = −6

(a)   a > b && a < c

(b)   a < b && a > c

(c)   a == c || b > a

(d)   b > 15 && c < 0 || a > 0

(e)   (a/2.0 == 0.0 && b/2.0 != 0.0) || c < 0.0

3.6 The straight-line method of computing the yearly depreciation of the value of an item is given by

$$\text{Depreciation} = \frac{\text{Purchase Price} - \text{Salvage Value}}{\text{Years of Service}}$$

Write a program to determine the salvage value of an item when the purchase price, years of service, and the annual depreciation are given.

3.7 Write a program that will read a real number from the keyboard and print the following output in one line:

Smallest integer not less than the number	The given number	Largest integer not greater than the number

3.8 The total distance travelled by a vehicle in t seconds is given by

$$\text{distance} = ut + (at^2)/2$$

Where u is the initial velocity (meters per second), a is the acceleration (meters per second^2). Write a program to evaluate the distance travelled at regular intervals of time, given the values of u and a. The program should provide the flexibility to the user to select his own time intervals and repeat the calculations for different values of u and a.

3.9 In inventory management, the Economic Order Quantity for a single item is given by

$$\text{EOQ} = \sqrt{\frac{2 \times \text{demand rate} \times \text{setup costs}}{\text{holding cost per item per unit time}}}$$

and the optimal Time Between Orders

$$\text{TBO} = \sqrt{\frac{2 \times \text{setup costs}}{\text{demand rate} \times \text{holding cost per item per unit time}}}$$

Write a program to compute EOQ and TBO, given demand rate (items per unit time), setup costs (per order), and the holding cost (per item per unit time).

3.10 For a certain electrical circuit with an industance L and resistance R, the damped natural frequency is given by

$$\text{Frequency} = \sqrt{\frac{1}{LC} - \frac{R^2}{4C^2}}$$

It is desired to study the variation of this frequency with C (capacitance). Write a program to calculate the frequency for different values of C starting from 0.01 to 0.1 in steps of 0.01.

MANAGING INPUT AND OUTPUT OPERATIONS

4.1 INTRODUCTION

Reading, processing, and writing of data are the three essential functions of a computer program. Most programs take some data as input and display the processed data, often known as *information* or *results*, on a suitable medium. So far we have seen two methods of providing data to the program variables. One method is to assign values to variables through the assignment statements such as **x = 5; a = 0;** and so on. Another method is to use the input function **scanf** which can read data from a terminal. We have used both the methods in most of our earlier example programs. For outputting results we have used extensively the function **printf** which sends results out to a terminal.

Unlike other high-level languages, C does not have any built-in input/output statements as part of its syntax. All input/output operations are carried out through function calls such as **printf** and **scanf**. There exist several functions that have more or less become standard for input and output operations in C. These functions are collectively known as the *standard I/O library*. In this chapter we shall discuss some common I/O functions that can be used on many machines without any change. However, one should consult the system reference manual for exact details of these functions and also to see what other functions are available.

It may be recalled that we have included a statement

#include <math.h>

in the Sample Program 5 in Chapter 1, where a math library function cos(x) has been used. This is to instruct the compiler to fetch the function cos(x) from the math library, and that it is not a part of C language. Similarly, each program that uses a standard input/output function must contain the statement

#include <stdio.h>

at the beginning. However, there might be exceptions. For example, this is not necessary for the functions **printf** and **scanf** which have been defined as a part of the C language.

The file name **stdio.h** is an abbreviation for *standard input-output header* file. The instruction

#include <**stdio.h**> tells the compiler 'to search for a file named *stdio.h* and place its contents at this point in the program'. The contents of the header file become part of the source code when it is compiled.

4.2 READING A CHARACTER

The simplest of all input/output operations is reading a character from the standard input unit (usually the keyboard) and writing it to the standard output unit (usually the screen). Reading a single character can be done by using the function **getchar**. (This can also be done with the help of the **scanf** function which is discussed in Section 4.4) The **getchar** takes the following form:

```
variable_name = getchar( );
```

variable_name is a valid C name that has been declared as **char** type. When this statement is encountered, the computer waits until a key is pressed and then assigns this character as a value to **getchar** function. Since **getchar** is used on the right-hand side of an assignment statement, the character value of **getchar** is in turn assigned to the variable name on the left For example

```
char   name;
name = getchar( );
```

will assign the character 'H' to the variable **name** when we press the key H on the keyboard. Since **getchar** is a function, it requires a set of parentheses as shown.

Example 4.1
The program in Fig. 4.1 shows the use of **getchar** function in an interactive environment.

The program displays a question of YES/NO type to the user and reads the user's response in a single character (Y or N). If the response is Y, it outputs the message

My name is BUSY BEE

otherwise, outputs "you are good for nothing".

The **getchar** function may be called successively to read the characters contained in a line of text. For example, the following program segment reads characters from keyboard one after another until the 'Return' key is pressed.

```
------------
------------
char character;
character = ' ';
while (character ! = '\n')
{
       character  =  getchar( );
}
------------
------------
```

Warning: The **getchar()** function accepts any character keyed in. This includes RETURN and TAB. This means that when we enter single character input, the newline character is waiting in the input queue after **getchar()** returns. This could create problems when we use **getchar()** interactively in a loop. A dummy **getchar()** may be used to "eat" the unwanted newline character.

```
Program
/***************************************************************/
/*          READING  A  CHARACTER  FROM  TERMINAL          */
/***************************************************************/
#include        <stdio.h>
main( )
{
     char answer;
     printf("Would you like to know my name?\n");
     printf("Type Y for YES and N for NO:    ");
     answer = getchar( );      /* .......... Reading a character........... */
     if(answer == 'Y'    ||    answer  ==  'y')
       printf("\n\n My name is BUSY BEE \n");
     else
       printf("\n\nYou are good for nothing \n");
}
Output
Would you like to know my name?
Type Y for YES and N for NO: Y

My name is BUSY  BEE

Would you like to know my name?
Type Y for YES and N for NO: n

You are good for nothing
```

Fig. 4.1 *Use of **getchar** function*

Example 4.2

The program of Fig. 4.2 requests the user to enter a character and displays a message on the screen telling the user whether the character is an alphabet or digit, or any other special character.

This program receives a character typed from the keyboard and tests whether it is a letter or digit and prints out a message accordingly. These tests are done with the help of the following functions:

isalpha(character)
isdigit(character)

For example, **isalpha** assumes a value non-zero (TRUE) if the argument **character** contains an alphabet; otherwise it assumes 0 (FALSE). Similar is the case with the function **isdigit**.

C supports many other similar functions which are given in Table 4.1 (Also see Appendix III). These character functions are contained in the file **ctype.h** and therefore the statement

#include < ctype.h >

must be included in the program.

```
Program
/*******************************************************************/
/*                    TESTING  CHARACTER  TYPE                    */
/*******************************************************************/
#include        <stdio.h>
#include        <ctype.h>
main( )
{
    char character;
    printf("Press any key \n");

    character = getchar( );

    if (isalpha(character) > 0)
      printf("The character is a letter.");
    else
      if (isdigit (character) > 0)
        printf("The character is a digit.");
      else
        printf("The character is not alphanumeric.");
}
Output
Press any key
h
The character is a letter.

Press any key
5
The character is a digit.

Press any key
*
The character is not alphanumeric.
```

Fig. 4.2 *Program to test the character type*

Table 4.1   Character Test Functions

Function	Test
isalnum(c)	Is c an alphanumeric character?
isalpha(c)	Is c an alphabetic character?
isdigit(c)	Is c a digit?
islower(c)	Is c a lower case letter?
isprint(c)	Is c a printable character?
ispunct(c)	Is c a punctuation mark?
isspace(c)	Is c a *white space* character?
isupper(c)	Is c an upper case letter?

4.3 WRITING A CHARACTER

Like **getchar**, there is an analogous function **putchar** for writing characters one at a time to the terminal. It takes the form as shown below:

```
putchar(variable_name);
```

where *variable-name* is a type **char** variable containing a character. This statement displays the character contained in the **variable-name** at the terminal. For example, the statements

```
answer = 'Y';
putchar(answer);
```

will display the character Y on the screen. The statement

```
putchar('\n');
```

would cause the cursor on the screen to move to the beginning of the next line.

Example 4.3

A program that reads a character from keyboard and then prints it in reverse case is given in Fig. 4.3. That is, if the input is upper case, the output will be lower case and vice-versa.

The program uses three new functions: **islower, toupper,** and **tolower**. The function **islower** is a conditional function and takes the value TRUE if the argument is a lower case alphabet; otherwise takes the value FALSE. The function **toupper** converts the lower case argument into an upper case alphabet while the function **tolower** does the reverse.

```
Program
/***************************************************************/
/*         WRITING A CHARACTER TO THE TERMINAL              */
/***************************************************************/
#include <stdio.h>
#include <ctype.h>
main( )
{
    char alphabet;
    printf("Enter an alphabet");
    putchar('\n');
    alphabet = getchar( );
    if (islower(alphabet));
      putchar(toupper(alphabet));
    else
      putchar(tolower(alphabet));
}
Output
Enter an alphabet
a
A
Enter an alphabet
Q
q
Enter an alphabet
z
Z
```

Fig. 4.3 *Reading and writing of alphabets in reverse case*

4.4 FORMATTED INPUT

Formatted input refers to an input data that has been arranged in a particular format. For example, consider the following data:

15.75   123   John

This line contains three pieces of data, arranged in a particular form. Such data has to be read conforming to the format of its appearance. For example, the first part of the data should be read into a variable **float**, the second into **int**, and the third part into **char**. This is possible in C using the **scanf** function.

We have already used this input function in a number of examples. Here, we shall explore all of the options that are available for reading the formatted data with **scanf** function. The general form of **scanf** is

scanf("*control string*", arg1, arg2, ... argn);

The *control string* specifies the field format in which the data is to be entered and the arguments *arg1*, *arg2*, ... *argn* specify the address of locations where the data is stored. Control string and arguments are separated by commas.

Control string contains field specifications which direct the interpretation of input data. It may include:

- Field (or format) specifications, consisting of the conversion character %, a data type character (or type specifier), and an *optional* number, specifying the field width.
- Blanks, tabs, or newlines.

Blanks, tabs and newlines are ignored. The data type character indicates the type of data that is to be assigned to the variable associated with the corresponding argument. The field width specifier is optional. The discussions that follow will clarify these concepts.

Inputting Integer Numbers

The field specification for reading an integer number is:

% w d

The percent sign (%) indicates that a conversion specification follows. *w* is an integer number that specifies the *field width* of the number to be read and d, known as data type character, indicates that the number to be read is in integer mode. Consider the following example:

scanf("%2d %5d", &num1, &num2);

Data line:

50   31426

The value 50 is assigned to **num1** and 31426 to **num2**. Suppose the input data is as follows:

31426   50

The variable **num1** will be assigned 31 (because of %2d) and **num2** will be assigned 426 (unread part of 31426). The value 50 that is unread will be assigned to the first variable in the **next scanf** call. This kind of errors may be eliminated if we use the field specifications without the field width specifications. That is, the statement

scanf("%d %d", &num1, &num2);

will read the data

31426   50

correctly and assign 31426 to **num1** and 50 to **num2**.

Input data items must be separated by spaces, tabs or newlines. Punctuation marks do not count as separators. When the **scanf** function searches the input data line for a value to be read, it will always bypass any white space characters.

What happens if we enter a floating point number instead of an integer? The fractional part may be stripped away! Also, **scanf** may skip reading further input.

When the **scanf** reads a particular value, reading of the value will terminate as soon as the number of characters specified by the field width is reached (if specified) or until a character that is not valid for the value being read is encountered. In the case of integers, valid characters are an optionally signed sequence of digits.

An input field may be skipped by specifying * in the place of field width. For example, the statement

scanf("%d %*d %d", &a, &b)

will assign the data

123   456   789

as follows:

123   to **a**
456   skipped (because of *)
789   to **b**

The data type character **d** may be preceded by 'l' (letter ell) to read long integers.

Example 4.4

Various input formatting options for reading integers are experimented with in the program shown in Fig. 4.4.

The first **scanf** requests input data for three integer values **a**, **b**, and **c**, and accordingly three values 1, 2, and 3 are keyed in. Because of the specification %*d the value 2 has been skipped and 3 is assigned to the variable **b**. Notice that since no data is available for c, it contains garbage.

The second **scanf** specifies the format %2d and %4d for the variables **x** and **y** respectively. Whenever we specify field width for reading integer numbers, the input numbers should not contain more digits than the specified size. Otherwise, the extra digits on the right-hand side will be truncated and assigned to the next variable in the list. Thus, the second **scanf** has

.runcated the four digit number 6789 and assigned 67 to x and 89 to y. The value 4321 has assigned to the first variable in the immediately following **scanf** statement.

```
Program
/*************************************************************************/
/*                    READING  INTEGER  NUMBERS                        */
/*************************************************************************/
main( )
{
    int a,b,c,x,y,z;
    int p,q,r;

    printf("Enter three integer numbers\n");
    scanf("%d %*d %d",&a,&b,&c);
    printf("%d %d %d \n\n",a,b,c);

    printf("Enter two 4-digit numbers\n");
    scanf("%2d %4d",&x,&y);
    printf("%d %d\n\n", x,y);

    printf("Enter two integers\n");
    scanf("%d %d", &a,&x);
    printf("%d %d \n\n",a,x);

    printf("Enter a nine digit number\n");
    scanf("%3d %4d %3d",&p,&q,&r);
    printf("%d %d %d \n\n",p,q,r);

    printf("Enter two three digit numbers\n");
    scanf("%d %d",&x,&y);
    printf("%d %d",x,y);
}

Output

Enter three integer numbers
1 2 3
1 3 -3577

Enter two 4-digit numbers
6789   4321
67 89

Enter two integers
44   66
4321  44

Enter a nine digit number
123456789
66 1234  567

Enter two three digit numbers
123   456
89 123
```

Fig. 4.4 *Reading integers using* **scanf**

Inputting Real Numbers

Unlike integer numbers, the field width of real numbers is not to be specified and therefore **scanf** reads real numbers using the simple specification **%f** for both the notations, namely, decimal point notation and exponential notation. For example, the statement

scanf("%f %f %f", &x, &y, &z);

with the input data

475.89   43.21E-1   678

will assign the value 475.89 to x, 4.321 to y, and 678.0 to z. The input field specifications may be separated by any arbitrary blank spaces.

If the number to be read is of **double** type, then the specification should be **%lf** instead of simple **%f**. A number may be skipped using **%*f** specification.

Example 4.5

Reading of real numbers (in both decimal point and exponential notation) is illustrated in Fig. 4.5.

```
Program
/****************************************************************************/
/*                   READING OF REAL NUMBERS                             */
/****************************************************************************/
main( )
{
      float x,y;
      double p,q;

      printf("Values of x and y:");
      scanf("%f %e", &x, &y);
      printf("\n");
      printf("x = %f\ny = %f\n\n", x, y);

      printf("Values of p and q:");
      scanf("%lf %lf", &p, &q);
      printf("\np = %lf\nq = %e",p,q);
      printf("\n\np = %.12lf\np = %.12e", p,q);
}
Output
Values of x and y:12.3456    17.5e−2

x = 12.345600
y = 0.175000

Values of p and q:4.142857142857    18.5678901234567890

p = 4.142857142857
q = 1.856789012346e+001
```

Fig. 4.5 *Reading of real numbers*

Inputting Character Strings

We have already seen how a single character can be read from the terminal using the **getchar** function. The same can be achieved using the **scanf** function also. In addition, a **scanf** function can input strings containing more than one character. Following are the specifications for reading character strings:

| **%ws** | or | **%wc** |

The corresponding argument should be a pointer to a character array. However, %c may be used to read a single character when the argument is a pointer to a **char** variable.

Example 4.6

Reading of strings using **%wc** and **%ws** is illustrated in Fig. 4.6.

The program in Fig. 4.6 illustrates the use of various field specifications for reading strings. When we use **%wc** for reading a string, the system will wait until the wth character is keyed in.

Note that the specification %s terminates reading at the encounter of a blank space. Therefore, **name2** has read only the first part of "New York" and the second part is automatically assigned to **name3**. However, during the second run, the string "New-York" is correctly assigned to **name2**.

Some versions of **scanf** support the following conversion specifications for strings:

%[characters] and %[^characters]

The specification %[characters] means that only the characters specified within the brackets are permissible in the input string. If the input string contains any other character, the string will be terminated at the first encounter of such a character. The specification %[^characters]

```
Program
/*******************************************************************/
/*                    READING  STRINGS                           */
/*******************************************************************/
main( )
{
     int no;
     char name1[15], name2[15], name3[15];

     printf("Enter serial number and name one\n");
     scanf("%d %15c", &no, name1);
     printf("%d %15s\n\n", no, name1);

     printf("Enter serial number and name two\n");
     scanf("%d %s", &no, name2);
     printf("%d %15s\n\n", no, name2);

     printf("Enter serial number and name three\n");
     scanf("%d %15s", &no, name3);
     printf("%d %15s\n\n", no, name3);
}
```

```
Enter serial number and name one
1  123456789012345
1  123456789012345r

Enter serial number and name two
2  New York
2              New

Enter serial number and name three
2              York

Enter serial number and name one
1  123456789012
1  123456789012  r

Enter serial number and name two
2  New-York
2              New-York

Enter serial number and name three
3  London
3              London
```

Fig. 4.6 *Reading of strings*

does exactly the reverse. That is, the characters specified after the circumflex (ˆ) are not permitted in the input string. The reading of the string will be terminated at the encounter of one of these characters.

We have just seen that **%s** specifier cannot be used to read strings with blank spaces. But, this can be done with the help of %[ ] specification. Blank spaces may be included within the brackets, thus enabling the **scanf** to read strings with spaces. Remember that the lowercase and uppercase letters are distinct. Example 4.7 illustrates the use of %[ ] specification.

Example 4.7
The program in Fig. 4.7 illustrates the function of %[ ] specification.

Reading Mixed Data Types

It is possible to use one **scanf** statement to input a data line containing mixed mode data. In such cases, care should be exercised to ensure that the input data items match the control specifications *in order* and *type*. When an attempt is made to read an item that does not match the type expected, the **scanf** function does not read any further and immediately returns the values read. The statement

scanf("%d %c %f %s", &count, &code, &ratio, name);

will read the data

15   p   1.575   coffee

correctly and assign the values to the variables in the order in which they appear. Some systems accept integers in the place of real numbers and vice-versa, and the input data is converted to the type specified in the control string.

Detection of Errors in Input

When a **scanf** function completes reading its list, it returns the value of number of items that

```
Program-A
/****************************************************************/
/*            ILLUSTRATION OF %[  ] SPECIFICATION             */
/****************************************************************/
main( )
{
    char address[80];
    printf("Enter address \n");
    scanf("%[ a-z ]", address);
    printf("%–80s \n\n",address);
}

Output
Enter address
new delhi 110 002
new delhi

Program-B
/****************************************************************/
/*            ILLUSTRATION OF %[^ ] SPECIFICATION             */
/****************************************************************/
main( )
{
    char address[80];
    printf("Enter address\n");
    scanf("%[^\n]",address);
    printf("%–80s \n\n",address);
}

Output
Enter address
New Delhi 110 002
New Delhi 110 002
```

Fig. 4.7 *Illustration of conversion specification [. .] for strings*

are successfully read. This value can be used to test whether any errors occurred in reading the input. For example, the statement

scanf("%d %f %s", &a, &b, name);

will return the value 3 if the following data is typed in:

20   150.25   motor

and will return the value 1 if the following line is entered

20   motor   150.25

This is because the function would encounter a string when it was expecting a floating point value, and would therefore terminate its scan after reading the first value.

Example 4.8

The program presented in Fig. 4.8 illustrates the testing for correctness of reading of data by **scanf** function.

```
Program
/******************************************************************/
/*          TESTING FOR CORRECTNESS OF INPUT DATA          */
/******************************************************************/
main( )
{
     int a;
     float b;
     char c;
     printf("Enter values of a, b and c\n");
     if (scanf("%d %f %c", &a, &b, &c) == 3)
       printf("a = %d   b = %f   c = %c\n", a, b, c);
     else
       printf("Error in input.\n");
}
Output
Enter values of a, b and c
12   3.45   A
a = 12   b = 3.450000   c = A

Enter values of a, b and c
23   78   9
a = 23   b = 78.000000   c = 9

Enter values of a, b and c
8   A   5.25
Error in input.

Enter values of a, b and c
Y   12   67
Error in input.

Enter values of a, b and c
15.75   23   X
a = 15   b = 0.750000   c = 2
```

Fig. 4.8 *Detection of errors in* ***scanf*** *input*

The function **scanf** is expected to read three items of data and therefore, when the values for all the three variables are read correctly, the program prints out their values. During the third run, the second item does not match with the type of variable and therefore the reading is terminated and the error message is printed. Same is the case with the fourth run.

In the last run, although data items do not match the variables, no error message has been printed. When we attempt to read a real number for an **int** variable, the integer part is assigned to the variable, and the truncated decimal part is assigned to the next variable. Note that the character '2' is assigned to the character variable **c**.

Commonly used **scanf** format codes are given in Table 4.1

Table 4.1   scanf Format Codes

Code	Meaning
%c	read a single character
%d	read a decimal integer
%e	read a floating point value
%f	read a floating point value
%g	read a floating point value
%h	read a short integer
%i	read a decimal, hexadecimal, or octal integer
%o	read an octal integer
%s	read a string
%u	read an unsigned decimal integer
%x	read a hexadecimal integer
%[..]	read a string of word(s)

The following letters may be used as prefix for certain conversion characters.

  h for short integers
  l for long integers or double
  L for long double

Points to Remember While Using scanf

If we do not plan carefully, some crazy things can happen with **scanf**. Since the I/O routines are not a part of C language, they are made available either as a separate module of the C library or as a part of the operating system (like UNIX). New features are added to these routines from time to time as new versions of systems are released. We should consult the system reference manual before using these routines. Given below are some of the general points to keep in mind while writing a **scanf** statement.

1. All function arguments, except the control string, *must* be pointers to variables.
2. Format specifications contained in the control string should match the arguments in order.
3. Input data items must be separated by spaces and must match the variables receiving the input in the same order.
4. The reading will be terminated, when **scanf** encounters an 'invalid mismatch' of data or a character that is not valid for the value being read.
5. When searching for a value, **scanf** ignores line boundaries and simply looks for the next appropriate character.

6. Any unread data items in a line will be considered as a part of the data input line to the next **scanf** call.
7. When the field width specifier *w* is used, it should be large enough to contain the input data size.

4.5 FORMATTED OUTPUT

We have seen the use of **printf** function for printing captions and numerical results. It is highly desirable that the outputs are produced in such a way that they are understandable and are in an easy-to-use form. It is therefore necessary for the programmer to give careful consideration to the appearance and clarity of the output produced by his program.

The **printf** statement provides certain features that can be effectively exploited to control the alignment and spacing of print-outs on the terminals. The general form of **printf** statement is

> **printf**("*control string*", arg1, arg2, ... argn);

Control string consists of three types of items:

1. Characters that will be printed on the screen as they appear.
2. Format specifications that define the output format for display of each item.
3. *Escape sequence* characters such as \n, \t, and \b.

The control string indicates how many arguments follow and what their types are. The arguments *arg1, arg2, ... argn* are the variables whose values are formatted and printed according to the specifications of the control string. The arguments should match in number, order and type with the format specifications.

A simple format specification has the following form:

> **% w.p type-specifier**

where *w* is an integer number that specifies the total number of columns for the output value and *p* is another integer number that specifies the number of digits to the right of the decimal point (of a real number) or the number of characters to be printed from a string. Both *w* and *p* are optional. Some examples of **printf** statement are:

```
printf("Programming in C");
printf("    ");
printf("\n");
printf("%d", x);
printf("a  =  %f\n   b  =  %f", a, b);
printf("sum  =  %d", 1234);
printf("\n\n");
```

printf never supplies a newline automatically and therefore multiple **printf** statements may be used to build one line of output. A newline can be introduced by the help of a *newline* character '\n' as shown in some of the examples above.

Output of Integer Numbers

The format specification for printing an integer number is

> **% w d**

where *w* specifies the minimum field width for the output. However, if a number is greater than the specified field width, it will be printed in full, overriding the minimum specification. **d** specifies that the value to be printed is an integer. The number is written *right-justified* in the given field width. Leading blanks will appear as necessary. The following examples illustrate the output of the number 9876 under different formats:

Format	Output
printf("%d", 9876)	9 8 7 6
printf("%6d", 9876)	⎵ ⎵ 9 8 7 6
printf("%2d", 9876)	9 8 7 6
printf("%-6d", 9876)	9 8 7 6 ⎵ ⎵
printf("%06d", 9876)	0 0 9 8 7 6

It is possible to force the printing to be *left-justified* by placing a *minus* sign directly after the % character, as shown in the fourth example above. It is also possible to pad with zeros the leading blanks by placing a 0 (zero) before the field width specifier as shown in the last item above.

Long integers may be printed by specifying **ld** in the place of **d** in the format specification.

Example 4.9

The program in Fig.4.9 illustrates the output of integer numbers under various formats.

```
Program
/******************************************************************/
/*              PRINTING  OF  INTEGER  NUMBERS                  */
/******************************************************************/
main( )
{
    int m = 12345;
    long n = 987654;

    printf("%d\n",m);
    printf("%10d\n",m);
    printf("%010d\n",m);
    printf("%-10d\n",m);
    printf("%10ld\n",n);
    printf("%10ld\n",-n);
}
Output
12345
     12345
0000012345
12345
    987654
   -987654
```

Fig. 4.9 *Formatted output of integers*

Output of Real Numbers

The output of a real number may be displayed in decimal notation using the following format specification:

$$\boxed{\% \ w.p \ f}$$

The integer w indicates the minimum number of positions that are to be used for the display of the value and the integer p indicates the number of digits to be displayed after the decimal point (*precision*). The value, when displayed, is *rounded to p decimal places* and printed *right-justified* in the field of w columns. Leading blanks and trailing zeros will appear as necessary. The default precision is 6 decimal places. The negative numbers will be printed with the minus sign. The number will be displayed in the form [−] mmm . nnn.

We can also display a real number in exponential notation by using the specification

$$\boxed{\% \ w.p \ e}$$

The display takes the form

[−] m.nnnne[±]xx

where the length of the string of n's is specified by the precision p. The default precision is 6. The field width w should satisfy the condition.

$$w \geq p+7$$

The value will be rounded off and printed right justified in the field of w columns.

Padding the leading blanks with zeros and printing with *left-justification* is also possible by introducing 0 or − before the field width specifier w.

The following examples illustrate the output of the number y = 98.7654 under different format specifications:

Format	Output
printf("%7.4f",y)	`98.7654`
printf("%7.2f",y)	`  98.77`
printf("%−7.2f",y)	`98.77  `
printf("%f",y)	`98.7654`
printf("%10.2e",y)	`   9.88e+01`
printf("%11.4e",−y)	`−9.8765e+01`

printf("%−10.2e",y)

```
9 . 8 8 e + 0 1    
```

printf("%e",y)

```
9 . 8 7 6 5 4 0 e + 0 1
```

Some systems also support a special field specification character that lets the user define the field size at run-time. This takes the following form:

$$\text{printf("\%*.*f", width, precision, number);}$$

In this case, both the field width and the precision are given as arguments which will supply the values for *w* and *p*. For example,

printf("%*.*f",7,2,number);

is equivalent to

printf("%7.2f",number);

The advantage of this format is that the values for *width* and *precision* may be supplied at run-time, thus making the format a *dynamic* one. For example, the above statement can be used as follows:

int width = 7;
int precision = 2;
....
....
printf("%*.*f", width, precision, number);

Example 4.10
All the options of printing a real number are illustrated in Fig. 4.10.

```
Program
/**************************************************************************/
/*                 PRINTING OF REAL NUMBERS                    */
/**************************************************************************/
main( )
{
    float y = 98.7654;

    printf("%7.4f\n", y);
    printf("%f\n", y);
    printf("%7.2f\n", y);
    printf("%−7.2f\n", y);
    printf("%07.2f\n", y);
    printf("%*.*f", 7, 2, y);
    printf("\n");
    printf("%10.2e\n", y);
    printf("%12.4e\n", −y);
```

```
        printf("%-10.2e\n", y);
        printf("%e\n", y);
    }
```

Output

```
98.7654
98.765404
    98.77
98.77
0098.77
98.77

    9.88e+001
  -9.8765e+001
  9.88e+001
  9.876540e+001
```

Fig. 4.10   *Formatted output of real numbers*

Note: Microsoft C supports three digits in exponent part.

Printing of a Single Characater

A single character can be displayed in a desired position using the format

> **%wc**

The characater will be displayed *right-justified* in the field of *w* columns. We can make the display *left-justified* by placing a minus sign before the integer *w*. The default value for *w* is 1.

Printing of Strings

The format specification for outputting strings is similar to that of real numbers. It is of the form

> **%w.ps**

where *w* specifies the field width for display and *p* instructs that only the first *p* characters of the string are to be displayed. The display is *right-justified*.

The following examples show the effect of a variety of specifications in printing a string "NEW DELHI 110001", containing 16 characters (including blanks)

Specification	Output
	1 2 3 4 5 6 7 8 9 0 1 2 3 4 5 6 7 8 9 0
%s	`NEW DELHI 110001`
%20s	`    NEW DELHI 110001`
%20.10s	`          NEW DELHI`
%.5s	`NEW D`
%-20.10s	`NEW DELHI`
%5s	`NEW DELHI 110001`

Example 4.11

Printing of characters and strings is illustrated in Fig. 4.11.

Mixed Data Output

It is permitted to mix data types in one printf statement. For example, the statement of the type

printf("%d %f %s %c", a, b, c, d);

is valid. As pointed out earlier, **printf** uses its control string to decide how many variables to be printed and what their types are. Therefore, the format specifications should match the variables in number, order, and type. If there are not enough variables or if they are of the wrong type, incorrect results will be output.

```
Program
/*******************************************************************/
/*           PRINTING OF CHARACTERS AND STRINGS            */
/*******************************************************************/
main( )
{
      char x = 'A';
      static char   name[20] = "ANIL KUMAR GUPTA";
      printf("OUTPUT OF CHARACTERS\n\n");
      printf("%c\n%3c\n%5c\n", x,x,x);
      printf("%3c\n%c\n", x,x);
      printf("\n");
      printf("OUTPUT OF STRINGS\n\n");
      printf("%s\n", name);
      printf("%20s\n", name);
      printf("%20.10s\n", name);
      printf("%.5s\n", name);
      printf("%−20.10s\n", name);
      printf("%5s\n", name);
}
Output
OUTPUT OF CHARACTERS

A
  A
    A
    A
A
OUTPUT OF STRINGS

ANIL KUMAR GUPTA
        ANIL KUMAR GUPTA
              ANIL KUMAR
ANIL
ANIL KUMAR
ANIL KUMAR GUPTA
```

Fig. 4.11 *Printing of characters and strings*

Commonly used **printf** format codes are given in Table 4.2 and format flags in Table 4.3

Table 4.2   printf Format Codes

Code	Meaning
%c	print a single character
%d	print a decimal integer
%e	print a floating point value in exponent form
%f	print a floating point value without exponent
%g	print a floating point value either e-type or f-type depending on value
%i	print a signed decimal integer
%o	print an octal integer, without leading zero
%s	print a string
%u	print an unsigned decimal integer
%x	print a hexadecimal integer, without leading 0x

The following letters may be used as prefix for certain conversion characters.

h for short integers,
l for long integers or double,
L for long double

Table 4.3   Output Format Flags

Flag	Meaning
–	Output is left-justified within the field. Remaining field will be blank.
+	+ or – will precede the signed numeric item.
0	Causes leading zeroes to appear.
# (with o or x)	Causes octal and hex items to be preceded by O and Ox, respectively.
# (with e,f or g)	Causes a decimal point to be present in all floating point numbers, even if it is whole number. Also prevents the truncation of trailing zeros in g-type conversion.

Enhancing the Readability of Output

Computer outputs are used as information for analysing certain relationships between variables and for making decisions. Therefore the correctness and clarity of outputs is of utmost importance. While the correctness depends on the solution procedure, the clarity depends on the way the output is presented. Following are some of the steps we can take to improve the clarity and hence the readability and understandability of outputs.

1. Provide enough blank space between two numbers.
2. Introduce appropriate headings and variable names in the output.
3. Print special messages whenever a peculiar condition occurs in the output.
4. Introduce blank lines between the important sections of the output.

The system usually provides two blank spaces between the numbers. However, this can be increased by selecting a suitable field width for the numbers or by introducing a 'tab' character between the specifications. For example, the statement

printf("a = %d\t b = %d", a, b);

will provide four blank spaces between the two fields. We can also print them on two separate lines by using the statement

printf("a = %d\n b = %d", a, b);

Messages and headings can be printed by using the character strings directly in the **printf** statement. Examples:

printf("\n   OUTPUT RESULTS   \n");
printf("code\t Name\t Age\n"):
printf("Error in input data\n");
printf(Enter your name\n");

CASE STUDIES

1. Inventory Report

Problem: The ABC Electric Company manufactures four consumer products. Their inventory position on a particular day is given below:

Code	Quantity	Rate (Rs)
F105	275	575.00
H220	107	99.95
I109	321	215.50
M315	89	725.00

It is required to prepare the inventory report table in the following format:

INVENTORY REPORT

Code	Quantity	Rate	Value
—	—	—	—
—	—	—	—
—	—	—	—
—	—	—	—
		Total Value:	—

The value of each item is given by the product of quantity and rate.
Program: The program given in Fig.4.12 reads the data from the terminal and generates the required output. The program uses subscripted variables which are discussed in Chapter 7.

2. Reliability Graph

Problem: The reliability of an electronic component is given by

$$\text{reliability } (r) = e^{-\lambda t}$$

Program

```
/********************************************************************/
/*                     INVENTORY  REPORT                          */
/********************************************************************/

#define ITEMS 4

main( )
{   /* BEGIN */

    int  i, quantity[5];
    float rate[5], value, total-value;
    char code[5][5];

    /*  READING VALUES  */

    i = 1;
    while ( i <= ITEMS)
    {
        printf("Enter code, quantity, and rate:");
        scanf("%s %d %f", code[i], &quantity[i], &rate[i]); i++;
    }

/*..................Printing of Table and Column Headings...............  */
    printf("\n\n");
    printf("                   INVENTORY  REPORT       \n");
    printf(" --------------------------------------------------------------\n");
    printf(" Code          Quantity      Rate      Value   \n");
    printf(" --------------------------------------------------------------\n");

/*..................Preparation of Inventory Position.................  */

    total-value = 0;
    i = 1;

    while ( i <= ITEMS);
    {
        value = quantity[i]  *  rate[i];
        printf("%5s %10d %10.2f   %e\n",code[i],quantity[i], rate[i],value);
        total-value += value;
        i ++;
    }
/*.....................Printing of End of Table.........................  */
    printf(" --------------------------------------------------------------\n");
    printf("                            Total Value = %e\n",total-value);
    printf(" --------------------------------------------------------------\n");
}   /* END */
```

Output

```
Enter code, quantity, and rate:F105    275       575.00
Enter code, quantity, and rate:H220    107        99.95
Enter code, quantity, and rate:I019    321       215.50
Enter code, quantity, and rate:M315     89       725.00

                INVENTORY  REPORT
-----------------------------------------------------------
Code            Quantity        Rate           Value
-----------------------------------------------------------
F105              275          575.00       1.581250e+005
H220              107           99.95       1.069465e+004
I019              321          215.50       6.917550e+004
M315               89          725.00       6.452500e+004
-----------------------------------------------------------
                            Total Value  =  3.025202e+005
-----------------------------------------------------------
```

Fig. 4.12 *Program for inventory report*

where λ is the component failure rate per hour and t is the time of operation in hours. A graph is required to determine the reliability at various operating times, from 0 to 3000 hours. The failure rate λ (lamda) is 0.001.

Program

```
/****************************************************************/
/*                  RELIABILITY GRAPH                          */
/****************************************************************/
#include   <math.h>
#define    LAMDA      0.001
main( )
{
    double t;
    float r;
    int   i, R;
    for (i=1; i<=27; ++i)
    {
        printf("- -");
    }
    printf("\n");
    for (t=0; t<=3000; t+=150)
    {
        r  = exp(-LAMDA*t);
        R = (int)(50*r+0.5);
        printf("  |");
        for (i=1; 1 <=R; ++i)
        {
            printf("*");
        }
        printf("# \n");
    }
}
```

```
        for (i = 1; i < 3; ++i)
        {
                printf(" |\n");
        }
}
```

Output

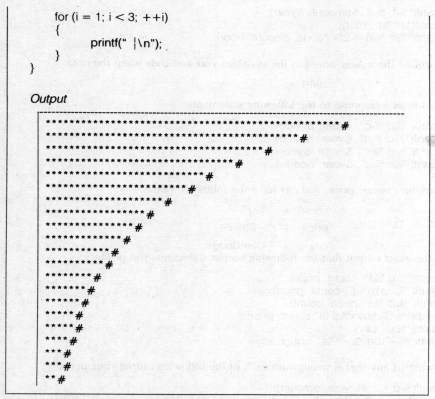

Fig. 4.13   *Program to draw reliability graph*

Program: The program given in Fig. 4.13 produces a shaded graph. The values of t are self-generated by the **for** statement

$$\textbf{for } (t=0; t<= 3000; t = t+150)$$

in steps of 150. The integer 50 in the statement

$$R = (int)(50^{*}r+0.5)$$

is a scale factor which converts r to a large value where an integer is used for plotting the curve. Remember r is always less than 1.

REVIEW QUESTIONS AND EXERCISES

For questions 4.1 to 4.5 assume that the following declarations have been made in the program:

```
int        year, count;
float      amount, price;
char       code, city[10];
double     root;
```

4.1 State errors, if any, in the following input statements.

   (a) scanf("%c%f%d", city, &price, &year);
   (b) scanf("%s%d", city, amount);

(c) scanf("%f, %d, &amount, &year);
(d) scanf(\n"%f", root);
(e) scanf("%c %d %ld", *code, &count, Root);

4.2 What will be the values stored in the variables **year** and **code** when the data

1988, x

is keyed in as a response to the following statements:

(a) scanf("%d %c", &year, &code);
(b) scanf("%c %d", &year, &code);
(c) scanf("%d %c", &code, &year);
(d) scanf("%s %c", &year, &code);

4.3 The variables **count**, **price**, and **city** have the following values:

count ← 1275

price ← −235.74

city ← Cambridge

Show the exact output that the following output statements will produce:

(a) printf("%d %f", count, price);
(b) printf("%2d\n%f", count, price);
(c) printf("%d %f", price, count);
(d) printf("%10dxxxx%5.2f",count, price);
(e) printf("%s", city);
(f) printf("%−10d %−15s", count, city);

4.4 State what (if anyting) is wrong with each of the following output statements:

(a) printf(%d 7.2%f, year, amount);
(b) printf("%−s, %c"\n, city, code);
(c) printf("%f, %d, %s", price, count, city);
(d) printf("%c%d%f\n", amount, code, year);

4.5 In response to the input statement

scanf("%4d%*%d", &year, &code, &count);

the following data is keyed in:

19883745

What values does the computer assign to the variables **year**, **code**, and **count**?

4.6 Given the string "WORDPROCESSING", write a program to read the string from the terminal and display the same in the following formats:

(a) WORD PROCESSING
(b) WORD
    PROCESSING
(c) W.P

4.7 Write a program to read the values of x and y and print the results of the following expressions in one line:

(a) $\dfrac{x+y}{x-y}$ (b) $\dfrac{x+y}{2}$ (c) $(x+y)(x-y)$

4.8 Write a program to read the following numbers, round them off to the nearest integers and print out the results in integer form:

35.7   50.21   −23.73   −46.45

5

DECISION MAKING AND BRANCHING

5.1 INTRODUCTION

We have seen that a C program is a set of statements which are normally executed sequentially in the order in which they appear. This happens when no options or no repetitions of certain calculations are necessary. However, in practice, we have a number of situations where we may have to change the order of execution of statements based on certain conditions, or repeat a group of statements until certain specified conditions are met. This involves a kind of decision making to see whether a particular condition has occurred or not and then direct the computer to execute certain statements accordingly.

C language possesses such decision making capabilities and supports the following statements known as *control* or *decision making* statements.

1. **if** statement
2. **switch** statement
3. Conditional operator statement
4. **goto** statement

We have already used some of these statements in the earlier examples. Here we shall discuss their features, capabilities and applications in more detail.

5.2 DECISION MAKING WITH IF STATEMENT

The **if** statement is a powerful decision making statement and is used to control the flow of execution of statements. It is basically a *two-way* decision statement and is used in conjunction with an expression. It takes the following form:

$$\boxed{\textbf{If } (test\ expression)}$$

It allows the computer to evaluate the expression first and then, depending on whether the value of the expression (relation or condition) is 'true' (non-zero) or 'false' (zero), it transfers the control to a particular statement. This point of program has two *paths* to follow, one for the true condition and the other for the false condition as shown in Fig. 5.1.

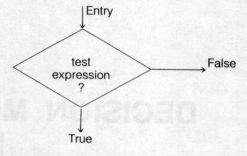

Fig. 5.1 *Two-way branching*

Some examples of decision making, using **if** statement are:

1. **if** (bank balance is zero)
   borrow money
2. **if** (room is dark)
   put on lights
3. **if** (code is 1)
   person is male
4. **if** (age is more than 55)
   person is retired

The **if** statement may be implemented in different forms depending on the complexity of conditions to be tested.

1. Simple **if** statement
2. **if**.....**else** statement
3. Nested **if**....**else** statement
4. **else if** ladder.

5.3 SIMPLE IF STATEMENT

The general form of a simple **if** statement is

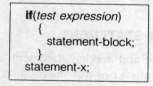

The 'statement-block' may be a single statement or a group of statements. If the *test expression* is true, the *statement-block* will be executed; otherwise the statement-block will be skipped and the execution will jump to the *statement-x*. Remember, when the condition is true both the statement-block and the statement-x are executed in sequence. This is illustrated in Fig. 5.2.

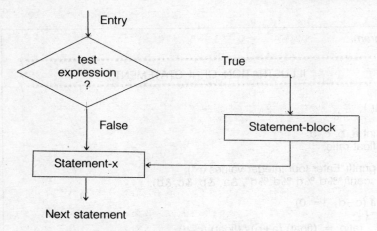

Fig. 5.2 *Flowchart of simple **if** control*

Consider the following segment of a program that is written for processing of marks obtained in an entrance examination.

```
.........
.........
if (category == SPORTS)
   {
      marks = marks + bonus_marks;
   }
printf("%f", marks);
.........
.........
```

The program tests the type of category of the student. If the student belongs to the SPORTS category, then additional bonus_marks are added to his marks before they are printed. For others, bonus_marks are not added.

Example 5.1

The program in Fig. 5.3 reads four values a, b, c, and d from the terminal and evaluates the ratio of (a+b) to (c−d) and prints the result, if c−d is not equal to zero.

The program given in Fig. 5.3 has been run for two sets of data to see that the paths function properly. The result of the first run is printed as

$$\text{Ratio} = -3.181818$$

The second run has neither produced any results nor any message. During the second run, the value of (c−d) is equal to zero and therefore the statements contained in the statement-block are skipped. Since no other statement follows the statement-block, program stops without producing any output.

Note the use of **float** conversion in the statement evaluating the **ratio**. This is necessary to avoid truncation due to integer division.

```
Program
/********************************************************************/
/*                ILLUSTRATION OF if STATEMENT                    */
/********************************************************************/
main( )
{
    int a, b, c, d;
    float ratio;

    printf("Enter four integer values\n");
    scanf("%d %d %d %d", &a, &b, &c, &d);

    if (c−d  != 0)
      {
        ratio  =  (float) (a+b) / (float) (c−d);
        printf("Ratio = %f\n", ratio);
      }
}
Output
Enter four integer values
12   23   34 _ 45
Ratio = −3.181818

Enter four integer values
12   23   34   34
```

Fig. 5.3 *Illustration of simple **If** statement*

The simple **if** is often used for counting purposes. The example 5.2 illustrates this.

Example 5.2

The program in Fig. 5.4 counts the number of boys whose weight is less than 50 kgs and height is greater than 170 cm.

The program has to test two conditions, one for weight and another for height. This is done using the compound relation

if (weight < 50 && height > 170)

This would have been equivalently done using two **if** statements as follows:

if (weight < 50)
If (height > 170)
count = count +1;

If the value of **weight** is less than 50, then the following statement is executed, which in turn is another **if** statement. This **if** statement tests **height** and if the **height** is greater than **170**, then the **count** is incremented by 1.

```
Program
/****************************************************************************/
/*                        COUNTING  WITH  if                              */
/****************************************************************************/
main( )
{
     int count, i;
     float weight, height;

     count  =  0;
     printf("Enter weight and height for 10 boys\n");
     for (i =1;  i  <=  10; i++)
     {
        scanf("%f %f", &weight, &height);
        if(weight < 50 && height > 170)
          count  =  count  +  1;
     }
     printf("Number of boys with weight  <  50 kgs\n");
     printf("and height  >  170 cm  =  %d\n", count);
}

Output
Enter weight and height for 10 boys
45    176.5
55    174.2
47    168.0
49    170.7
54    169.0
53    170.5
49    167.0
48    175.0
47    167
51    170
Number of boys with weight  <  50 kgs
and height  >  170 cm  =  3
```

Fig. 5.4 *Use of **if** for counting*

5.4 THE IF... ELSE STATEMENT

The **if...else** statement is an extension of the simple **if** statement. The general form is

```
if (test expression)
     {
         True-block statement(s)
     }
else
     {
         False-block statement(s)
     }
statement-x
```

If the *test expression* is true, then the *true-block statement(s)*, immediately following the **if** statement are executed; otherwise, the *false-block statement(s)* are executed. In either case, either *true-block* or *false-block* will be executed, not both. This is illustrated in Fig. 5.5. In both the cases, the control is transferred subsequently to statement-x.

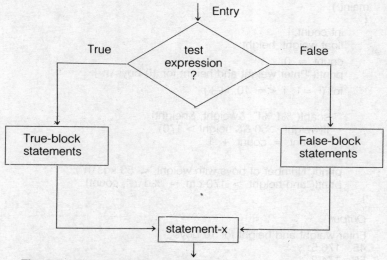

Fig. 5.5 *Flowchart of if......else control*

Let us consider an example of counting the number of boys and girls in a class. We use code 1 for a boy and 2 for a girl. The program statement to do this may be written as follows:

```
.........
.........
if (code == 1)
    boy = boy + 1;
if (code == 2)
    girl = girl + 1;
.........
.........
```

The first test determines whether or not the student is a boy. If yes, the number of boys is increased by 1 and the program continues to the second test. The second test again determines whether the student is a girl. This is unnecessary. Once a student is identified as a boy, there is no need to test again for a girl. A student can be either a boy or a girl, not both. The above program segment can be modified using the **else** clause as follows:

```
..........
..........
if (code == 1)
    boy = boy + 1;
else
    girl = girl + 1;
xxxxxxxxxx
..........
```

Here, if the code is equal to 1, the statement **boy = boy + 1;** is executed and the control is transferred to the statement xxxxxx, after skipping the **else** part. If the code is not equal to 1, the statement **boy = boy + 1;** is skipped and the statement in the **else** part **girl = girl + 1;** is executed before the control reaches the statement xxxxxxx.

Consider the program given in Fig. 5.3. When the value (c − d) is zero, the ratio is not calculated and the program stops without any message. In such cases we may not know whether the program stopped due to a zero value or some other error. This program can be improved by adding the **else** clause as follows:

```
..........
..........
if (c−d != 0)
   {
   ratio = (float)(a+b)/(float)(c−d);
   printf("Ratio = %f\n", ratio);
   }
else
   printf("c−d is zero\n");
..........
..........
```

Example 5.3
A program to evaluate the power series

$$e^x = 1 + x + \frac{x^2}{2!} + \frac{x^3}{3!} + \ ..... \ + \frac{x^n}{n!}, \ 0 < x < 1$$

is given in Fig. 5.6. It uses **if......else** to test the accuracy.

The power series contains the recurrence relationship of the type

$$T_n = T_{n-1} \ (\frac{x}{n}) \ \text{for } n > 1$$

$$T_1 = x \qquad \text{for } n = 1$$
$$T_0 = 1$$

If T_{n-1} (usually known as *previous term*) is known, then T_n (known as *present term*) can be easily found by multiplying the *previous term* by x/n. Then

$$e^x = T_0 + T_1 + T_2 + ... + T_n = \text{sum}$$

The program uses **count** to count the number of terms added. The program stops when the value of the term is less than 0.0001 (**ACCURACY**). Note that when a term is less than **ACCURACY**, the value of **n** is set equal to 999 (a number higher than 100) and therefore the **while** loop terminates. The results are printed outside the **while** loop.

5.5 NESTING OF IF... ELSE STATEMENTS

When a series of decisions are involved, we may have to use more than one **if...else** statement in *nested* form as follows:

Program

```
/****************************************************************************/
/*                  EXPERIMENT WITH if...else STATEMENT                     */
/****************************************************************************/
#define ACCURACY 0.0001
main( )
{
    int n, count;
    float x, term, sum;

    printf("Enter value of x:");
    scanf("%f", &x);

    n = term = sum = count = 1;

    while (n <= 100)
    {
        term = term * x/n;
        sum = sum + term;
        count = count + 1;
        if (term < ACCURACY)
            n = 999;
        else
            n = n + 1;
    }
    printf("Terms = %d Sum = %f \n", count, sum);

}
```

Output

```
Enter value of x:0
Terms = 2 Sum = 1.000000

Enter value of x:0.1
Terms = 5 Sum = 1.105171

Enter value of x:0.5
Terms = 7 Sum = 1.648720

Enter value of x:0.75
Terms = 8 Sum = 2.116997

Enter value of x:0.99
Terms = 9 Sum = 2.691232

Enter value of x:1
Terms = 9 Sum = 2.718279
```

Fig. 5.6 *Illustration of* **if...else** *statement*

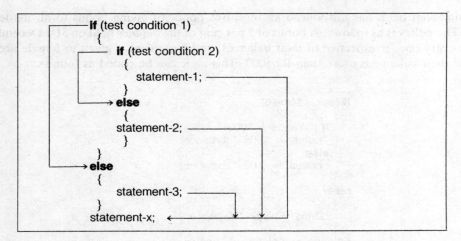

The logic of execution is illustrated in Fig. 5.7. If the *condition-1* is false, the statement-3 will be executed; otherwise it continues to perform the second test. If the *condition-2* is true, the statement-1 will be evaluated; otherwise the statement-2 will be evaluated and then the control is transferred to the statement-x.

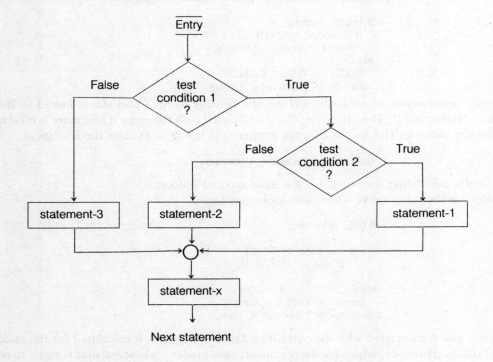

Fig. 5.7 *Flowchart of nested **if..else** statements*

A commercial bank has introduced an incentive policy of giving bonus to all its deposit holders. The policy is as follows: A bonus of 2 per cent of the *balance* held on 31st December is given to every one, irrespective of their balances, and 5 per cent is given to female account holders if their balance is more than Rs.5000. This logic can be coded as follows:

```
.........
if (sex is female)
   {
     if (balance > 5000)
       bonus = 0.05 * balance;
     else
       bonus = 0.02 * balance;
   }
else
   {
     bonus = 0.02 * balance;
   }
balance = balance + bonus;
.........
.........
```

When nesting, care should be exercised to match every **if** with an **else**. Consider the following alternative to the above program (which looks right at the first sight):

```
if (sex is female)
   if (balance > 5000)
     bonus = 0.05 * balance;
else
   bonus = 0.02 * balance;
balance = balance + bonus;
```

There is an ambiguity as to over which **if** the **else** belongs to. In C, an **else** is linked to the closest non-terminated **if**. Therefore, the **else** is associated with the inner **if** and there is no **else** option for the outer **if**. This means that the computer is trying to execute the statement

balance = balance + bonus;

without really calculating the bonus for the male account holders.

Consider another alternative which also looks correct:

```
If (sex is female)
   {
     if (balance > 5000)
       bonus = 0.05 * balance;
   }
else
   bonus = 0.02 * balance;
balance = balance + bonus;
```

In this case, **else** is associated with the outer **if** and therefore bonus is calculated for the male account holders. However, bonus for the female account holders, whose balance is equal to or less than 5000 is not calculated because of the missing **else** option for the inner **if**.

Example 5.4

The program in Fig. 5.8 selects and prints the largest of the three numbers using nested **if....else** statements.

Program

```
/*************************************************************************/
/*            SELECTING  THE  LARGEST  OF  THREE  VALUES           */
/*************************************************************************/

main( )
{
    float A, B, C;

    printf("Enter three values\n");
    scanf("%f %f %f", &A, &B, &C);

    printf("\nLargest value is   ");

    if  (A>B)
      {
        if  (A>C)
          printf("%f\n", A);
        else
          printf("%f\n", C);
      }
    else
      {
        if  (C>B)
          printf("%f\n", C);
        else
          printf("%f\n", B);
      }
}
```

Output

```
Enter three values
23445   67379   88843

Largest value is   88843.000000
```

Fig. 5.8 *Selecting the largest of three numbers*

5.6 THE ELSE IF LADDER

There is another way of putting **if**s together when multipath decisions are involved. A multipath decision is a chain of **if**s in which the statement associated with each **else** is an **if**. It takes the following general form:

```
if (condition 1)
      statement-1;
else if (condition 2)
        statement-2;
    else if (condition 3)
          statement-3;
          ------------
        else if (condition n)
              statement-n;
            else
                default-statement;
statement-x;
```

This construct is known as the **else if** ladder. The conditions are evaluated from the top (of the ladder), downwards. As soon as a true condition is found, the statement associated with it is executed and the control is transferred to the *statement-x* (skipping the rest of the ladder). When all the n conditions become false, then the final **else** containing the *default-statement* will be executed. Fig.5.9 shows the logic of execution of **else if** ladder statements.

Let us consider an example of grading the students in an academic institution. The grading is done according to the following rules:

Average marks	Grade
80 to 100	Honours
60 to 79	First Division
50 to 59	Second Division
40 to 49	Third Division
0 to 39	Fail

This grading can be done using the **else if** ladder as follows:

```
if (marks > 79)
    grade = "Honours";
else if (marks > 59)
        grade = "First Division";
    else if (marks > 49)
            grade = "Second Division";
        else if (marks > 39)
                grade = "Third Division";
            else
                grade = "Fail";
printf ("%s\n", grade);
```

Consider another example given below:

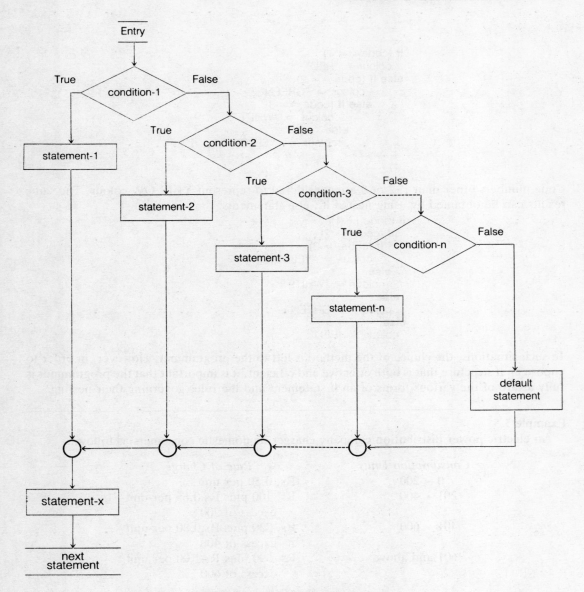

Fig. 5.9 *Flowchart of **else**..**if** ladder*

```
          ----------
          ----------
          if (code == 1)
             colour = "RED";
          else if (code == 2)
                  colour = "GREEN";
               else if (code == 3)
                       colour = "WHITE";
                    else
                       colour = "YELLOW";
          ----------
          ----------
```

Code numbers other than 1, 2 or 3 are considered to represent YELLOW colour. The same results can be obtained by using nested **if...else** statements.

```
          if (code != 1)
            if (code != 2)
              if (code != 3)
                colour = "YELLOW";
              else
                colour = "WHITE";
            else
              colour = "GREEN";
          else
            colour = "RED";
```

In such situations, the choice of the method is left to the programmer. However, in order to choose an **if** structure that is both effective and efficient, it is important that the programmer is fully aware of the various forms of an **if** statement and the rules governing their nesting.

Example 5.5

An electric power distribution company charges its domestic consumers as follows:

Consumption Units	Rate of Charge
0 - 200	Rs. 0.50 per unit
201 - 400	Rs. 100 plus Rs.0.65 per unit excess of 200
401 - 600	Rs. 230 plus Rs.0.80 per unit excess of 400
601 and above	Rs. 390 plus Rs.1.00 per unit excess of 600

The program in Fig.5.10 reads the customer number and power consumed and prints the amount to be paid by the customer.

5.7 THE SWITCH STATEMENT

We have seen that when one of the many alternatives is to be selected, we can design a program using **if** statements to control the selection. However, the complexity of such a

Program
```
/*******************************************************************/
/*                   USE  OF  else  if  LADDER                    */
/*******************************************************************/
main( )
{
    int units, custnum;
    float charges;
    printf("Enter CUSTOMER NO. and UNITS consumed\n");
    scanf("%d %d", &custnum, &units);

    if (units <= 200)
      charges = 0.5 * units;
    else if (units <= 400)
          charges = 100 + 0.65* (units − 200);
        else if (units <= 600)
              charges = 230 + 0.8 * (units − 400);
            else
              charges = 390 + (units − 600);
    printf("\n\nCustomer No: %d: Charges = %.2f\n",
          custnum, charges);
}
```
Output
```
Enter CUSTOMER NO. and UNITS consumed 101    150
Customer No:101  Charges = 75.00

Enter CUSTOMER NO. and UNITS consumed 202    225
Customer No:202  Charges = 116.25

Enter CUSTOMER NO. and UNITS consumed 303    375
Customer No:303  Charges = 213.75

Enter CUSTOMER NO. and UNITS consumed 404    520
Customer No:404  Charges = 326.00

Enter CUSTOMER NO. and UNITS consumed 505    625
Customer No:505  Charges = 415.00
```

Fig. 5.10   *Illustration of **else**..**if** ladder*

program increases dramatically when the number of alternatives increases. The program becomes difficult to read and follow. At times, it may confuse even the person who designed it. Fortunately, C has a built-in multiway decision statement known as a **switch**. The **switch** statement tests the value of a given variable (or expression) against a list of **case** values and when a match is found, a block of statements associated with that **case** is executed. The general form of the **switch** statement is as shown below:

The *expression* is an integer expression or characters. *Value-1, value-2* ..... are constants or constant expressions (evaluable to an integral constant) and are known as *case lables*. Each of these values should be unique within a **switch** statement. **block-1, block-2** .... are statement lists and may contain zero or more statements. There is no need to put braces around these blocks. Note that **case** labels end with a colon (:).

When the **switch** is executed, the value of the expression is successively compared against the values *value-1, value-2*,.... If a case is found whose value matches with the value of the *expression*, then the block of statements that follows the case are executed.

```
switch (expression)
{
    case  value-1:
                block-1
                break;
    case  value-2:
                block-2
                break;
    ......
    ......
    default:
                default-block
                break;
}
statement-x;
```

The **break** statement at the end of each block signals the end of a particular case and causes an exit from the **switch** statement, transferring the control to the **statement-x** following the **switch**.

The **default** is an optional case. When present, it will be executed if the value of the *expression* does not match with any of the case values. If not present, no action takes place if all matches fail and the control goes to the **statement-x**.

The selection process of **switch** statement is illustrated in the flowchart shown in Fig. 5.11.

The **switch** statement can be used to grade the students as discussed in the last section. This is illustrated below:

```
------------
------------
index = marks/10;
switch (index)
{
    case 10:
    case  9:
    case  8:
            grade = "Honours";
            break;
    case  7:
    case  6:
            grade = "First Division";
            break;
    case  5:
            grade = "Second Division";
            break;
    case  4:
            grade = "Third Division";
            break;
    default:
            grade = "Fail";
            break;
}
printf("%s\n", grade);
------------
------------
```

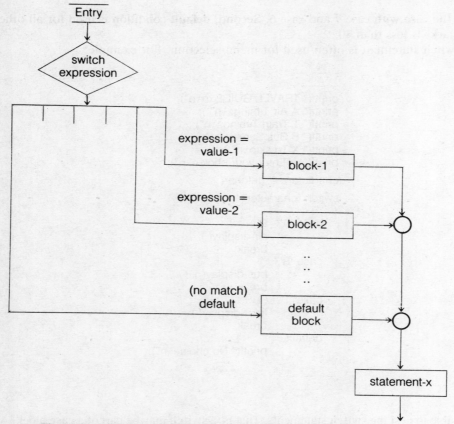

Fig. 5.11 *Selection process of the **switch** statement*

Note that we have used a conversion statement

$$\text{index = marks / 10;}$$

where, **index** is defined as an integer. The variable index takes the following integer values.

Marks		Index
	100	10
90	– 99	9
80	– 89	8
70	– 79	7
60	– 69	6
50	– 59	5
40	– 49	4
	.	.
	.	.
	0	0

This segment of the program illustrates two important features. First, it uses empty cases. The first three cases will execute the same statements

```
grade = "Honours";
break;
```

Same is the case with case 7 and case 6. Second, **default** condition is used for all other cases where marks is less than 40.

The **switch** statement is often used for menu selection. For example:

```
-----------
-----------
printf(" TRAVEL GUIDE\n\n");
printf(" A Air Timings\n" );
printf(" T Train Timings\n");
printf(" B Bus Service\n" );
printf(" X To skip\n" );
printf("\n Enter your choice\n");

character  =  getchar( );

switch (character)
{
    case 'A'    :
                air-display( );
                break;
    case 'B'    :
                bus-display( );
                break;
    case 'T'    :
                train-display( );
                break;
    default    :
                printf(" No choice\n");
}
-----------
-----------
```

It is possible to nest the **switch** statements, That is, a **switch** may be part of a **case** block. ANSI C allows 15 levels of nesting and as many as 257 *case labels*.

5.8 THE ? : OPERATOR

The C language has an unusual operator, useful for making two-way decisions. This operator is a combination of ? and :, and takes three operands. This operator is popularly known as the *conditional operator*. The general form of use of the conditional operator is as follows:

> *conditional expression* **?** *expression1* **:** *expression2*

The *conditional expression* is evaluated first. If the result is nonzero, *expression1* is evaluated and is returned as the value of the conditional expression. Otherwise, *expression2* is evaluated and its value is returned. For example, the segment

```
if (x < 0)
  flag  =  0;
else
  flag  =  1;
```

can be written as

```
flag  =  ( x < 0 ) ? 0 : 1;
```

Consider the evaluation of the following function:

$$y = 1.5x + 3 \quad \text{for } x \leqslant 2$$
$$y = 2x + 5 \quad \text{for } x > 2$$

This can be evaluated using the conditional operator as follows:

y = (x > 2) ? (2 * x + 5) : (1.5 * x + 3);

The conditional operator may be nested for evaluating more complex assignment decisions. For example, consider the weekly salary of a salesgirl who is selling some domestic products. If x is the number of products sold in a week, her weekly salary is given by

$$\text{salary} = \begin{cases} 4x + 100 & \text{for } x < 40 \\ 300 & \text{for } x = 40 \\ 4.5x + 150 & \text{for } x > 40 \end{cases}$$

This complex equation can be written as

salary = (x != 40) ? ((x < 40) ? (4*x+100) : (4.5*x+150)) : 300;

The same can be evaluated using **if...else** statements as follows:

```
if (x <= 40)
  if (x < 40)
    salary = 4 * x+100;
  else
    salary = 300;
else
  salary = 4.5 * x+150;
```

When the conditional operator is used, the code becomes more concise and perhaps, more efficient. However, the readability is poor. It is better to use **if** statements when more than a single nesting of conditional operator is required.

Example 5.6

An employee can apply for a loan at the beginning of every six months, but he will be sanctioned the amount according to the following company rules:

Rule 1: An employee cannot enjoy more than two loans at any point of time.

Rule 2: Maximum permissible total loan is limited and depends upon the category of the employee.

A program to process loan applications and to sanction loans is given in Fig. 5.12.

The program uses the following variables:

loan3 - present loan amount requested
loan2 - previous loan amount pending
loan1 - previous to previous loan pending
maxloan- maximum permissible loan
sancloan- loan sanctioned

The rules for sanctioning new loan are:

1. loan1 should be zero.
2. loan2 + loan3 should not be more than maxloan.

Note the use of **long int** type to declare variables.

```
Program
/***********************************************************************/
/*                     CONDITIONAL  OPERATOR                        */
/***********************************************************************/
#define     MAXLOAN  50000
main( )
{
      long int loan1, loan2, loan3, sancloan, sum23;
      printf("Enter the values of previous two loans:\n");
      scanf(" %ld %ld", &loan1, &loan2);

      printf("\nEnter the value of new loan:\n");
      scanf(" %ld", &loan3);

      sum23 = loan2 + loan3;
      sancloan = (loan1>0) ? 0 : ( (sum23>MAXLOAN) ?
                    MAXLOAN − loan2 : loan3);

      printf("\n\n");
      printf("Previous loans pending:\n%ld   %ld\n", loan1, loan2);
      printf("Loan requested = %ld\n", loan3);
      printf("Loan sanctioned = %ld\n", sancloan);

}
Output
Enter the values of previous two loans:
0      20000

Enter the value of new loan:
45000


Previous loans pending:
0      20000
Loan requested  = 45000
Loan sanctioned = 30000

Enter the values of previous two loans:
1000     15000

Enter the value of new loan:
25000


Previous loans pending:
1000     15000
Loan requested  = 25000
Loan sanctioned = 0
```

Fig. 5.12 *Illustration of the conditional operator*

5.9 THE GOTO STATEMENT

So far we have discussed ways of controlling the flow of execution based on certain specified conditions. Like many other languages, C supports the **goto** statement to branch uncondi-tionally from one point to another in the program. Although it may not be essential to use the

goto statement in a highly structured language like C, there may be occasions when the use of **goto** might be desirable.

The **goto** requires a *label* in order to identify the place where the branch is to be made. A *label* is any valid variable name, and must be followed by a colon. The *label* is placed immediately before the statement where the control is to be transferred. The general forms of **goto** and *label* statements are shown below:

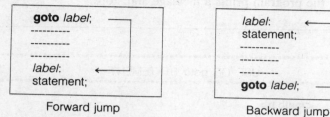

Forward jump	Backward jump

The *label*: can be anywhere in the program either before or after the **goto** label; statement.

During running of a program when a statement like

goto begin;

is met, the flow of control will jump to the statement immediately following the label **begin:**. This happens unconditionally.

Note that a **goto** breaks the normal sequential execution of the program. If the *label*: is before the statement goto *label*; a *loop* will be formed and some statements will be executed repeatedly. Such a jump is known as a *backward jump*. On the other hand, if the *label*: is placed after the **goto** *label*; some statements will be skipped and the jump is known as a *forward jump*.

A **goto** is often used at the end of a program to direct the control to go to the input statement, to read further data. Consider the following example:

```
main( )
{
    double x, y;
    read:
    scanf("%f", &x);
    if (x < 0) goto read;
    y = sqrt(x);
    printf("%f %f\n", x, y);
    goto read;
}
```

This program is written to evaluate the square root of a series of numbers read from the terminal. The program uses two **goto** statements, one at the end, after printing the results to transfer the control back to the input statement and the other to skip any further computation when the number is negative.

Due to the unconditional **goto** statement at the end, the control is always transferred back to the input statement. In fact, this program puts the computer in a permanent loop known as an *infinite loop*. The computer goes round and round until we take some special steps to terminate the loop. Such infinite loops should be avoided. Example 5.7 illustrates how such infinite loops can be eliminated.

Example 5.7
Program presented in Fig. 5.13 illustrates the use of the **goto** statement.

The program evaluates one square root for five numbers. The variable **count** keeps the count of numbers read. When **count** is less than or equal to 5, **goto read;** directs the control to the label **read;** otherwise, the program prints a message and stops.

```
Program
/******************************************************************************/
/*                      USE OF goto STATEMENT                               */
/******************************************************************************/
#include   <math.h>
main( )
{
    double x, y;
    int count;

    count = 1;

    printf("Enter FIVE real values in a LINE \n");
read:
    scanf("%lf", &x);
    printf("\n");
    if (x < 0)
      printf("Item − %d is negative\n",count);
    else
    {
      y = sqrt(x);
      printf("%lf\t %lf\n", x, y);
    }

    count = count + 1;

    if (count <= 5)
goto read;
    printf("\nEnd of computation");
}

Output
Enter FIVE real values in a LINE
50.70   40   −36   75   11.25
50.750000              7.123903
40.000000              6.324555
Item −3 is negative
75.000000              8.660254
11.250000              3.354102
End of computation
```

Fig. 5.13 *Use of the **goto** statement*

Another use of the **goto** statement is to transfer the control out of a loop (or nested loops) when certain peculiar conditions are encountered. Example:

```
----------------
----------------
while(------)
{
        for(------)
        {
        ----------------
        ----------------
        if(--------------) goto end_of_program;  ─┐
        ----------------                          │
        }                                         │ Jumping out
        ----------------                          │ of loops
        ----------------                          │
}                                                 │
end_of_program:  ◄────────────────────────────────┘
```

We should try to avoid using **goto** as far as possible. But there is nothing wrong, if we use it to enhance the readability of the program or to improve the execution speed.

CASE STUDIES

1. Range of Numbers

Problem: A survey of the computer market shows that personal computers are sold at varying costs by the vendors. The following is the list of costs (in hundreds) quoted by some vendors:

35.00	40.50	25.00	31.25	68.15
47.00	26.65	29.00	53.45	62.50

Determine the average cost and the range of values.

Problem analysis: Range is one of the measures of dispersion used in statistical analysis of a series of values. The range of any series is the difference between the highest and the lowest values in the series. That is

$$\text{Range} = \text{highest value} - \text{lowest value}$$

It is therefore necessary to find the highest and the lowest values in the series.

Program: A program to determine the range of values and the average cost of a personal computer in the market is given in Fig. 5.14.

When the value is read the first time, it is assigned to two *buckets*, **high** and **low**, through the statement

$$\textbf{high} = \textbf{low} = \textbf{value};$$

For subsequent values, the value read is compared with **high**; if it is larger, the value is assigned to **high**. Otherwise, the value is compared with **low**; if it is smaller, the value is assigned to **low**. Note that at a given point, the buckets **high** and **low** hold the highest and the lowest values read so far.

```
Program
/*************************************************************/
/*                    RANGE  OF  NUMBERS                     */
/*************************************************************/
main( )
{
    int count;
    float value, high, low, sum, average, range;

    sum = 0;
    count = 0;

    printf("Enter numbers in a line :
            input a NEGATIVE number to end\n");
input:
    scanf("%f", &value);

    if (value < 0) goto output;
       count = count + 1;
    if (count == 1)
       high = low = value;
    else if (value > high)
            high = value;
          else if (value < low)
                 low = value;

    sum = sum + value;
    goto input;

output:
    average = sum/count;
    range = high − low;
    printf("\n\n");
    printf("Total values : %d\n", count);
    printf("Highest-value: %f\nLowest-value : %f\n", high, low);

    printf("Range          : %f\nAverage          : %f\n",
               range, average);
}
Output
Enter numbers in a line : input a NEGATIVE number to end
35   40.50   25   31.25   68.15   47   26.65   29   53.45   62.50  −1

Total values   :  10
Highest-value:  68.150002
Lowest-value :  25.000000
Range          :  43.150002
Average        :  41.849998
```

Fig. 5.14 *Calculation of range of values*

The values are read in an input loop created by the **goto input;** statement. The control is transferred out of the loop by inputting a negative number. This is caused by the statement

if (value < 0) goto output;

2. Pay-Bill Calculations

Problem: A manufacturing company has classified its executives into four levels for the benefit of certain perks. The levels and corresponding perks are shown below:

Level	Perks	
	Conveyance allowance	Entertainment allowance
1	1000	500
2	750	200
3	500	100
4	250	

An executive's gross salary includes basic pay, house rent allowance at 25% of basic pay and other perks. Income tax is withheld from the salary on a percentage basis as follows:

Gross salary	Tax rate
Gross <= 2000	No tax deduction
2000 < Gross <= 4000	3%
4000 < Gross <= 5000	5%
Gross > 5000	8%

Write a program that will read an executive's job number, level number, and basic pay and then compute the net salary after withholding income tax.

Problem analysis:
Gross salary = basic pay + house rent allowance + perks
Net salary = gross salary − income tax.

The computation of perks depends on the level, while the income tax depends on the gross salary. The major steps are:

1. Read data.
2. Decide level number and calculate perks.
3. Calculate gross salary.
4. Calculate income tax.
5. Compute net salary.
6. Print the results.

Program: A program and the results of the test data are given in Fig. 5.15. Note that the last statement should be an executable statement. That is, the lable **stop:** cannot be the last line.

```
Program
/****************************************************************/
/*                  PAY-BILL CALCULATIONS                       */
/****************************************************************/
#define    CA1    1000
#define    CA2    750
#define    CA3    500
#define    CA4    250
#define    EA1    500
#define    EA2    200
#define    EA3    100
#define    EA4    0

main( )
{
     int    level, jobnumber;
     float  gross,
            basic,
            house_rent,
            perks,
            net,
            incometax;
input:
     printf("\nEnter level, job number, and basic pay\n");
     printf("Enter 0 (zero) for level to END\n\n");
     scanf("%d", &level);
     if (level == 0) goto stop;
     scanf("%d %f", &jobnumber, &basic);
     switch (level)
     {
         case 1:
                 perks = CA1 + EA1;
                 break;
         case 2:
                 perks = CA2 + EA2;
                 break;
         case 3:
                 perks = CA3 + EA3;
                 break;
         case 4:
                 perks = CA4 + EA4;
                 break;
         default:
                 printf("Error in level code\n");
                 goto stop;
     }
     house_rent = 0.25 * basic;
     gross = basic + house_rent + perks;
     if (gross <= 2000)
       incometax = 0;
     else if (gross <= 4000)
             incometax = 0.03 * gross;
```

```
              else if (gross <= 5000)
                      incometax = 0.05 * gross;
                  else
                      incometax = 0.08 * gross;
          net = gross - incometax;
          printf("%d %d %.2f\n", level, jobnumber, net);
          goto input;
          stop: printf("\n\nEND OF THE PROGRAM");
    }
```

Output

```
Enter level, job number, and basic pay
Enter 0 (zero) for level to END

1  1111  4000
1  1111  5980.00

Enter level, job number, and basic pay
Enter 0 (zero) for level to END

2  2222  3000
2  2222  4465.00

Enter level, job number, and basic pay
Enter 0 (zero) for level to END

3  3333  2000
3  3333  3007.00

Enter level, job number, and basic pay
Enter 0 (zero) for level to END

4  4444  1000
4  4444  1500.00

Enter level, job number, and basic pay
Enter 0 (zero) for level to END

0

END OF THE PROGRAM
```

Fig. 5.15 *Pay-bill calculations*

REVIEW QUESTIONS AND EXERCISES

5.1   Determine whether the following are true or false:

   (a) When **if** statements are nested, the last **else** gets associated with the nearest **if** without an **else**.
   (b) One **if** can have more than one **else** clause.
   (c) A **switch** statement can always be replaced by a series of **if..else** statements.
   (d) A **switch** expression can be of any type.
   (e) A program stops its execution when a **break** statement is encountered.

5.2   In what ways does a **switch** statement differ from an **if** statement?

5.3   Find errors, if any, in each of the following segments:

(a) if (x + y = z   && y > 0)
    printf("   ");

(b) if (code > 1);
    a = b + c
  else
    a = 0

(c) if (p < 0) || (q < 0)
    printf (" sign is negative");

5.4 The following is a segment of a program:

```
x = 1;
y = 1;
if (n > 0)
   x = x + 1;
   y = y − 1;
printf(" %d %d", x, y);
```

What will be the values of x and y if n assumes a value of (a) 1 and (b) 0.

5.5 Rewrite each of the following without using compound relations:

(a) if (grade <= 59 && grade >= 50)
    second = second + 1;

(b) if (number > 100 || number < 0)
    printf(" Out of range");
  else
    sum = sum + number;

(c) if ((M1 > 60 && M2 > 60) || T > 200)
    printf(" Admitted\n");
  else
    printf(" Not admitted\n");

5.6 Read all the programs discussed in this chapter. Identify any changes that might be necessary to improve either readability or efficiency of the programs.

5.7   Write a program to determine whether a number is 'odd' or 'even' and print the message

NUMBER IS EVEN
or
NUMBER IS ODD

(a) without using **else** option, and (b) with **else** option.

5.8 Write a program to find the number of and sum of all integers greater than 100 and less than 200 that are divisible by 7.

5.9 A set of two linear equations with two unknowns x_1 and x_2 is given below:

$$ax_1 + bx_2 = m$$
$$cx_1 + dx_2 = n$$

The set has a unique solution

$$x_1 = \frac{md - bn}{ad - cb}$$

$$x_2 = \frac{na - mc}{ad - cb}$$

provided the denominator $ad - cb$ is not equal to zero.
Write a program that will read the values of constants a, b, c, d, m, and n and compute the values of x_1 and x_2. An appropriate message should be printed if $ad - cb = 0$.

5.10 Given a list of marks ranging from 0 to 100, write a program to compute and print the number of students:

(a) who have obtained more than 80 marks,
(b) who have obtained more than 60 marks,
(c) who have obtained more than 40 marks,
(d) who have obtained 40 or less marks,
(e) in the range 81 to 100,
(f) in the range 61 to 80,
(g) in the range 41 to 60, and
(h) in the range 0 to 40.

The program should use a minimum number of **if** statements.

5.11 Admission to a professional course is subject to the following conditions:
(a) Marks in mathematics >= 60
(b) Marks in physics   >= 50
(c) Marks in Chemistry   >= 40
(d) Total in all three subjects >= 200
              or
    Total in mathematics and physics >= 150

Given the marks in the three subjects, write a program to process the applications to list the eligible candidates.

5.12 Write a program to print a two-dimensional Square Root Table as shown below, to provide the square root of any number from 0 to 9.9. For example, the value x will give the square root of 3.2 and y the square root of 3.9.

Square Root Table

Number	0.0	0.1	0.2	. . . . . .	0.9
0.0 1.0 2.0					
3.0			x		y
. . 9.0					

5.13 Shown below is a Floyd's triangle.

```
1
2  3
4  5  6
7  8  9  10
11 . . . . . . 15
          .
          .
79 . .  . . . .  . . . . . .  91
```

(a) Write a program to print this triangle.
(b) Modify the program to produce the following form of Floyd's triangle.

```
1
0  1
1  0  1
0  1  0  1
1  0  1  0  1
```

5.14 A cloth showroom has announced the following seasonal discounts on purchase of items:

Purchase amount	Discount	
	Mill cloth	Handloom items
0 - 100	–	5%
101 - 200	5%	7.5%
201 - 300	7.5%	10.0%
Above 300	10.0%	15.0%

Write a program using **switch** and **if** statements to compute the net amount to be paid by a customer.

5.15 Write a program that will read the value of x and evaluate the following function

$$y = \begin{cases} 1 & \text{for } x > 0 \\ 0 & \text{for } x = 0 \\ -1 & \text{for } x < 0 \end{cases}$$

Using

(a) nested **if** statements,
(b) **else if** statements, and
(c) conditional operator ? :

6

DECISION MAKING AND LOOPING

6.1 INTRODUCTION

We have seen in the previous chapter that it is possible to execute a segment of a program repeatedly by introducing a counter and later testing it using the **if** statement. While this method is quite satisfactory for all practical purposes, we need to initialize and increment a counter and test its value at an appropriate place in the program for the completion of the loop. For example, suppose we want to calculate the sum of squares of all integers between 1 and 10. We can write a program using the **if** statement as follows:

```
------------
------------
sum = 0;
n = 1;
loop:
sum = sum + n*n;
if (n == 10)
    goto print;
else
{
    n = n+1;
goto loop;
}
print:
------------
------------
```

L
o
o
p

n = 10,
end of loop

This program does the following things:

1. Initializes the variable **n**.
2. Computes the square of **n** and adds it to **sum**.
3. Tests the value of **n** to see whether it is equal to 10 or not. If it is equal to 10, then the program prints the results.
4. If **n** is less than 10, then it is incremented by one and the control goes back to compute the **sum** again.

The program evaluates the statement

sum = sum + n*n;

10 times. That is, the loop is executed 10 times. This number can be decreased or increased easily by modifying the relational expression appropriately in the statement **if** (n == 10). On such occasions where the exact number of repetitions are known, there are more convenient methods of looping in C. These looping capabilities enable us to develop concise programs containing repetitive processes without the use of **goto** statements.

In looping, a sequence of statements are executed until some conditions for termination of the loop are satisfied. A *program loop* therefore consists of two segments, one known as the *body of the loop* and the other known as the *control statement*. The control statement tests certain conditions and then directs the repeated execution of the statements contained in the body of the loop.

Depending on the position of the control statement in the loop, a control structure may be classified either as the *entry-controlled loop* or as the *exit-controlled loop*. The flowcharts in Fig. 6.1 illustrate these structures. In the entry-controlled loop, the control conditions are tested before the start of the loop execution. If the conditions are not satisfied, then the body of the loop will not be executed. In the case of an exit-controlled loop, the test is performed at the end of the body of the loop and therefore the body is executed unconditionally for the first time.

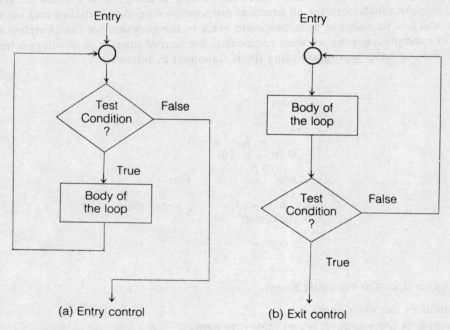

(a) Entry control   (b) Exit control

Fig. 6.1 *Loop control structures*

The test conditions should be carefully stated in order to perform the desired number of loop executions. It is assumed that the test condition will eventually transfer the control out of the loop. In case, due to some reason it does not do so, the control sets up an *infinite loop* and the body is executed over and over again.

A looping process, in general, would include the following four steps:

1. Setting and initialization of a counter.
2. Execution of the statements in the loop.
3. Test for a specified condition for execution of the loop.
4. Incrementing the counter.

The test may be either to determine whether the loop has been repeated the specified number of times or to determine whether a particular condition has been met.

The C language provides for three loop constructs for performing loop operations. They are:

1. The **while** statement.
2. The **do** statement.
3. The **for** statement.

We shall discuss the features and applications of each of these statements in this chapter.

6.2 THE WHILE STATEMENT

The simplest of all the looping structures in C is the **while** statement. We have used **while** in many of our earlier programs. The basic format of the **while** statement is

```
while (test condition)
{
    body of the loop
}
```

The **while** is an *entry-controlled* loop statement. The *test-condition* is evaluated and if the condition is true, then the body of the loop is executed. After execution of the body, the test-condition is once again evaluated and if it is true, the body is executed once again. This process of repeated execution of the body continues until the test-condition finally becomes *false* and the control is transferred out of the loop. On exit, the program continues with the statement immediately after the body of the loop.

The body of the loop may have one or more statements. The braces are needed only if the body contains two or more statements. However, it is a good practice to use braces even if the body has only one statement.

We can rewrite the program loop discussed in Section 6.1 as follows:

```
------------
------------
sum = 0;
n = 1;
while(n <= 10)
{
    sum = sum + n * n;
    n = n+1;
}
printf("sum = %d\n", sum);
------------
------------
```

The body of the loop is executed 10 times for n = 1, 2, ..., 10 each time adding the square of the value of n, which is incremented inside the loop. The test condition may also be written as **n < 11**; the result would be the same.

Another example of **while** statement which uses the keyboard input is shown below:

```
-----------
-----------
character = ' '
while (character != 'Y')
        character = getchar();
xxxxxxx;
-----------
-----------
```

First the **character** is initialized to ' '. The **while** statement then begins by testing whether **character** is not equal to Y. Since the **character** was initialized to ' ', the test is true and the loop statement

character = getchar( );

is executed. Each time a letter is keyed in, the test is carried out and the loop statement is executed until the letter Y is pressed. When Y is pressed, the condition becomes false because **character** equals Y, and the loop terminates, thus transferring the control to the statement xxxxxxx;.

Example 6.1

A program to evaluate the equation

$$y = x^n$$

when n is a non-negative integer, is given in Fig. 6.2.

The variable **y** is initialized to 1 and then multiplied by **x**, n times using the **while** loop. The loop control variable, count is initialized outside the loop and incremented inside the loop. When the value of **count** becomes greater than **n**, the control exits the loop.

6.3 THE DO STATEMENT

The **while** loop construct that we have discussed in the previous section makes a test of condition *before* the loop is executed. Therefore, the body of the loop may not be executed at all if the condition is not satisfied at the very first attempt. On some occasions it might be necessary to execute the body of the loop before the test is performed. Such situations can be handled with the help of the **do** statement. This takes the form:

```
do
{
   body of the loop
}
while (test-condition);
```

On reaching the **do** statement, the program proceeds to evaluate the body of the loop first. At the end of the loop, the *test-condition* in the **while** statement is evaluated. If the condition is

```
Program
/***********************************************************************/
/*                      EXAMPLE OF while STATEMENT                     */
/***********************************************************************/
main( )
{
    int count, n;
    float x, y;
    printf("Enter the values of x and n : ");
    scanf("%f %d", &x, &n);
    y = 1.0;
    count = 1;
    /* LOOP BEGINS */
    while ( count <= n)
    {
        y = y*x;
        count++;
    }
    /* END OF LOOP */
    printf(" x = %f; n = %d; x to power n = %f n",x,n,y);

}
Output
Enter the values of x and n : 2.5   4
x = 2.500000; n = 4; x to power n = 39.062500

Enter the values of x and n : 0.5   4
x = 0.500000; n = 4; x to power n = 0.062500
```

Fig. 6.2 *Program to compute x to the power n using* **while** *loop*

true, the program continues to evaluate the body of the *loop* once again. This process continues as long as the *condition* is true. When the condition becomes false, the loop will be terminated and the control goes to the statement that appears immediately after the **while** statement.

Since the *test-condition* is evaluated at the bottom of the loop, the **do...while** construct provides an *exit-controlled* loop and therefore the body of the loop is *always executed at least once*.

A simple example of a **do...while** loop is:

```
------------
do
{
    printf("Input a number\n");
    number = getnum( );
}
while (number > 0);
------------
```

This segment of a program reads a number from the keyboard until a zero or a negative number is keyed in.

The test conditions may have compound relations as well. For instance, the statement

while (number > 0 && number < 100);

in the above example would cause the loop to be executed as long as the number keyed in lies between 0 and 100.

Consider another example:

```
------------
I = 1;
sum = 0;
do
{
    sum = sum + I;
    I = I+2;
}
while(sum < 40 || I < 10);
printf("%d %d\n", I, sum);
------------
```

The loop will be executed as long as one of the two relations is true.

Example 6.2

A program to print the multiplication table from 1×1 to 12×10 as shown below is given in Fig. 6.3.

1	2	3	4	....	10
2	4	6	8	....	20
3	6	9	12	....	30
4				....	40
.				.	
.					
12				....	120

This program contains two **do....while** loops in nested form. The outer loop is controlled by the variable **row** and executed 12 times. The inner loop is controlled by the variable **column** and is executed 10 times, each time the outer loop is executed. That is, the inner loop is executed a total of 120 times, each time printing a value in the table.

Notice that the **printf** of the inner loop does not contain any new line character (\n). This allows the printing of all row values in one line. The empty **printf** in the outer loop initiates a new line to print the next row.

6.4 THE FOR STATEMENT

Simple 'for' Loops

The **for** loop is another *entry-controlled* loop that provides a more concise loop control structure. The general form of the **for** loop is

```
for ( initialization ; test-condition ; increment)
{
    body of the loop
}
```

Program

```
/*****************************************************************/
/*               PRINTING OF MULTIPLICATION TABLE               */
/*****************************************************************/
#define COLMAX  10
#define ROWMAX 12
main( )
{
    int row,column, y;

    row = 1;
    printf("              MULTIPLICATION TABLE              \n");
    printf(" ———————————————————————————————————————————— \n");
    /*......OUTER LOOP BEGINS........*/
    do
    {
        column = 1;
        /*.......INNER LOOP BEGINS.......*/
        do
        {
            y = row * column;
            printf("%4d", y);
            column = column + 1;
        }
            while (column <= COLMAX);
            /*... INNER LOOP ENDS ...*/

            printf("\n");
            row = row + 1;
    }
    while (row <= ROWMAX);
    /*.....      OUTER LOOP ENDS      .....*/
    printf(" ———————————————————————————————————————————— \n");
}
```

Output

MULTIPLICATION TABLE

1	2	3	4	5	6	7	8	9	10
2	4	6	8	10	12	14	16	18	20
3	6	9	12	15	18	21	24	27	30
4	8	12	16	20	24	28	32	36	40
5	10	15	20	25	30	35	40	45	50
6	12	18	24	30	36	42	48	54	60
7	14	21	28	35	42	49	56	63	70
8	16	24	32	40	48	56	64	72	80
9	18	27	36	45	54	63	72	81	90
10	20	30	40	50	60	70	80	90	100
11	22	33	44	55	66	77	88	99	110
12	24	36	48	60	72	84	96	108	120

Fig. 6.3 *Printing of a multiplication table using **do...while** loop*

The execution of the **for** statement is as follows:

1. *Initialization* of the *control variables* is done first, using assignment statements such as i = 1 and count = 0. The variables **i** and **count** are known as loop-control variables.
2. The value of the control variable is tested using the *test-condition*. The test-condition is a relational expression, such as i < 10 that determines when the loop will exit. If the condition is *true*, the body of the loop is executed; otherwise the loop is terminated and the execution continues with the statement that immediately follows the loop.
3. When the body of the loop is executed, the control is transferred back to the **for** statement after evaluating the last statement in the loop. Now, the control variable is *incremented* using an assignment statement such as i = i+1 and the new value of the control variable is again tested to see whether it satisfies the loop condition. If the condition is satisfied, the body of the loop is again executed. This process continues till the value of the control variable fails to satisfy the test-condition.

Consider the following segment of a program:

```
for ( x = 0 ; x <= 9 ; x = x+1)
{
    printf("%d", x);
}
printf("\n");
```

This **for** loop is executed 10 times and prints the digits 0 to 9 in one line. The three sections enclosed within parentheses must be separated by semicolons. Note that there is no semicolon at the end of the *increment* section, x = x+1.

The **for** statement allows for *negative increments*. For example, the loop discussed above can be written as follows:

```
for ( x = 9 ; x >= 0 ; x = x−1 )
    printf("%d", x);
printf("\n");
```

This loop is also executed 10 times, but the output would be from 9 to 0 instead of 0 to 9. Note that braces are optional when the body of the loop contains only one statement.

Since the conditional test is always performed at the beginning of the loop, the body of the loop may not be executed at all, if the condition fails at the start. For example,

```
for (x = 9; x < 9; x = x−1)
    printf("%d", x);
```

will never be executed because the test condition fails at the very beginning itself.

Let us again consider the problem of sum of squares of integers discussed in section 6.1. This problem can be coded using the **for** statement as follows:

```
------------
------------
sum = 0;
for (n = 1; n <= 10; n = n+1)
{
    sum = sum+ n*n;
}
printf("sum = %d\n", sum);
------------
------------
```

The body of the loop

sum = sum + n∗n;

is executed 10 times for n = 1,2, ..., 10 each time incrementing the **sum** by the square of the value of **n**.

One of the important points about the **for** loop is that all the three actions, namely *initialization*, *testing*, and *incrementing*, are placed in the **for** statement itself, thus making them visible to the programmers and users, in one place. The **for** statement and its equivalent of **while** and **do** statements are shown in Table 6.1.

Table 6.1   Comparison of the Three Loops

for	while	do

for (n=1; n<=10; ++n)
{
--------- 	
--------- 	
}
	n = 1;
	while (n<=10)
	{
	---------- 	
	---------- 	
	n = n+1;
	}
		n = 1;
		do
		{
		--------- 	
		--------- 	
		n = n+1;
		}
		while (n<=10);

Example 6.3

The program in Fig. 6.4 uses a **for** loop to print the "Powers of 2" table for the power 0 to 20, both positive and negative.

The program evaluates the value

$$p = 2^n$$

successively by multiplying 2 by itself n times.

$$q = 2^{-n} = \frac{1}{p}$$

Note that we have declared **p** as a **long int** and **q** as a **double**.

Additional Features of for Loop

The **for** loop in C has several capabilities that are not found in other loop constructs. For example, more than one variable can be initialized at a time in the **for** statement. The statements

        p = 1;
        for (n=0; n<17; ++n)

can be rewritten as

        for (p=1, n=0; n<17; ++n)

Program

```
/************************************************************/
/*                  USE OF for LOOP                         */
/************************************************************/

main( )
{
    long int    p;
    int         n;
    double      q;

    printf(" ------------------------------------------------------------- \n");
    printf(" 2 to power n            n              2 to power −n\n");
    printf(" ------------------------------------------------------------- \n");
    p = 1;
    for (n = 0; n < 21 ; ++n)     /* LOOP BEGINS */
    {
        if (n == 0)
            p = 1;
        else
            p = p * 2;
        q = 1.0/(double)p ;
        printf("%10ld %10d %20.12lf\n", p, n, q);
    }                                             /* LOOP ENDS    */
    printf(" -------------------------------------------------------------\n");
}
```

Output

2 to power n	n	2 to power -n
1	0	1.000000000000
2	1	0.500000000000
4	2	0.250000000000
8	3	0.125000000000
16	4	0.062500000000
32	5	0.031250000000
64	6	0.015625000000
128	7	0.007812500000
256	8	0.003906250000
512	9	0.001953125000
1024	10	0.000976562500
2048	11	0.000488281250
4096	12	0.000244140625
8192	13	0.000122070313
16384	14	0.000061035156
32768	15	0.000030517578
65536	16	0.000015258789
131072	17	0.000007629395
262144	18	0.000003814697
524288	19	0.000001907349
1048576	20	0.000000953674

Fig. 6.4 *Program to print 'Power of 2' table using **for** loop*

Notice that the initialization section has two parts p = 1 and n = 1 separated by a *comma*.

Like the initialization section, the increment section may also have more than one part. For example, the loop

```
for (n=1, m=50; n<=m; n=n+1, m=m−1)
{
    p = m/n;
    printf("%d %d %d\n", n, m, p);
}
```

is perfectly valid. The multiple arguments in the increment section are separated by *commas*.

The third feature is that the test−condition may have any compound relation and the testing need not be limited only to the loop control variable. Consider the example below:

```
sum = 0;
for (i = 1; i < 20 && sum < 100;  ++i)
{
    sum  =  sum+i;
    printf("%d %d\n", sum);
}
```

The loop uses a compound test condition with the control variable **i** and external variable **sum**. The loop is executed as long as both the conditions i < 20 and sum < 100 are true. The **sum** is evaluated inside the loop.

It is also permissible to use expressions in the assignment statements of initialization and increment sections. For example, a statement of the type

```
for (x  =  (m+n)/2; x > 0; x = x/2)
```

is perfectly valid.

Another unique aspect of **for** loop is that one or more sections can be omitted, if necessary. Consider the following statements:

```
------------
------------
m = 5;
for ( ; m != 100 ; )
{
    printf("%d\n", m);
    m = m+5;
}
------------
------------
```

Both the initialization and increment sections are omitted in the **for** statement. The initialization has been done before the **for** statement and the control variable is incremented inside the loop. In such cases, the sections are left blank. However, the semicolons separating the sections must remain. If the test−condition is not present, the **for** statement sets up an infinite loop. Such loops can be broken using **break** or **goto** statements in the loop.

We can set up *time delay loops* using the *null* statement as follows:

```
for ( j  =  1000; j > 0; j = j−1)
    ;
```

This loop is executed 1000 times without producing any output; it simply causes a time delay. Notice that the body of the loop contains only a semicolon, known as a *null* statement. This can also be written as

$$\textbf{for (j=1000; j > 0; j = J-1);}$$

This implies that the C compiler will not give an error message if we place a semicolon by mistake at the end of a **for** statement. The semicolon will be considered as a *null statement* and the program may produce some nonsense.

Nesting of for Loops

Nesting of loops, that is, one **for** statement within another **for** statement, is allowed in C. For example, two loops can be nested as follows:

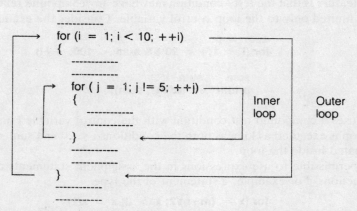

The nesting may continue upto 15 levels in ANSI C; many compilers allow more. The loops should be properly indented so as to enable the reader to easily determine which statements are contained within each **for** statement.

The program to print the multiplication table discussed in Example 6.2 can be written more concisely using nested **for** statements as follows:

```
------------
------------
for (row = 1; row <= ROWMAX ;  ++row)
{
    for (column = 1; column <= COLMAX ;   ++column)
    {
        y = row * column;
        printf("%4d", y);
    }
    printf("\n");
}
------------
------------
```

The outer loop controls the rows while the inner loop controls the columns.

Example 6.4

A class of n students take an annual examination in m subjects. A program to read the marks obtained by each student in various subjects and to compute and print the total marks obtained by each of them is given in Fig. 6.5.

Program
```
/****************************************************************************/
/*                     ILLUSTRATION OF NESTED LOOPS                      */
/****************************************************************************/
#define FIRST        360
#define SECOND       240
main( )
{
    int n, m, i, j,
        roll–number, marks, total;
    printf("Enter number of students and subjects\n");
    scanf("%d %d", &n, &m);
    printf("\n");
    for (i = 1; i <= n ; ++i)
    {
        printf("Enter roll–number : ");
        scanf("%d", &roll–number);
        total = 0 ;
        printf("\nEnter marks of %d subjects for ROLL NO %d
            \n",m,roll–number);
        for (j =  1; j <=  m; j++)
        {
            scanf("%d", &marks);
            total  =   total + marks;
        }
        printf("TOTAL MARKS  =  %d ", total);
        if (total >=  FIRST)
            printf("( First Division )\n\n");
        else if (total >  =  SECOND)
            printf("( Second Division )\n\n");
            else
            printf("( ***  F A I L  *** )\n\n");
    }
}
```
Output
```
Enter number of students and subjects
3 6

Enter roll–number : 8701

Enter marks of 6 subjects for ROLL NO 8701
81 75 83 45 61 59
TOTAL MARKS  =  404 ( First Division )

Enter roll–number : 8702

Enter marks of 6 subjects for ROLL NO 8702
51 49 55 47 65 41
TOTAL MARKS  =  308 ( Second Division )

Enter roll–number : 8704

Enter marks of 6 subjects for ROLL NO 8704
40 19 31 47 39 25
TOTAL MARKS  =  201 ( ***  F A I L  *** )
```

Fig. 6.5 *Illustration of nested **for** loops*

The program uses two **for** loops, one for controlling the number of students and the other for controlling the number of subjects. Since both the number of students and the number of subjects are requested by the program, the program may be used for a class of any size and any number of subjects.

The outer loop includes three parts: (1) reading of roll-numbers of students, one after another, (2) inner loop, where the marks are read and totalled for each student, and (3) printing of total marks and declaration of grades.

6.5 JUMPS IN LOOPS

Loops perform a set of operations repeatedly until the control variable fails to satisfy the test-condition. The number of times a loop is repeated is decided in advance and the test condition is written to achieve this. Sometimes, when executing a loop it becomes desirable to skip a part of the loop or to leave the loop as soon as a certain condition occurs. For example, consider the case of searching for a particular name in a list containing, say, 100 names. A program loop written for reading and testing the names a 100 times must be terminated as soon as the desired name is found. C permits a jump from one statement to another within a loop as well as a jump out of a loop.

Jumping Out of a Loop

An early exit from a loop can be accomplished by using the **break** statement or the **goto** statement. We have already seen the use of the **break** in the **switch** statement and the **goto** in the **if...else** construct. These statements can also be used within **while**, **do**, or **for** loops. They are illustrated in Fig. 6.6 and Fig. 6.7.

When the **break** statement is encountered inside a loop, the loop is immediately exited and the program continues with the statement immediately following the loop. When the loops are nested, the **break** would only exit from the loop containing it. That is, the **break** will exit only a single loop.

Since a **goto** statement can transfer the control to any place in a program, it is useful to provide branching within a loop. Another important use of **goto** is to exit from deeply nested loops when an error occurs. A simple **break** statement would not work here.

Example 6.5

The program in Fig. 6.8 illustrates the use of the **break** statement in a C program.

The program reads a list of positive values and calculates their average. The **for** loop is written to read 1000 values. However, if we want the program to calculate the average of any set of values less than 1000, then we must enter a negative number after the last value in the list, to mark the end of input.

Each value, when it is read, is tested to see whether it is a positive number or not. If it is positive, the value is added to the **sum**; otherwise, the loop terminates. On exit, the average of the values read is calculated and the results are printed out.

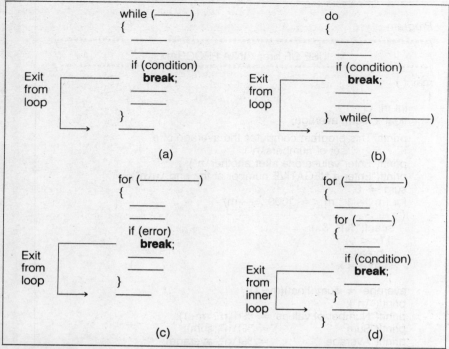

Fig. 6.6 *Exiting a loop with* **break** *statement*

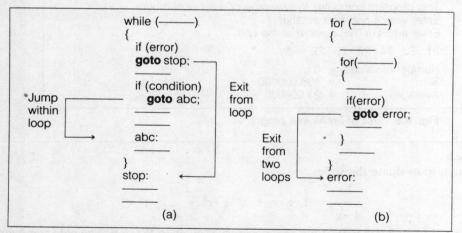

Fig. 6.7 *Jumping within and exiting from the loops with* **goto** *statement*

Program

```
/***************************************************************************/
/*                  USE OF break IN A PROGRAM                           */
/***************************************************************************/
main( )
{
    int m;
    float x, sum, average;

    printf("This program computes the average of a
                set of numbers\n");
    printf("Enter values one after another\n");
    printf("Enter a NEGATIVE number at the end.\n\n");
    sum = 0;
    for (m = 1 ; m <= 1000 ; ++m)
    {
      scanf("%f", &x);
      if (x < 0)
        break;
      sum += x ;
      }
    average = sum/(float)(m−1);
    printf("\n");
    printf("Number of values = %d\n", m−1);
    printf("Sum             = %f\n", sum);
    printf("Average         = %f\n", average);
}
```

Output

```
This program computes the average of a set of numbers
Enter values one after another
Enter a NEGATIVE number at the end.

21  23  24  22  26  22  −1

Number of values = 6
Sum             = 138.000000
Average         = 23.000000
```

Fig. 6.8 *Use of **break** in a program*

Example 6.6

A program to evaluate the series

$$\frac{1}{1-x} = 1 + x + x^2 + x^3 + \ldots + x^n$$

for $-1 < x < 1$ to evaluate to 0.01 per cent accuracy is given in Fig. 6.9. The **goto** statement is used to exit the loop on achieving the desired accuracy.

We have used the **for** statement to perform the repeated addition of each of the terms in the series. Since it is an infinite series, the evaluation of the function is terminated when the term

x^n reaches the desired accuracy. The value of n that decides the number of loop operations is not known and therefore we have decided arbitrarily a value of 100, which may or may not result in the desired level of accuracy.

```
Program
/****************************************************************/
/*              EXAMPLE OF exit WITH goto STATEMENT           */
/****************************************************************/
#define        LOOP            100
#define        ACCURACY        0.0001
main( )
{
     int n;
     float x, term, sum;
     printf("Input value of x : ");
     scanf("%f", &x);
     sum = 0 ;
     for (term = 1, n = 1 ; n <= LOOP ; ++n)
     {
        sum += term ;
        if (term <= ACCURACY)
          goto output; /* EXIT FROM THE LOOP */
        term *= x ;
     }
     printf("\nFINAL VALUE OF N IS NOT SUFFICIENT\n");
     printf("TO ACHIEVE DESIRED ACCURACY\n");
     goto end;
     output:
     printf("\nEXIT FROM LOOP\n");
     printf("Sum = %f;  No.of terms = %d\n",  sum, n);
     end:
        ;

}
Output
Input value of x :  .21
EXIT FROM LOOP
Sum  =  1.265800;   No.of terms  =  7

Input value of x :  .75
EXIT FROM LOOP
Sum  =  3.999774;   No.of terms  =  34

Input value of x :  .99
FINAL VALUE OF N IS NOT SUFFICIENT
TO ACHIEVE DESIRED ACCURACY
```

Fig. 6.9 *Use of **goto** to exit from a loop*

The test of accuracy is made using an **if** statement and the **goto** statement exits the loop as soon as the accuracy condition is satisfied. If the number of loop repetitions is not large enough to produce the desired accuracy, the program prints an appropriate message.

Note that the **break** statement is not very convenient to use here. Both the normal exit and the **break** exit will transfer the control to the same statement that appears next to the loop. But, in the present problem, the *normal exit* prints the message

"FINAL VALUE OF N IS NOT SUFFICIENT
TO ACHIEVE DESIRED ACCURACY"

and the *forced exit* prints the results of evaluation. Notice the use of a *null* statement at the end. This is necessary because a program should not end with a label.

Skipping a part of a Loop

During the loop operations, it may be necessary to skip a part of the body of the loop under certain conditions. For example, in processing of applications for some job, we might like to exclude the processing of data of applicants belonging to a certain category. On reading the category code of an applicant, a test is made to see whether his application should be considered or not. If it is not to be considered, the part of the program loop that processes the application details is skipped and the execution continues with the next loop operation.

Like the **break** statement, C supports another similar statement called the **continue** statement. However, unlike the **break** which causes the loop to be terminated, the **continue**, as the name implies, causes the loop to be *continued* with the *next iteration* after *skipping* any statements in between. The **continue** statement tells the compiler, "SKIP THE FOLLOWING STATEMENTS AND CONTINUE WITH THE NEXT ITERATION". The format of the **continue** statement is simply

continue;

The use of the **continue** statement in loops is illustrated in Fig. 6.10. In **while** and **do** loops, **continue** causes the control to go directly to the *test-condition* and then to continue the iteration process. In the case of **for** loop, the *increment* section of the loop is executed before the *test-condition* is evaluated.

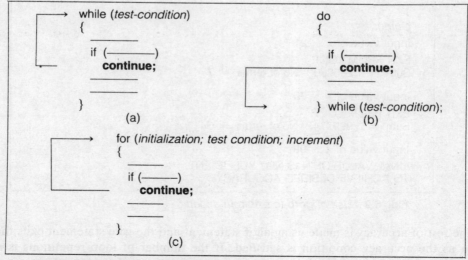

Fig. 6.10 *Bypassing and continuing in loops*

Example 6.7
The program in Fig. 6.11 illustrates the use of **continue** statement.

The program evaluates the square root of a series of numbers and prints the results. The process stops when the number 9999 is typed in.

In case, the series contains any negative numbers, the process of evaluation of square root hould be bypassed for such numbers because the square root of a negative number is not defined. The **continue** statement is used to achieve this. The program also prints a message saying that the number is negative and keeps an account of negative numbers.

The final output includes the number of positive values evaluated and the number of negative items encountered.

```
Program
/******************************************************************* /
/*                     USE OF continue STATEMENT                 */
/******************************************************************* /
#include <math.h>
main( )
{
      int count, negative;
      double number, sqroot;
      printf("Enter 9999 to STOP\n");
      count = 0 ;
      negative = 0 ;
      while (count <= 100)
      {
          printf("Enter a number : ");
          scanf("%lf", &number);
          if (number == 9999)
            break;          /* EXIT FROM THE LOOP */ '
          if (number < 0)
          {
            printf("Number is negative\n\n");
            negative++ ;
            continue;       /* SKIP REST OF THE LOOP */
          }
          sqroot = sqrt(number);
          printf("Number          = %lf\nSquare root = %lf\n\n",
                                    number, sqroot);
          count++ ;
      }
      printf("Number of items done  = %d\n", count);
      printf("\n\nNegative items        = %d\n", negative);
      printf("END OF DATA\n");
}
Output
Enter 9999 to STOP
Enter a number : 25.0
```

```
Number      = 25.000000
Square root = 5.000000

Enter a number : 40.5
Number      = 40.500000
Square root = 6.363961

Enter a number : −9
Number is negative

Enter a number : 16
Number      = 16.000000
Square root = 4.000000

Enter a number : −14.75
Number is negative

Enter a number : 80
Number      = 80.000000
Square root = 8.944272

Enter a number : 9999


Number of items done =  4
Negative items       =  2
END OF DATA
```

Fig. 6.11 *Use of* **continue** *statement*

Avoiding goto

As mentioned earliar, it is a good practice to avoid using gotos. There are many reasons for this. When **goto** is used, many compilers generate a less efficient code. In addition, using many of them makes a program logic complicated and renders the program unreadable. It is possible to avoid using **goto** by careful program design. In case any goto is absolutely necessary, it should be documented. The following goto jumps would cause problems and therefore must be avoided:

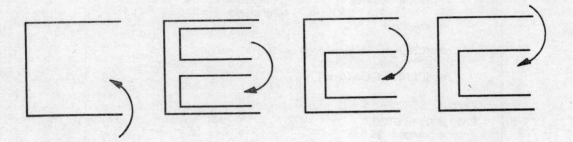

Concise Test Expressions

We often use test expressions in the if, for, while and do statements that are evaluated and compared with zero for making branching decisions. Since every integer expression has a true/false value, we need not make explicit comparisions with zero. For instance, the expression **x** is true whenever **x** is not zero, and false when **x** is zero. Applying **!** operator, we can write concise test expressions without using any relational operators.

> if (*expression* == 0)

is equivalent to

> if (! *expression*)

Similarly,

> if (*expression* ! = 0)

is equivalent to

> if (*expression*)

Example

If **(m%5 == 0 && n%5 == 0)** is same as **if (! (m%5) && ! (n%5))**

CASE STUDIES ·

1. Table of Binomial Coefficients

Problem: Binomial coefficients are used in the study of binomial distributions and reliability of multicomponent redundant systems. It is given by

$$B(m,x) = \binom{m}{x} = \frac{m!}{x! \, (m-x)!} , m >= x$$

A table of binomial coefficients is required to determine the binomial coefficient for any set of *m* and *x*.

Problem Analysis: The binomial coefficient can be recursively calculated as follows:

$$B(m,o) = 1$$
$$B(m,x) = B(m,x-1) \left[\frac{m-x+1}{x}\right], \quad x = 1,2,3,...,m$$

Further,

$$B(o,o) = 1$$

That is, the binomial coefficient is one when either *x* is zero or *m* is zero. The program in Fig. 6.12 prints the table of binomial coefficients for *m* = 10. The program employs one **do** loop and one **while** loop.

Program

```
/************************************************************************/
/*              EVALUATION OF BINOMIAL COEFFICIENTS                     */
/************************************************************************/
#define    MAX       10
main( )
{
    int  m,  x,  binom;
    printf(" m x");
    for (m = 0; m <= 10 ; ++m)
    printf("%4d", m);
    printf("\n ----------------------------------------------------------------\
               ------------\n");
    m = 0;
    do
    {
      printf("%2d   ", m);
      x = 0; binom = 1;
      while (x <= m)
      {
          if(m == 0 || x == 0)
            printf("%4d", binom);
          else
            {
              binom = binom * (m – x + 1)/x;
              printf("%4d", binom);
            }
          x = x + 1;
      }
      printf("\n");
      m = m + 1;
    }
    while (m <= MAX);
    printf(" ------------------------------------------------------------------\
               ------------ \n");
}
```

Output

m x	0	1	2	3	4	5	6	7	8	9	10
0	1										
1	1	1									
2	1	2	1								
3	1	3	3	1							
4	1	4	6	4	1						
5	1	5	10	10	5	1					
6	1	6	15	20	15	6	1				
7	1	7	21	35	35	21	7	1			
8	1	8	28	56	70	56	28	8	1		
9	1	9	36	84	126	126	84	36	9	1	
10	1	10	45	120	210	252	210	120	45	10	1

Fig. 6.12 *Program to print binomial coefficient table*

2. Histogram

Problem: In an organization, the employees are grouped according to their basic pay for the purpose of certain perks. The pay-range and the number of employees in each group are as follows:

Group	Pay-Range	Number of Employees
1	750 – 1500	12
2	1501 – 3000	23
3	3001 – 4500	35
4	4501 – 6000	20
5	above 6000	11

Draw a histogram to highlight the group sizes.

Problem Analysis: Given the size of groups, it is required to draw bars representing the sizes of various groups. For each bar, its group number and size are to be written.

Program in Fig. 6.13 reads the number of employees belonging to each group and draws a histogram. The program uses four **for** loops and two **if.....else** statements.

```
Program
/****************************************************************/
/*                PROGRAM TO DRAW HISTOGRAM                    */
/****************************************************************/
#define      N     5
main( )
{
    int value[N];
    int i, j, n, x;
    for (n=0; n < N;  ++n)
    {
      printf("Enter employees in Group - %d : ",n+1);
      scanf("%d", &x);
      value[n] = x;
      printf("%d\n", value[n]);
    }
    printf("\n");
    printf("              |\n");
    for (n = 0 ; n < N ;  ++n)
    {
        for(i = 1 ; i <= 3 ; i++)
        {
            if ( i == 2)
                printf("Group-%1d   |",n+1);
            else
                printf("          |");
            for (j = 1 ; j <= value[n]; ++j)
                printf("*");
            if (i == 2)
                printf("(%d)\n", value[n]);
            else
```

```
                    printf("\n");
                }
            printf("       |\n");
        }
    }
```
Output

Enter employees in Group - 1 : 12
12
Enter employees in Group - 2 : 23
23
Enter employees in Group - 3 : 35
35
Enter employees in Group - 4 : 20
20
Enter Employees in Group - 5 : 11
11

```
           |
           |  ***********
Group-1    |  ***********(12)
           |  ***********
           |
           |  ***********************
Group-2    |  ***********************(23)
           |  ***********************
           |
           |  ***********************************
Group-3    |  ***********************************(35)
           |  ***********************************
           |
           |  ********************
Group-4    |  ********************(20)
           |  ********************
           |
           |  **********
Group-5    |  **********(11)
           |  **********
```

Fig. 6.13 *Program to draw a histogram*

3. Minimum Cost

Problem: The cost of operation of a unit consists of two components C_1 and C_2 which can be expressed as functions of a parameter p as follows:

$$C_1 = 30 - 8p$$
$$C_2 = 10 + p^2$$

The parameter p ranges from 0 to 10. Determine the value of p with an accuracy of ± 0.1 where the cost of operation would be minimum.

Problem Analysis:

$$\text{Total cost} = C_1 + C_2 = 40 - 8p + p^2$$

The cost is 40 when $p = 0$, and 33 when $p = 1$ and 60 when $p = 10$. The cost, therefore, decreases first and then increases. The program in Fig. 6.14 evaluates the cost at successive intervals of p (in steps of 0.1) and stops when the cost begins to increase. The program employs **break** and **continue** statements to exit the loop.

```
Program
/****************************************************************************/
/*                    PROBLEM OF MINIMUM COST                               */
/****************************************************************************/
main( )
{
    float p, cost, p1, cost1;
    for (p = 0; p <= 10; p = p + 0.1)
    {
      cost = 40 – 8 * p + p * p;
      if(p == 0)
        {
         cost1 = cost;
         continue;
        }
      if(cost >= cost1)
        break;
      cost1 = cost;
      p1 = p;
    }
    p = (p + p1)/2.0;
    cost = 40 – 8 * p + p * p;
    printf("\nMINIMUM COST = %.2f  AT p  = %.1f\n", cost, p);
}
Output
MINIMUM COST = 24.00   AT p = 4.0
```

Fig. 6.14 *Program of minimum cost problem*

4. Plotting of Two Functions

Problem: We have two functions of the type

$$y1 = \exp(-ax)$$
$$y2 = \exp(-ax^2/2)$$

Plot the graphs of these functions for x varying from 0 to 5.0.

Problem Analysis: Initially when $x = 0$, $y1 = y2 = 1$ and the graphs start from the same point. The curves cross when they are again equal at $x = 2.0$. The program should have appropriate branch statements to print the graph points at the following three conditions:

1. $y1 > y2$
2. $y1 < y2$
3. $y1 = y2$

The functions $y1$ and $y2$ are normalized and converted to integers as follows:

$$y1 = 50 \exp(-ax) + 0.5$$
$$y2 = 50 \exp(-ax^2/2) + 0.5$$

The program in Fig. 6.15 plots these two functions simultaneously. (0 for *y1*, * for *y2*, and #
for the common point).

```
Program
/*******************************************************************************/
/*       \               PLOTTING OF TWO FUNCTIONS                          */
/*******************************************************************************/
#include      <math.h>
main( )
{
    int   i;
    float a, x, y1, y2;

    a = 0.4;
    printf("                                          Y ————————> \n");
    printf("   0  ————————————————————————————————————— \
          ——————————————— \n");

    for (x = 0; x < 5; x = x+0.25)
    {  /* BEGINNING OF FOR LOOP */
/*.................Evaluation of functions...................*/
      y1 = (int) ( 50 * exp( −a * x ) + 0.5 );
      y2 = (int) (50 * exp( −a * x * x/2 ) + 0.5 );

/*.................Plotting when y1 = y2 ...................*/
      if (y1 == y2)
      {
       if (x == 2.5)
         printf("   X |");
       else
         printf("    |");

       for (i = 1; i <= y1 − 1; ++i)
         printf("  ");

         printf("# \n");
       continue;
      }

/*.................Plotting when y1 > y2 ...................*/
      if (y1 > y2)
      {
       if (x == 2.5)
         printf("   X |");
       else
         printf("    |");

       for (i = 1; i <= y2 − 1; ++i)
         printf("  ");

       printf("*");

       for (i = 1; i <=  (y1 − y2 − 1); ++i)
         printf("−");

       printf("0\n");
       continue;
```

```
        }
      /*.................Plotting when y2 > y1 .................*/
          if (x == 2.5)
            printf("   X |");
          else
            printf("      |");
          for (i = 1; i <= (y1 − 1); ++i)
            printf(" ");
          printf("0");
          for (i = 1; i <=  (y2 − y1 − 1); ++i)
            printf("−");
          printf("*\n");
        } /*.................END OF FOR LOOP ....................*/
          printf("      |\n");
    }
```

Output

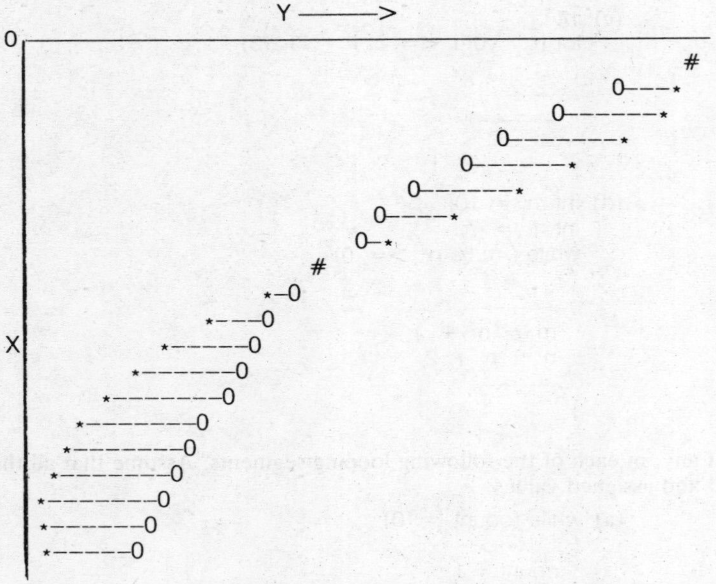

Fig. 6.15 *Plotting of two functions*

REVIEW QUESTIONS AND EXERCISES

6.1 Compare in terms of their functions, the following pairs of statements:
(a) while and do...while.
(b) while and for.
(c) break and goto.
(d) break and continue.
(e) continue and goto.

6.2 Analyze each of the program segments that follow and determine how many times the body of each loop will be executed.

(a)
```
x  = 5;
y  = 50;
while ( x <= y)
{
   x = y/x;
   _____
   _____
}
```

(b)
```
m = 1;
do
{
   _____
   _____
   m = m+2;
}
while (m < 10);
```

(c)
```
int i;
for (i = 0; i <= 5; i = i+2/3)
{
   _____
   _____
   _____
}
```

(d)
```
int m = 10;
int n  = 7;
while ( m % n  >= 0)
{
   _____
   m = m + 1;
   n = n + 2;
   _____
}
```

6.3 Find errors, if any, in each of the following looping segments. Assume that all the variables have been declared and assigned values.

(a)
```
while (count !=10);
{
   count = 1;
   sum = sum + x;
   count = count + 1;
}
```

(b)
```
name = 0;
do { name = name + 1;
printf("My name is John\n");}
while (name = 1)
```

(c)
```
do;
total = total + value;
scanf("%f", &value);
while(value != 999);
```

```
(d) for (x = 1, x > 10; x = x + 1)
    {
        _____
        _____
        _____
    }
(e) m = 1;
    n = 0;
    for ( ; m+n < 19; ++n);
    printf("Hello\n");
    m = m+10
(f) for (p = 10; p > 0;)
    p = p − 1;
    printf("%f", p);
```

6.4 What is a null statement? Explain its usefulness.

6.5 Given a number, write a program using **while** loop to reverse the digits of the number. For example, the number

12345

should be written as

54321

(*Hint*: Use modulus operator to extract the last digit and the integer division by 10 to get the $n-1$ digit number from the n digit number.)

6.6 The factorial of an integer m is the product of consecutive integers from 1 to m. That is,
$$\text{factorial } m = m! = m \times (m-1) \times \ldots \ldots \times 1.$$
Write a program that computes and prints a table of factorials for any given m.

6.7 Write a program to compute the sum of the digits of a given integer number.

6.8 The numbers in the sequence

1 1 2 3 5 8 13 21 ......

are called Fibonacci numbers. Write a program using a **do....while** loop to calculate and print the first m Fibonacci numbers.

(*Hint*: After the first two numbers in the series, each number is the sum of the two preceding numbers.)

6.9 Rewrite the program of the Example 6.1 using the **for** statement.

6.10 Write a program to evaluate the following investment equation
$$V = P(1+r)^n$$
and print the tables which would give the value of V for various combination of the following values of P, r, and n.

P : 1000, 2000, 3000,........, 10,000
r : 0.10, 0.11, 0.12,........, 0.20
n : 1, 2, 3, ..., 10

(*Hint*: P is the principal amount and V is the value of money at the end of n years. This equation can be recursively written as

$$V = P(1+r)$$
$$P = V$$

That is, the value of money at the end of first year becomes the principal amount for the next year and so on.)

6.11 Write programs to print the following outputs using **for** loops.

(a)
```
1
2 2
3 3 3
4 4 4 4
5 5 5 5 5
```

(b)
```
* * * * *
  * * * *
    * * *
      * *
        *
```

(c)
```
     1
    2 2
   3 3 3
  4 4 4 4
 5 5 5 5 5
```

6.12 Write a program to read the age of 100 persons and count the number of persons in the age group 50 to 60. Use **for** and **continue** statements.

6.13 Rewrite the program of case study 6.4 (plotting of two curves) using **else...if** constructs instead of **continue** statements.

6.14 Write a program to print a table of values of the function

$$y = \exp{(-x)}$$

for x varying from 0.0 to 10.0 in steps of 0.10. The table should appear as follows:

Table for $Y = \mathrm{EXP}(-X)$

x	0.1	0.2	0.3	.... 0.9
0.0				
1.0				
2.0				
3.0				
.				
.				
.				
9.0				

6.15 Write a program that will read a positive integer and determine and print its binary equivalent.

(*Hint*: The bits of the binary representation of an integer can be generated by repeatedly dividing the number and the successive quotients by 2 and saving the remainder, which is either 0 or 1, after each division.)

7

ARRAYS

7.1 INTRODUCTION

An *array* is a group of related data items that share a common name. For instance, we can define an array name **salary** to represent a *set of salaries* of a group of employees. A particular value is indicated by writing a number called *index* number or *subscript* in brackets after the array name. For example,

salary[10]

represents the salary of the 10th employee. While the complete set of values is referred to as an array, the individual values are called *elements*. Arrays can be of any variable type.

The ability to use a single name to represent a collection of items and to refer to an item by specifying the item number enables us to develop concise and efficient programs. For example, a loop with the subscript as the control variable can be used to read the entire array, perform calculations and, print out the results. In this chapter, we shall discuss how arrays can be defined and used in C.

7.2 ONE-DIMENSIONAL ARRAYS

A list of items can be given one variable name using only one subscript and such a variable is called a *single-subscripted variable* or a *one-dimensional array*. In mathematics, we often deal with variables that are single-subscripted. For instance, we use the equation.

$$A = \frac{\sum\limits_{i=1}^{n} x_i}{n}$$

to calculate the average of *n* values of *x*. The subscripted variable x_i refers to the *i*th element of *x*. In C, single-subscripted variable x_i can be expressed as

***x*[1], *x*[2], *x*[3].........*x*[*n*]**

The subscript can begin with number 0. That is

x[0]

is allowed. For example, if we want to represent a set of five numbers, say (35,40,20,57,19), by an **array** variable **number**, then we may declare the variable **number** as follows

int number[5];

and the computer reserves five storage locations as shown below:

	number[0]
	number[1]
	number[2]
	number[3]
	number[4]

The values to the array elements can be assigned as follows:

number[0] = 35;
number[1] = 40;
number[2] = 20;
number[3] = 57;
number[4] = 19;

This would cause the array **number** to store the values as shown below:

number [0]	35
number [1]	40
number [2]	20
number [3]	57
number [4]	19

These elements may be used in programs just like any other C variable. For example, the following are valid statements:

a = number[0] + 10;
number[4] = number[0] + number [2];
number[2] = x[5] + y[10];
value[6] = number[i] * 3;

The subscript of an array can be integer constants, integer variables like i, or expressions that yield integers. *C performs no bounds checking and, therefore, care should be exercised to ensure that the array indices are within the declared limits.*

Declaration of Arrays

Like any other variable, arrays must be declared before they are used. The general form of array declaration is

$$\boxed{\textit{type variable-name}[\text{size}];}$$

The *type* specifies the type of element that will be contained in the array, such as **int**, **float**, or **char** and the *size* indicates the maximum number of elements that can be stored inside the array. For example,

float height[50];

declares the **height** to be an array containing 50 real elements. Any subscripts 0 to 49 are valid. Similarly,

int group[10];

declares the **group** as an array to contain a maximum of 10 integer constants. Remember, any reference to the arrays outside the declared limits would not necessarily cause an error. Rather, it might result in unpredictable program results.

The C language treats character strings simply as arrays of characters. The *size* in a character string represents the maximum number of characters that the string can hold. For instance,

char name[10];

declares the **name** as a character array (string) variable that can hold a maximum of 10 characters. Suppose we read the following string constant into the string variable **name**.

"WELL DONE"

Each character of the string is treated as an element of the array **name** and is stored in the memory as follows:

'W'
'E'
'L'
'L'
' '
'D'
'O'
'N'
'E'
'\0'

When the compiler sees a character string, it terminates it with an additional null character. Thus, the element **name[9]** holds the null character '\0' at the end. When declaring character arrays, we must always allow one extra element space for the null terminator.

Example 7.1

Write a program using a single-subscripted variable to evaluate the following expressions:

$$\text{Total} = \sum_{i=1}^{10} x_i^2$$

The values of $x_1, x_2, \dots$ are read from the terminal.

Program in Fig. 7.1 uses a one-dimensional array **x** to read the values and compute the sum of their squares.

Initialization of Arrays

We can initialize the elements of arrays in the same way as the ordinary variables when they are declared. The general form of initialization of arrays is:

static *type array-name*[size] = { list of values };

The values in the list are separated by commas. For example, the statement

static int number[3] = { 0,0,0 };

will declare the variable **number** as an array of size 3 and will assign zero to each element. If the number of values in the list is less than the number of elements, then only that many elements will be initialized. The remaining elements will be set to zero automatically. For instance,

static float total[5] = {0.0,15.75,−10};

will initialize the first three elements to 0.0, 15.75, and −10.0 and the remaining two elements to zero.

Note that we have used the word 'static' before *type* declaration. This declares the variable as a *static variable*. More about static and other class of variables are discussed in Chapter 9. *Note*: Under the old version (the K & R standard), automatic arrays cannot be initialized. Only external and static arrays may be initialized. However, the ANSI standard permits arrays with **auto** storage class to be initialized. That is, the keyword **static** could be omitted, when an ANSI compiler is used. Since ANSI compilers accept both the versions, we use the storage class **static** in our programs so that they can run under both the K & R and ANSI compilers.

The *size* may be omitted. In such cases, the compiler allocates enough space for all initialized elements. For example, the statement

static int counter[ ] = {1,1,1,1};

will declare the **counter** array to contain four elements with initial values 1. This approach works fine as long as we initialize every element in the array.

Character arrays may be initialized in a similar manner. Thus, the statement

static char name[ ] = {'J','O', 'h', 'n'};

declares the **name** to be an array of four characters, initialized with the string "John"

Initialization of arrays in C suffers two drawbacks.

1. There is no convenient way to initialize only selected elements.
2. There is no shortcut method for initializing a large number of array elements like the one available in FORTRAN.

```
Program
/**************************************************************************/
/*         PROGRAM SHOWING ONE-DIMENSIONAL ARRAY           */
/**************************************************************************/
main( )
{
    int    i;
    float  x[10], value, total ;
/*.....................READING VALUES INTO ARRAY ................... */
    printf("ENTER 10 REAL NUMBERS\n") ;

    for( i = 0; i < 10 ; i++ )
    {
      scanf("%f", &value) ;
      x[i] = value ;
    }
/*.....................COMPUTATION OF TOTAL........................... */

    total = 0.0 ;
    for( i = 0 ; i < 10 ; i++ )
      total = total + x[i] * x[i] ;
/*.....................PRINTING OF x[i] VALUES AND TOTAL ....... */

    printf("\n");
    for( i = 0 ; i < 10 ; i++ )
      printf("x[%2d] = %5.2f\n", i+1, x[i]) ;

    printf("\ntotal = %.2f\n", total) ;
}
Output
ENTER 10 REAL NUMBERS
1.1 2.2 3.3 4.4 5.5 6.6 7.7 8.8 9.9 10.10

x[ 1] =    1.10
x[ 2] =    2.20
x[ 3] =    3.30
x[ 4] =    4.40
x[ 5] =    5.50
x[ 6] =    6.60
x[ 7] =    7.70
x[ 8] =    8.80
x[ 9] =    9.90
x[10] =   10.10

Total  =  446.86
```

Fig. 7.1 *Program to illustrate one-dimensional array*

Consider an array of size, say 100. All the 100 elements have to be explicitly initialized. There is no way to specify a repeat count. In such situations, it would be better to use a **for** loop to initialize the elements. Consider the following segment of a C program:

```
------------
------------
for (i = 0; i < 100; i = i+1)
{
if i < 50
   sum[i] = 0.0;
else
   sum[i] = 1.0;
}
------------
------------
```

The first 50 elements of the array **sum** are initialized to zero while the remaining 50 elements are initialized to 1.0.

Example 7.2

Given below is the list of marks obtained by a class of 50 students in an annual examination.

```
43 65 51 27 79 11 56 61 82 09
25 36 07 49 55 63 74 81 49 37
40 49 16 75 87 91 33 24 58 78
65 56 76 67 45 54 36 63 12 21
73 49 51 19 39 49 68 93 85 59
```

Write a program to count the number of students belonging to each of the following groups of marks: 0-9, 10-19, 20-29,......,100.

The program coded in Fig. 7.2 uses the array **group** containing 11 elements, one for each range of marks. Each element counts those values falling within the range of values it represents.

For any value, we can determine the correct group element by dividing the value by 10. For example, consider the value 59. The integer division of 59 by 10 yields 5. This is the element into which 59 is counted.

Note that the numbers with fractional part are rounded off to the nearest integer before the integer division occurs.

7.3 TWO-DIMENSIONAL ARRAYS

So far we have discussed the array variables that can store a list of values. There will be situations where a table of values will have to be stored. Consider the following data table, which shows the value of sales of three items by four salesgirls:

	Item1	Item2	Item3
Salesgirl #1	310	275	365
Salesgirl #2	210	190	325
Salesgirl #3	405	235	240
Salesgirl #4	260	300	380

The table contains a total of 12 values, three in each line. We can think of this table as a matrix consisting of four *rows* and three *columns*. Each row represents the values of sales by a particular salesgirl and each column represents the values of sales of a particular item.

```
Program
/**************************************************************************/
/*              PROGRAM FOR FREQUENCY COUNTING              */
/**************************************************************************/
#define   MAXVAL    50
#define   COUNTER   11
main( )
{
      float       value[MAXVAL];
      int         i, low, high;
      static int  group[COUNTER] = { 0,0,0,0,0,0,0,0,0,0,0};

/*..........................READING AND COUNTING..........................*/
      for(i = 0; i < MAXVAL; i++)
      {
        /*...READING OF VALUES...*/
        scanf("%f", &value[i]);
        /*...COUNTING FREQUENCY OF GROUPS...*/
        ++ group[ (int) (value[i] + 0.5) / 10] ;
      }
/*..........................PRINTING OF FREQUENCY TABLE...............*/
      printf("\n");
      printf("GROUP    RANGE      FREQUENCY\n\n") ;
      for( i = 0 ; i < COUNTER ; i++ )
      {
        low = i * 10 ;
        if(i == 10)
          high = 100 ;
        else
          high = low + 9 ;
        printf("   %2d     %3d to %3d       %d\n",
               i+1, low, high, group[i] ) ;
      }
}
Output
43  65  51  27  79  11  56  61  82  09
25  36  07  49  55  63  74  81  49  37
40  49  16  75  87  91  33  24  58  78     (input data)
65  56  76  67  45  54  36  63  12  21
73  49  51  19  39  49  68  93  85  59
      GROUP         RANGE         FREQUENCY
         1          0 to   9          2
         2         10 to  19          4
         3         20 to  29          4
         4         30 to  39          5
```

5	40 to 49	8
6	50 to 59	8
7	60 to 69	7
8	70 to 79	6
9	80 to 89	4
10	90 to 99	2
11	100 to 100	0

Fig. 7.2 *Program for frequency counting*

In mathematics, we represent a particular value in a matrix by using two subscripts such as v_{ij}. Here v denotes the entire matrix and v_{ij} refers to the value in the ith row and jth column. For example, in the above table v_{23} refers to the value 325.

C allows us to define such tables of items by using *two-dimensional* arrays. The table discussed above can be defined in C as

v[4][3]

Two-dimensional arrays are declared as follows:

> *type array_name* [row_size][column_size];

Note that unlike most other languages, which use one pair of parentheses with commas to separate array sizes, C places each size in its own set of brackets.

Two dimensional arrays are stored in memory as shown in Fig. 7.3. As with the single-dimensional arrays, each dimension of the array is indexed from zero to its maximum size minus one; the first index selects the row and the second index selects the column within that row.

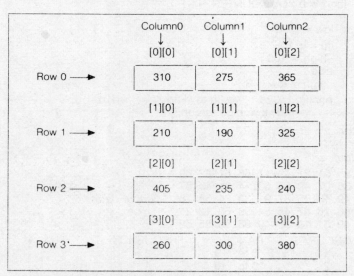

Fig. 7.3 *Representation of a two-dimensional array in memory*

Example 7.3

Write a program using a two-dimensional array to compute and print the following informa-tion from the table of data discussed above:

  (a) Total value of sales by each girl.
  (b) Total value of each item sold.
  (c) Grand total of sales of all items by all girls.

The program and its output are shown in Fig. 7.4. The program uses the variable **value** in two-dimensions with the index **i** representing girls and **j** representing items. The following equations are used in computing the results:

$$\text{(a) Total sales by mth girl} = \sum_{j=0}^{2} \text{value}[m][j]$$
$$(\text{girl\_total}[m])$$

$$\text{(b) Total value of nth item} = \sum_{i=0}^{3} \text{value}[i][n]$$
$$(\text{item\_total}[n])$$

$$\text{(c) Grand total} = \sum_{i=0}^{3} \sum_{j=0}^{2} \text{value}[i][j]$$

$$= \sum_{i=0}^{3} \text{girl\_total}[i]$$

$$= \sum_{j=0}^{2} \text{item\_total}[j]$$

Program
```
/********************************************************************/
/*        PROGRAM SHOWING TWO-DIMENSIONAL ARRAYS          */
/********************************************************************/
#define    MAXGIRLS    4
#define    MAXITEMS    3
main( )
{
    int    value[MAXGIRLS][MAXITEMS];
    int    girl_total[MAXGIRLS], item_total [MAXITEMS];
    int    i, j, grand_total;
/*.............READING OF VALUES AND COMPUTING girl_total..... */
    printf("Input data\n");
    printf("Enter values, one at a time, row-wise\n\n");
    for( i = 0 ; i < MAXGIRLS ; i++ )
    {
```

```
            girl_total[i] = 0;
            for( j = 0 ; j < MAXITEMS ; j++ )
            {
               scanf("%d", &value[i][j]);
               girl_total[i] = girl_total[i] + value[i][j];
            }
        }
    /*...........................COMPUTING  item_total ...............................*/
        for( j = 0 ; j < MAXITEMS ; j++ )
        {
            item_total[j] = 0;
            for( i = 0 ; i < MAXGIRLS ; i++ )
               item_total[j] = item_total[j] + value[i][j];
        }
    /*...........................COMPUTING grand_total ..............................*/
        grand_total = 0;
        for( i = 0 ; i < MAXGIRLS ; i++ )
            grand_total = grand_total + girl_total[i];
    /*...........................PRINTING OF RESULTS..............................*/
        printf("\n GIRLS  TOTALS\n\n");
        for( i = 0 ; i < MAXGIRLS ; i++ )
            printf("Salesgirl[%d] = %d\n", i+1, girl_total[i] );
        printf("\n ITEM TOTALS\n\n");
        for( j = 0 ; j < MAXITEMS ; j++ )
            printf("Item[%d] = %d\n", j+1, item_total[j] );
        printf("\nGrand Total = %d\n", grand_total);
}
```

Output

Input data
Enter values, one at a time, row_wise

```
310   257   365
210   190   325
405   235   240
260   300   380
```

 GIRLS TOTALS

Salesgirl[1] = 950
Salesgirl[2] = 725
Salesgirl[3] = 880
Salesgirl[4] = 940

 ITEM TOTALS

Item[1] = 1185
Item[2] = 1000
Item[3] = 1310

Grand Total = 3495

Fig. 7.4 *Illustration of two-dimensional arrays*

Example 7.4

Write a program to compute and print a multiplication table for numbers 1 to 5 as shown below:

	1	2	3	4	5
1	1	2	3	4	5
2	2	4	6	8	10
3	3	6	.	.	.
4	4	8	.	.	.
5	5	10	.	.	25

The program shown in Fig. 7.5 uses a two-dimensional array to store the table values. Each value is calculated using the control variables of the nested for loops as follows:

product [i][j] = row * column

where i denotes rows and j denotes columns of the product table. Since the indices i and j range from 0 to 4, we have introduced the following transformation:

    row = i+1
    column = j+1

7.4 INITIALIZING TWO-DIMENSIONAL ARRAYS

Like the one-dimensional arrays, two-dimensional arrays may be initialized by following their declaration with a list of initial values enclosed in braces. For example,

static int table[2][3] = { 0,0,0,1,1,1};

initializes the elements of the first row to zero and the second row to one. The initialization is done row by row. The above statement can be equivalently written as

static int table[2][3] = {{0,0,0}, {1,1,1}};

by surrounding the elements of each row by braces.

We can also initialize a two-dimensional array in the form of a matrix as shown below:

static int table[2][3] = {
                        {0,0,0},
                        {1,1,1}
        };

Note the syntax of the above statements. Commas are required after each brace that closes off a row, except in the case of the last row.

If the values are missing in an initializer, they are automatically set to zero. For instance, the statement

Program

```
/**********************************************************************/
/*          PROGRAM TO PRINT MULTIPLICATION TABLE              */
/**********************************************************************/
#define    ROWS       5
#define    COLUMNS    5
main( )
{
    int    row, column, product[ROWS][COLUMNS] ;
    int    i, j ;
    printf("   MULTIPLICATION TABLE\n\n") ;
    printf("       ") ;
    for( j = 1 ; j <= COLUMNS ; j++ )
      printf("%4d", j) ;
    printf("\n") ;
    printf("————————————————— \n");
    for( i = 0 ; i < ROWS ; i++ )
    {
      row = i + 1 ;
      printf("%2d |", row) ;
      for(j = 1 ; j <= COLUMNS ; j++ )
      {
        column = j ;
        product[i][j] = row * column ;
        printf("%4d", product[i][j] ) ;
      }
      printf("\n") ;
    }
}
```

Output

```
MULTIPLICATION TABLE

      1   2   3   4   5
  ————————————————————
1 |   1   2   3   4   5
2 |   2   4   6   8  10
3 |   3   6   9  12  15
4 |   4   8  12  16  20
5 |   5  10  15  20  25
```

Fig. 7.5 *Program to print multiplication table, using two-dimensional array*

static int table[2][3] = {
                                {1,1},
                                {2}
                                    };

will initialize the first two elements of the first row to one, the first element of the second row to two, and all other elements to zero.

When all the elements are to be initialized to zero, the following short-cut method may be used.

static int m[3][5] = { {0}, {0}, {0} };

The first element of each row is explicitly initialized to zero while other elements are automatically initialized to zero.

Example 7.5

A survey to know the popularity of four cars (Ambassador, Fiat, Dolphin and Maruti) was conducted in four cities (Bombay, Calcutta, Delhi and Madras). Each person surveyed was asked to give his city and the type of car he was using. The results, in coded form, are tabulated as follows:

```
M  1 C  2 B  1 D  3 M  2 B  4
C  1 D  3 M  4 B  2 D  1 C  3
D  4 D  4 M  1 M  1 B  3 B  3
C  1 C  1 C  2 M  4 M  4 C  2
D  1 C  2 B  3 M  1 B  1 C  2
D  3 M  4 C  1 D  2 M  3 B  4
```

Codes represent the following information:

M – Madras   1 – Ambassador
D – Delhi   2 – Fiat
C – Calcutta   3 – Dolphin
B – Bombay   4 – Maruti

Write a program to produce a table showing popularity of various cars in four cities.

A two-dimensional array **frequency** is used as an accumulator to store the number of cars used, under various categories in each city. For exmple, the element **frequency** [i][j] denotes the number of cars of type j used in city i. The **frequency** is declared as an array of size 5x5 and all the elements are initialized to zero.

The program shown in Fig. 7.6 reads the city code and the car code, one set after another, from the terminal. Tabulation ends when the letter X is read in place of a city code.

7.5 MULTIDIMENSIONAL ARRAYS

C allows arrays of three or more dimensions. The exact limit is determined by the compiler. The general form of a multidimensional array is

type **array_name**[s1][s2][s3]....[sm];

where s$_i$ is the size of the ith dimension. Some example are:

int survey[3][5][12];
float table[5][4][5][3];

survey is a three-dimensional array declared to contain 180 integer type elements. Similarly **table** is a four-dimensional array containing 300 elements of floating-point type.

The array **survey** may represent a survey data of rainfall during the last three years from January to December in five cities.

Program

```
/******************************************************************/
/*              PROGRAM TO TABULATE SURVEY DATA                 */
/******************************************************************/
main( )
{
    int       i, j, car;
    static int  frequency[5][5] = { {0}, {0}, {0}, {0}, {0} };
    char      city;

    printf("For each person, enter the city code \n");
    printf("followed by the car code.\n");
    printf("Enter the letter X to indicate end.\n");
/*....................TABULATION BEGINS.............................. */
    for( i = 1 ; i < 100 ; i++ )
    {
        scanf("%c", &city );
        if( city == 'X' )
          break;

        scanf("%d", &car );
        switch(city)
        {
            case 'B' :  frequency[1][car]++;
                        break;
            case 'C' :  frequency[2][car]++;
                        break;
            case 'D' :  frequency[3][car]++;
                        break;
            case 'M' :  frequency[4][car]++;
                        break;
        }
    }
/*...........TABULATION COMPLETED AND PRINTING BEGINS .. */
    printf("\n\n");
    printf("                  POPULARITY TABLE\n\n");
    printf("-----------------------------------------------\n");
    printf("City   Ambassador   Fiat   Dolphin   Maruti \n");
    printf("-----------------------------------------------\n");
    for(i = 1; i <= 4; i++)
    {
        switch(i)
        {
            case 1:  printf("Bombay      ");
                     break;
            case 2:  printf("Calcutta    ");
                     break;
            case 3:  printf("Delhi       ");
                     break;
            case 4:  printf("Madras      ");
                     break;
        }
        for( j = 1 ; j <= 4 ; j++ )
          printf("%7d", frequency[i][j] );
```

```
            printf("\n") ;
        }
        printf(" ———————————————————————————————\n");
/*...................PRINTING ENDS..................... */
}
```
Output

For each person, enter the city code
followed by the car code.
Enter the letter X to indicate end.
```
M  1  C  2  B  1  D  3  M  2  B  4
C  1  D  3  M  4  B  2  D  1  C  3
D  4  D  4  M  1  M  1  B  3  B  3
C  1  C  1  C  2  M  4  M  4  C  2
D  1  C  2  B  3  M  1  B  1  C  2
D  3  M  4  C  1  D  2  M  3  B  4  X
```

POPULARITY TABLE

City	Ambassador	Fiat	Dolphin	Maruti
Bombay	2	1	3	2
Calcutta	4	5	1	0
Delhi	2	1	3	2
Madras	4	1	1	4

Fig. 7.6 *Program to tabulate a survey data*

If the first index denotes year, the second city and the third month, then the element **survey[1][2][9]** denotes the rainfall in the month of October during the second year in city-3.

Remember that a three-dimensional array can be represented as a series of two-dimensional arrays as shown below:

CASE STUDIES

1. Median of a List of Numbers

When all the items in a list are arranged in order, the middle value which divides the items into two parts with equal number of items on either side is called the *median*. Odd number of items have just one middle value while even number of items have two middle values. The median for even number of items is therefore designated as the average of the two middle values.

The major steps for finding the median are as follows:

1. Read the items into an array while keeping a count of the items.
2. Sort the items in increasing order.
3. Compute median.

The program and sample output are shown in Fig. 7.7. The sorting algorithm used is as follows:

1. Compare the first two elements in the list, say a[1], and a[2]. If a[2] is smaller than a[1], then interchange their values.
2. Compare a[2] and a[3]; interchange them if a[3] is smaller than a[2].
3. Continue this process till the last two elements are compared and interchanged.
4. Repeat the above steps n−1 times.

In repeated trips through the array, the smallest elements 'bubble up' to the top. Because of this bubbling up effect, this algorithm is called *bubble sorting*. The bubbling effect is illustrated below for four items.

	Initial values		After step 1		After step 2		After step 3	
Trip-1	80	<===	35		35		35	
	35	<—	80	<===	65		65	
	65		65	<—	80	<===	10	
	10		10		10	<—	80	<===

Trip-2	35	<—	35		35	
	65	<===	65	<===	10	
	10		10	<—	65	<===
	80		80		80	

During the first trip, three pairs of items are compared and interchanged whenever needed. It should be noted that the number 80, the largest among the items, has been moved to the bottom at the end of the first trip. This means that the element 80 (the last item in the new list) need not be considered any further. Therefore, trip-2 requires only two pairs to be compared. This time, the number 65 (the second largest value) has been moved down the list. Notice that each trip brings the smallest value 10 up by one level.

The number of steps required in a trip is reduced by one for each trip made. The entire process will be over when a trip contains only one step. If the list contains n elements, then the number of comparisons involved would be $n(n-1)/2$.

```
Program
/************************************************************************/
/*        PROGRAM TO SORT A LIST AND FIND ITS MEDIAN        */
/************************************************************************/
#define N 10
main( )
{
     int i,j,n;
     float median,a[N], t;
     printf("Enter the number of items\n");
     scanf("%d", &n);
/*   Reading items into array a   */
     printf("Input %d values \n",n);
     for (i = 1; i <= n ; i++)
        scanf("%f", &a[i]);
/*   Sorting begins   */
     for (i = 1 ; i <= n−1 ; i++)
     {    /* Trip-i begins   */
        for (j = 1 ; j <= n−i ; j++)
        {
           if (a[j] <= a[j+1])
           { /* Interchanging values */
              t = a[j];
              a[j] = a[j+1];
              a[j+1] = t;
           }.
           else
```

```
                continue ;
            }
        } /* sorting ends */
    /* calculation of median */
        if (n % 2 == 0)
            median = (a[n/2] + a[n/2+1])/2.0 ;
        else
            median = a[n/2 + 1];
    /* Printing */
        for (i = 1 ; i <= n ; i++)
            printf("%f   ", a[i]);
            printf("\n\nMedian is %f\n", median);
}
```

Output

```
Enter the number of items
5
Input 5 values
1.111   2.222   3.333   4.444   5.555
5.555000   4.444000   3.333000   2.222000   1.111000

Median is 3.333000


Enter the number of items
6
Input 6 values
3  5  8  9  4  6
9.000000  8.000000  6.000000  5.000000  4.000000  3.000000

Median is 5.500000
```

Fig. 7.7 *Program to sort a list of numbers and to determine median*

2. Calculation of Standard Deviation

In statistics, standard deviation is used to measure deviation of data from its mean. The formula for calculating standard deviation of n items is

$$s = \sqrt{\text{variance}}$$

where

$$\text{variance} = \frac{1}{n} \sum_{i=1}^{n} (x_i - m)^2$$

and

$$m = \text{mean} = \frac{1}{n} \sum_{i=1}^{n} x_i$$

The algorithm for calculating the standard deviation is as follows:

1. Read n items.
2. Calculate sum and mean of the items.
3. Calculate variance.
4. Calculate standard deviation.

Complete program with sample output is shown in Fig. 7.8.

```
Program
/**************************************************************************/
/*        PROGRAM TO CALCULATE STANDARD DEVIATION        */
/**************************************************************************/
#include <math.h>
#define   MAXSIZE   100
main( )
{
     int i,n;
     float value [MAXSIZE], deviation,
          sum,sumsqr,mean,variance,stddeviation;

     sum = sumsqr = n = 0;

     printf("Input values: input −1 to end \n");
     for (i=1; i< MAXSIZE; i++)
     {
       scanf("%f", &value[i]);
       if (value[i] == −1)
         break;
       sum += value[i];
       n += 1;
     }
     mean = sum/(float)n;

     for (i = 1 ; i <= n; i++)
     {
        deviation = value[i] − mean;
        sumsqr += deviation * deviation;
     }
     variance = sumsqr/(float)n ;
     stddeviation = sqrt(variance) ;

     printf("\nNumber of items : %d\n",n);
     printf("Mean : %f\n", mean);
     printf("Standard deviation : %f\n", stddeviation);
}
Output
Input values: input −1 to end
65  9   27  78  12  20  33  49  −1

Number of items : 8
Mean : 36.625000
Standard deviation : 23.510303
```

Fig. 7.8 *Program to calculate standard deviation*

3. Evaluating a Test

A test consisting of 25 multiple-choice items is administered to a batch of 3 students. Correct answers and student responses are tabulated as shown below:

	Items
Correct answers	1 2 3 4 5 6 7 8 9 0 1 2 3 4 5 6 7 8 9 0 1 2 3 4 5

Algorithm for evaluating the answers of students is as follows:

1. Read correct answers into an array.
2. Read the responses of a student and count the correct ones.
3. Repeat step-2 for each student.
4. Print the results.

A program to implement this algorithm is given in Fig. 7.9. The program uses the following arrays:

key[i]   — To store correct answers of items
response[i] — To store responses of students
correct[i]   — To identify items that are answered correctly.

```
Program
/*********************************************************************/
/*      PROGRAM TO EVALUATE A MULTIPLE-CHOICE TEST      */
/*********************************************************************/
#define    STUDENTS      3
#define    ITEMS         25
main( )
{
       char     key[ITEMS+1], response[ITEMS+1];
       int      count, i, student,n,
                correct[ITEMS+1];
/*     Reading of Correct answers     */
       printf("Input key to the items\n");
       for(i=0; i < ITEMS; i++)
          scanf("%c",&key[i]);
       scanf("%c",&key[i]);
       key[i] = '\0';
/*     Evaluation begins     */
```

```
    for(student = 1; student <= STUDENTS; student++)
    {
/*Reading student responses and counting correct ones*/
    count = 0;
    printf("\n");
    printf("Input responses of student-%d\n",student);

    for(i=0; i < ITEMS ; i++)
        scanf("%c",&response[i]);

    scanf("%c",&response[i]);
    response[i] = '\0';

    for (i = 0; i < ITEMS; i++)
        correct[i] = 0;

    for(i=0; i < ITEMS ; i++)
        if(response[i] == key[i])
        {
            count = count + 1;
            correct[i] = 1;
        }

        /* printing of results */

    printf("\n");
    printf("Student-%d\n", student);
    printf("Score is %d out of %d\n",count, ITEMS);
    printf("Response to the items below are wrong\n");

    n = 0;
    for(i=0; i < ITEMS ; i++)
        if(correct[i] == 0)
        {
            printf("%d",i+1);
            n = n+1;
        }
    if(n == 0)
        printf("NIL\n");
    printf(("\n");
    }   /* Go to next student */
/* Evaluation and printing ends */
}
```

Output

Input key to the items
abcdabcdabcdabcdabcdabcda

Input responses of student-1
abcdabcdabcdabcdabcdabcda

Student-1
Score is 25 out of 25
Response to the following items are wrong
NIL

Input responses of student-2
abcddcbaabcdabcddddddddddd

```
Student-2
Score is 14 out of 25
Response to the following items are wrong
5 6 7 8 17 18 19 21 22 23 25
Input responses of student-3
aaaaaaaaaaaaaaaaaaaaaaaaa
Student-3
Score is 7 out of 25
Response to the following items are wrong
2 3 4 6 7 8 10 11 12 14 15 16 18 19 20 22 23 24
```

Fig. 7.9 *Program to evaluate responses to a multiple-choice test*

4. Production and Sales Analysis

A company manufactures five categories of products and the number of items manufactured and sold are recorded product-wise every week in a month. The company reviews its production schedule at every month-end. The review may require one or more of the following information:

(a) Value of weekly production and sales.
(b) Total value of all the products manufactured.
(c) Total value of all the products sold.
(d) Total value of each product, manufactured and sold.

Let us represent the products manufactured and sold by two two-dimensional arrays M and S respectively. Then,

$$
M = \begin{array}{|c|c|c|c|c|}
\hline
M11 & M12 & M13 & M14 & M15 \\
\hline
M21 & M22 & M23 & M24 & M25 \\
\hline
M31 & M32 & M33 & M34 & M35 \\
\hline
M41 & M42 & M43 & M44 & M45 \\
\hline
\end{array}
$$

$$
S = \begin{array}{|c|c|c|c|c|}
\hline
S11 & S12 & S13 & S14 & S15 \\
\hline
S21 & S22 & S23 & S24 & S25 \\
\hline
S31 & S32 & S33 & S34 & S35 \\
\hline
S41 & S42 & S43 & S44 & S45 \\
\hline
\end{array}
$$

where Mij represents the number of jth type product manufactured in ith week and Sij the number of jth product sold in ith week. We may also represent the cost of each product by a single dimensional array C as follows:

$$
C = \begin{array}{|c|c|c|c|c|}
\hline
C1 & C2 & C3 & C4 & C5 \\
\hline
\end{array}
$$

where Cj is the cost of jth type product.

We shall represent the value of products manufactured and sold by two value arrays, namely, **Mvalue** and **Svalue**. Then,

$$Mvalue[i][j] = M_{ij} \times C_j$$
$$Svalue[i][j] = S_{ij} \times C_j$$

A program to generate the required outputs for the review meeting is shown in Fig. 7.10. The following additional variables are used:

Mweek[i]	=	Value of all the products manufactured in week i.
	=	$\sum\limits_{j=1}^{5}$ Mvalue[i][j]
Sweek[i]	=	Value of all the products sold in week i
	=	$\sum\limits_{j=1}^{5}$ Svalue[i][j]
Mproduct[j]	=	Value of jth type product manufactured during the month
	=	$\sum\limits_{i=1}^{4}$ Mvalue[i][j]
Sproduct[j]	=	Value of jth type product sold during the month
	=	$\sum\limits_{i=1}^{4}$ Svalue[i][j]
Mtotal	=	Total value of all the products manufactured during the month
	=	$\sum\limits_{i=1}^{4}$ Mweek[i] = $\sum\limits_{j=1}^{5}$ Mproduct[j]
Stotal	=	Total value of all the products sold during the month
	=	$\sum\limits_{i=1}^{4}$ Sweek[i] = $\sum\limits_{j=1}^{5}$ Sproduct[j]

Program

```
/*********************************************************************/
/*            PRODUCTION  AND  SALES  ANALYSIS                  */
/*********************************************************************/
main( )
{
     int M[5][6],S[5][6],C[6],
         Mvalue[5][6],Svalue[5][6],
         Mweek[5], Sweek[5],
         Mproduct[6], Sproduct[6],
         Mtotal, Stotal, i,j,number;
/*       Input data       */
     printf(" Enter products manufactured week_wise \n");
     printf(" M11,M12,————, M21,M22,———— etc\n");
     for(i=1; i<=4; i++)
       for(j=1;j<=5; j++)
         scanf("%d",&M[i][j]);
```

```
        printf(" Enter products sold week_wise\n ");
        printf(" S11,S12,——, S21,S22,—— etc\n ");

        for(i=1; i<=4; i++)
            for(j=1; j<=5; j++)
                scanf("%d", &S[i][j]);

        printf(" Enter cost of each product\n");
        for(j=1; j <=5; j++)
            scanf("%d",&C[j]);

/*      Value matrices of production and sales    */

        for(i=1; i<=4; i++)
            for(j=1; j<=5; j++)
            {
                Mvalue[i][j] = M[i][j] * C[j];
                Svalue[i][j]  = S[i][j] * C[j];
            }

/*      Total value of weekly production and sales    */

        for(i=1; i<=4; i++)
        {
            Mweek[i] = 0 ;
            Sweek[i]  = 0 ;
            for(j=1; j<=5; j++)
            {
                Mweek[i] += Mvalue[i][j];
                Sweek[i]  += Svalue[i][j];
            }
        }

/*      Monthly value of product_wise production and sales    */

        for(j=1; j<=5; j++)
        {
            Mproduct[j] = 0 ;
            Sproduct[j]  = 0 ;
            for(i=1; i<=4; i++)
            {
                Mproduct[j] += Mvalue[i][j];
                Sproduct[j] += Svalue[i][j];
            }
        }

/*      Grand total of production and sales values    */

        Mtotal = Stotal = 0;
        for(i=1; i<=4; i++)
        {
            Mtotal += Mweek[i];
            Stotal += Sweek[i];
        }

/ *****************************************************************
            Selection and printing of information required
  *****************************************************************/

        printf("\n\n");
        printf(" Following is the list of things you can\n");
```

```
            printf(" request for. Enter appropriate item number\n");
            printf(" and press RETURN Key\n\n");

            printf(" 1.Value matrices of production & sales\n");

            printf(" 2.Total value of weekly production & sales\n");

            printf(" 3.Product_wise monthly value of production &");
            printf(" sales\n");

            printf(" 4.Grand total value of production & sales\n");

            printf(" 5.Exit\n");

            number = 0;
            while(1)
            {       /*  Beginning of while loop  */
                printf("\n\n ENTER YOUR CHOICE:");
                scanf("%d",&number);
                printf("\n");

                if(number == 5)
                {
                 printf("G O O D   B Y E\n\n");
                 break;
                }

                switch(number)
                {  /*  Beginning of switch  */
/*     V A L U E   M A T R I C E S  */
                    case 1:
                        printf("VALUE MATRIX OF PRODUCTION\n\n");
                        for(i=1; i<=4; i++)
                        {
                            printf(" Week(%d)\t", i);
                            for(j=1; j <=5; j++)
                              printf("%7d", Mvalue[i][j]);
                            printf("\n");
                        }
                        printf("\n VALUE MATRIX OF SALES\n\n");
                        for(i=1; i <=4; i++)
                        {
                            printf(" Week(%d)\t",i);
                            for(j=1; j <=5; j++)
                              printf("%7d", Svalue[i][j]);
                            printf("\n");
                        }
                        break;
/*     W E E K L Y   A N A L Y S I S    */
                    case 2:
                        printf(" TOTAL WEEKLY PRODUCTION & SALES\n\n");
                        printf("                  PRODUCTION    SALES\n");
                        printf("              ——————————  ——————————\n");
                        for(i=1; i <=4; i++)
                        {
                            printf(" Week(%d)\t", i);
```

```
                              printf("%7d\t%7d\n", Mweek[i], Sweek[i]);
                         }
                         break;
/*     P R O D U C T W I S E   A N A L Y S I S   */
          case 3:
                    printf(" PRODUCT_WISE TOTAL PRODUCTION &");
                    printf(" SALES\n\n");
                    printf("                        PRODUCTION    SALES\n");
                    printf("                        _____   _____\n");
                    for(j=1; j <=5; j++)
                    {
                         printf(" Product(%d)\t", j);
                         printf("%7d\t%7d\n",Mproduct[j],Sproduct[j]);
                    }
                    break;
/*     G R A N D   T O T A L S   */
          case 4:
                    printf(" GRAND TOTAL OF PRODUCTION & SALES\n");
                    printf("\n Total production = %d\n", Mtotal);
                    printf(" Total sales       =%d\n", Stotal);
                    break;
/*     D E F A U L T   */
          default :
                    printf(" Wrong choice, select again\n\n");
                    break;

          } /* End of switch */

     } /* End of while loop */

     printf(" Exit from the program\n\n");

} /* End of main */
```

Output

```
Enter products manufactured week_wise
M11,M12,———, M21,M22,——— etc
11   15   12   14   13
13   13   14   15   12
12   16   10   15   14
14   11   15   13   12

Enter products sold week_wise
S11,S12,———, S21,S22,——— etc
10   13    9   12   11
12   10   12   14   10
11   14   10   14   12
12   10   13   11   10

Enter cost of each product
10   20   30   15   25

Following is the list of things you can
request for. Enter appropriate item number
and press RETURN key
```

1. Value matrices of production & sales
2. Total value of weekly production & sales
3. Product_wise monthly value of production & sales
4. Grand total value of production & sales
5. Exit

ENTER YOUR CHOICE:1

VALUE MATRIX OF PRODUCTION

Week(1)	110	300	360	210	325
Week(2)	130	260	420	225	300
Week(3)	120	320	300	225	350
Week(4)	140	220	450	185	300

VALUE MATRIX OF SALES

Week(1)	100	260	270	180	275
Week(2)	120	200	360	210	250
Week(3)	110	280	300	210	300
Week(4)	120	200	390	165	250

ENTER YOUR CHOICE 2

TOTAL WEEKLY PRODUCTION & SALES

	PRODUCTION	SALES
Week(1)	1305	1085
Week(2)	1335	1140
Week(3)	1315	1200
Week(4)	1305	1125

ENTER YOUR CHOICE:3

PRODUCT_WISE TOTAL PRODUCTION SALES

	PRODUCTION	SALES
Product(1)	500	450
Product(2)	1100	940
Product(3)	1530	1320
Product(4)	855	765
Product(5)	1275	1075

ENTER YOUR CHOICE:4

GRAND TOTAL OF PRODUCTION & SALES

Total production = 5260
Total sales   = 4550

ENTER YOUR CHOICE:5

G O O D   B Y E

Exit from the program

Fig. 7.10 *Program for production and sales analysis*

REVIEW QUESTIONS AND EXERCISES

7.1 Explain the need for array variables.

7.2 Identify errors, if any, in each of the following array declaration statements.

   (a) int score (100);
   (b) float values[10,15];
   (c) float average[ROW],[COLUMN];
   (d) char name[15];
   (e) int sum[ ];

7.3 Identify errors, if any, in each of the following initialization statements.

   (a) static int number[ ] = {0,0,0,0,0};
   (b) static float item[3][2] = {0,1,2,3,4,5};
   (c) static char word[ ] = {'A','R', 'R', 'A', 'Y'};
   (d) stataic int m[2,4] = {(0,0,0,0)(1,1,1,1)};
   (e) static float result[10] = 0;

7.4 Assume that the arrays **A** and **B** are declared as follows:

   int   A[5][4];
   float   B[4];

   Find the errors (if any) in the following program segments.

   (a) for (i=1; i<=5; i++)
           for(j=1; j<=4; j++)
             A[i][j] = 0;

   (b) for (i=1; i<4; i++)
           scanf("%f", B[i]);

   (c) for (i=0; i<=4; i++)
           B[i] = B[i]+i;

   (d) for (i=4; i>=0; i--)
           for (j=0; j<4; j++)
             A[i][j] = B[j] + 1.0;

7.5 Write the segment of a program that initializes the array **A** as follows:

1	0	0	0	0	. . . .	0
0	1	0	0	0	. . . .	0
0	0	1	0	0	. . . .	0
.	.	.	.	.		.
.	.	.	.	.		.
.	.	.	.	.		.
.	.	.	.	.		.
0	0	0	0	0	. . . .	1

All diagonal elements are initialized to one and others to zero.

7.6 Write a program for fitting a straight line through a set of points (x_i, y_i), $i = 1,...,n$. The straight line equation is

$$y = mx + c$$

and the values of m and c are given by

$$m = \frac{n \sum (x_i y_i) - (\sum x_i)(\sum y_i)}{n (\sum x_i^2) - (\sum x_i)^2}$$

$$c = \frac{1}{n} (\sum y_i - m \sum x_i)$$

All summations are from 1 to n.

7.7 The daily maximum temperatures recorded in 10 cities during the month of January (for all 31 days) have been tabulated as follows:

Write a program to read the table elements into a two-dimensional array **temperature**, and to find the city and day corresponding to (a) the highest temperature and (b) the lowest temperature.

7.8 An election is contested by 5 candidates. The candidates are numbered 1 to 5 and the voting is done by marking the candidate number on the ballot paper. Write a program to read the ballots and count the votes cast for each candidate using an array variable **count**. In case, a number read is outside the range 1 to 5, the ballot should be considered as a 'spoilt ballot' and the program should also count the number of spoilt ballots.

7.9 The following set of numbers is popularly known as Pascal's triangle.

```
1
1   1
1   2   1
1   3   3   1
1   4   6   4   1
1   5   10  10  5   1
.       .       .       .
.       .   .       .       .
```

If we denote rows by i and columns by j, then any element (except the boundry elements) in the triangle is given by

$$p_{ij} = p_{i-1, j-1} + p_{i-1, j}$$

Write a program to calculate the elements of the Pascal triangle for 10 rows and print the results.

7.10 The annual examination results of 100 students are tabulated as follows:

Roll No.	Subject 1	Subject 2	Subject 3

Write a program to read the data and determine the following:

(a) Total marks obtained by each student.
(b) The highest marks in each subject and the Roll No. of the student who secured it.
(c) The student who obtained the highest total marks.

7.11 Given are two one-dimensional arrays **A** and **B** which are sorted in ascending order. Write a program to *merge* them into a single sorted array **C** that contains every item from arrays **A** and **B**, in ascending order.

7.12 Two matrices that have the same number of rows and columns can be multiplied to produce a third matrix. Consider the following two matrices.

$$
A = \begin{bmatrix}
a_{11} & a_{12} & \dots & a_{1n} \\
a_{21} & a_{22} & \dots & a_{2n} \\
\cdot & & & \cdot \\
\cdot & & & \cdot \\
\cdot & & & \cdot \\
a_{n1} & & \dots & a_{nn}
\end{bmatrix}
$$

$$
B = \begin{bmatrix}
b_{11} & b_{12} & \dots & b_{1n} \\
b_{21} & b_{22} & \dots & b_{2n} \\
\cdot & & & \cdot \\
\cdot & & & \cdot \\
\cdot & & & \cdot \\
b_{n1} & & \dots & b_{nn}
\end{bmatrix}
$$

The product of **A** and **B** is a third matrix **C** of size *nxn* where each element of **C** is given by the following equation.

$$
C_{ij} = \sum_{k=1}^{n} a_{ik}\, b_{ki}
$$

Write a program that will read the values of elements of **A** and **B** and produce the product matrix **C**.

HANDLING OF CHARACTER STRINGS

8.1 INTRODUCTION

A string is an array of characters. We have used strings in a number of examples in the past. Any group of characters (except double quote sign) defined between double quotation marks is a constant string. Example:

"Man is obviously made to think."

If we want to include a double quote in the string, then we may use it with a back slash as shown below.

" \" Man is obviously made to think,\" said Pascal."

For example,

printf ("\" Well Done !\" ");

will output the string

" Well Done !"

while the statement

printf(" Well Done !");

will output the string

Well Done !

Character strings are often used to build meaningful and readable programs. The common operations performed on character strings are:

- Reading and Writing strings.
- Combining strings together.
- Copying one string to another.
- Comparing strings for equality.
- Extracting a portion of a string.

In this chapter we shall discuss these operations in detail and develop programs that involve these operations.

8.2 DECLARING AND INITIALIZING STRING VARIABLES

A string variable is any valid C variable name and is always declared as an *array*. The general form of declaration of a string variable is

```
char string_name[ size ];
```

The *size* determines the number of characters in the *string-name*. Some examples are:

```
char city[10];
char name[30];
```

When the compiler assigns a character string to a character array, it automatically supplies a *null* character ('\0 ') at the end of the string. Therefore, the *size* should be equal to the maximum number of characters in the string *plus* one.

Character arrays may be initialized when they are declared. C permits a character array to be initialized in either of the following two forms:

```
static char city[9]  =  " NEW YORK ";
static char city[9]  =  {'N','E','W',' ','Y','O','R','K','\0'};
```

The reason that **city** had to be 9 elements long is that the string NEW YORK contains 8 characters and one element space is provided for the null terminator. Note that when we initialize a character array by listing its elements, we must supply explicitly the null terminator.

C also permits us to initialize a character array without specifying the number of elements. In such cases, the size of the array will be determined automatically, based on the number of elements initialized. For example, the statement

```
static char string [ ]  =  {'G', 'O','O','D','\0'};
```

defines the array **string** as a five element array.

Note that the word **static** may be omitted when using ANSI compilers.

8.3 READING STRINGS FROM TERMINAL

Reading Words

The familiar input function **scanf** can be used with **%s** format specification to read in a string of characters. Example:

```
char address[15];
scanf("%s", address);
```

The problem with the **scanf** function is that it terminates its input on the first white space it finds. (A white space includes blanks, tabs, carriage returns, form feeds, and new lines.) Therefore, if the following line of text is typed in at the terminal,

NEW YORK

then only the string "NEW" will be read into the array address, since the blank space after the word 'NEW' will terminate the string.

Note that unlike previous **scanf** calls, in the case of character arrays, the ampersand (&) is not required before the variable name. The **scanf** function automatically terminates the string that is read with a *null* character and therefore the character array should be large enough to hold the input string plus the null character.

If we want to read the entire line "NEW YORK", then we may use two character arrays of appropriate sizes. That is,

scanf("%s %s", adr1, adr2);

with the line of text

NEW YORK

will assign the string "NEW" to **adr1** and "YORK" to **adr2**.

Example 8.1

Write a program to read a series of words from a terminal using **scanf** function

---

The program shown in Fig. 8.1 reads four words and displays them on the screen. Note that the string 'Oxford Road' is treated as *two words* while the string 'Oxford-Road' as *one word*.

```
Program
/*************************************************************/
/*      READING A SERIES OF WORDS USING scanf FUNCTION      */
/*************************************************************/
main( )
{
    char word1[40], word2[40], word3[40], word4[40];
    printf("Enter text :  \n");
    scanf("%s %s", word1, word2);
    scanf("%s", word3);
    scanf("%s", word4);

    printf("\n");
    printf("word1  =  %s\nword2  =  %s \n", word1, word2);
    printf("word3  =  %s\nword4  =  %s \n", word3, word4);
}
Output
Enter text :
Oxford Road, London M17ED

word1  =  Oxford
word2  =  Road,
word3  =  London
word4  =  M17ED

Enter text :
Oxford-Road, London-M17ED United Kingdom

word1  =  Oxford-Road,
word2  =  London-M17ED
word3  =  United
word4  =  Kingdom
```

Fig. 8.1 *Reading a series of words using* **scanf**

Reading a Line of Text

In many text processing applications, we need to read in an entire line of text from the terminal. It is not possible to use **scanf** function to read a line containing more than one word. This is because the **scanf** terminates reading as soon as a space is encountered in input.

We have discussed in Chapter 4 as to how to read a single character from the terminal, using the function **getchar**. We can use this function repeatedly to read successive single characters from the input and place them into a character array. Thus, an entire line of text can be read and stored in an array. The reading is terminated when the newline character ('\n') is entered and the *null* character is then inserted at the end of the string.

Example 8.2

Write a program to read a line of text containing a series of words from the terminal.

The program shown in Fig.8.2 can read a line of text (upto a maximum of 80 characters) into the string **line**. Every time a character is read, it is assigned to its location in the string **line** and

```
Program
/**********************************************************************/
/*        PROGRAM TO READ A LINE OF TEXT FROM TERMINAL          */
/**********************************************************************/
#include    <stdio.h>
main( )
{
    char    line[81], character;
    int     c;
    c = 0;
    printf("Enter text. Press <Return> at end\n");
    do
    {
        character  =  getchar( );
        line[c]    =  character;
        c++;
    }
    while(character !='\n');
    c = c - 1;
    line[c] = '\0';
    printf("\n%s\n", line);
}
Output
Enter text. Press <Return> at end
Programming in C is interesting.

Programming in C is interesting.

Enter text. Press <Return> at end
National Computing Centre, United kingdom.

National Computing Centre, United Kingdom.
```

Fig. 8.2 *Program to read a line of text from terminal*

then tested for *newline* character. When the *newline* character is read (signalling the end of line), the reading loop is terminated and the *newline* character is replaced by the *null* character to indicate the end of character string.

When the loop is exited, the value of the index **c** is one number higher than the last character position in the string (since it has been incremented after assigning the new character to the string). Therefore the index value **c−1** gives the position where the *null* character is to be stored.

C does not provide operators that work on strings directly. For instance we cannot assign one string to another directly. For example, the assignment statements

string   =   "ABC";
string1 = string2;

are not valid. If we really want to copy the characters in **string2** into **string1**, we may do so on a character-by-character basis.

Example 8.3
Write a program to copy one string to another and count the number of characters copied.

The program is shown in Fig. 8.3. We use a **for** loop to copy the characters contained inside **string2** into the **string1**. The loop is terminated when the *null* character is reached. Note that we are again assigning a null character to the **string1**.

8.4 WRITING STRINGS TO SCREEN

We have used extensively the **printf** function with **%s** format to print strings to the screen. The format **%s** can be used to display an array of characters that is terminated by the *null* character. For example, the statement

printf("%s", name);

can be used to display the entire contents of the array **name**.

We can also specify the precision with which the array is displayed. For instance, the specification

%10.4

indicates that the *first four* characters are to be printed in a field width of 10 columns.

However, if we include the minus sign in the specification (e.g., %−10.4s), the string will be printed left justified. Example 8.4 illustrates the effect of various **%s** specifications.

Example 8.4
Write a program to store the string "United Kingdom" in the array **country** and display the string under various format specifications.

The program and its output are shown in Fig. 8.4. The output illustrates the following features of the %s specifications.

1. When the field width is less than the length of the string, the entire string is printed.

```
Program
/****************************************************************/
/*            COPYING ONE STRING INTO ANOTHER              */
/****************************************************************/
main( )
{
        char        string1[80], string2[80];
        int         i;

        printf("Enter a string \n");
        printf("?");

        scanf("%s", string2);

        for( i=0 ; string2[i] != '\0'; i++)
        string1[i]  =  string2[i];

        string1[i]  =  '\0';

        printf("\n");
        printf("%s \n", string1);
        printf("Number of characters  =  %d \n", i );
}
Output
Enter a string
?Manchester

Manchester
Number of characters  =  10


Enter a string
?Westminster

Westminster
Number of characters  =  11
```

Fig. 8.3 *Copying one string into another*

2. The integer value on the right side of the decimal point specifies the number of characters to be printed.
3. When the number of characters to be printed is specified as zero, nothing is printed.
4. The minus sign in the specification causes the string to be printed left-justified.

The **printf** on UNIX supports another nice feature that allows for variable field width or precision. For instance

printf("%*.*s\n", w,d, string);

prints the first *d* characters of the **string** in the field width of *w*.

This feature comes in handy for printing a sequence of characters. Example 8.5 illustrates this.

```
Program
/****************************************************************************/
/*              WRITING STRINGS USING %s FORMAT                   */
/****************************************************************************/
main( )
{
    static char country[15]  =  "United Kingdom";
    printf("\n\n");
    printf(" ——————————— \n");
    printf("|%15s|\n", country);
    printf("|%5s|\n", country);
    printf("|%15.6s|\n", country);
    printf("|%-15.6s|\n", country);
    printf("|%15.0s|\n", country);
    printf("|%.3s|\n", country);
    printf("|%s|\n", country);
    printf(" ——————————— \n");
}
Output
 ———————————
| United Kingdom|
|United Kingdom|
|         United|
|United         |
|               |
|Uni|
|United Kingdom |
 ———————————
```

Fig. 8.4 *Writing strings using* **%s** *format*

Example 8.5

Write a program using **for** loop to print the following output.

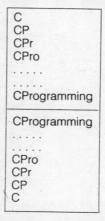

Program

```
/***************************************************************************/
/*              PRINTING SEQUENCES OF CHARACTERS                        */
/***************************************************************************/
main( )
{
    int   c,  d;
    static char     string[ ] = "CProgramming";
    printf("\n\n");
    printf("———————————\n");
    for( c = 0 ; c <= 11 ; c++ )
    {
      d = c + 1;
      printf("|%-12.*s|\n", d, string);
    }
    printf("|———————————|\n");
    for( c = 11 ; c >= 0 ; c-- )
    {
      d = c + 1;
      printf("|%-12.*s|\n", d, string);
    }
    printf("———————————\n");
}
```

Output

```
C
CP
CPr
CPro
CProg
CProgr
CProgra
CProgram
CProgramm
CProgrammi
CProgrammin
CProgramming

CProgramming
CProgrammin
CProgrammi
CProgramm
CProgram
CProgra
CProgr
CProg
CPro
CPr
CP
C
```

Fig. 8.5 *Illustration of variable field specifications*

The outputs of the program in Fig. 8.5, for variable specifications %12.*s, %.*s, and %*.1s are shown in Fig. 8.6, which further illustrates the variable field width and the precision specifications.

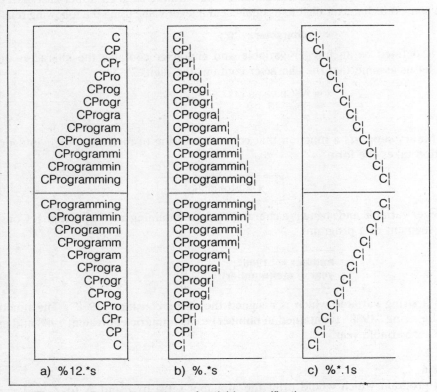

Fig. 8.6 *Further illustrations of variable specifications*

8.5 ARITHMETIC OPERATIONS ON CHARACTERS

C allows us to manipulate characters the same way we do with numbers. Whenever a character constant or character variable is used in an expression, it is automatically converted into an integer value by the system. The integer value depends on the local character set of the system.

To write a character in its integer representation, we may write it as an integer. For example, if the machine uses the ASCII representation, then,

x = 'a';
printf("%d\n",x);

will display the number 97 on the screen.

It is also possible to perform arithmetic operations on the character constants and variables. For example,

x = 'z'−1;

is a valid statement. In ASCII, the value of 'z' is 122 and therefore, the statement will assign the value 121 to the variable x.

We may also use character constants in relational expressions. For example, the expression

ch >= 'A' && ch <= 'Z'

would test whether the character contained in the variable **ch** is an upper-case letter.

We can convert a character digit to its equivalent integer value using the following relationship:

x = character − '0';

where **x** is defined as an integer variable and **character** contains the character digit. For example, let us assume that the **character** contains the digit '7', Then,

$$x = \text{ASCII value of '7'} - \text{ASCII value of '0'}$$
$$= 55 - 48$$
$$= 7$$

The C library supports a function that converts a string of digits into their integer values. The function takes the form

$$x = \textbf{atoi}(string)$$

x is an integer variable and **string** is a character array containing a string of digits. Consider the following segment of a program:

```
------------
number = "1988";
year = atoi(number);
------------
```

number is a string variable which is assigned the string constant "1988". The function **atoi** converts the string "1988" (contained in **number**) to its numeric equivalent 1988 and assigns it to the integer variable **year**.

Example 8.6

Write a program which would print the alphabet set a to z and A to Z in decimal and character form.

The program is shown in Fig.8.7. In ASCII character set, the decimal numbers 65 to 90 represent upper-case alphabets and 97 to 122 represent lower-case alphabets. The values from 91 to 96 are excluded using an **if** statement in the **for** loop.

8.6 PUTTING STRINGS TOGETHER

Just as we cannot assign one string to another directly, we cannot join two strings together by the simple arithmetic addition. That is, the statements such as

string3 = string1 + string2;
string2 = string1 + "hello";

are not valid. The characters from **string1** and **string2** should be copied into the **string3** one

```
Program
/*********************************************************************/
/*PRINTING ALPHABET SET IN DECIMAL AND CHARACTER FORM */
/*********************************************************************/
main( )
{
    char    c;
    printf("\n\n");
    for( c = 65 ; c <= 122 ; c = c + 1 )
    {
        if( c > 90 && c < 97 )
           continue;
        printf("%5d − %c ", c, c);
    }
    printf("\n");
}
Output
    65  - A    66  - B    67  - C    68  - D    69  - E    70  - F
    71  - G    72  - H    73  - I    74  - J    75  - K    76  - L
    77  - M    78  - N    79  - O    80  - P    81  - Q    82  - R
    83  - S    84  - T    85  - U    86  - V    87  - W    88  - X
    89  - Y    90  - Z    97  - a    98  - b    99  - c   100  - d
   101  - e   102  - f   103  - g   104  - h   105  - i   106  - j
   107  - k   108  - l   109  - m   110  - n   111  - o   112  - p
   113  - q   114  - r   115  - s   116  - t   117  - u   118  - v
   119  - w   120  - x   121  - y   122  - z
```

Fig. 8.7 *Printing of the alphabet set in decimal and character form*

after the other. The *size* of the array **string3** should be large enough to hold the total characters.

The process of combining two strings together is called *concatenation*. Example 8.7 illustrates the concatenation of three strings.

Example 8.7

The names of employees of an organization are stored in three arrays, namely **first_name**, **second_name**, and **last_name**. Write a program to concatenate the three parts into one string to be called **name**.

The program is given in Fig. 8.8. Three **for** loops are used to copy the three strings. In the first loop, the characters contained in the **first_name** are copied into the variable **name** until the *null* character is reached. The *null* character is not copied; instead it is replaced by a *space* by the assignment statement

                    name[i] = ' ';

Similarly, the *second_name* is copied into **name**, starting from the column just after the space created by the above statement. This is achieved by the assignment statement

name[i+j+1] = second_name[j];

If **first_name** contains 4 characters, then the value of **i** at this point will be 4 and therefore the first character from **second_name** will be placed in the *fifth cell* of **name**. Note that we have stored a space in the *fourth cell*.

In the same way, the statement

name[i+j+k+2] = last_name[k];

is used to copy the characters from **last_name** into the proper locations of **name**.

At the end, we place a *null* character to terminate the concatenated string **name**. In this example, it is important to note the use of the expressions **i+j+1** and **i+j+k+2**.

```
Program
/*********************************************************************/
/*                 CONCATENATION OF STRINGS                       */
/*********************************************************************/
main( )
{
    int   i, j, k ;
    static char     first_name[10]  = {"VISWANATH"} ;
    static char    second_name[10]  = {"PRATAP"} ;
    static char     last_name[10]  = {"SINGH"} ;
    char  name[30] ;
    /* Copy first_name into name */
    for(i = 0; first_name[i] != '\0'; i++)
       name[i] = first_name[i];
    /* End first_name with a space */
    name[i] = ' ';
    /* Copy second_name into name */
    for(j = 0; second_name[j] != '\0'; j++)
       name[i+j+1] = second_name[j];
    /* End second_name with a space */
    name[i+j+1] = ' ' ;
    /* Copy last_name into name */
    for( k = 0; last_name[k] != '\0'; k++ )
       name[i+j+k+2] = last_name[k];
    /* End name with a null character */
    name[i+j+k+2] = '\0';
    printf("\n\n");
    printf("%s\n", name);
}
Output
VISWANATH PRATAP SINGH
```

Fig. 8.8 *Concatenation of strings*

8.7 COMPARISON OF TWO STRINGS

Once again, C does not permit the comparison of two strings directly. That is, the statements such as

$$\textbf{if(name1} \;==\; \textbf{name2)}$$
$$\textbf{if(name} \;\;\;==\; \textbf{"ABC")}$$

are not permitted. It is therefore necessary to compare the two strings to be tested, character by character. The comparison is done until there is a mismatch or one of the strings terminates into a *null* character, whichever occurs first. The following segment of a program illustrates this.

```
------------
i=0;
while(str1[i] == str2[i] && str1[i] !='\0'
            && str2[i] !='\0')
    i = i+1;
if (str1[i] == '\0' && str2[i] == '\0')
    printf("strings are equal\n");
else
    printf("strings are not equal\n"),
------------
```

8.8 STRING–HANDLING FUNCTIONS

Fortunately, the C library supports a large number of string-handling functions that can be used to carry out many of the string manipulations discussed so far. Following are the most commonly used string-handling functions.

Function	Action
strcat( )	concatenates two strings
strcmp( )	compares two strings
strcpy( )	copies one string over another
strlen( )	finds the length of a string

We shall discuss briefly how each of these functions can be used in the processing of strings.

strcat( ) Function

The **strcat** function joins two strings together. It takes the following form:

strcat(string1, string2);

string1 and **string2** are character arrays. When the function **strcat** is executed, **string2** is appended to **string1**. It does so by removing the *null* character at the end of **string1** and placing **string2** from there. The string at **string2** remains unchanged. For example, consider the following three strings:

```
            0   1   2   3   4   5   6   7   8   9   0   1   2
part1 =   | V | E | R | Y |   | \0|   |   |   |   |   |   |   |

            0   1   2   3   4   5   6
part2 =   | G | O | O | D | \0|   |   |

            0   1   2   3   4   5   6
part3 =   | B | A | D | \0|   |   |   |
```

Execution of the statement

strcat(part1, part2);

will result in:

```
            0   1   2   3   4   5   6   7   8   9   0   1   2
part1 =   | V | E | R | Y |   | G | O | O | D | \0|   |   |   |

            0   1   2   3   4   5   6
part2 =   | G | O | O | D | \0|   |   |
```

while the statement

strcat(part1, part3);

will result in:

```
            0   1   2   3   4   5   6   7   8   9   0   1   2
part1 =   | V | E | R | Y |   | B | A | D | \0|   |   |   |   |

            0   1   2   3   4   5   6
part3 =   | B | A | D | \0|   |   |   |
```

We must make sure that the size of **string1** (to which **string2** is appended) is large enough to accommodate the final string.

strcat function may also append a string constant to a string variable. The following is valid:

strcat(part1,"GOOD");

C permits nesting of **strcat** functions. For example, the statement

strcat(strcat(string1,string2), string3);

is allowed and concatenates all the three strings together. The resultant string is stored in **string1**.

strcmp( ) Function

The **strcmp** function compares two strings identified by the arguments and has a value 0 if they are equal. If they are not, it has the numeric difference between the first nonmatching characters in the strings. It takes the form:

> **strcmp**(string1, string2);

string1 and **string2** may be string variables or string constants. Examples are:

> **strcmp(name1, name2);**
> **strcmp(name1, "John");**
> **strcmp("Rom", "Ram");**

Our major concern is to determine whether the strings are equal; if not, which is alphabetically above. The value of the mismatch is rarely important. For example, the statement

> **strcmp("their", "there");**

will return a value of −9 which is the numeric difference between ASCII "i" and ASCII "r". That is, "i" minus "r" in ASCII code is −9. If the value is negative, **string1** is alphabetically above **string2**.

strcpy( ) Function

The **strcpy** function works almost like a string-assignment operator. It takes the form

> **strcpy**(string1, string2);

and assigns the contents of **string2** to **string1**. **string2** may be a character array variable or a string constant. For example, the statement

> **strcpy(city, "DELHI");**

will assign the string "DELHI" to the string variable **city**. Similarly, the statement

> **strcpy(city1, city2);**

will assign the contents of the string variable **city2** to the string variable **city1**. The size of the array **city1** should be large enough to receive the contents of **city2**.

strlen( ) Function

This function counts and returns the number of characters in a string.

> n = **strlen**(string);

Where **n** is an integer variable which receives the value of the length of the **string**. The argument may be a string constant. The counting ends at the first null character.

Example 8.8

s1, s2, and s3 are three string variables. Write a program to read two string constants into s1 and s2 and compare whether they are equal or not. If they are not, join them together. Then copy the contents of s1 to the variable s3. At the end, the program should print the contents of all the three variables and their lengths.

The program is shown in Fig. 8.9. During the first run, the input strings are "New" and "York". These strings are compared by the statement

> **x = strcmp(s1, s2);**

Since they are not equal, they are joined together and copied into s3 using the statement

> **strcpy(s3, s1);**

The program outputs all the three strings with their lengths.

During the second run, the two strings s1 and s2 are equal, and therefore, they are not joined together. In this case all the three strings contain the same string constant "London".

8.9 TABLE OF STRINGS

We often use lists of character strings, such as a list of names of students in a class, list of names of employees in an organization, list of places, etc. A list of names can be treated as a table of strings and a two-dimensional character array can be used to store the entire list. For example, a character array **student[30][15]** may be used to store a list of 30 names, each of length not more than 15 characters. Shown below is a table of five cities:

C	h	a	n	d	i	g	a	r	h
M	a	d	r	a	s				
A	h	m	e	d	a	b	a	d	
H	y	d	e	r	a	b	a	d	
B	o	m	b	a	y				

This table can be conveniently stored in a character array **city** by using the following declaration:

> **static char city[ ] [ ]**
> **{**
> **"Chandigarh",**
> **"Madras",**
> **"Ahmedabad",**
> **"Hyderabad",**
> **"Bombay"**
> **} ;**

To access the name of the ith city in the list, we write

> **city[i−1]**

Program

```
/******************************************************************/
/*          ILLUSTRATIONS OF STRING-HANDLING FUNCTIONS      */
/******************************************************************/
#include        <string.h>
main( )
{
     char      s1[20],     s2[20],     s3[20];
     int       x,   l1,       l2,   l3;
     printf("\n\nEnter two string constants \n");
     printf("?");
     scanf("%s %s", s1, s2);

     /* comparing s1 and s2 */
     x = strcmp(s1, s2);
     if(x != 0)
     {
        printf("\n\nStrings are not equal \n");
        strcat(s1, s2);       /* joining s1 and s2 */
     }
     else
        printf("\n\nStrings are equal \n");

     /* copying s1 to s3 */
     strcpy(s3, s1);

     /* Finding length of strings */
     l1 = strlen(s1);
     l2 = strlen(s2);
     l3 = strlen(s3);

     /* output */
     printf("\ns1 = %s\t length = %d characters\n", s1, l1);
     printf("s2 = %s\t length = %d characters\n", s2, l2);
     printf("s3 = %s\t length = %d characters\n", s3, l3);
}
```

Output

```
Enter two string constants
? New York

Strings are not equal

s1 = NewYork           length = 7 characters
s2 = York              length = 4 characters
s3 = NewYork           length = 7 characters

Enter two string constants
? London    London

Strings are equal

s1 = London            length = 6 characters
s2 = London            length = 6 characters
s3 = London            length = 6 characters
```

Fig. 8.9 *Illustration of string handling functions*

and therefore **city[0]** denotes "Chandigarh", **city[1]** denotes "Madras" and so on. This shows that once an array is declared as two-dimensional, it can be used like a one-dimensional array in further manipulations. That is, the table can be treated as a column of strings.

Example 8.9

Write a program that would sort a list of names in alphabetical order.

A program to sort the list of strings in alphabetical order is given in Fig. 8.10. It employs the method of *bubble* sorting described in Case Study 1 in the previous chapter.

Program

```
/*************************************************************************/
/*              SORTING STRINGS IN ALPHABETICAL ORDER              */
/*************************************************************************/

#define ITEMS     5
#define MAXCHAR  20

main( )
{
    char  string[ITEMS][MAXCHAR], dummy[MAXCHAR];
    int    i = 0, j = 0;
    /* Reading the list */

    printf ("Enter names of %d items \n ",ITEMS);
    while (i < ITEMS)
        scanf ("%s", string[i++]);

    /* Sorting begins */

    for (i=1; i < ITEMS; i++) /* Outer loop begins */
    {
        for (j=1; j <= ITEMS−i ; j++) /*Inner loop begins*/
        {
            if (strcmp (string[j−1], string[j]) > 0)
            {
                /* Exchange of contents */
                strcpy (dummy, string[j−1]);
                strcpy (string[j−1], string[j]);
                strcpy (string[j], dummy );
            }
        } /* Inner loop ends */

    } /* Outer loop ends */

    /* Sorting completed */

    printf ("\nAlphabetical list \n\n");
    for (i=0; i < ITEMS ; i++)
        printf ("%s", string[i]);
}
```

Output

Enter names of 5 items
London Manchester Delhi Paris Moscow

Alphabetical list

Delhi
London
Manchester
Moscow
Paris

Fig. 8.10 *Sorting of strings*

Note that a two-dimensional array is used to store the list of strings. Each string is read using a **scanf** function with **%s** format. Remember, if any string contains a white space, then the part of the string after the white space will be treated as another item in the list by the **scanf**. In such cases, we should read the entire line as a string using a suitable algorithm.

CASE STUDIES

1. Counting Words in a Text

One of the practical applications of string manipulations is counting the words in a text. We assume that a word is a sequence of any characters, except escape characters and blanks, and that two words are separated by one blank character. The algorithm for counting words is as follows:

1. Read a line of text.
2. Beginning from the first character in the line, look for a blank. If a blank is found, increment **words** by 1.
3. Continue *steps* 1 and 2 until the last line is completed.

The implementation of this algorithm is shown in Fig. 8.11. The first **while** loop will be executed once for each line of text. The end of text is indicated by pressing the 'Return' key an *extra time* after the entire text has been entered. The extra 'Return' key causes a *newline* character as input to the last line and as a result, the last line contains only the *null* character.

The program checks for this special line using the statement

if (line[0] == '\0')

and if the first (and only the first) character in the line is a *null* character, then counting is terminated. Note the difference between a *null* character and a blank character.

The program also counts the number of lines read and the total number of characters in the text. Remember, the last line containing the *null* string is not counted.

After the first **while** loop is exited, the program prints the results of counting.

Program

```
/****************************************************************/
/*       COUNTING CHARACTERS, WORDS AND LINES IN A TEXT        */
/****************************************************************/

#include    <stdio.h>
main( )
{
      char  line[81], ctr;
      int    i,c,
             end = 0,
             characters = 0,
             words = 0,
             lines = 0;

      printf("KEY IN THE TEXT.\n");
      printf("GIVE ONE SPACE AFTER EACH WORD.\n");
      printf("WHEN COMPLETED, PRESS 'RETURN'.\n\n");

      while( end == 0)
      {
           /* Reading a line of text */

           c = 0;
           while((ctr=getchar( )) != '\n')
                line[c++] = ctr;
           line[c] = '\0';

           /* counting the words in a line */

           if(line[0] == '\0')
              break ;
           else
           {
             words++;
             for(i=0; line[i] != '\0';i++)
                  if(line[i] == ' ' || line[i] == '\t')
                      words++;
           }
           /* counting lines and characters */

           lines = lines +1;
           characters = characters + strlen(line);
      }
      printf ("\n");
      printf("Number of lines = %d\n", lines);
      printf("Number of words = %d\n", words);
      printf("Number of characters = %d\n", characters);
}
```

Output

KEY IN THE TEXT.
GIVE ONE SPACE AFTER EACH WORD.
WHEN COMPLETED, PRESS 'RETURN'.

Admiration is a very short-lived passion.
Admiration involves a glorious obliquity of vision.
Always we like those who admire us but we do not

like those whom we admire.
Fools admire, but men of sense approve.

Number of lines = 5
Number of words = 36
Number of characters = 205

Fig. 8.11 *Counting of characters, words and lines in a text*

2. Processing of a Customer List

Telephone numbers of important customers are recorded as follows:

Full name	*Telephone number*
Joseph Louis Lagrange	869245
Jean Robert Argand	900823
Carl Freidrich Gauss	806788
------------	------------
------------	------------

It is desired to prepare a revised alphabetical list with surname (last name) first, followed by a comma and the initials of the first and middle names. For example,

Argand,J.R

We create a table of strings, each row representing the details of one person, such as first_name, middle_name, last_name, and telephone_number. The columns are interchanged as required and the list is sorted on the last_name. Fig. 8.12 shows a program to achieve this.

```
Program
/ ***********************************************************************/
/*                PROCESSING OF CUSTOMER LIST                        */
/ ***********************************************************************/
#define     CUSTOMERS    10
main( )
{
    char  first_name[20][10], second_name[20][10],
          surname[20][10], name[20][20],
          telephone[20][10], dummy[20];
    int   i,j;
    printf("Input names and telephone numbers \n");
    printf("?");
    for(i=0; i < CUSTOMERS ; i++)
    {
        scanf("%s %s %s %s", first_name[i],
              second_name[i], surname[i], telephone[i]);
        /* converting full name to surname with initials */
        strcpy(name[i], surname[i] );
        strcat(name[i], ",");
        dummy[0] = first_name[i][0];
        dummy[1] = '\0';
        strcat(name[i], dummy);
```

```
            strcat(name[i], ".");
            dummy[0] = second_name[i][0];
            dummy[1] = '\0';
            strcat(name[i], dummy);
    }
    /* Alphabetical ordering of surnames */

        for(i=1; i <= CUSTOMERS−1; i++)
          for(j=1; j <= CUSTOMERS−i; j++)
            if(strcmp (name[j−1], name[j]) > 0)
            {
            /* Swaping names */
                strcpy(dummy, name[j−1]);
                strcpy(name[j−1], name[j]);
                strcpy(name[j], dummy);

            /* Swaping telephone numbers */
                strcpy(dummy, telephone[j−1]);
                strcpy(telephone[j−1],telephone[j]);
                strcpy(telephone[j], dummy);
            }
        /* printing alphabetical list */
        printf("\nCUSTOMERS LIST IN ALPHABETICAL ORDER \n\n");
        for(i=0; i < CUSTOMERS ; i++)
        printf("  %−20s\t %−10s\n", name[i], telephone[i]);
}
```

Output

Input names and telephone numbers
?Gottfried Wilhelm Leibniz 711518
Joseph Louis Lagrange 869245
Jean Robert Argand 900823
Carl Freidrich Gauss 806788
Simon Denis Poisson 853240
Friedrich Wilhalm Bessel 719731
Charles Francois Sturm 222031
George Gabriel Stokes 545454
Mohandas Karamchand Gandhi 362718
Josian Willard Gibbs 123145

CUSTOMERS LIST IN ALPHABETICAL ORDER

Argand,J.R	900823
Bessel,F.W	719731
Gandhi,M.K	362718
Gauss,C.F	806788
Gibbs,J.W	123145
Lagrange,J.L	869245
Leibniz,G.W	711518
Poisson,S.D	853240
Stokes,G.G	545454
Sturm,C.F	222031

Fig. 8.12 *Program to alphabetize a customer list*

REVIEW QUESTIONS AND EXERCISES

8.1 Describe the limitations of using **getchar** and **scanf** functions for reading strings.

8.2 Character strings in C are automatically terminated by the *null* character. Explain how this feature helps in string manipulations.

8.3 String variables can be assigned values in three ways:

(a) During type declaration
```
static char string[ ] = {"......."};
```
(b) Using **strcpy** function
```
strcpy(string, "......");
```
(c) Reading-in a string using **scanf** function
```
scanf("%s", string);
```

Compare them critically and describe situations where one is superior to the others.

8.4 Assuming the variable **string** contains the value "The sky is the limit" determine what output of the following program segments will be.

(a) printf("%s", string);
(b) printf("%25.10s", string);
(c) printf("%s", string[0]);
(d) for (i=0; string[i] != "."; i++)
        printf("%c", string[i]);
(e) for (i=0; string[i] != '\0'; i++;)
        printf("%d\n", string[i]);
(f) for (i=0; i <= strlen[string]; ;)
    {
       string[i++] = i;
       printf("%s\n", string[i]);
    }
(g) printf("%c\n", string[10] + 5);
(h) printf("%c\n", string[10] + '5');

8.5 Write a program which reads your name from the keyboard and outputs a list of ASCII codes which represent your name.

8.6 Write a program to do the following:

(a) To output the question "Who is the inventor of C ?"
(b) To accept an answer.
(c) To print out "Good" and then stop, if the answer is correct.
(d) To output the message "try again", if the answer is wrong.
(e) To display the correct answer when the answer is wrong even at the third attempt and stop.

8.7 Write a program to extract a portion of a character string and print the extracted string. Assume that *m* characters are extracted, starting with the *n*th character.

8.8 Write a program which will read a text and count all occurences of a particular word.

8.9 Write a program which will read a string and rewrite it in the alphabetical order. For example, the word STRING should be written as GINRST.

8.10 Write a program to replace a particular word by another word in a given string. For example, the word "PASCAL" should be replaced by "C" in the text "It is good to program in PASCAL language."

8.11 A Maruti car dealer maintains a record of sales of various vehicles in the following form:

Vehicle type	Month of sales	Price
MARUTI–800	02/87	75000
MARUTI–DX	07/87	95000
GYPSY	04/88	110000
MARUTI–VAN	08/88	85000

Write a program to read this data into a table of strings and output the details of a particular vehicle sold during a specified period. The program should request the user to input the vehicle type and the period (starting month, ending month).

USER-DEFINED FUNCTIONS

9.1 INTRODUCTION

We have mentioned earlier that one of the strengths of C language is that C functions are easy to define and use. We have used functions in every program that we have discussed so far. However, they have been primarily limited to the three functions, namely, **main**, **printf**, and **scanf**. In this chapter, we shall consider in detail how a function is designed, how two or more functions are put together and how they communicate with one another.

C functions can be classified into two categories, namely, *library* functions and *user-defined* functions. **main** is an example of user-defined functions. **printf** and **scanf** belong to the category of library functions. We have also used other library functions such as **sqrt**, **cos**, **strcat**, etc. The main distinction between these two categories is that library functions are not required to be written by us whereas a user-defined function has to be developed by the user at the time of writing a program. However, a user-defined function can later become a part of the C program library.

9.2 NEED FOR USER-DEFINED FUNCTIONS

As pointed out earlier, **main** is a specially recognized function in C. Every program must have a **main** function to indicate where the program has to begin its execution. While it is possible to code any program utilizing only **main** function, it leads to a number of problems. The program may become too large and complex and as a result the task of debugging, testing, and maintaining becomes difficult. If a program is divided into functional parts, then each part may be independently coded and later combined into a single unit. These subprograms called 'functions' are much easier to understand, debug, and test.

There are times when some type of operation or calculation is repeated at many points throughout a program. For instance, we might use the factorial of a number at several points in the program. In such situations, we may repeat the program statements wherever they are needed. Another approach is to design a function that can be called and used whenever required. This saves both time and space.

This sub-sectioning approach clearly results in a number of advantages.

1. It facilitates top-down modular programming as shown in Fig. 9.1. In this programming style, the high level logic of the overall problem is solved first while the details of each lower-level function are addressed later.
2. The length of a source program can be reduced by using functions at appropriate places. This factor is particularly critical with microcomputers where memory space is limited.
3. As mentioned earlier, it is easy to locate and isolate a faulty function for further investigations.
4. A function may be used by many other programs. This means that a C programmer can build on what others have already done, instead of starting over, from scratch.

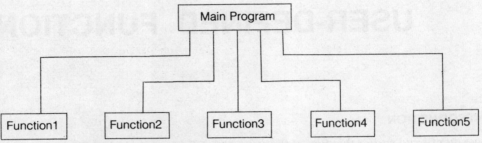

Fig. 9.1 *Top-down modular programming, using functions*

9.3 A MULTI-FUNCTION PROGRAM

A function is a self-contained block of code that performs a particular task. Once a function has been designed and packed, it can be treated as a 'black box' that takes some data from the main program and returns a value. The inner details of operation are invisible to the rest of the program. All that the program knows about a function is: What goes in and what comes out. Every C program can be designed using a collection of these black boxes.

Consider a set of statements as shown below:

```
printline( )
{
    int i;
    for (i=1; i<40; i++)
        printf("−");
    printf("\n");
}
```

The above set of statements defines a function called **printline** which could print a line of 39-character length. This function can be used in a program as follows:

```
main( )
{
    printline( );
    printf("This illustrates the use of C functions\n");
    printline( );
}
printline( )
{
```

```
            int i;
            for(i=1; i<40; i++)
                printf("–");
                printf("\n");
        }
```

This program will print the following output:

This illustrates the use of C functions

The above program contains two user-defined functions:

main( )
printline( )

As we know, the program execution always begins with the **main** function. During execution of the **main**, the first statement encountered is

printline( );

which indicates that the function **printline** is to be executed. At this point, the program control is transferred to the function **printline**. After executing the **printline** function which outputs a line of 39 character length, the control is transferred back to the **main**. Now, the execution continues at the point where the function call was executed. After executing the **printf** statement, the control is again transferred to the **printline** function for printing the line once more.

The **main** function calls the user-defined **printline** function two times and the library function **printf** once. We may notice that the **printline** function itself calls the library function **printf** repeatedly.

Any function can call any other function. In fact, it can call itself. A 'called function' can also call another function. A function can be called more than once. In fact, this is one of the main features of using functions. Figure 9.2 illustrates the flow of control in a multi-function program.

Except the starting point, there are no other predetermined relationships, rules of precedence, or hierarchies among the functions that make up a complete program. The functions can be placed in any order. A called function can be placed either before or after the calling function. However, it is the usual practice to put all the called functions at the end.

Important Note

During the last few years of applications of C, the way the functions have been defined and declared has undergone changes. The major change is the way the function arguments are declared. There are now two established methods of declaring the parameters. The older method (known as "classic" method) declares function arguments separately after the definition of function name (known as *function header*). The newer method (known as "modern" or ANSI method) combines the function definition and arguments declaration in one line. Luckily the modern compilers support both the methods. That is, we can write a function using either of them and execute it successfully.

Since a large number of existing programs and functions have been written using the older method, we should be familiar with this approach. The sections that follow (Sections 9.4 through 9.15) will discuss and use the classic form of function definitions and declarations. The modern ANSI method is discussed in Section 9.16.

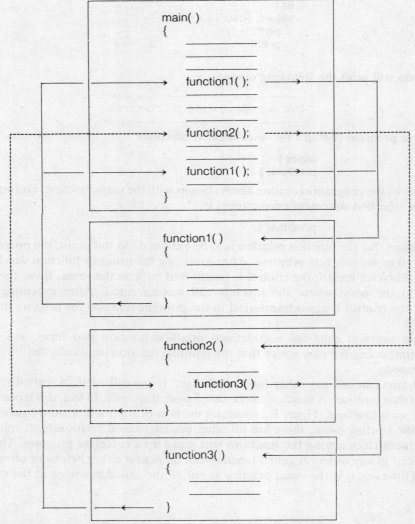

Fig. 9.2 *Flow of control in a multi-function program*

9.4 THE FORM OF C FUNCTIONS

All functions have the form:

```
function-name(argument list)
argument declaration;
{
local variable declarations;
executable statement1;
executable statement2;
------------
------------
return(expression);
}
```

All parts are not essential. Some may be absent. For example, the argument list and its associated argument declaration parts are optional. We may recall that the **main** functions discussed thus far have not included any arguments. Same is the case with the **printline** function discussed earlier.

Similarly, the declaration of local variables is required only when any local variables are used in the function. In the example discussed in the previous section, the **main** function does not use any local variables, while the **printline** function uses one local variable **i**.

A function can have any number of executable statements. A function that does nothing, may not include any executable statements at all. For example:

do_nothing( ) { }

The **return** statement is the mechanism for returning a value to the calling function. This is also an optional statement. Its absence indicates that no value is being returned to the calling function.

Function Name

A function must follow the same rules of formation as other variable names in C. Additional care must be taken to avoid duplicating library routine names or operating system commands.

Argument List

The argument list contains valid variable names separated by commas. The list must be surrounded by parentheses. Note that no semicolon follows the closing parenthesis. The argument variables receive values from the calling function, thus providing a means for data communication from the calling function to the called function. Some examples of functions with arguments are:

```
quadratic(a,b,c)
power(x,n)
mul(a,b)
square(y)
copy(name1, name2)
```

All argument variables must be declared for their types after the function header and before the opening brace of the function body. Example:

```
power(x,n)
float  x;
int    n;
{
    -----------
    -----------
    -----------
}
```

9.5 RETURN VALUES AND THEIR TYPES

Does a function send back any information to the calling function? If so, how does it achieve this?

A function may or may not send back any value to the calling function. If it does, it is done through the **return** statement. While it is possible to pass to the called function any number of values, the called function can only return *one value* per call, at the most.

The **return** statement can take one of the following forms

```
                    return;
                    or
                    return(expression);
```

The first, the 'plain' **return** does not return any value; it acts much as the closing brace of the function. When a **return** is encountered, the control is immediately passed back to the calling function. An example of the use of a simple **return** is as follows:

```
                    if(error)
                        return;
```

The second form of **return** with an expression returns the value of the expression. For example, the function

```
                    mul(x,y)
                    int    x,y;
                    {
                        int    p;
                        p  =  x*y;
                        return(p);
                    }
```

returns the value of **p** which is the product of the values of **x** and **y**. The last two statements can be combined into one statement as follows:

```
                    return (x*y);
```

A function may have more than one **return** statements. This situation arises when the value returned is based on certain conditions. For example:

```
                    if( x <= 0 )
                        return(0);
                    else
                        return(1);
```

What type of data does a function return? All functions by default return **int** type data. But what happens if a function must return some other type? We can force a function to return a particular type of data by using a *type specifier* in the function header. Example:

```
                    double product(x,y)
                    float sqr_root(p)
```

When a value is returned, it is automatically cast to the function's type. In functions that do computations using **double**, yet return **int**, the returned value will be truncated to an integer.

9.6 CALLING A FUNCTION

A function can be called by simply using the function name in a statement. Example:

```
main( )
{
    int p;
    p = mul(10,5);
    printf("%d\n", p);
}
```

When the compiler encounters a function call, the control is transferred to the function **mul(x,y)**. This function is then executed line by line as described and a value is returned when a **return** statement is encountered. This value is assigned to **p**.

A function which returns a value can be used in expressions like any other variable. Each of the following statements is valid:

```
printf("%d\n", mul(p,q));
y = mul(p,q) / (p+q);
if (mul(m,n)>total) printf("large");
```

However, a function cannot be used on the right side of an assignment statement. For instance,

mul(a,b) = 15;

is invalid.

A function that does not return any value may not be used in expressions; but can be called to perform certain tasks specified in the function. The function **printline( )** discussed in Section 9.3 belongs to this category. Such functions may be called in by simply stating their names as independent statements.

Example:

```
main( )
{
    printline( );
}
```

Note the presence of a semicolon at the end.

9.7 CATEGORY OF FUNCTIONS

A function, depending on whether arguments are present or not and whether a value is returned or not, may belong to one of the following categories.

Category 1: Functions with no arguments and no return values
Category 2: Functions with arguments and no return values
Category 3: Functions with arguments and return values.

In the sections to follow, we shall discuss these categories with examples.

9.8 NO ARGUMENTS AND NO RETURN VALUES

When a function has no arguments, it does not receive any data from the calling function. Similarly, when it does not return a value, the calling function does not receive any data from the called function. In effect, there is no data transfer between the calling function and the called function. This is depicted in Fig. 9.3. The dotted lines indicate that there is only a transfer of control but not data.

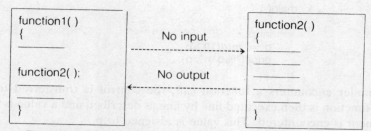

Fig. 9.3 *No data communication between functions*

As pointed out earlier, a function that does not return any value cannot be used in an expression. It can only be used as an independent statement.

Example 9.1

Write a program with multiple functions that do not communicate any data between them.

A program with three user-defined functions is given in Fig. 9.4. **main** is the calling function that calls **printline** and **value** functions. Since both the called functions contain no arguments, there are no argument declarations. The **printline** function, when encountered, prints a line with a length of 35 characters as prescribed in the function. The **value** function calculates the value of principal amount after a certain period of years and prints the results. The following equation is evaluated repeatedly:

$$value = principal(1+interest-rate)$$

```
Program
/********************************************************************/
/*                                                                  */
            FUNCTIONS WITH NO ARGUMENTS, NO RETURN VALUES
/********************************************************************/
/*                        %%%%%%%%%%
                          % main function    %
                          %%%%%%%%%%                             */
main( )
{
    printline( );
    value( );
    printline( );
}
/*      Function1: printline( )         */
printline( )            /* contains no arguments */
{
    int i ;
    for(i=1; i <= 35; i++)
        printf("%c",'-');
        printf("\n");
```

```
}
/*      Function2: value( )           */
value( )    /* contains no arguments */
{
    int      year, period;
    float    inrate, sum, principal;
    printf("Principal amount?");
    scanf("%f", &principal);
    printf("Interest rate?      ");
    scanf("%f", &inrate);
    printf("Period?             ");
    scanf("%d", &period);
    sum = principal;
    year = 1;
    while(year <= period)
    {
        sum = sum *(1+inrate);
        year = year +1;
    }
    printf("\n%8.2f %5.2f %5d %12.2f\n",
           principal,inrate,period,sum);
}
Output
_____
Principal amount?5000
Interest rate?      0.12
Period?             5

5000.00  0.12     5            8811.71
```

Fig. 9.4 *Functions with no arguments and no return values*

It is important to note that the function **value** receives its data directly from the terminal. The input data includes principal amount, interest rate and the period for which the final value is to be calculated. The **while** loop calculates the final value and the results are printed by the library function **printf**. When the closing brace of **value( )** is reached, the control is transferred back to the calling function **main**. Since everything is done by the **value** itself there is in fact nothing left to be sent back to the called function.

Note that no **return** statement is employed. When there is nothing to be returned, the **return** statement is optional. The closing brace of the function signals the end of execution of the function, thus returning the control, back to the calling function.

9.9 ARGUMENTS BUT NO RETURN VALUES

In Fig. 9.4 the **main** function has no control over the way the functions receive input data. For example, the function **printline** will print the same line each time it is called. Same is the case with the function, **value**. We could make the calling function to read data from the terminal and pass it on to the called function. This approach seems to be wiser because the calling function can check for the validity of data, if necessary, before it is handed over to the called function.

The nature of data communication between the calling function and the called function with arguments but no return value is shown in Fig. 9.5.

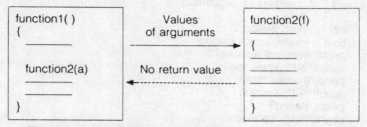

Fig. 9.5 *One-way data communication*

We shall modify declaration of both the called functions to include arguments as follows:

printline(ch)
value(p,r,n)

The arguments **ch**, **p**, **r**, and **n** are called the *formal arguments*. The calling function can now send values to these arguments using function calls containing appropriate arguments. For example, the function call

value(500,0.12,5)

would send the values 500,0.12 and 5 to the function

value(p,r,n)

and assign 500 to **p**, 0.12 to **r** and 5 to **n**. The values 500,0.12, and 5 are the *actual arguments* which become the values of the *formal arguments* inside the called function.

The *actual* and *formal* arguments should match in number, type, and order. The values of actual arguments are assigned to the formal arguments on a *one to one* basis, starting with the first argument as shown in Fig. 9.6.

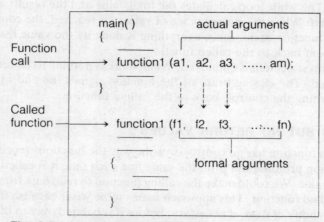

Fig. 9.6 *Arguments matching between the function call and the called function*

We should ensure that the function call has matching arguments. In case, the actual arguments are more than the formal arguments (m > n), the extra actual arguments are discarded. On the other hand, if the actual arguments are less than the formal arguments, the unmatched formal arguments are initialized to some garbage values. Any mismatch in data type may also result in passing of garbage values. Remember, no error message will be generated.

While the formal arguments must be valid variable names, the actual arguments may be variable names, expressions, or constants. The variables used in actual arguments must be assigned values before the function call is made.

Remember that, when a function call is made, *only a copy of the values of actual arguments is passed into the called function*. What occurs inside the function will have no effect on the variables used in the actual argument list.

Example 9.2

Modify the program of Example 9.1 to include the arguments in the function calls.

The modified program with function arguments is presented in Fig. 9.7. Most of the program is identical to the program in Fig. 9.4. The input prompt and **scanf** assignment statement have been moved from **value** function to **main**. The variables **principal**, **inrate**, and **period** are declared in **main** because they are used in **main** to receive data. The function call

value(principal, inrate, period);

passes information it contains to the function **value**.

The function header of **value** has three formal arguments p,r, and n which correspond to the actual arguments in the function call, namely, **principal**, **inrate**, and **period**. The formal arguments are declared immediately after the function header. On execution of the function call, the values of the actual arguments are assigned to the corresponding formal arguments. In fact, the following assignments are accomplished across the function boundaries:

p = principal;
r = inrate;
n = period;

The variables declared inside a function are known as *local* variables and therefore their values are local to the function and cannot be accessed by any other function. We shall discuss more about this later in the chapter.

The function **value** calculates the final amount for a given period and prints the results as before. Control is transferred back on reaching the closing brace of the function. Note that the function does not return any value.

The function **printline** is called twice. The first call passes the character 'Z', while the second passes the character 'C' to the function. These are assigned to the formal argument **ch** for printing lines (see the output).

9.10 ARGUMENTS WITH RETURN VALUES

The function **value** in Fig. 9.7 receives data from the calling function through arguments, but does not send back any value. Rather, it displays the results of calculations at the terminal.

```
Program
/**********************************************************************/
/*      FUNCTIONS WITH ARGUMENTS BUT NO RETURN VALUES     */
/**********************************************************************/
main( )
{
    float principal, inrate;
    int period;

    printf("Enter principal amount, interest");
    printf(" rate, and period \n");
    scanf("%f %f %d",&principal, &inrate, &period);
    printline('Z');
    value(principal,inrate,period);
    printline('C');
}
/* ---------------------------------------------------------------- */
printline(ch)
char ch;
{
    int i ;
    for(i=1; i <= 52; i++)
        printf("%c",ch);
    printf("\n");
}
/* ---------------------------------------------------------------- */
value(p,r,n)
int n;
float p,r;
{
    int year ;
    float sum ;
    sum = p ;
    year = 1;
    while(year <= n)
    {
        sum = sum * (1+r);
        year = year +1;
    }
    printf("%f\t%f\t%d\t%f\n",p,r,n,sum);
}
/* ---------------------------------------------------------------- */
Output
Enter principal amount, interest rate, and period
5000   0.12   5
ZZZZZZZZZZZZZZZZZZZZZZZZZZZZZZZZZZZZZZZZZZZZZZZZZZZZZZ
5000.000000        0.120000        5        8811.708984
CCCCCCCCCCCCCCCCCCCCCCCCCCCCCCCCCCCCCCCCCCCCCCCCCCCCC
```

Fig. 9.7 *Functions with arguments but no return values*

However, we may not always wish to have the result of a function displayed. We may use it in the calling function for further processing. Moreover, to assure a high degree of portability between programs, a function should generally be coded without involving any I/O operations. For example, different programs may require different output formats for displaying results. These shortcomings can be overcome by handing over the result of a function to its calling function where the returned value can be used as required by the program.

A self-contained and independent function should behave like a 'black box' that receives a predefined form of input and outputs a desired value. Such functions will have two-way data communication as shown in Fig. 9.8.

We shall modify the program in Fig. 9.7 to illustrate the use of two-way data communication between the calling and the called functions.

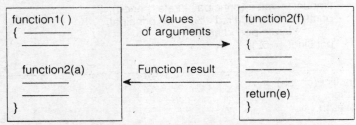

Fig. 9.8 *Two-way data communication between functions*

Example 9.3

In the program presented in Fig. 9.7, modify the function **value**, to return the final amount calculated to the **main**, which will display the required output at the terminal. Also extend the versatility of the function **printline** by having it to take the length of the line as an argument.

The modified program with the proposed changes is presented in Fig. 9.9. One major change is the movement of the **printf** statement from **value** to **main**.

The calculated value is passed on to **main** through the statement:

> **return(sum);**

The integer value of **sum** at this point is returned to **main** and assigned to the variable **amount** by the function call

> **amount = value(principal,inrate,period);**

The following events occur, in order, when the above function call is executed:

1. The function call transfers the control along with copies of the values of the actual arguments to the function **value** where the formal arguments **p, r,** and **n** are assigned the values of **principal, inrate,** and **period** respectively.
2. The called function **value** is executed line by line in a normal fashion until the **return(sum);** statement is encountered. At this point, the value of **sum** is passed back to the function-call in the **main** and the following indirect assignment occurs:

> **value(principal,inrate,period) = sum;**

```
Program
/***********************************************************/
/*        FUNCTIONS WITH ARGUMENTS AND RETURN VALUES        */
/***********************************************************/
main( )
{
    float principal, inrate, amount;
    int period;
    printf("Enter principal amount, interest");
    printf(" rate, and period\n");
    scanf("%f %f %d", &principal, &inrate, &period);
    printline ('*' , 52);
    amount = value (principal, inrate, period);
    printf("\n%f\t%f\t%d\t%f\n\n",principal,
            inrate,period,amount);
    printline('=',52);
}
/* -------------------------------------------------------- */
printline(ch,len)
int len;
char ch;
{
    int i;
    for(i=1;i<=len;i++) printf("%c",ch);
    printf("\n");
}
/* -------------------------------------------------------- */
value(p,r,n)
int n;
float p,r;
{
    int year;
    float sum;
    sum = p; year = 1;
    while(year <=n)
    {
        sum = sum * (1+r);
        year = year +1;
    }
    return(sum);
}
/* -------------------------------------------------------- */
Output
Enter principal amount, interest rate, and period
5000  0.12  5
**********************************************************
5000.000000         0.120000         5         8811.000000
----------------------------------------------------------
```

Fig. 9.9 *Functions with arguments and return values*

3. The calling statement is executed normally and the returned value is thus assigned to **amount**.

Note that the value returned by the function is only the integer part of **sum**. Another important change is the inclusion of a second argument to **printline** function to receive the value of length of the line from the calling function. Thus, the function call

printline('*', 52);

will transfer the control to the function **printline** and assign the following values to the formal arguments **ch**, and **len**:

ch = '*';
len = 52;

9.11 HANDLING OF NON-INTEGER FUNCTIONS

We mentioned earlier that a C function returns a value of the type **int** as the default case when no other type is specified explicitly. For example, the function **value** of Example 9.3 does all calculations using **floats** but the return statement

return(sum);

returns only the integer part of **sum**. This is due to the absence of the *type-specifier* in the function header. In this case, we can accept the integer value of **sum** because the truncated decimal part is insignificant compared to the integer part. However, there will be times when we may find it necessary to receive the **float** or **double** type of data. For example, a function that calculates the mean or standard deviation of a set of values should return the function value in either **float** or **double**.

We must do two things to enable a calling function to receive a non-integer value from a called function:

1. The explicit type-specifier, corresponding to the data type required must be mentioned in the function header. The general form of the function definition is

```
type-specifier function-name (argument list)
argument declaration;
{
     function statements;
}
```

The type-specifier tells the compiler, the type of data the function is to return.
2. The called function *must be declared* at the start of the body in the calling function, like any other variable. This is to tell the calling function the type of data that the function is actually returning.

The program given below illustrates the transfer of a floating-point value between functions is done in a multifunction program.

```
main( )
{
     float a,b,mul( );
     double div( );
```

```
            a = 12.345;
            b = 9.82;
            printf("%f \n", mul(a,b));
            printf("%lf \n", div(a,b));
       }
       float mul(x,y)
       float x,y;
       {
            return(x*y);
       }
       double div(p,q)
       double p,q;
       {
            return(p/q);
       }
```

The declaration part of **main** function declares not only the variables but the functions **mul** and **div** as well. This only tells the compiler that **mul** will return a float-type value and **div** a double-type value. Parentheses that follow **mul** and **div** specify that they are functions instead of variables.

If we have a mismatch between the type of data that the called function returns and the type of data that the calling function expects, we will have unpredictable results. We must, therefore, be very careful to make sure that both types are compatible.

Example 9.4

Write a function **power** that computes x raised to the power y for integers x and y and returns double-type value.

Fig. 9.10 shows a **power** function that returns a **double**. The declaration

$$\text{double power( );}$$

appears in **main**, before **power** is called.

```
Program
/***********************************************************/
/*                 POWER FUNCTIONS                        */
/***********************************************************/
main( )
{
      int x,y;
      double power( );
      printf("Enter x,y:");
      scanf("%d %d", &x,&y);
      printf("%d to power %d is %f \n", x,y,power (x,y));
}
/* -------------------------------------------------------- */
double power(x,y)   /* computes x to power y */
int x,y;
{
```

```
        double p;
        p = 1.0 ;   /* x to power zero */
        if(y >= 0)
          while(y--)  /* computes positive powers */
            p *= x;
        else
          while(y++) /* computes negative powers */
            p /= x ;
        return(p);   /* returns double type */
    }
    /* ------------------------------------------------------------------------------- */
    Output
    Enter x,y:16  2
    16 to power 2 is 256.000000

    Enter x,y:16  -2
    16 to power -2 is 0.003906
```

Fig. 9.10   *Illustration of return of float values*

Another way to guarantee that **power's** type is declared before it is called in **main** is to define the **power** function before we define **main**. **Power's** type is then known from its definition, so we no longer need its type declaration in **main**.

Functions Returning Nothing

We have seen earlier that in many occasions, functions do not return any values. They perform only some printing or house keeping operations. Consider the program in Fig. 9.4.

```
    main ()
    {
      printline();
      value();
      printline();
    }
    printline()
    {
      . . . .
      . . . .
    }
    value()
    {
      . . . .
      . . . .
    }
```

The functions **printline**() and **value**() do not return any values and therefore they were not declared in the **main**. Although the program works nicely, we can declare them in the **main** with the qualifier **void**. This states explicitly that the functions do not return values. This prevents any accidental use of these functions in expressions. The program in Fig. 9.4 may be modified as follows:

```
main()
{
    void printline();        /* declaration */
    void value();            /* declaration */
    . . . .
    . . . .
}
void printline()
{
    . . . .
    . . . .
}
void value()
{
    . . . .
    . . . .
}
```

9.12 NESTING OF FUNCTIONS

C permits nesting of functions freely. **main** can call **function1**, which calls **function2**, which calls **function3**, ...and so on. There is in principle no limit as to how deeply functions can be nested. Consider the following program:

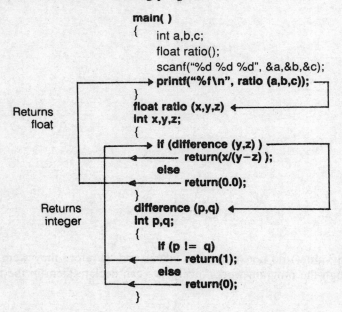

```
main( )
{
    int a,b,c;
    float ratio();
    scanf("%d %d %d", &a,&b,&c);
    printf("%f\n", ratio (a,b,c));
}
float ratio (x,y,z)
int x,y,z;
{
    if (difference (y,z) )
        return(x/(y−z) );
    else
        return(0.0);
}
difference (p,q)
int p,q;
{
    if (p != q)
        return(1);
    else
        return(0);
}
```

Returns float

Returns integer

The above program calculates the ratio

$$\frac{a}{b-c}$$

and prints the result. We have the follwing three functions:

main( )
ratio( )
difference( )

main reads the values of a, b and c and calls the function **ratio** to calculate the value a/(b−c). This ratio cannot be evaluated if (b−c) = 0. Therefore, **ratio** calls another function **difference** to test whether the difference (b−c) is zero or not. **difference** returns 1, if b is not equal to c; otherwise returns zero to the function **ratio**. In turn, **ratio** calculates the value a/(b−c) if it receives 1 and returns the result in **float**. In case, **ratio** receives zero from **difference**, it sends back 0.0 to **main** indicating that (b−c) = 0.

Nesting of function calls is also possible. For example, a statement like

p = mul(mul(5,2),6);

is valid. This represents two sequential function calls. The inner function call is evaluated first and the returned value is again used as an actual argument in the outer function call. If **mul** returns the product of its arguments, then the value of **p** would be 60 (= 5×2×6).

9.13 RECURSION

When a called function in turn calls another function a process of 'chaining' occurs. *Recursion* is a special case of this process, where a function calls itself. A very simple example of recursion is presented below:

```
main( )
{
    printf("This is an example of recursion\n");
    main( );
}
```

When executed, this program will produce an output something like this:

```
This is an example of recursion
This is an example of recursion
This is an example of recursion
This is an ex
```

Execution is terminated abruptly; otherwise the execution will continue indefinitely.

Another useful example of recursion is the evaluation of factorials of a given number. The factorial of a number n is expressed as a series of repetitive multiplications as shown below:

factorial of n = n(n−1)(n−2).........1.

For example,

factorial of 4 = 4×3×2×1 = 24

A function to evaluate factorial of n is as follows:

```
factorial(n)
int   n;
{
    int fact;
    if (n==1)
        return(1);
    else
        fact = n*factorial(n-1);
    return(fact);
}
```

Let us see how the recursion works. Assume n = 3. Since the value of n is not 1, the statement

$$fact = n * factorial(n-1);$$

will be executed with n = 3. That is,

$$fact = 3 * factorial(2);$$

will be evaluated. The expression on the right-hand side includes a call to **factorial** with n = 2. This call will return the following value:

$$2 * factorial(1)$$

Once again, **factorial** is called with n = 1. This time, the function returns 1. The sequence of operations can be summarized as follows:

```
fact = 3 * factorial(2)
     = 3 * 2 * factorial(1)
     = 3 * 2 * 1
     = 6
```

Recursive functions can be effectively used to solve problems where the solution is expressed in terms of successively applying the same solution to subsets of the problem. When we write recursive functions, we must have an **if** statement somewhere to force the function to return without the recursive call being executed. Otherwise, the function will never return.

9.14 FUNCTIONS WITH ARRAYS

Like the values of simple variables, it is also possible to pass the values of an array to a function. To pass an array to a called function, it is sufficient to list the name of the array, *without any subscripts,* and the size of the array as arguments. For example, the call

largest(a,n);

will pass all the elements contained in the array **a** of size **n**. The called function expecting this call must be appropriately defined. The **largest** function header might look like:

```
float largest(array, size)
float array[ ];
int size;
```

The function **largest** is defined to take two arguments, the array name and the size of the array to specify the number of elements in the array. The declaration of the formal argument **array** is made as follows:

float array[ ];

The pair of brackets informs the compiler that the argument **array** is an array of numbers. It is not necessary to specify the size of the **array** here.

Let us consider a problem of finding the largest value in an array of elements. The program is as follows:

```
main( )
{
        float largest( );
        static float value[4] = {2.5,-4.75,1.2,3.67};
        printf("%f\n", largest(value,4) );
}

float largest(a,n)
float a[ ];
int   n;
{
        int   i;
        float max;
        max = a[0];
        for(i = 1; i < n; i++)
                if(max < a[i])
                        max = a[i];
        return(max);
}
```

When the function call **largest**(value,4) is made, the values of all elements of the array **value** are passed to the corresponding elements of array **a** in the called function. The **largest** function finds the largest value in the array and returns the result to the **main**.

Example 9.5

Write a program to calculate the standard deviation of an array of values. The array elements are read from the terminal. Use functions to calculate standard deviation and mean.

Standard deviation of a set of n values is given by

$$S.D. = \sqrt{\frac{1}{n} \sum_{i=1}^{n} (\bar{x}-x_i)^2}$$

where $\bar{x}$ is the mean of the values.

A multifunction program consisting of **main**, **std-dev**, and **mean** functions is shown in Fig. 9.11. **main** reads the elements of the array **value** from the terminal and calls the function **std-dev** to print the standard deviation of the array elements. **std-dev**, in turn, calls another function **mean** to supply the average value of the array elements.

Both **std-dev** and **mean** are defined as **floats** and therefore they are declared as **floats** in the declaration part of their calling functions.

When dealing with array arguments, we should remember one major distinction. If a function changes the values of an array elements, then these changes will be made to the original array that passed to the function. When an entire array is passed as an argument, the contents of the array are not copied into the formal parameter array; instead, information about the addresses of array elements are passed on to the function. Therefore, any changes introduced to the array elements are truly reflected in the original array in the calling function.

Program

```
/*************************************************************************/
/*                      FUNCTIONS WITH ARRAYS                        */
/*************************************************************************/
#include         <math.h>
#define SIZE         5
main( )
{
    float value[SIZE], std_dev();
    int i;

    printf("Enter %d float values\n", SIZE);
    for (i=0 ;i  <  SIZE ; i++)
      scanf("%f", &value[i]);
    printf("Std.deviation is %f\n", std_dev(value,SIZE));
}
float std_dev(a,n)
float a[];
int   n;
{
    int i;
    float mean(), x, sum = 0.0;
    x = mean (a,n);
    for(i=0;`i <n; i++)
      sum += (x-a[i])*(x-a[i]);
    return(sqrt(sum/(float)n));
}
float mean(a,n)
float a[ ];
int n;
{
    int i ;
    float sum = 0.0;
    for(i=0 ; i < n ; i++)
      sum = sum + a[i];
    return(sum/(float)n);
}
```

Output

```
Enter 5 float values
35.0 67.0 79.5 14.20 55.75
Std.deviation is 23.231582
```

Fig. 9.11 *Passing of arrays to a function*

However, this does not apply when an individual element is passed on as argument. Example 9.6 highlights these concepts.

Example 9.6

Write a program that uses a function to sort an array of integers.

A program to sort an array of integers using the function **sort( )** is given in Fig. 9.12. Its output clearly shows that a function can change the values in an array passed as an argument.

```
Program
/*********************************************************************/
/*                SORTING OF ARRAY ELEMENTS                        */
/*********************************************************************/
main( )
{
    int i;
    static int marks[5] = {40, 90, 73, 81, 35};
    printf("Marks before sorting \n");
    for(i = 0; i < 5; i++)
        printf("%d ", marks[i]);
    printf("\n\n");

    sort (5, marks);
    printf("Marks after sorting \n");
    for(i = 0; i < 5; i++)
        printf("%4d", marks[i]);
    printf("\n");
}
sort(m,x)
int m, x[ ];
{
    int i, j, t;
    for(i = 1; i <= m−1; i++)
        for(j = 1; j <=m−i; j++)
            if(x[j−1] >= x[j])
            {
                t = x[j−1];
                x[j−1] = x[j];
                x[j] = t;
            }
}
Output
Marks before sorting
40 90 73 81 35

Marks after sorting
 35   40   73   81   90
```

Fig. 9.12 *Sorting of array elements using a function*

9.15 THE SCOPE AND LIFETIME OF VARIABLES IN FUNCTIONS

Variables in C differ in behaviour from those in most other languages. For example, in a BASIC program, a variable retains its value throughout the program. It is not always the case in C. It all depends on the 'storage' class a variable may assume.

As mentioned earlier, a variable in C can have any one of the four storage classes:

1. Automatic variables
2. External variables
3. Static variables
4. Register variables

We shall briefly discuss the *scope* and *longevity* of each of the above class of variables. The scope of variable determines over what part(s) of the program a variable is actually available for use (active). Longevity refers to the period during which a variable retains a given value during execution of a program (alive). So longevity has a direct effect on the utility of a given variable.

The variables may also be broadly categorized, depending on the place of their declaration, as *internal* (local) or *external* (global). Internal variables are those which are declared within a particular function, while external variables are declared outside of any function.

It is very important to understand the concept of storage classes and their utility in order to develop efficient multifunction programs.

Automatic Variables

Automatic variables are declared inside a function in which they are to be utilized. They are *created* when the function is called and *destroyed* automatically when the function is exited, hence the name automatic. Automatic variables are therefore private (or local) to the function in which they are declared. Because of this property, automatic variables are also referred to as *local* or *internal* variables.

A variable declared inside a function without storage class specification is, by default, an automatic variable. For instance, the storage class of the variable **number** in the example below is automatic.

```
main( )
{
    int number;
    ------------
    ------------
}
```

We may also use the keyword **auto** to declare automatic variables explicitly.

```
main( )
{
    auto int number;
    ------------
    ------------
}
```

One important feature of automatic variables is that their value cannot be changed accidentally by what happens in some other function in the program. This assures that we may declare and use the same variable name in different functions in the same program without causing any confusion to the compiler.

Example 9.7
Write a multifunction to illustrate how automatic variables work.

A program with two subprograms **function1** and **function2** is shown in Fig. 9.13. **m** is an automatic variable and it is declared at the beginning of each function. **m** is initialized to 10, 100, and 1000 in **function1**, **function2**, and **main** respectively.

When executed, **main** calls **function2** which in turn calls **function1**. When **main** is active, **m** = 1000; but when **function2** is called, the **main**'s **m** is temporarily put on the shelf and the new local **m** = 100 becomes active. Similarly, when **function1** is called, both the previous values of **m** are put on the shelf and the latest value of **m** (=10) becomes active. As soon as **function1** (m=10) is finished, **function2** (m=100) takes over again. As soon it is done, **main** (m=1000) takes over. The output clearly shows that the value assigned to **m** in one function does not affect its value in the other functions; and the local value of **m** is destroyed when it leaves a function.

```
Program
/*******************************************************************/
/*          ILLUSTRATION OF WORKING OF auto VARIABLES          */
/*******************************************************************/
main( )
{
    int  m  =  1000;
    function2( );
    printf("%d\n",m);
}
function1( )
{
    int  m  =  10;
    printf("%d\n",m);
}
function2( )
{
    int  m  =  100;
    function1( );
    printf("%d\n",m);
}
Output

10
100
1000
```

Fig. 9.13 *Working of automatic variables*

There are two consequences of the scope and longevity of **auto** variables worth remembering. First, any variable local to **main** will normally *live* throughout the whole program, although it is *active* only in **main**. Secondly, during recursion, the nested variables are unique **auto** variables, a situation similar to function-nested **auto** variables with identical names.

Automatic variables can also be defined within a set of braces known as "blocks". They are meaningful only inside the blocks where they are defined. Consider the example below:

```
main()
{
        int n, a, b;
        . . . .                                 ◄────── Scope level 1
        . . . .
        if(n <= 100)
        {
                int n, sum;
                . . . .                         ◄────── Scope level 2
                . . . .
        }
        . . . . /* sum not valid here */
        . . . .
}
```

The variables **n, a** and **b** defined in **main** have scope from the begining to the end of **main**. However, the variable **n** defined in the **main** cannot enter into the block of scope level 2 because the scope level 2 contains another variable named **n**. The second **n** (which takes precedence over the first **n**) is available only inside the scope level 2 and no longer available the moment control leaves the **if** block. Of course, if no variable named **n** is defined inside the **if** block, then **n** defined in the **main** would be available inside scope level 2 as well. The variable **sum** defined in the **if** block is not available outside that block.

External Variables

Variables that are both *alive* and *active* throughout the entire program are known as *external* variables. They are also known as *global* variables. Unlike local variables, global variables can be accessed by *any* function in the program. External variables are declared outside a function. For example, the external declaration of integer **number** and float **length** might appear as:

```
int number;
float length = 7.5;
main( )
{
        _____
        _____
}
```

```
function1( )
{
      _____
      _____

}
function2( )
{
      _____
      _____

}
```

The variables **number** and **length** are available for use in all the three functions. In case a local variable and a global variable have the same name, the local variable will have precedence over the global one in the function where it is declared. Consider the following example:

```
int count;
main( )
{
      count = 10;
      _____
      _____

}
function( )
{
      int count = 0;
      _____
      _____
      count = count+1;
}
```

When the **function** references the variable **count**, it will be referencing only its local variable, not the global one. The value of **count** in **main** will not be affected.

Example 9.8
Write a multifunction program to illustrate the properties of global variables.

A program to illustrate the properties of global variables is presented in Fig. 9.14. Note that variable **x** is used in all functions, but none except **fun2**, has a definition for **x**. Because **x** has been declared 'above' all the functions, it is available to each function without having to pass **x** as a function argument.

```
Program
/******************************************************************/
/*      ILLUSTRATION OF PROPERTIES OF GLOBAL VARIABLES      */
/******************************************************************/

int x ;
main( )
{
     x = 10 ;
     printf("x = %d\n", x);
     printf("x = %d\n", fun1( ));
```

```
        printf("x = %d\n", fun2( ));
        printf("x = %d\n", fun3( ));
}
fun1( )
{
        x = x + 10 ;
        return(x);
}
fun2( )
{
        int x ;
        x = 1 ;
        return(x);
}
fun3( )
{
        x = x + 10 ;
        return(x);
}
Output
x = 10
x = 20
x = 1
x = 30
```

Fig. 9.14 *Illustration of global variables*

Once a variable has been declared as global, any function can use it and change its value. Then, subsequent functions can reference only that new value. Because of this property, we should try to use global variables only for tables or for variables shared between functions when it is inconvenient to pass them as parameters.

One other aspect of a global variable is that it is visible only from the point of declaration to the end of the program. Consider a program segment as shown below:

```
        main( )
        {
                y = 5;
                -----------
                -----------
        }
        int y;
        func1( )
        {
                y = y+1;
        }
```

We have a problem here. As far as **main** is concerned, y is not defined. So, the compiler will issue an error message. Unlike local variables, global variables are initialized to zero by default. The statement

$$y = y+1;$$

in **fun1** will, therefore, assign 1 to y.

External Declaration

In the program segment above, the **main** cannot access the variable y as it has been declared after the **main** function. This problem can be solved by declaring the variable with the storage class **extern**. For example:

```
main()
{
        extern int y; /* external declaration */
        . . . .
        . . . .
}
func1()
{
        extern int y; /* external declaration */
        . . . .
        . . . .
}
int y;  /* definition */
```

Although the variable **y** has been defined after both the functions, the *external declaration* of **y** inside the functions informs the compiler that **y** is an integer type defined somewhere else in the program. Note that the **extern** declaration does not allocate storage space for variables. In case of arrays, the definition should include their size as well.
Example:

```
main()
{
        int i;
        void print_out();
        extern float height [ ];
        . . . .
        . . . .
        print_out();
}
void print_out()
{
        extern float height [ ];
        int i;
        . . . .
        . . . .
}
float height[SIZE];
```

An **extern** within a function provides the type information to just that one function. We can provide type information to all functions within a file by placing external declarations before any of them, as shown below:

```
        extern float height [ ];
        main()
        {
                int i;
                void print_out();
                . . . .
                . . . .
                print_out();
        }
        void print_out()
        {
                int i;
                . . . .
                . . . .
        }
        float height[SIZE];
```

The distinction between definition and declaration also applies to functions. A function is defined when its parameters and function body are specified. This tells the compiler to allocate space for the function code and provides type information for the parameters. Since functions are external by default, we daclare them (in the calling functions) without the qualifier **extern**. Therefore, the declaration

void print_out();

is equivalent to

extern void print_out();

Function declarations outside of any function behave the same way as variable declarations.

Multifile Programs

So far we have been assuming that all the functions (including the **main**) are defined in one file. However, in real-life programming environment, we may use more than one source files which may be compiled separately and linked later to form an executable object code. This approach is very useful because any change in one file does not affect other files thus eliminating the need for recompilation of the entire program.

Multiple source files can share a variable provided it is declared as an external variable appropriately. Variables that are shared by two or more files are global variables and therefore we must declare them accordingly in one file and then explicitly define them with **extern** in other files. Figure 9.15 illustrates the use of **extern** declarations in a multifile program.

The function **main** in **file1** can reference the variable **m** that is declared as global in **file2**. Remember, **function1** can not access the variable **m**. If, however, the **extern int m;** statement is placed before **main**, then both the functions could refer to **m**. This can also be achieved by using **extern int m;** statement inside each function in **file1**.

The **extern** specifier tells the compiler that the following variable types and names have already been declared elsewhere and no need to create storage space for them. It is the

file1.c

```
main()
{
    extern int m;
    int i;
    . . . .
    . . . .
}
function1()
{
    int j;
    . . . .
    . . . .
}
```

file2.c

```
int m /* global variable */
function2()
{
    int i;
    . . . .
    . . . .
}
function3()
{
    int count;
    . . . .
    . . . .
}
```

Fig.9.15 *Use of **extern** in a multifile program*

responsibility of the *linker* to resolve the reference problem. It is important to note that a multifile global variable should be declared *without* **extern** in one (and only one) of the files. The **extern** declaration is done in places where secondary references are made. If we declare a variable as global in two different files used by a single program, then the linker will have a conflict as to which variable to use and, therefore, issues a warning.

The multifile program shown in Fig.9.15 may be modified as shown in Fig.9.16.

file1.c

```
int m; /* global variable */

main()
{
    int i;
    . . . .
    . . . .
}
function1()
{
    int j;
    . . . .
    . . . .
}
```

file2.c

```
extern int m;

function2()
{
    int i;
    . . . .
    . . . .
}
function3()
{
    int count;
    . . . .
    . . . .
}
```

Fig.9.16 *Another version of a multifile program*

When a function is defined in one file and accessed in another, the later file must include a function *declaration*. The declaration identifies the function as an external function whose definition appears elsewhere. We usually place such declarations at the begining of the file, before all functions. Although all functions are assumed to be external, it would be a good practice to explicitly declare such functions with the storage class **extern**.

Static Variables

As the name suggests, the value of static variables persists until the end of the program. A variable can be declared static using the keyword **static** like

> **static int x;**
> **static float y;**

A static variable may be either an internal type or an external type, depending on the place of declaration.

Internal static variables are those which are declared inside a function. The scope of internal static variables extend upto the end of the function in which they are defined. Therefore, internal **static** variables are similar to **auto** variables, except that they remain in existence (alive) throughout the remainder of the program. Therefore, internal **static** variables can be used to retain values between function calls. For example, it can be used to count the number of calls made to a function.

Example 9.9

Write a program to illustrate the properties of a static variable.

The program in Fig. 9.17 explains the behaviour of a static variable.

```
Program
/ *******************************************************************************/
/*                     ILLUSTRATION OF STATIC VARIABLE                       */
/ *******************************************************************************/
main ( )
{
     int i;
     for(i=1; i<=3; i++)
        stat( );
{
stat( )
}
     static int x = 0;
     x = x+1;
     printf("x = %d\n", x);
{
Output
x = 1
x = 2
x = 3
```

Fig. 9.17 *Illustration of static variable*

A static variable is initialized only once, when the program is compiled. It is never initialized again. During the first call to **stat**, **x** is incremented to 1. Because **x** is static, this value persists and therefore, the next call adds another 1 to **x** giving it a value of 2. The value of **x** becomes three when the third call is made.

Had we declared **x** as an **auto** variable, the output would have been:

```
x = 1
x = 1
x = 1
```

This is because each time **stat** is called, the auto variable **x** is initialized to zero. When the function terminates, its value of 1 is lost.

An external **static** variable is declared outside of all functions and is available to all the functions in that program. The difference between a **static** external variable and a simple external variable is that the **static** external variable is available only within the file where it is defined while the simple external variable can be accessed by other files.

It is also possible to control the scope of a function. For example, we would like a particular function accessible only to the functions in the file in which it is defined, and not to any function in other files. This can be accomplished by defining 'that' function with the storage class **static**.

Register Variables

We can tell the compiler that a variable should be kept in one of the machine's registers, instead of keeping in the memory (where normal variables are stored). Since a register access is much faster than a memory access, keeping the frequently accessed variables (e.g., loop control variables) in the register will lead to faster execution of programs. This is done as follows:

register int count;

Although, ANSI standard does not restrict its application to any particular data type, most compilers allow only **int** or **char** variables to be placed in the register.

Since only a few variables can be placed in the register, it is important to carefully select the variables for this purpose. However, C will automatically convert **register** variables into nonregister variables once the limit is reached.

Table 9.1 summarizes the information on the visibility and lifetime of variables in functions and files.

Table 9.1 Scope and Lifetime of Declarations

Storage class	Where declared	Visibility (Active)	Lifetime (Alive)
None	Before all functions in a file (may be initialized)	Entire file plus other files where variable is declared with **extern**.	Entire program (Global)

extern	Before all functions in a file (cannot be initialized)	Entire file plus other files where variable is declared **extern** and the file where originally declared as global.	Global
static	Before all functions in a file	Only in that file	Global
None or **auto**	Inside a function (or a block)	Only in that function or block	Until end of function or block
register	Inside a fucntion or block	Only in that function or block	Until end of function or block
static	Inside a fucntion	Only in that function	Global

9.16 ANSI C FUNCTIONS

Function Definition

As mentioned in the beginning of this chapter, ANSI standard combines the function definition and arguments declaration in one line (the function header). The general form of ANSI C functions is:

```
data-type  function-name (type1 a1, type2 a2,.. typeN aN )
{
      . . . .
      . . . . (body of the function)
      . . . .
}
```

Here *data-type* refers to the type of the value returned by the function **function-name** and *type1*, *type2*, ..., *typeN* are types of arguments *a1*, *a2*, ..., *aN*.

As usual, if no data type is specified for the function, then, by default, the function is assumed to return an integer value. The arguments declaration is done using the *comma* separator. Remember, each argument must be independently declared with type specifier and name. That is, similar type arguments cannot be combined under one type name, like variable declarations. For example,

double funct(int a, int b, double c)

is a valid function definition, where as

double funct(int a, b, double c)

is incorrect.

This new version of function definition, which combines the argument list and the arguments declaration, is called a *function prototype*. Function prototypes were not part of the original C language. It is one of the important recommendations of the ANSI C committee.

Function Declaration

We know that every function that is being referenced should be declared for its type in the calling function. For example:

```
main()
{
        float a, b, x;
        float mul(); /* function declaration (old type)*/
        . . . .
        . . . .
        x = mul(a,b); /* function call */
}
```

Note that the function declaration as stated above specifies the type of value returned by the function **mul** and does not talk anything about its arguments. The actual arguments are specified only when the function is called.

The introduction of "function prototypes" requires that the function declaration must include not only the type of return value but also the type and number of arguments to expect. Above program segment may be modified using the function prototype as follows:

```
main()
{
        float a, b, x;
        float mul(float a, float b);          /* function prototype */
                                              /* ANSI declaration  */
        . . . . .
        . . . .
        x = mul(a, b);
}
```

The general form of function declaration using ANSI prototype is:

> *data-type* **function-name** (*type1 a1, type2 a2, ...,typeN aN*);

One major reason for using function prototypes in function declarations is that they enable the compiler check for any mismatch of type and number of arguments between the function calls and the function definitions. They also help the compiler to perform automatic type conversions on function parameters. When a function is called, the actual arguments are automatically converted to the types in the function definition using the normal rules of assignment.

The argument names *(a1, a2, ..., aN)* used in the function declaration are for documentation purpose only and they do not define the variables in the function. This means, we may use any "dummy" argument names (which are recognised only within the declaration). For example, the following function declaration is valid.

```
main()
{
        float a, b, x;
        float mul(float length, float breadth); /* declaration */
        . . . .
        . . . .
        x = mul(a,b);
}
```

But the normal practice is to use the names of the "actual" arguments appearing in the function call. Since only the types (and not the names) of the arguments are important, it is possible to declare a function without the names of arguments. Example:

float mul(float, float); /* declaration */

In case, a function does not return anything, or it does not have any arguments to declare, it can be declared using **void** as follows.

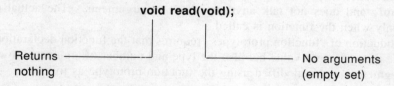

The type **void** is often used for declaring functions returning pointers that can point to any type of data.

Example 9.10

Rewrite the power function program in Fig. 9.10 using function prototypes.

The rewritten program is shown in Fig. 9.18. The program uses function prototypes in both the function definition and function declaration. The program also illustrates the following aspects:

1. When the function is called, the names of the actual arguments need not be the same as the names given in the declaration. Nevertheless, their data types must match the types in declaration.
2. The names of the arguments in prototype declaration need not be the same names given in the prototype definition. Here again, the data types must match.

3. The variable name *p* has been defined in both the functions. Since they are defined as local **auto** variables, they do not conflict.

```
Program

/************************************************************************/
/* POWER FUNCTION PROGRAM WITH PROTOTYPES  */
/************************************************************************/

main()
{
    int x, y, m, n, p;
    double q;
    double power(int x, int y); /* prototype declaration*/

    x =  16;  y = 2;
    p = power(x, y);

    m = 16;  n = -2;
    q = power(m,n);    /* arguments names not same */

    printf("\n p = %d\n q = %f\n", p,q);
}

double power(int a, int b)  /* prototype definition */

{
    double p;
    p = 1.0;

    if(b >= 0)
      while(b- -) p *= a;
    else
      while(b++) p /= a;
    return(p);
}

Output

p = 256
q = 0.003906
```

Fig. 9.18 *Use of function prototypes*

Variable Number of Arguments

Some functions have a variable number of arguments and data types which cannot be known at compile time. The **print** and **scanf** functions are typical examples. The ANSI standard proposes new symbol called the *ellipsis* to handle such functions. The ellipsis consists of three periods (...) and used as shown below:

$$\text{double area(float d, ...)}$$

Both the function declaration and definition should use ellipsis to indicate that the arguments are arbitrary both in number and type.

9.17 POINTS TO REMEMBER

The strength of C language lies primarily in the effective use of functions. While we encourage the use of modular, multifunction programming approach, it is worthwhile to remember some important points about functions.

1. A function may or may not return a value. If it does, it can return only one value.
2. Actual and formal arguments must agree in data types. Otherwise, garbage will be passed, without generating any error message.
3. Functions return integer value by default.
4. When a function is supposed to return a non-integer value, its type must be explicitly specified in the function header. Such functions should be declared at the start of the calling functions.
5. A function without a **return** statement cannot return any value. However, a global variable used in the function will retain its value for future use.
6. A function that returns a value may be used in expressions (arithmetic or relational) like any other C variable.
7. When the value returned is assigned to a variable, the value will be converted to the type of the variable receiving it.
8. A function cannot be the target of an assignment.
9. A **return** statement can occur anywhere within the body of a function. A function can also have more than one **return** statement.
10. A function may be placed either after or before the **main** function.
11. Where more functions are used, they may appear in any order.
12. A function is treated as an external variable. Therefore, a function cannot be defined inside another function.
13. A variable declared inside a function is known only to that function. It is created when the function is called and destroyed when the function is finished.
14. A global (external) variable is visible only from the point of its declaration to the end of the program.
15. A variable that has been declared as **static** inside a function retains its value even after the function is *exited*. (Since static variables are initialized during compilation, they are initialized only once.)
16. A multifile global variable must be declared without **extern** in one (and only one) of the files. The **extern** declaration is done in places where secondary references are made.

CASE STUDY

Calculation of Area Under a Curve

One of the applications of computers in numerical analysis is computing the area under a curve. One simple method of calculating the area under a curve is to divide the area into a number of trapezoids of same width and summing up the areas of individual trapezoids. The area of a trapezoid is given by

$$\text{Area} = 0.5 * (h1 + h2) * b$$

Where h1 and h2 are the heights of two sides and b is the width as shown below:

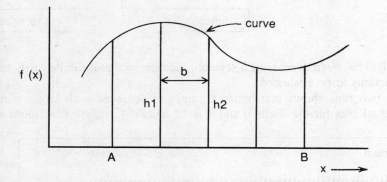

The program in Fig. 9.19 calculates the area for a curve of the function

$$f(x) = x^2 + 1$$

between any two given limits, say, A and B.

Input

Lower limit (A)
Upper limit (B)
Number of trapezoids

Output

Total area under the curve between the given limits.

Algorithm

1. Input the lower and upper limits and the number of trapezoids.
2. Calculate the width of trapezoids.
3. Initialize the total area.
4. Calculate the area of trapezoid and add to the total area.

5. Repeat step-4 until all the trapezoids are completed.
6. Print total area.

The algorithm is implemented in top-down modular form as shown below:

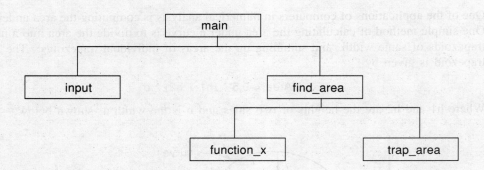

The evaluation of f(x) has been done using a separate function so that it can be easily modified to allow other functions to be evaluated.

The output for two runs shows that better accuracy is achieved with larger number of trapezoids. The actual area for the limits 0 and 3 is 12 units (by analytical method).

```
Program

/********************************************************************/
/*                  AREA UNDER A CURVE                          */
/********************************************************************/

#include <stdio.h>

float    start_point,      /* GLOBAL VARIABLES */
         end_point,
         total_area;
int      numtraps;

main()
{
    void     input(void);
    float    find_area(float a, float b,  int n);

    printf("AREA  UNDER  A  CURVE");
    input();
    total_area = find_area(start_point, end_point, numtraps);
    printf("TOTAL AREA = %f", total_area);
}
```

```
void input(void)
{
     printf("\n Enter lower limit: ");
     scanf("%f", &start_point);
     printf(" Enter upper limit: ");
     scanf("%f", &end_point);
     printf(" Enter number of trapezoids: ");
     scanf("%d", &numtraps);
}

float find_area(float a, float b, int n)
{
     float    base, lower, h1, h2;      /* LOCAL VARIABLES */
     float    function_x(float x);
     float    trap_area(float h1, float h2, float base);


     base = (b–a)/n;
     lower = a;

     for(lower = a; lower <= b – base; lower = lower + base)
     {
        h1 =   function_x(lower);
        h2 =   function_x(lower + base);
        total_area += trap_area(h1, h2, base);
     }
     return(total_area);
}

float trap_area(float height_1, float height_2, float base)
{
   float   area;          /* LOCAL VARIABLE */

   area = 0.5 * (height_1 + height_2) * base;
   return(area);
}

float  function_x(float x)
{
   /* F(X) = X * X + 1  */

   return(x * x + 1);
}
```

Output

AREA UNDER A CURVE
 Enter lower limit: 0
 Enter upper limit: 3
 Enter number of trapezoids: 30
TOTAL AREA = 12.005000

AREA UNDER A CURVE
 Enter lower limit: 0
 Enter upper limit: 3
 Enter number of trapezoids: 100
TOTAL AREA = 12.000438

Fig. 9.19 *Computing area under a curve*

REVIEW QUESTIONS AND EXERCISES

9.1 Explain what is likely to happen when the following situations are encountered in a program.

(a) Actual arguments are less than the formal arguments in a function.
(b) Data type of one of the actual arguments does not match with the data type of the corresponding formal argument.
(c) The type of the *expression* in **return**(expression) does not match with the type of the function.
(d) Same variable name is declared in two different functions.

9.2 State whether the following statements are *true* or *false*.

(a) Functions should be arranged in the order in which they are called.
(b) C functions can return only one value.
(c) We can pass any number of arguments to a function.
(d) A function in C should have at least one argument.
(e) A function always returns an integer value.
(f) A function can call itself.
(g) A global variable can be used only in **main** function.
(h) The values of formal arguments can be changed inside the function where they are declared.
(i) Every function should have a **return** statement.

9.3 Distinguish between the following:

(a) Actual and formal arguments.
(b) Global and local variables.
(c) Automatic and static variables.
(d) Global and extern variables.

9.4 **Main** is a user-defined function. How does it differ from other user-defined functions?

9.5 Which of the following function headers are invalid? And why?

(a) average(x,y,z);
(b) power(a,n−1)

(c) product(m,10)
(d) double minimum(float a; float b;)

9.6 The following function returns the value of x/y.

```
divide(x,y)
float x,y;
{
    return(x/y);
}
```

What will be the value of the following function calls:

(a) divide(10,2)
(b) divide(9,2)
(c) divide(4.5,1.5)

9.7 Determine the output of the following program:

```
main( )
{
    int x = 10;
    int y = 20;
    int  p,q;
    p = prod(x,y);
    q = prod(p,prod(x,2));
    printf("%d %d\n", p,q);
}
prod(a,b)
int a,b;
{
    return (a*b);
}
```

9.8 Write a function **exchange** to interchange the values of two variables, say **x** and **y**. Illustrate the use of this function, in a calling function. (*Hint*: Assume that **x** and **y** are defined as global variables.)

9.9 Write a function **space(x)** that can be used to provide a space of x positions between two output numbers.

9.10 Use recursive calls to evaluate

$$f(x) = x - \frac{x^3}{3!} + \frac{x^5}{5!} - \frac{x^7}{7!} + ...$$

9.11 An n_order polynomial can be evaluated as follows:

$$P = (.....(((a_0x+a_1)x+a_2)x+a_3)x+...+a_n)$$

Write a function to evaluate the polynomial, using an array variable **a**.

9.12 The Fibonacci numbers are defined recursively as follows:

$$F_1 = 1$$
$$F_2 = 1$$
$$F_n = F_{n-1}+F_{n-2}, \quad n > 2$$

Write a function that will generate and print the first *n* Fibonacci numbers.

9.13 Write a function that will round a floating-point number to an indicated decimal place. For example the number 17.457 would yield the value 17.46 when it is rounded off to two decimal places.

9.14 Write a function **prime** that returns 1 if its argument is a prime number and returns zero otherwise.

9.15 Write a function that will scan a character string passed as an argument and convert all lower-case characters into their upper-case equivalents.

9.16   Write a function to raise a number to a power when both are floating point numbers.

Note: It is a good practice to use function prototypes as recommended in ANSI C. Try them if your compiler supports ANSI standards.

STRUCTURES AND UNIONS

10.1 INTRODUCTION

We have seen that arrays can be used to represent a group of data items that belong to the same type, such as **int** or **float**. However, if we want to represent a collection of data items of different types using a single name, then we cannot use an array. Fortunately, C supports a constructed data type known as *structure*, which is a method for packing data of different types. A structure is a convenient tool for handling a group of logically related data items. For example, it can be used to represent a set of attributes, such as student_name, roll_number and marks. The concept of a structure is analogous to that of a 'record' in many other languages.

Structures help to organize complex data in a more meaningful way. It is a powerful concept that we may often need to use in our program design. This chapter is devoted to the study of structures and their applications in program development. Another related concept known as *unions* is also discussed.

10.2 STRUCTURE DEFINITION

A structure definition creates a format that may be used to declare structure variables. Let us use an example to illustrate the process of structure definition and the creation of structure variables. Consider a book database consisting of book name, author, number of pages, and price. We can define a structure to hold this information as follows:

```
struct book_bank
{
    char  title[20];
    char  author[15];
    int   pages;
    float price;
};
```

The keyword **struct** declares a structure to hold the details of four fields, namely **title**, **author**, **pages**, and **price**. These fields are called *structure elements or members*. Each member may belong to a different type of data. **book_bank** is the name of the structure and is called the *structure tag*. The tag name may be used subsequently to declare variables that have the tag's structure.

Note that the above declaration has not declared any variables. It simply describes a format called *template* to represent information as shown below.

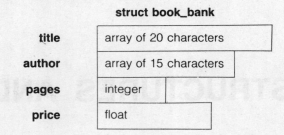

struct book_bank

title	array of 20 characters
author	array of 15 characters
pages	integer
price	float

The general format of a structure definition is as follows:

```
struct    tag_name
{
        data_type     member1;
        data_type     member2;
        ...           ...
        ...           ...
};
```

We can declare structure variables using the tag name anywhere in the program. For example, the statement

struct book_bank book1, book2, book3;

declares **book1, book2**, and **book3** as variables of type **struct book_bank**.

Each one of these variables has four members as specified by the template. The complete declaration might look like this:

```
struct book_bank
{
    char  title[20];
    char  author[15];
    int   pages;
    float price;
};
struct book_bank book1, book2, book3;
```

Remember that the members of a structure themselves are not variables. They do not occupy any memory until they are associated with the structure variables such as **book1**.

In defining a structure you may note the following syntax:

1. The template is terminated with a semicolon.
2. While the entire declaration is considered as a statement, each member is declared independently for its name and type in a separate statement inside the template.
3. The tag name such as **book_bank** can be used to declare structure variables of its type, later in the program.

It is also allowed to combine both the template declaration and variables declaration in one statement. The declaration

```
struct book_bank
{
    char title[20];
    char author[15];
    int pages;
    float price;
} book1, book2, book3;
```

is valid. The use of tag name is optional. For example,

```
struct
{
    ........
    ........
    ........
} book1, book2, book3;
```

declares **book1**, **book2**, and **book3** as structure variables representing three books, but does not include a tag name for later use in declarations.

Normally, structure definitions appear at the beginning of the program file, before any variables or functions are defined. They may also appear before the **main**, along with macro definitions, such as **#define**. In such cases, the definition is *global* and can be used by other functions as well.

10.3 GIVING VALUES TO MEMBERS

We can assign values to the members of a structure in a number of ways. As mentioned earlier, the members themselves are not variables. They should be linked to the structure variables in order to make them meaningful members. For example, the word **title**, has no meaning where as the phrase 'title of book3' has a meaning. The link between a member and a variable is established using the *member operator* '.' which is also known as 'dot operator' or 'period operator'. For example,

```
book1.price
```

is the variable representing the price of **book1** and can be treated like any other ordinary variable. Here is how we would assign values to the members of **book1**:

```
strcpy(book1.title, "BASIC");
strcpy(book1.author, "Balagurusamy");
book1.pages = 250;
book1.price = 28.50;
```

We can also use **scanf** to give the values through the keyboard.

```
scanf("%s\n", book1.title);
scanf("%d\n", &book1.pages);
```

are valid input statements.

Example 10.1

Define a structure type, **struct personal**, that would contain person name, date of joining and salary. Using this structure, write a program to read this information for one person from the keyboard and print the same on the screen.

Structure definition along with the program is shown in Fig. 10.1. The **scanf** and **printf** functions illustrate how the member operator '.' is used to link the structure members to the structure variables. The variable name with a period and the member name is used like an ordinary variable.

```
Program
/*****************************************************************/
/* DEFINING AND ASSIGNING VALUES TO STRUCTURE MEMBERS */
/*****************************************************************/
struct personal
{
      char name[20];
      int   day;
      char month[10];
      int   year;
      float salary;
};
main( )
{
      struct personal person;

      printf("Input Values\n");
      scanf("%s %d %s %d %f",
                  person.name,
                  &person.day,
                  person.month,
                  &person.year,
                  &person.salary);
      printf("%s %d %s %d %.2f\n",
                  person.name,
                  person.day,
                  person.month,
                  person.year,
                  person.salary);
}

Output
Input Values

M.L.Goel 10 January 1945 4500
M.L.Goel 10 January 1945 4500.00
```

Fig. 10.1 *Defining and accessing structure members*

10.4 STRUCTURE INITIALIZATION

Like any other data type, a structure variable can be initialized. However, a structure must be declared as **static** if it is to be initialized inside a function (similar to arrays).

Note: This condition is not applicable to ANSI compilers. The ANSI standard permits initialization of structure variables with **auto** storage class. We could therefore delete the word **static** when using ANSI compilers. However, the use of the keyword **static** in the programs would enable us to run them under both the old and ANSI standard compilers.

```
                              main( )
                              {
                                  static struct
                                  {
                                      int weight;
                                      float height;
                                  }
                                  student = {60, 180.75};
                                  .....
                                  .....
                              }
```

This assigns the value 60 to **student.weight** and 180.75 to **student.height**. There is a one-to-one correspondence between the members and their initializing values.

A lot of variation is possible in initializing a structure. The following statements initialize two structure variables. Here, it is essential to use a tag name.

```
                              main( )
                              {
                                  struct st_record
                                  {
                                      int    weight;
                                      float  height;
                                  };
                                  static struct st_record student1 = { 60, 180.75 };
                                  static struct st_record student2 = { 53, 170.60 };
                                  .....
                                  .....
                              }
```

Another method is to initialize a structure variable outside the function as shown below:

```
                          struct st_record        /*  No static word   */
                          {
                              int    weight;
                              float  height;
                          }  student1  =  {60, 180.75};
                          main( )
                          {
                              static struct st_record student2  =  {53, 170.60};
                              .....
                              .....
                          }
```

C language does not permit the initialization of individual structure members within the template. The initialization must be done only in the declaration of the actual variables.

10.5 COMPARISON OF STRUCTURE VARIABLES

Two variables of the same structure type can be compared the same way as ordinary variables. If **person1** and **person2** belong to the same structure, then the following operations are valid:

Operation	Meaning
person1 = person2	Assign **person2** to **person1**.
person1 == person2	Compare all members of **person1** and **person2** and return 1 if they are equal, 0 otherwise.
person1 != person2	Return 1 if all the members are not equal, 0 otherwise.

Note that not all compilers support these operations. For example, Microsoft C version does not permit any logical operations on structure variables. In such cases, individual members can be compared using logical operators.

Example 10.2

Write a program to illustrate the comparison of structure variables.

The program shown in Fig. 10.2 illustrates how a structure variable can be copied into another of the same type. It also performs member-wise comparison to decide whether two structure variables are identical.

10.6 ARRAYS OF STRUCTURES

We use structures to describe the format of a number of related variables. For example, in analysing the marks obtained by a class of students, we may use a template to describe student name and marks obtained in various subjects and then declare all the students as structure variables. In such cases, we may declare an array of structures, each element of the array representing a structure variable. For example,

struct class student[100];

defines an array called **student**, that consists of 100 elements. Each element is defined to be of the type **struct class**. Consider the following declaration:

```
struct marks
{
        int   subject1;
        int   subject2;
        int   subject3;
};
main( )
{
        static struct marks student[3] =
                {{45,68,81}, {75,53,69}, {57,36,71}};
```

This declares the **student** as an array of three elements **student[0]**, **student[1]**, and **student[2]** and initializes their members as follows:

student[0].subject1 = 45;
student[0].subject2 = 68;
....
....
student[2].subject3 = 71;

Program

```
/******************************************************************/
/*            COMPARISON OF STRUCTURE VARIABLES               */
/******************************************************************/
struct class
{
    int number;
    char name[20];
    float marks;
};
main( )
{
    int  x;
    static struct class student1 = {111,"Rao",72.50};
    static struct class student2 = {222,"Reddy", 67.00};
    struct class student3;

    student3 = student2;

    x = ( (student3.number  ==  student2.number) &&
        (student3.marks    ==  student2.marks)) ? 1 : 0;

    if(x  ==  1)
    {
        printf("\nstudent2 and student3 are same\n\n");
        printf("%d %s %f\n", student3.number,
                             student3.name,
                             student3.marks);
    }
    else
        printf("\nstudent2 and student3 are different\n\n");

}
```

Output

student2 and student3 are same

222 Reddy 67.000000

Fig. 10.2 *Comparing and copying structure variables*

Note that the array is declared just as it would have been, with any other array. Since **student** is an array, we use the usual array-accessing methods to access individual elements and then the member operator to access members.

An array of structures is stored inside the memory in the same way as a multi-dimensional array. The array **student** actually looks as shown in Fig. 10.3.

Example 10.3

For the **student** array discussed above, write a program to calculate the subject-wise and student-wise totals and store them as a part of the structure.

---

student[0].subject1	45
.subject2	68
.subject3	81
student[1].subject1	75
.subject2	53
.subject3	69
student[2].subject1	57
.subject2	36
.subject3	71

Fig. 10.3 *The array **student** inside memory*

The program is shown in Fig. 10.4. We have declared a four-member structure, the fourth one for keeping the student-totals. We have also declared an array **total** to keep the subject-totals and the grand-total. The grand-total is given by **total.total**. Note that a member name can be any valid C name and can be the same as an existing structure variable name. The linked name **total.total** represents the **total** member of the structure variable **total**.

```
Program
/****************************************************************************/
/*                    ARRAYS OF STRUCTURES                                 */
/****************************************************************************/
struct marks
{
     int   sub1;
     int   sub2;
     int   sub3;
     int   total;
};

main( )
{
     int   i;
     static struct marks student[3] = { {45,67,81,0},
                                         {75,53,69,0},
                                         {57,36,71,0} };
     static struct marks total;
     for(i  =  0; i  <=  2; i++)
     {
          student[i].total  =  student[i].sub1 +
```

```
                              student[i].sub2 +
                              student[i].sub3;
              total.sub1  = total.sub1 + student[i].sub1;
              total.sub2  = total.sub2 + student[i].sub2;
              total.sub3  = total.sub3 + student[i].sub3;
              total.total = total.total + student[i].total;
    }
    printf(" STUDENT               TOTAL\n\n");
    for(i = 0; i <= 2; i++)
       printf("Student[%d]           %d\n", i+1,student[i].total);
    printf("\n SUBJECT               TOTAL\n\n");

       printf("%s        %d\n%s        %d\n%s         %d\n",
              "Subject 1   ",   total.sub1,
              "Subject 2   ",   total.sub2,
              "Subject 3   ",   total.sub3);

       printf("\nGrand Total = %d\n", total.total);
    }
```

Output

STUDENT   TOTAL

Student[1]   193
Student[2]   197
Student[3]   164

SUBJECT   TOTAL

Subject 1   177
Subject 2   156
Subject 3   221

Grand Total = 554

Fig. 10.4 *Illustration of subscripted structure variables*

10.7 ARRAYS WITHIN STRUCTURES

C permits the use of arrays as structure members. We have already used arrays of characters inside a structure. Similarly, we can use single- or multi-dimensional arrays of type **int** or **float**. For example, the following structure declaration is valid:

```
            struct marks
            {
              int    number;
              float subject[3];
            } student[2];
```

Here, the member **subject** contains three elements, **subject[0]**, **subject[1]** and **subject[2]**. These elements can be accessed using appropriate subscripts. For example, the name

student[1].subject[2];

would refer to the marks obtained in the third subject by the second student.

Example 10.4

Rewrite the program of Example 10.3 using an array member to represent the three subjects.

The modified program is shown in Fig. 10.5. You may notice that the use of array name for subjects has simplified the code.

10.8 STRUCTURES WITHIN STRUCTURES

Structures within a structure means nesting of structures. Nesting of structures is permitted in C. Let us consider the following structure defined to store information about the salary of employees.

```
struct salary
{
    char      name[20];
    char      department[10];
    int       basic_pay;
    int       dearness_allowance;
    int       house_rent_allowance;
    int       city_allowance;
}
employee;
```

This structure defines name, department, basic pay and three kinds of allowances. We can group all the items related to allowance together and declare them under a substructure as shown below:

```
struct salary
{
    char   name[20];
    char   department[10];
    struct
    {
        int   dearness;
        int   house_rent;
        int   city;
    }
    allowance;
}
employee;
```

The salary structure contains a member named **allowance** which itself is a structure with three members. The members contained in the inner structure namely **dearness**, **house_rent**, and **city** can be referred to as

```
employee.allowance.dearness
employee.allowance.house_rent
employee.allowance.city
```

An inner-most member in a nested structure can be accessed by chaining all the concerned

Program

```
/*************************************************************************/
/*                ARRAYS WITHIN A STRUCTURE                         */
/*************************************************************************/
main( )
{
    struct   marks
    {
      int   sub[3];
      int   total;
    };
    static struct marks student[3]  =
    {45,67,81,0,75,53,69,0,57,36,71,0};
    static struct marks total;
    int   i,j;

    for(i  =  0; i  <= 2; i++)
    {
      for(j  =  0; j  <=  2; j++)
      {
        student[i].total  +=  student[i].sub[j];
        total.sub[j]  +=  student[i].sub[j];
      }
      total.total  +=  student[i].total;
    }
    printf("STUDENT              TOTAL\n\n");
    for(i  =  0; i  <=  2; i++)
      printf("Student[%d]            %d\n", i+1, student[i].total);

    printf("\nSUBJECT            TOTAL\n\n");
    for(j  =  0; j  <=  2; j++)
      printf("Subject-%d            %d\n", j+1, total.sub[j]);

    printf("\nGrand Total  =        %d\n", total.total);
}
```

Output

STUDENT	TOTAL
Student[1]	193
Student[2]	197
Student[3]	164

SUBJECT	TOTAL
Subject-1	177
Subject-2	156
Subject-3	221
Grand Total =	554

Fig. 10.5 *Use of subscripted members in structures*

structure variables (from outer-most to inner-most) with the member using dot operator. The
following being invalid:

employee.allowance   (actual member is missing)

employee.house_rent   (inner structure variable
                                          is missing)

An inner structure can have more than one variable. The following form of declaration is legal:

```
struct salary
{
    ....
    struct
    {
        int   dearness;
        ....
    }
    allowance,
    arrears;
}
employee[100];
```

The inner structure has two variables, **allowance** and **arrears**. This implies that both of them have the same structure template. Note the comma after the name **allowance**. A base member can be accessed as follows:

```
employee[1].allowance.dearness
employee[1].arrears.dearness
```

We can also use tag names to define inner structures. Example:

```
struct pay
{
    int   dearness;
    int   house_rent;
    int   city;
};
struct salary
{
    char   name[20];
    char   department[10];
    struct pay allowance;
    struct pay arrears;
};
struct salary employee[100];
```

pay template is defined outside the **salary** template and is used to define the structure of **allowance** and **arrears** inside the **salary** structure.

It is also permissible to nest more than one type of structures.

```
struct personal_record
{
    struct name_part name;
    struct addr_part address;
    struct date date_of_birth;
    .....
    .....
};
struct personal_record person1;
```

The first member of this structure is **name** which is of the type **struct name_part**. Similarly, other members have their structure types.

10.9 STRUCTURES AND FUNCTIONS

We know that the main philosophy of C language is the use of functions. Therefore, it is natural that C supports the passing of structure values as arguments to functions. There are three methods by which the values of a structure can be transferred from one function to another.

The first method is to pass each member of the structure as an actual argument of the function call. The actual arguments are then treated independently like ordinary variables. This is the most elementary method and becomes unmanageable and inefficient when the structure size is large.

The second method involves passing of a copy of the entire structure to the called function. Since the function is working on a copy of the structure, any changes to structure members within the function are not reflected in the original structure (in the calling function). It is, therefore, necessary for the function to return the entire structure back to the calling function. All compilers may not support this method of passing the entire structure as a parameter.

The third approach employs a concept called *pointers* to pass the structure as an argument. In this case, the address location of the structure is passed to the called function. The function can access indirectly the entire structure and work on it. This is similar to the way arrays are passed to functions. This method is more efficient as compared to the second one.

In this section, we discuss in detail the second method, while the third approach using pointers is discussed in the next chapter, where pointers are dealt in detail.

The general format of sending a copy of a structure to the called function is:

> *function name (structure variable name)*

The called function takes the following form:

```
data_type function name(st_name)
struct_type st_name;
{
      ......
      ......
      return(expression);
}
```

The following points are important to note:

1. The called function must be declared for its type, appropriate to the data type it is expected to return. For example, if it is returning a copy of the entire structure, then it must be declared as **struct** with an appropriate tag name.
2. The structure variable used as the actual argument and the corresponding formal argument in the called function must be of the same **struct** type.
3. The **return** statement is necessary only when the function is returning some data. The *expression* may be any simple variable or structure variable or an expression using simple variables.

4. When a function returns a structure, it must be assigned to a structure of identical type in the calling function.
5. The called function must be declared in the calling function for its type, if it is placed after the calling function.

Example 10.5

Write a simple program to illustrate the method of sending an entire structure as a parameter to a function.

A program to update an item is shown in Fig. 10.6. The function **update** receives a copy of the structure variable **item** as one of its parameters. Note that both the function **update** and the formal parameter **product** are declared as type **struct stores**. It is done so because the function uses the parameter **product** to receive the structure variable **item** and also to return the updated values of **item**.

The function **mul** is of type **float** because it returns the product of **price** and **quantity**. However, the parameter **stock**, which receives the structure variable **item** is declared as type **struct stores**.

The entire structure returned by **update** can be copied into a structure of identical type. The statement

item = update(item,p-increment,q_increment);

replaces the old values of **item** by the new ones.

```
Program
/************************************************************/
/*          STRUCTURES AS FUNCTION PARAMETERS            */
/*             Passing a copy of the entire structure    */
/************************************************************/
struct stores
{
    char name[20];
    float price;
    int   quantity;
};
main( )
{
    struct stores update( );
    float         mul(), p_increment, value;
    int           q_increment;
    static struct stores item = {"XYZ", 25.75, 12};

    printf("\nInput increment values:");
    printf("  price increment and quantity increment\n");
    scanf("%f %d", &p_increment, &q_increment);
/*------------------------------------------------------*/
    item  = update(item, p_increment, q_increment);
/*------------------------------------------------------*/
    printf("Updated values of item\n\n");
    printf("Name       : %s\n",item.name);
```

```
        printf("Price      : %f\n",item.price);
        printf("Quantity   : %d\n",item.quantity);
/* ------------------------------------------------------------------------------------ */
        value  = mul(item);
/* ------------------------------------------------------------------------------------ */
        printf("\nValue of the item = %f\n", value);
}
struct stores update(product, p, q)
struct stores product;
float  p;
int    q;
{
   product.price += p;
   product.quantity += q;
   return(product);
}
float mul(stock)
struct stores stock;
{
   return(stock.price * stock.quantity);
}
```

Output

Input increment values: price increment and quantity increment
10 12
Updated values of item

Name   : XYZ
Price   : 35.750000
Quantity : 24

Value of the item = 858.000000

Fig. 10.6 *Using structure as a function parameter*

You may notice that the template of **stores** is defined before **main()**. This has made the data type **struct stores** as *global* and has enabled the functions **update** and **mul** to make use of this definition.

10.10 UNIONS

Unions are a concept borrowed from structures and therefore follow the same syntax as structures. However, there is major distinction between them in terms of storage. In structures, each member has its own storage location, whereas all the members of a union use the same location. This implies that, although a union may contain many members of different types, it can handle only one member at a time. Like structures, a union can be declared using the keyword **union** as follows:

```
            union item
            {
                int   m;
                float x;
                char c;
            } code;
```

This declares a variable **code** of type **union item**. The union contains three members, each with a different data type. However, we can use only one of them at a time. This is due to the fact that only one location is allocated for a union variable, irrespective of its size.

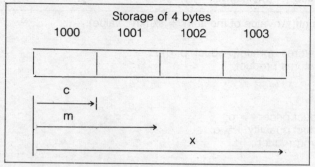

Fig. 10.7 *Sharing of a storage locating by union members*

The compiler allocates a piece of storage that is large enough to hold the largest variable type in the union. In the declaration above, the member **x** requires 4 bytes which is the largest among the members. Figure 10.7 shows how all the three variables share the same address. This assumes that a **float** variable requires 4 bytes of storage.

To access a union member, we can use the same syntax that we use for structure members. That is,

```
code.m
code.x
code.c
```

are all valid member variables. During accessing, we should make sure that we are accessing the member whose value is currently stored. For example, the statements such as

```
code.m  =  379;
code.x  =  7859.36;
printf("%d", code.m);
```

would produce erroneous output (which is machine dependent).

In effect, a union creates a storage location that can be used by any one of its members at a time. When a different member is assigned a new value, the new value supercedes the previous member's value.

Unions may be used in all places where a structure is allowed. The notation for accessing a union member which is nested inside a structure remains the same as for the nested structures.

10.11 SIZE OF STRUCTURES

We normally use structures, unions, and arrays to create variables of large sizes. The actual size of these variables in terms of bytes may change from machine to machine. We may use the unary operator **sizeof** to tell us the size of a structure (or any variable). The expression

$$sizeof\ (\textbf{struct } x)$$

will evaluate the number of bytes required to hold all the members of the structure **x**. If **y** is a simple structure variable of type **struct x**, then the expression

sizeof(y)

would also give the same answer. However, if **y** is an array variable of type **struct x**, then

sizeof(y)

would give the total number of bytes the array **y** requires.

This kind of information would be useful to determine the number of records in a database. For example, the expression

sizeof(y)/**sizeof**(x)

would give the number of elements in the array **y**.

10.12 BIT FIELDS

So far, we have been using integer fields of size 16 bits to store data. There are occasions where data items require much less than 16 bits space. In such cases, we waste memory space. Fortunately, C permits us to use small bit fields to hold data items and thereby to pack several data items in a word of memory. Bit fields allow direct manipulation of string of a string of preselected bits as if it represented an integral quantity.

A bit field is a set of adjacent bits whose size can be from 1 to 16 bits in length. A word can therefore be divided into a number of bit fields. The name and size of bit fields are defined using a structure. The general form of bit field definition is:

```
struct tag-name
{

    data-type   name1: bit-length;
    data-type   name2: bit-length;
    . . . .
    . . . .
    data-type   nameN: bit-length;
}
```

The *data-type* is either **int** or **unsigned int** or **signed int** and the *bit-length* is the number of bits used for the specified name. Remember that a **signed** bit field should have at least 2 bits (one bit for sign). Note that the field name is followed by a colon. The *bit-length* is decided by the range of value to be stored. The largest value that can be stored is 2^{n-1}, where n is bit-length.

The internal representation of bit fields is machine dependent. That is, it depends on the size of **int** and the ordering of bits. Some machines store bits from left to right and others from right to left. The sketch below illustrates the layout of bit fields, assuming a 16-bit word that is ordered from right to left.

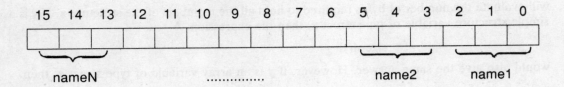

There are several specific points to observe:

1. The first field always starts with the first bit of the word.
2. A bit field cannot overlap integer boundaries. That is, the sum of lengths of all the fields in a structure should not be more than the size of a word. In case, it is more, the overlapping field is automatically forced to the beginning of the next word.
3. There can be unnamed fields declared with size. Example:

Unsigned : *bit-length*;

Such fields provide padding within the word.

4. There can be unused bits in a word.
5. We cannot take the address of a bit field variable. This means we cannot use **scanf** to read values into bit fields. We can neither use pointer to access the bit fields.
6. Bit fields cannot be arrayed.
7. Bit fields should be assigned values that are within the range of their size. If we try to assign larger values, behaviour would be unpredicted.

Suppose, we want to store and use personal information of employees in compressed form. This can be done as follows:

```
struct personal
{
unsigned    sex :        1
unsigned    age :        7
unsigned    m_status:    1
unsigned    children :   3
unsigned         :       4
} emp;
```

This defines a variable name **emp** with four bit fields. The range of values each field could have is as follows:

Bit field	Bit length	Range of values
sex	1	0 or 1
age	7	0 to 127 (2^7-1)
m_status	1	0 or 1
children	3	0 to 7 (2^3-1)

Once bit fields are defined, they can be referenced just as any other structure-type data item would be referenced. The following assignment statements are valid.

```
emp.sex = 1;
emp.age = 50;
```

Remember, we cannot use **scanf** to read values into a bit field. We may have to read into a temporary variable and then assign its value to the bit field. For example:

```
scanf("%d %d", &AGE,&CHILDREN);
emp.age = AGE;
emp.children = CHILDREN;
```

One restriction in accessing bit fields is that a pointer cannot be used. However, they can be used in normal expressions like any other variable. For example,

```
sum = sum + emp.age;
if(emp.m_status)......;
printf("%d\n", emp.age);
```

are valid statements.

It is possible to combine normal structure elements with bit field elements. For example:

```
struct personal
{
    char       name[20];  /* normal variable   */
    struct addr  address;   /* structure variable */
    unsigned    sex : 1;
    unsigned    age : 7;
    . . . .
    . . . .

} emp[100];
```

This declares **emp** as a 100 element array of type **struct personal**. This combines normal variable **name** and structure type variable **address** with bit fields.

Bit fields are packed into words as they appear in the definition. Consider the following definition:

```
struct pack
{
    unsigned  a : 2;
    int    count;
    unsigned  b : 3;
};
```

Here, the bit field **a** will be in one word, the variable **count** will be in the second word and the bit field **b** will be in the third word. The fields **a** and **b** would not get packed into the same word.

CASE STUDY

Book Shop Inventory

A book shop uses a personal computer to maintain the inventory of books that are being sold at the shop. The list includes details such as author, title, price, publisher, stock position, etc. Whenever a customer wants a book, the shop keeper inputs the title and author of the book and the system replies whether it is in the list or not. If it is not, an appropriate message is displayed. If book is in the list, then the system displays the book details and asks for number of copies. If the requested copies are available, the total cost of the books is displayed; otherwise the message "Required copies not in stock" is displayed.

A program to accomplish this is shown in Fig. 10.8. The program uses a template to define the structure of the book. Note that the date of publication, a member of **record** structure, is also defined as a structure.

When the title and author of a book are specified, the program searches for the book in the list using the function

look_up(table, s1, s2, m)

The parameter **table** which receives the structure variable **book** is declared as type **struct record**. The parameters **s1** and **s2** receive the string values of **title** and **author** while **m** receives the total number of books in the list. Total number of books is given by the expression

sizeof(book)/sizeof(struct record)

The search ends when the book is found in the list and the function returns the serial number of the book. The function returns −1 when the book is not found. Remember that the serial number of the first book in the list is zero. The program terminates when we respond "NO" to the question

Do you want any other book?

Note that we use the function

get(string)

to get title, author, etc. from the terminal. This enables us to input strings with spaces such as "C Language". We cannot use **scanf** to read this string since it contains two words.

Since we are reading the quantity as a string using the **get(string)** function, we have to convert it to an integer before using it in any expressions. This is done using the **atoi()** function.

```
Program
/***********************************************************************/
/*                      BOOK SHOP INVENTORY                          */
/***********************************************************************/
#include  <stdio.h>
#include  <string.h>
struct  record
{
     char   author[20];
     char   title[30];
```

```
        float   price;
        struct
        {
          char  month[10];
          int     year;
        }
        date;
        char  publisher[10];
        int     quantity;
};
main( )
{
    char  title[30], author[20];
    int     index, no_of_records, look_up( );
    char  response[10], quantity[10];
    static struct record book[] =  {
    {"Ritche","C Language",45.00,"May",1977,"PHI",10},
    {"Kochan","Programming in C",75.50,"July", 1983,"Hayden",5},
    {"Balagurusamy","BASIC",30.00,"January",1984,"TMH",0},
    {"Balagurusamy","COBOL",60.00,"December",1988,"Macmillan",25}
                                    };
    no_of_records = sizeof(book)/ sizeof(struct record);
    do
    {
      printf("Enter title and author name as per the list\n");
      printf("\nTitle:       ");
      get(title);

      printf("Author:       ");
      get(author);

      index  =  look_up(book, title, author, no_of_records);
      if(index != −1)          /*  Book found  */
      {
        printf("\n%s %s %.2f %s %d %s\n\n",
                book[index].author,
                book[index].title,
                book[index].price,
                book[index].date.month,
                book[index].date.year,
                book[index].publisher);
        printf("Enter number of copies:");
        get(quantity);
        if(atoi(quantity) < book[index].quantity)

          printf("Cost of %d copies = %.2f\n",atoi(quantity),
                book[index].price * atoi(quantity) );
        else
          printf("\nRequired copies not in stock\n\n");
      }
      else
        printf("\nBook not in list\n\n");

      printf("\nDo you want any other book? (YES / NO):");
      get(response);
    }
```

```
            while(response[0] == 'Y' || response[0] == 'y');
            printf("\n\nThank you. Good bye!\n");
}
get(string)
char    string[ ];
{
    char    c;
    int     i = 0;
    do
    {
        c = getchar( );
        string[i++] = c;
    }
    while(c != '\n');
    string[i−1] = '\0';
}
int look_up(table, s1, s2, m)
struct record table[ ];
char    s1[ ], s2[ ];
int     m;
{
    int   i;
    for(i = 0; i < m; i++)
        if(strcmp(s1, table[i].title) == 0 &&
           strcmp(s2, table[i].author) == 0)
           return(i);              /* book found         */
    return(−1);                    /* book not found     */
}
```

Output

Enter title and author name as per the list

Title: BASIC
Author: Balagurusamy

Balagurusamy BASIC 30.00 January 1984 TMH

Enter number of copies:5

Required copies not in stock

Do you.want any other book? (YES / NO):y
Enter title and author name as per the list

Title: COBOL
Author: Balagurusamy

Balagurusamy COBOL 60.00 December 1988 Macmillan

Enter number of copies:7
Cost of 7 copies = 420.00

Do you want any other book? (YES / NO):y
Enter title and author name as per the list

Title: C Programming
Author: Ritche

Book not in list

Do you want any other book? (YES / NO):n

Thank you.   Good bye!

Fig. 10.8 *Program of book shop inventory*

REVIEW QUESTIONS AND EXERCISES

10.1 How does a structure differ from an array?

10.2 Explain the meaning and purpose of the following:

    (a) Template.
    (b) Tag.
    (c) sizeof.
    (d) struct.

10.3 Describe what is wrong in the following structure declaration:

```
                struct
                {
                    int   number;
                    float price;
                }
                main( )
                {
                    .....
                    .....
                }
```

10.4 The following code appears at the beginning of a function. Identify errors, if any, in the code.

```
                static int count[ ]  =  {
                        10, 15, 20, 30;
                        float value;
```

10.5 What is meant by the following terms?

    (a) Nested structure.
    (b) Array of structures.

10.6 Define a structure that can describe a hotel. It should have members that include the name, address, grade, average room charge, and number of rooms.

    Write functions to perform the following operations:

    (a) To print out hotels of a given grade in order of charges.
    (b) To print out hotels with room charges less than a given value.

10.7 Define a structure called **cricket** that will describe the following informaton:

        player name
        team name
        batting average

using **cricket**, declare an array **player** with 50 elements and write a program to read the information about all the 50 players and print a team-wise list containing names of players with their batting average.

10.8   Rewrite the programs in Fig. 10.6 and Fig 10.8 using ANSI function prototypes.

POINTERS

11.1 INTRODUCTION

Pointers are another important feature of C language. Although they may appear a little confusing for a beginner, they are a powerful tool and handy to use once they are mastered. There are a number of reasons for using pointers.

1. A pointer enables us to access a variable that is defined outside the function.
2. Pointers are more efficient in handling the data tables.
3. Pointers reduce the length and complexity of a program.
4. They increase the execution speed.
5. The use of a pointer array to character strings results in saving of data storage space in memory.

The real power of C lies in the proper use of pointers. In this chapter, we will examine the pointers in detail and learn how to use them in program development.

11.2 UNDERSTANDING POINTERS

As you know, computers use their memory for storing the instructions of a program, as well as the values of the variables that are associated with it. The computer's memory is a sequential collection of 'storage cells' as shown in Fig. 11.1. Each cell, commonly known as a *byte*, has a number called *address* associated with it. Typically, the addresses are numbered consecutively, starting from zero. The last address depends on the memory size. A computer system having 64 K memory will have its last address as 65,535.

Whenever we declare a variable, the system allocates, somewhere in the memory, an appropriate location to hold the value of the variable. Since, every byte has a unique address number, this location will have its own address number. Consider the following statement:

int   quantity = 179;

This statement instructs the system to find a location for the integer variable **quantity** and puts the value 179 in that location. Let us assume that the system has chosen the address location 5000 for **quantity**. We may represent this as shown in Fig. 11.2.

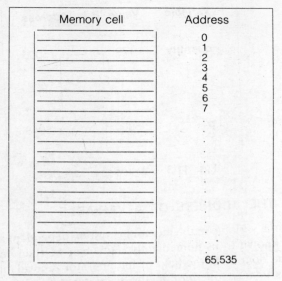

Fig. 11.1 *Memory organization*

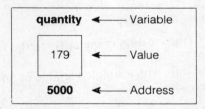

Fig. 11.2 *Representation of a variable*

During execution of the program, the system always associates the name **quantity** with the address 5000. (This is something similar to having a house number as well as a house name.) We may have access to the value 179 by using either the name **quantity** or the address 5000. Since memory addresses are simply numbers, they can be assigned to some variables which can be stored in memory, like any other variable. Such variables that hold memory addresses are called *pointers*. A pointer is, therefore, nothing but a variable that contains an address which is a location of another variable in memory.

Remember, since a pointer is a variable, its value is also stored in the memory in another location. Suppose, we assign the address of **quantity** to a variable **p**. The link between the variables **p** and **quantity** can be visualized as shown in Fig. 11.3. The address of **p** is 5048.

Since the value of the variable **p** is the address of the variable **quantity**, we may access the value of **quantity** by using the value of **p** and therefore, we say that the variable **p** 'points' to the variable **quantity**. Thus, **p** gets the name 'pointer'.

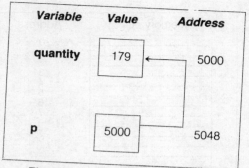

Fig. 11.3 *Pointer as a variable*

11.3 ACCESSING THE ADDRESS OF A VARIABLE

The actual location of a variable in the memory is system dependent and therefore, the address of a variable is not known to us immediately. How can we then determine the address of a variable? This can be done with the help of the operator **&** available in C. We have already seen the use of this *address operator* in the **scanf** function. The operator **&** immediately preceding a variable returns the address of the variable associated with it. For example, the statement

p = &quantity;

would assign the address 5000 (the location of **quantity**) to the variable **p**. The **&** operator can be remembered as 'address of'.

The **&** operator can be used only with a simple variable or an array element. The following are illegal use of address operator:

1. **&125**   (pointing at constants).
2. int x[10];
    &x   (pointing at array names)
3. **&(x+y)**   (pointing at expressions).

If **x** is an array, then expressions such as

&x[0] and &x[i+3]

are valid and represent the addresses of 0th and (i+3)th elements of **x**.

Example 11.1

Write a program to print the address of a variable along with its value.

The program shown in Fig. 11.4, declares and initializes four variables and then prints out these values with their respective storage locations. Notice that we have used %u format for printing address values. Memory addresses are unsigned integers.

```
Program
/**********************************************************/
/*           ACCESSING ADDRESSES OF VARIABLES           */
/**********************************************************/
main( )
{
      char a;
      int   x;
      float p, q;
      a  =  'A';
      x  =  125;
      p  =  10.25, q = 18.76;
      printf("%c is stored at addr %u.\n", a, &a);
      printf("%d is stored at addr %u.\n", x, &x);
      printf("%f is stored at addr %u.\n", p, &p);
      printf("%f is stored at addr %u.\n", q, &q);
}
Output
A is stored at addr 4436.
125 is stored at addr 4434.
10.250000 is stored at addr 4442.
18.760000 is stored at addr 4438.
```

Fig. 11.4 *Accessing the address of a variable*

11.4 DECLARING AND INITIALIZING POINTERS

In C, every variable must be declared for its type. Since pointer variables contain addresses that belong to a separate data type, they must be declared as pointers before we use them. The declaration of a pointer variable takes the following form:

> *data type*   *pt_name;

This tells the compiler three things about the variable **pt_name**.

1. The asterisk (*) tells that the variable **pt_name** is a pointer variable.
2. **pt_name** needs a memory location.
3. **pt_name** points to a variable of type *data type*.

For example,

int *p;

declares the variable **p** as a pointer variable that points to an integer data type. Remember that the type **int** refers to the data type of the variable being pointed to by **p** and not the type of the value of the pointer. Similarly, the statement

float *x;

declares x as a pointer to a floating point variable.

Once a pointer variable has been declared, it can be made to point to a variable using an assignment statement such as

p = &quantity;

which causes **p** to point to **quantity**. That is, **p** now contains the address of **quantity**. This is known as pointer *initialization*. Before a pointer is initialized, it should not be used.

We must ensure that the pointer variables always point to the corresponding type of data. For example,

```
float  a, b;
int    x, *p;
p   =&a;
b   =*p;
```

will result in erroneous output because we are trying to assign the address of a **float** variable to an integer pointer. When we declare a pointer to be of **int** type, the system assumes that any address that the pointer will hold will point to an integer variable. Since the compiler will not detect such errors, care should be taken to avoid wrong pointer assignments.

And also assigning an absolute address to a pointer variable is prohibited. The following is wrong.

```
int  *ptr;
....
ptr = 5368;
....
....
```

A pointer variable can be initialized in its declaration itself. For example,

int   x, *p = &x;

is perfectly valid. It declares **x** as an integer variable and **p** as a pointer variable and then initializes **p** to the address of **x**. Note carefully that this is an initialization of **p**, not *p. And also remember that the target variable **x** is declared first. The statement

int   *p = &x, x;

is not valid.

11.5 ACCESSING A VARIABLE THROUGH ITS POINTER

Once a pointer has been assigned the address of a variable, the question remains as to how to access the value of the variable using the pointer. This is done by using another unary operator * (asterisk), usually known as the *indirection* operator. Consider the following statements:

```
int   quantity, *p, n;

quantity = 179;
p = &quantity;
n = *p;
```

The first line declares **quantity** and **n** as integer variables and **p** as a pointer variable pointing to an integer. The second line assigns the value 179 to **quantity** and the third line assigns the address of **quantity** to the pointer variable **p**. The fourth line contains the indirection operator *. When the operator * is placed before a pointer variable in an expression (on the right-hand side of the equal sign), the pointer returns the value of the variable of which the pointer value is the address. In this case, ***p** returns the value of the variable **quantity**, because **p** is the address of **quantity**. The * can be remembered as 'value at address'. Thus the value of **n** would be 179. The two statements

$$p = \&quantity;$$
$$n = *p;$$

are equivalent to

$$n = *\&quantity;$$

which in turn is equivalent to

$$n = quantity;$$

In C, the assignment of pointers and addresses is always done symbolically, by means of symbolic names. You cannot access the value stored at the address 5368 by writing *5368. It will not work. Example 11.2 illustrates the distinction between pointer value and the value it points to.

Example 11.2

Write a program to illustrate the use of indirection operator '*' to access the value pointed to by a printer.

The program and output are shown in Fig. 11.5. The program clearly shows how we can access the value of a variable using a pointer. You may notice that the value of the pointer **ptr** is 4104 and the value it points to is 10. Further, you may also note the following equivalences:

$$x = *(\&x) = *ptr = y$$
$$\&x = \&*ptr$$

```
Program
/**************************************************************************/
/*                ACCESSING VARIABLES USING POINTERS              */
/**************************************************************************/
main( )
{
     int   x, y;
     int   *ptr;

     x = 10;
     ptr = &x;
     y = *ptr;

     printf("Value of x is %d\n\n",x);
     printf("%d is stored at addr %u\n", x, &x);
     printf("%d is stored at addr %u\n", *&x, &x);
     printf("%d is stored at addr %u\n", *ptr, ptr);
     printf("%d is stored at addr %u\n", y, &*ptr);
```

```
        printf("%d is stored at addr %u\n", ptr, &ptr);
        printf("%d is stored at addr %u\n", y, &y);

        *ptr = 25;
        printf("\nNow x = %d\n",x);
}
```
Output

Value of x is 10

10 is stored at addr 4104
10 is stored at addr 4104
10 is stored at addr 4104
10 is stored at addr 4104
4104 is stored at addr 4106
10 is stored at addr 4108

Now x = 25

Fig. 11.5 *Accessing a variable through its pointer*

The actions performed by the program are illustrated in Fig. 11.6. The statement **ptr = &x** assigns the address of **x** to **ptr** and **y = *ptr** assigns the value pointed to by the pointer **ptr** to **y**.

Note the use of the assignment statement

*ptr = 25;

This statement puts the value of 25 at the memory location whose address is the value of **ptr**. We know that the value of **ptr** is the address of **x** and therefore the old value of **x** is replaced by 25. This, in effect, is equivalent to assigning 25 to **x**. This shows how we can change the value of a variable *indirectly* using a pointer and the *indirection operator*.

11.6 POINTER EXPRESSIONS

Like other variables, pointer variables can be used in expressions. For example, if **p1** and **p2** are properly declared and initialized pointers, then the following statements are valid.

```
y    = *p1 * *p2;          same as      (*p1) * (*p2)
sum  = sum + *p1;
z    = 5* - *p2/ *p1;      same as      (5 * (−(*p2) ))/(*p1)
*p2  = *p2 + 10;
```

Note that there is a blank space between / and * in the item3 above. The following is wrong.

```
z = 5* − *p2 /*p1;
```

The symbol /* is considered as the beginning of a comment and therefore the statement fails.

C allows us to add integers to or subtract integers from pointers, as well as to subtract one pointer from another. p1 + 4, p2 − 2 and p1 − p2 are all allowed. If **p1** and **p2** are both pointers to the same array, then **p2 − p1** gives the number of elements between **p1** and **p2**.

We may also use short-hand operators with the pointers.

```
p1++;
−−p2;
sum += *p2;
```

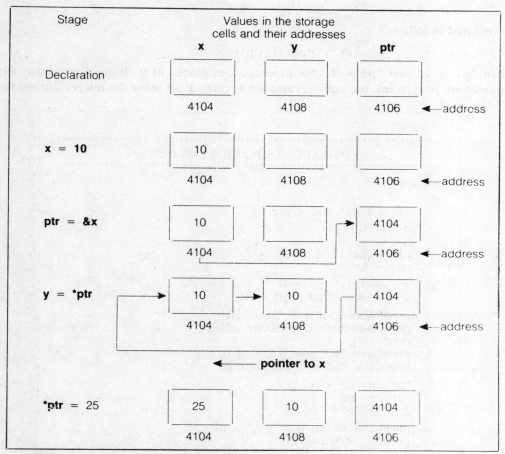

Fig 11.6 *Illustration of pointer assignments*

In addition to arithmetic operations discussed above, pointers can also be compared using the relational operators. The expressions such as **p1 > p2**, **p1 == p2**, and **p1 != p2** are allowed. However, any comparison of pointers that refer to separate and unrelated variables makes no sense. Comparisons can be used meaningfully in handling arrays and strings.

We may not use pointers in division or multiplication. For example, expressions such as

$$\textbf{p1 / p2 or p1 * p2 or p1 / 3}$$

are not allowed. Similarly, two pointers cannot be added. That is, **p1 + p2** is illegal.

Example 11.3

Write a program to illustrate the use of pointers in arithmetic operations.

The program in Fig. 11.7 shows how the pointer variables can be directly used in expressions. It also illustrates the order of evaluation of expressions. For example, the expression

$$4* \ - \ *p2 \ / \ *p1 \ + \ 10$$

is evaluated as follows:

$$((4 * (-(*p2))) / (*p1)) + 10$$

When $*p1 = 12$ and $*p2 = 4$, this expression evaluates to 9. Remember, since all the variables are of type **int**, the entire evaluation is carried out using the integer arithmetic.

```
Program
/****************************************************************/
/*              ILLUSTRATION OF POINTER EXPRESSIONS            */
/****************************************************************/
main( )
{
    int    a, b, *p1, *p2, x, y, z;
    a    = 12;
    b    = 4;
    p1   = &a;
    p2   = &b;

    x    = *p1 * *p2 - 6;
    y    = 4* - *p2 / *p1 + 10;

    printf("Address of a = %u\n", p1);
    printf("Address of b = %u\n", p2);
    printf("\n");
    printf("a = %d, b = %d\n", a, b);
    printf("x = %d, y = %d\n", x, y);

    *p2  = *p2 + 3;
    *p1  = *p2 - 5;
    z    = *p1 * *p2 -6;

    printf("\na = %d, b = %d,", a, b);
    printf(" z = %d\n", z);

}
Output
Address of a = 4020
Address of b = 4016

a = 12, b = 4
x = 42, y = 9
a = 2, b = 7, z = 8
```

Fig. 11.7 *Evaluation of pointer expressions*

11.7 POINTER INCREMENTS AND SCALE FACTOR

We have seen that the pointers can be incremented like

$$\textbf{p1 = p2 + 2;}$$
$$\textbf{p1 = p1 + 1;}$$

and so on. Remember, however, an expression like

$$\textbf{p1++;}$$

will cause the pointer **p1** to point to the next value of its type. For example, if **p1** is an integer pointer with an initial value, say 2800, then after the operation **p1 = p1 + 1**, the value of **p1** will be 2802, and not 2801. That is, when we increment a pointer, its value is increased by the length of the data type that it points to. This length is called the *scale factor*. ✓

For an IBM PC, the lengths of various data types are as follows:

characters	1 byte
integers	2 byte
floats	4 bytes
long integers	4 bytes
doubles	8 bytes

The number of bytes used to store various data types depends on the system and can be found by making use of the **sizeof** operator. For example, if **x** is a variable, then **sizeof(x)** returns the number of bytes needed for the varible.

11.8 POINTERS AND ARRAYS

When an array is declared, the compiler allocates a base address and sufficient amount of storage to contain all the elements of the array in contiguous memory locations. The base address is the location of the first element (index 0) of the array. The compiler also defines the array name as a constant pointer to the first element. Suppose we declare an array **x** as follows:

$$\textbf{static int x[5] = \{1, 2, 3, 4, 5\};}$$

Suppose the base address of **x** is 1000 and assuming that each integer requires two bytes, the five elements will be stored as follows:

Elements ⟶	x[0]	x[1]	x[2]	x[3]	x[4]
Value ⟶	1	2	3	4	5
Address ⟶	1000	1002	1004	1006	1008

└── Base address

The name **x** is defined as a constant pointer pointing to the first element, **x[0]** and therefore the value of **x** is 1000, the location where **x[0]** is stored. That is,

$$x = \&x[0] = 1000$$

If we declare **p** as an integer pointer, then we can make the pointer **p** to point to the array **x** by the following assignment:

$$\textbf{p = x;}$$

This is equivalent to

$$\textbf{p = \&x[0];}$$

(ANSI standard permits a pointer to an array to be obtained by applying the **&** operator to the array name itself.)

Now, we can access every value of **x** using **p++** to move from one element to another. The relationship between **p** and **x** is shown below:

```
p     = &x[0] (= 1000)
p+1   = &x[1] (= 1002)
p+2   = &x[2] (= 1004)
p+3   = &x[3] (= 1006)
p+4   = &x[4] (= 1008)
```

You may notice that the address of an element is calculated using its index and the scale factor of the data type. For instance,

$$\text{address of } \mathbf{x[3]} = \text{base address} + (3 \times \text{scale factor of } \mathbf{int})$$
$$= 1000 + (3 \times 2) = 1006$$

When handling arrays, instead of using array indexing, we can use pointers to access array elements. Note that *(p+3) gives the value of x[3]. The pointer accessing method is much faster than array indexing.

The example 11.4 illustrates the use of pointer accessing method.

Example 11.4

Write a program using pointers to compute the sum of all elements stored in an array.

The program shown in Fig. 11.8 illustrates how a pointer can be used to traverse an array. Since incrementing an array pointer causes it to point to the next element, we need only to add one to p each time we go through the loop.

```
Program
/*********************************************************************/
/*              POINTERS IN ONE-DIMENSIONAL ARRAY                  */
/*********************************************************************/
main( )
{
     int *p, sum, i;
     static int x[5] = {5,9,6,3,7};
     i = 0;
     p = x;
     sum = 0;
     printf("Element   Value   Address\n\n");
     while(i < 5)
     {
       printf("  x[%d]      %d      %u\n", i, *p, p);
       sum = sum + *p;
       i++, p++;
     }
     printf("\n  Sum    = %d\n", sum);
     printf("\n  &x[0]  = %u\n", &x[0]);
     printf("\n  p      = %u\n", p);
}

Output
Element          Value        Address
  x[0]             5            166
  x[1]             9            168
```

x[2]	6	170
x[3]	3	172
x[4]	7	174
Sum	= 55	
&x[0]	= 166	
p	= 176	

Fig. 11.8 *Accessing array elements using the pointer*

It is possible to avoid the loop control variable **i** as shown below:

```
    .....
    p = x;
    while(p <= &x[4])
    {
        sum += *p;
        p++;
    }
    .....
```

Here, we compare the pointer **p** with the address of the last element to determine when the array has been traversed.

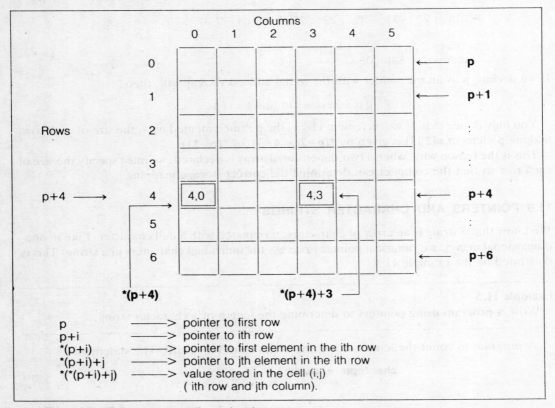

```
p             ——————> pointer to first row
p+i           ——————> pointer to ith row
*(p+i)        ——————> pointer to first element in the ith row
*(p+i)+j      ——————> pointer to jth element in the ith row
*(*(p+i)+j)   ——————> value stored in the cell (i,j)
                      ( ith row and jth column).
```

Fig. 11.9 *Pointers to two-dimensional arrays*

Pointers can be used to manipulate two-dimensional arrays as well. We know that in a one-dimensional array **x**, the expression

$$\text{*(x+i)} \quad \text{or} \quad \text{*(p+i)}$$

represents the element **x[i]**. Similarly, an element in a two-dimensional array can be represented by the pointer expression as follows:

$$\text{*(*(a+i)+j)} \quad \text{or} \quad \text{*(*(p+i)+j)}$$

Figure 11.9 illustrates how this expression represents the element **a[i][j]**. The base address of the array **a** is &a[0][0] and starting at this address, the compiler allocates contiguous space for all the elements, *row-wise*. That is, the first element of the second row is placed immediately after the last element of the first row, and so on. Suppose we declare an array **a** as follows:

```
int a[3][4] = {{15,27,11,35},
               {22,19,31,17},
               {31,23,14,36}
              };
```

The elements of **a** will be stored as shown below:

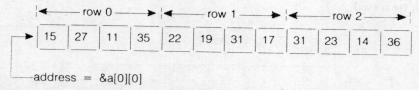

If we declare **p** as an **int** pointer with the initial address of &a[0][0], then

$$\text{a[i][j] is equivalent to *(p+4 x i+j)}$$

You may notice that, if we increment **i** by 1, the **p** is incremented by 4, the size of each row, making **p** element **a[2][3]** is given by *(p+2 × 4+3) = *(p+11).

This is the reason why, when a two-dimensional array is declared, we must specify the size of each row so that the compiler can determine the correct storage mapping.

11.9 POINTERS AND CHARACTER STRINGS

We know that a string is an array of characters, terminated with a null character. Like in one-dimensional arrays, we can use a pointer to access the individual characters in a string. This is illustrated by the example 11.5.

Example 11.5

Write a program using pointers to determine the length of a character string.

A program to count the length of a string is shown in Fig. 11.10. The statement

char *cptr = name;

```
Program
/***********************************************************************/
/*                  POINTERS AND CHARACTER STRINGS                   */
/***********************************************************************/

main( )
{
     char *name;
     int    length;
     char *cptr  =  name;

     name  =  "DELHI";

     while(*cptr != '\0')
     {
          printf("%c is stored at address %u\n", *cptr, cptr);
          cptr++;
     }
     length  =  cptr − name;
     printf("\nLength of the string = %d\n", length);
}

Output
D   is stored at address 54
E   is stored at address 55
L   is stored at address 56
H   is stored at address 57
I   is stored at address 58

Length of the string  =  5
```

Fig. 11.10   *String handling by pointers*

declares **cptr** as a pointer to a character and assigns the address of the first character of **name** as the initial value. Since a string is always terminated by the null character, the statement

while(*cptr != '\0')

is true until the end of the string is reached.

When the **while** loop is terminated, the pointer **cptr** holds the address of the null character. Therefore, the statement

length = cptr − name;

gives the length of the string **name**.

The output also shows the address location of each character. Note that each character occupies one memory cell (byte).

In C, a constant character string always represents a pointer to that string. And therefore the following statements are valid:

char *name;
name = "Delhi";

These statements will declare **name** as a pointer to character and assign to **name** the constant character string "Delhi". You might remember that this type of assignment does not apply to character arrays. The statements like

```
char    name[20];
name  =  "Delhi";
```

do not work.

One important use of pointers is in handling of a table of strings. Consider the following array of strings:

```
char    name[3][25];
```

This says that the **name** is a table containing three names, each with a maximum length of 25 characters (including null character). The total storage requirements for the **name** table are 75 bytes.

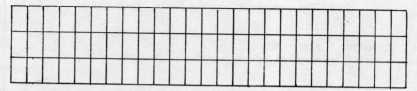

We know that rarely the individual strings will be of equal lengths. Therefore, instead of making each row a fixed number of characters, we can make it a pointer to a string of varying length. For example,

```
static char *name[3]  =  {
                           "New Zealand",
                           "Australia",
                           "India"
                          };
```

declares **name** to be an *array of three pointers* to characters, each pointer pointing to a particular name as shown below:

```
name[0] → New Zealand
name[1] → Australia
name[2] → India
```

This declaration allocates only 28 bytes, sufficient to hold all the characters as shown below:

N	e	w		Z	e	a	l	a	n	d	\0
A	u	s	t	r	a	l	i	a	\0
I	n	d	i	a	\0

The following statement would print out all the three names:

```
for(i = 0; i <=  2; i++)
    printf("%s\n", name[i]);
```

To access the jth character in the ith name, we may write as

$$*(name[i]+j)$$

The character arrays with the rows of varying length are called ragged arrays and are better handled by pointers.

Remember the difference between the notations ***p[3]** and **(*p)[3]**. Since * has a lower precedence than [ ], ***p[3]** declares **p** as an array of 3 pointers while **(*p)[3]** declares **p** as a pointer to an array of three elements.

11.10 POINTERS AND FUNCTIONS

Pointers as Function Arguments

We have noted earlier that when an array is passed to a function as an argument, only the address of the first element of the array is passed, but not the actual values of the array elements. If **x** is an array, when we call **sort(x)**, the address of **x[0]** is passed to the function **sort**. The function uses this address for manipulating the array elements. Similarly, we can pass the address of a variable as an argument to a function in the normal fashion.

When we pass addresses to a function, the parameters receiving the addresses should be pointers. The process of calling a function using pointers to pass the addresses of variable is known as *call by reference*. (You know, the process of passing the acutal value of variables is known as *call by value*.) The function which is called by 'reference' can change the value of the variable used in the call. Consider the following code:

```
main( )
{
    int   x;
    x = 20;
    change(&x);
    printf(" %d \n", x);
}
change(p)
int *p;
{
  *p = *p + 10;
}
```

When the function **change( )** is called, the address of the variable **x**, not its value, is passed into the function **change( )**. Inside **change( )**, the variable **p** is declared as a pointer and therefore **p** is the address of the variable **x**. The statement

$$*p = *p + 10;$$

means 'add 10 to the value stored at the address **p**'. Since **p** represents the address of **x**, the value of **x** is changed from 20 to 30. Therefore, the output of the program will be 30, not 20.

Thus, call by reference provides a mechanism by which the function can change the stored values in the calling function.

Example 11.6
Write a function using pointers to exchange the values stored in two locations in the memory.

The program in Fig. 11.11 shows how the contents of two locations can be exchanged using their address locations. The function **exchange( )** receives the addresses of the variables **x** and **y** and exchanges their contents.

```
Program
/**********************************************************************/
/*               POINTERS AS FUNCTION PARAMETERS              */
/**********************************************************************/
main( )
{
    int    x, y;
    x  =  100;
    y  =  200;
    printf("Before exchange : x  =  %d   y  =  %d\n\n", x, y);
    exchange(&x,&y);
    printf("After exchange    : x  =  %d   y  =  %d\n\n", x, y);
}
exchange(a,b)
int  *a, *b;
{
    int  t;
    t  =  *a;   /* Assign the value at address a to t */
    *a  =  *b; /* put the value at b into a */
    *b  =  t;   /* put t into b */
}

Program
Before exchange :x  =  100   y  =  200
After exchange  :  x  =  200   y  =  100
```

Fig. 11.11 *Passing of pointers as function parameters*

You may note the following points:

1. The function parameters are declared as pointers.
2. The dereferenced pointers are used in the function body.
3. When the function is called, the addresses are passed as actual arguments.

Pointer parameters are commonly employed in string functions. Consider the function **copy** which copies one string to another.

```
copy(s1, s2)
char *s1, *s2;
{
        while( (*s1++  =  *s2++) != '\0')

}
```

This copies the contents of **s2** into the string **s1**. Parameters **s1** and **s2** are the pointers to character strings, whose initial values are passed from the calling function. For example, the calling statement

copy(name1, name2);

will assign the address of the first element of **name1** to **s1** and the address of the first element of **name2** to **s2**.

Note that the value of ***s2++** is the character that **s2** pointed to before **s2** was incremented. Due to the postfix **++**, **s2** is incremented only after the current value has been fetched. Similarly, **s1** is incremented only after the assignment has been completed.

Each character, after it has been copied, is compared with '\0' and therefore copying is terminated as soon as the '\0' is copied.

Pointers to Functions

A function, like a variable, has an address location in the memory. It is therefore, possible to declare a pointer to a function, which can then be used as an argument in another function. A pointer to a function is declared as follows:

type **(*fptr)( );**

This tells the compiler that **fptr** is a pointer to a function which returns *type* value. The parentheses around ***fptr** are necessary. Remember that a statement like

type ***gptr( );**

would declare **gptr** as a function returning a pointer to *type*.

We can make a function pointer to point to a specific function by simply assigning the name of the function to the pointer. For example, the statements

double (*p1)( ), mul( );
p1 = mul;

declare **p1** as a pointer to a function and **mul** as a function and then make **p1** to point to the function **mul**. To call the function **mul**, we may now use the pointer **p1** with the list of parameters. That is,

(*p1)(x,y)

is equivalent to

mul(x,y)

Note the parentheses around ***p1**.

Example 11.7

Write a program that uses a function pointer as a function argument.

A program to print the function values over a given range of values is shown in Fig. 11.12. The printing is done by the function **table** by evaluating the function passed to it by the **main**.

With **table**, we declare the parameter **f** as a pointer to a function as follows:

double (*f)( );

The value returned by the function is of type **double**. When **table** is called in the statement

table (y, 0.0, 2, 0.5);

```
Program
/******************************************************************/
/*            ILLUSTRATION OF POINTERS TO FUNCTIONS            */
/******************************************************************/
#include  <math.h>
#define  PI 3.1415926
main( )
{
    double  y( ),  cos( ),  table( );

    printf("Table of y(x) = 2*x*x−x+1\n\n");
    table(y, 0.0, 2.0, 0.5);

    printf("\nTable of cos(x)\n\n");
    table(cos, 0.0, PI, 0.5);
}
double table(f, min, max, step)
double (*f)( ), min, max, step;
{
    double a, value;
    for(a = min; a <= max; a += step)
    {
      value = (*f)(a);
      printf("%5.2f  %10.4f\n", a, value);
    }
}
double y(x)
double x;
{
    return(2*x*x−x+1);
}
```

```
Output
Table of y(x)  = 2*x*x − x+1
0.00            1.0000
0.50            1.0000
1.00            2.0000
1.50            4.0000
2.00            7.0000
Table of cos(x)
0.00             1.0000
0.50             0.8776
1.00             0.5403
1.50             0.0707
2.00            −0.4161
2.50            −0.8011
3.00            −0.9900
```

Fig. 11.12 *Use of pointers to functions*

we pass a pointer to the function **y** as the first parameter of **table**. Note that **y** is not followed by a parameter list.

During the execution of **table**, the statement

value = (*f)(a);

calls the function **y**, which is pointed to by **f**, passing it the parameter **a**. Thus the function **y** is evaluated over the range 0.0 to 2.0 at the intervals of 0.5.

Similarly, the call

table (cos, 0.0, PI, 0.5);

passes a pointer to **cos** as its first parameter and therefore, the function **table** evaluates the value of **cos** over the range 0.0 to PI at the intervals of 0.5.

11.11 POINTERS AND STRUCTURES

We know that the name of an array stands for the address of its zeroth element. The same thing is true of the names of arrays of structure variables. Suppose **product** is an array variable of **struct** type. The name **product** represents the address of its zeroth element. Consider the following declaration:

```
struct inventory
{
   char   name[30];
   int    number;
   float  price;
} product[2], *ptr;
```

This statement declares **product** as an array of two elements, each of the type **struct inventory** and **ptr** as a pointer to data objects of the type **struct inventory**.

The assignment

ptr = product;

would assign the address of the zeroth element of **product** to **ptr**. That is, the pointer **ptr** will now point to **product[0]**. Its members can be accessed using the following notation.

ptr –> name
ptr –> number
ptr –> price

The symbol –> is called the *arrow operator* and is made up of a minus sign and a greater than sign. Note that **ptr –>** is simply another way of writing **product[0]**.

When the pointer **ptr** is incremented by one, it is made to point to the next record, i.e., **product[1]**. The following **for** statement will print the values of members of all the elements of **product** array.

for(ptr = product; ptr < product+2; ptr++)
printf("%s %d %f\n",ptr–> name,ptr–> number,ptr–> price);

We could also use the notation

(*ptr).number

to access the member **number**. The parentheses around ***ptr** are necessary because the member operator "." has a higher precedence than the operator *

Example 11.8

Write a program to illustrate the use of structure pointers.

A program to illustrate the use of a structure pointer to manipulate the elements of an array of structures is shown in Fig. 11.13. The program highlights all the features discussed above. Note that the pointer **ptr** (of type **struct invent**) is also used as the loop control index in **for** loops.

```
Program
/******************************************************************/
/*              POINTERS TO STRUCTURE VARIABLES                 */
/******************************************************************/
struct invent
{
    char  *name[20];
    int    number;
    float  price;
};
main( )
{
    struct invent product[3], *ptr;
    printf("INPUT\n\n");
    for(ptr = product; ptr < product+3; ptr++)
        scanf("%s %d %f", ptr->name, &ptr->number, &ptr->price);
    printf("\nOUTPUT\n\n");

    ptr = product;
    while(ptr < product + 3)
    {
        printf("%-20s %5d %10.2f\n",
                    ptr->name,
                    ptr->number,
                    ptr->price);
        ptr++;
    }
}

Output
INPUT
Washing_machine 5 7500
Electric_iron 12 350
Two_in_one 7 1250
OUTPUT

Washing_machine        5      7500.00
Electric_iron         12       350.00
Two_in_one             7      1250.00
```

Fig. 11.13 *Pointer to structure variables*

While using structure pointers, we should take care of the precedence of operators.

The operators '—>' and '.', and ( ) and [ ] enjoy the highest priority among the operators. They bind very tightly with their operands. For example, given the definition

```
struct
{
    int   count;
    float *p;
} *ptr;
```

then the statement

$$++ \textbf{ptr} -> \textbf{count};$$

increments **count**, not **ptr**. However,

$$(++ \textbf{ptr}) -> \textbf{count};$$

increments **ptr** first, and then links **count**. The statement

$$\textbf{ptr}++ -> \textbf{count};$$

is legal and increments **ptr** after accessing **count**.

The following statements also behave in the similar fashion.

*ptr—>p	Fetches whatever **p** points to.
*ptr—>p++	Increments **p** after accessing whatever it points to.
(*ptr—>p)++	Increments whatever **p** points to.
*ptr++ —> p	Increments **ptr** after accessing whatever it points to.

In the previous chapter, we discussed about passing of a structure as an argument to a function. We also saw an example where a function receives a copy of an entire structure and returns it after working on it. As we mentioned earlier, this method is inefficient in terms of both, the execution speed and memory. We can overcome this drawback by passing a pointer to the structure and then using this pointer to work on the structure members. Consider the following function:

```
print_invent(item)
struct invent *item;
{
    printf("Name: %s\n", item —> name);
    printf("Price: %f\n", item —> price);
}
```

This function can be called by

print_invent(&product);

The formal argument **item** receives the address of the structure **product** and therefore it must be declared as a pointer of type **struct invent**, which represents the structure of **product**.

11.12 POINTS ON POINTERS

While pointers provide enormous power and flexibility to the programmers, they may cause nightmares if they are not properly handled. It is advisable to master all the intricacies of pointers before using them. We should make sure that we know where each pointer is pointing in a program. Here are some general observations and common errors that might be useful to remember.

1. A pointer contains garbage until it is initialized. Since compilers cannot detect uninitialized or wrongly initialized pointers, the errors may not be known until we execute the program. Remember that even if we are able to locate a wrong result, it may not provide any evidence for us to suspect problems in the pointers.
2. The abundance of C operators is another cause of confusion that leads to errors. For example, the expressions such as

   *ptr++, *p[ ], (*p)[ ], (ptr).member,

   etc., should be carefully used. A proper understanding of the precedence and associativity rules of C plays a critical role in pointer applications.
3. When an array is passed as an argument to a function, a pointer is actually passed. In the header function, we must declare such arrays with proper sizes, except the first, which is optional.
4. If we define an array in a function with **auto** class, we cannot pass the address of that array back to the **main** for subsequent work.
5. A very common error is to use (or not to use) the address operator& and the indirection operator * in certain places. The user-friendly compiler may not warn you of such mistakes.

CASE STUDIES

1.Processing of Examination Marks

Marks obtained by a batch of students in the Annual Examination are tabulated as follows:

Student name	Marks obtained
S.Laxmi	45 67 38 55
V.S.Rao	77 89 56 69
- -	- - - -

It is required to compute the total marks obtained by each student and print the rank list based on the total marks.

The program in Fig. 11.14 stores the student names in the array **name** and the marks in the array **marks**. After computing the total marks obtained by all the students, the program prepares and prints the rank list. The declaration

   int   marks[STUDENTS][SUBJECTS+1];

defines **marks** as a pointer to the array's first row. We use **rowptr** as the pointer to the row of **marks**. The **rowptr** is initialized as follows:

   int (*rowptr)[SUBJECTS+1] = array;

Note that **array** is the formal argument whose values are replaced by the values of the actual argument **marks**. The parentheses around ***rowptr** makes the **rowptr** as a pointer to an array of SUBJECTS+1 integers. Remember, the statement

Program

```
/**************************************************************************/
/*            POINTERS AND TWO-DIMENSIONAL ARRAYS              */
/**************************************************************************/
#define    STUDENTS 5
#define    SUBJECTS 4
#include   <string.h>
main( )
{
    char name[STUDENTS][20];
    static   int   marks[STUDENTS][SUBJECTS+1];

    printf("Input students names & their marks in four subjects\n");

    get_list(name, marks, STUDENTS, SUBJECTS);

    get_sum(marks, STUDENTS, SUBJECTS+1);

    printf("\n");
    print_list(name,marks,STUDENTS,SUBJECTS+1);

    get_rank_list(name, marks, STUDENTS, SUBJECTS+1);

    printf("\nRanked List\n\n");
    print_list(name,marks,STUDENTS,SUBJECTS+1);
}
/*    Input student name and marks          */
get_list(string,array,m,n)
int   m, n;
char *string[ ];
int   array[][SUBJECTS+1];
{
    int   i, j, (*rowptr)[SUBJECTS+1]  =  array;

    for(i  =  0; i < m; i++)
    {
      scanf("%s", string[i]);
      for(j  =  0; j < SUBJECTS; j++)
         scanf("%d", &(*(rowptr + i))[j]);
    }
}
/*    Compute total marks obtained by each student     */
get_sum(array, m, n)
int    m,n;
int    array[][SUBJECTS+1];
{
    int    i, j, (*rowptr)[SUBJECTS+1]  =  array;

    for(i  =  0; i < m; i++)
    {
      (*(rowptr + i))[n-1]  =  0;
      for(j  =0; j < n-1; j++)
         (*(rowptr + i))[n-1] += (*(rowptr + i))[j];
    }
} .
```

```
/*      Prepare rank list based on total marks    */
get_rank_list(string,array,m,n)
int   m,n;
char *string[ ];
int   array[][SUBJECTS+1];
{
      int i, j, k, (*rowptr)[SUBJECTS+1] = array;
      char *temp;

      for(i  =  1; i <= m−1; i++)
        for(j  =  1; j <= m−i; j++)
          if( (*(rowptr + j−1))[n−1] < (*(rowptr + j))[n−1])
            {
              swap_string(string[j−1], string[j]);

              for(k  =  0; k < n; k++)
                swap_int(&(*(rowptr + j−1))[k],&(*(rowptr+j))[k]);
            }
}
/*       Print out the ranked list              */
print_list(string,array, m, n)
int   m,n;
char *string[ ];
int   array[][SUBJECTS+1];
{
      int   i, j, (*rowptr)[SUBJECTS+1]  =  array;
      for(i  =  0; i < m; i++)
      {
        printf("% −20s", string[i]);
        for(j  =  0; j < n; j++)
          printf("%5d", (*(rowptr + i))[j]);
        printf("\n");
      }
}
/*       Exchange of integer values              */
swap_int(p,q)
int *p, *q;
{
      int   temp;

      temp =  *p;
      *p   =  *q;
      *q   =  temp;
}
/*      Exchange of strings            */
swap_string(s1, s2)
char      s1[], s2[];
{
      char swaparea[256];
      int   i;

      for(i  =  0; i < 256; i++)
        swaparea[i]  =  ' \0';
      i = 0;
```

```
      while(s1[i] != '\0' && i < 256)
      {
         swaparea[i]  =  s1[i];
         i++;
      }
      i = 0;
      while(s2[i] != '\0' && i < 256)
      {
         s1[i]  =  s2[i];
         s1[++i]  =  '\0';
      }
      i = 0;
      while(swaparea[i] != '\0')
      {
         s2[i]  =  swaparea[i];
         s2[++i]  =  '\0';
      }
   }
```

Output

Input students names & their marks in four subjects
S.Laxmi 45 67 38 55
V.S.Rao 77 89 56 69
A.Gupta 66 78 98 45
S.Mani 86 72 0 25
R.Daniel 44 55 66 77

```
S.Laxmi              45 67 38 55 205
V.S.Rao              77 89 56 69 291
A.Gupta              66 78 98 45 287
S.Mani               86 72  0 25 183
R.Daniel             44 55 66 77 242
```

Ranked List

```
V.S.Rao              77 89 56 69 291
A.Gupta              66 78 98 45 287
R.Daniel             44 55 66 77 242
S.Laxmi              45 67 38 55 205
S.Mani               86 72  0 25 183
```

Fig. 11.14 *Preparation of the rank list of a class of students*

```
            int   *rowptr[SUBJECTS+1];
```

would declare **rowptr** as an array of **SUBJECTS+1** elements.

When we increment the **rowptr** (by **rowptr+1**), the incrementing is done in units of the size of each row of **array**, making **rowptr** point to the next row. Since **rowptr** points to a particular row, (*rowptr)[x] points to the xth element in the row.

2. Inventory Updating

The price and quantity of items stocked in a store changes every day. They may either increase or decrease. The program in Fig. 11.15 reads the incremental values of price and quantity and computes the total value of the items in stock.

Program

```
/**********************************************************************/
/*              STRUCTURES AS FUNCTION PARAMETERS                 */
/*                    Using structure pointers                    */
/**********************************************************************/
struct stores
{
     char name[20];
     float  price;
     int    quantity;
};

main( )
{
     void update( );
     float          mul(), p_increment, value;
     int            q_increment;

     static struct stores item = {
     "XYZ", 25.75, 12};
     struct stores *ptr = &item;

     printf("\nInput increment values:");
     printf(" price increment and quantity increment \n");
     scanf("%f %d", &p_increment, &q_increment);
/* -------------------------------------------------------------------- */
     update(&item, p_increment, q_increment);
/* -------------------------------------------------------------------- */
     printf("Updated values of item\n\n");
     printf("Name      : %s\n",ptr->name);
     printf("Price     : %f\n",ptr->price);
     printf("Quantity  : %d\n",ptr->quantity);
/* -------------------------------------------------------------------- */
     value  = mul(&item);
/* -------------------------------------------------------------------- */
     printf("\nValue of the item  = %f\n", value);
}
void update(product, p, q)
struct stores *product;
float p;
int   q;
{
     product->price += p;
     product->quantity += q;
}
float mul(stock)
struct stores *stock;
{
     return(stock->price * stock->quantity);
}
```

```
Output
Input increment values: price increment and quantity increment
10 12
Updated values of item
Name      : XYZ
Price     : 35.750000
Quantity  : 24
Value of the item  =  858.000000
```

Fig. 11.15 *Use of structure pointers as function parameters*

The program illustrates the use of structure pointers as function parameters. **&item**, the address of the structure **item**, is passed to the functions **update(product,p,q)** and **mul(stock)**. The formal arguments **product** and **stock**, which receive the value of **&item**, are declared as pointers of type **struct stores**.

REVIEW QUESTIONS AND EXERCISES

11.1 What is a pointer?

11.2 How is a pointer initialized?

11.3 Explain the effects of the following statements:

    (a) int   a, *b = &a;
    (b) int   p, *p;
    (c) char *s;
    (d) a = (float *) &x;
    (e) double(*f)( );

11.4 If **m** and **n** have been declared as integers and **p1** and **p2** as pointers to integers, then state errors, if any, in the following statements.

    (a) p1 = &m;
    (b) p2 = n;
    (c) *p1 = &n;
    (d) p2 = &*&m;
    (e) m = p2−p1;
    (f) p1 = &p2;
    (g) m = *p1 + *p2++;

11.5 Distinguish between (*m)[5] and *m[5].

11.6 State whether each of the following statements is true or false. Give reasons.

    (a) An integer can be added to a pointer.
    (b) A pointer can never be subtracted from another pointer.
    (c) When an array is passed as an argument to a function, a pointer is passed.
    (d) Pointers cannot be used as formal parameters in headers to function definitions.
    (e) Value of a local variable in a function can be changed by another function.

11.7 Explain the difference between 'call by reference' and 'call by value'.

11.8 Write a program using pointers to read in an array of integers and print its elemnts in reverse order.

11.9 We know that the roots of a quadratic equation of the form

$$ax^2 + bx + c = 0$$

are given by the following equations:

$$x_1 = \frac{-b + \text{square root } (b^2 - 4ac)}{2a}$$

$$x_2 = \frac{-b - \text{square-root } (b^2 - 4ac)}{2a}$$

Write a function to calculate the roots. The function must use two pointer parameters, one to receive the coefficients a, b, and c, and the other to send the roots to the calling function.

11.10 Write a function that receives a sorted array of integers and an integer value, and inserts the value in its correct place.

11.11 Write a function using pointers to add two matrices and to return the resultant matrix to the calling function.

11.12 Using pointers, write a function that receives a character string and a character as argument and deletes all occurrences of this character in the string. The function should return the corrected string with no holes.

11.13 Write a function **day_name** that receives a number n and returns a pointer to a character string containing the name of the corresponding day. The day names should be kept in a **static** table of character strings local to the function.

11.14 Write a program to read in an array of names and to sort them in alphabetical order. Use **sort** function that receives pointers to the functions **strcmp** and **swap**. **sort** in turn should call these functions via the pointers.

11.15 Given an array of sorted list of integer numbers, write a function to search for a particular item, using the method of *binary search*. And also show how this function may be used in a program. Use pointers and pointer arithmetic.

   Hint: In binary search, the target value is compared with the array's middle element. Since the table is sorted, if the required value is smaller, we know that all values greater than the middle element can be ignored. That is, in one attempt, we eliminate one half the list. This search can be applied recursively till the target value is found.

FILE MANAGEMENT IN C

12.1 INTRODUCTION

Until now, we have been using the functions such as **scanf** and **printf** to read and write data. These are console oriented I/O functions which always use the terminal (keyboard and screen) as the target place. This works fine as long as the data is small. However, many real-life problems involve large volumes of data and in such situations, the console oriented I/O operations pose two major problems.

1. It becomes cumbersome and time consuming to handle large volumes of data through terminals.
2. The entire data is lost when either the program is terminated or the computer is turned off.

It is therefore necessary to have a more flexible approach where data can be stored on the disks and read whenever necessary, without destroying the data. This method employs the concept of *files* to store data. A file is a place on the disk where a group of related data is stored. Like most other languages, C supports a number of functions that have the ability to perform basic file operations, which include:

- naming a file,
- opening a file,
- reading data from a file,
- writing data to a file, and
- closing a file.

There are two distinct ways to perform file operations in C. The first one is known as the *low-level I/O* and uses UNIX system calls. The second method is referred to as the *high-level I/O* operation and uses functions in C's standard I/O library. We shall discuss in this chapter, the important file handling functions that are available in the C library. They are listed in Table 12.1.

There are many other functions. Not all of them are supported by all compilers. You should check your C library before using a particular I/O function.

Table 12.1   High level I/O functions

Function name	Operation
fopen( )	• Creates a new file for use.
	• Opens an existing file for use.
fclose( )	• Closes a file which has been opened for use.
getc( )	• Reads a character from a file.
putc( )	• Writes a character to a file.
fprintf( )	• Writes a set of data values to a file.
fscanf( )	• Reads a set of data values from a file.
getw( )	• Reads an integer from a file.
putw( )	• Writes an integer to a file.
fseek( )	• Sets the position to a desired point in the file.
ftell( )	• Gives the current position in the file (in terms of bytes from the start).
rewind( )	• Sets the position to the beginning of the file.

12.2 DEFINING AND OPENING A FILE

If we want to store data in a file in the secondary memory, we must specify certain things about the file, to the operating system. They include:

1. Filename.
2. Data structure.
3. Purpose.

Filename is a string of characters that make up a valid filename for the operating system. It may contain two parts, a primary name and an optional period with the extension. Examples:

Input.data
store
PROG.C
Student.c
Text.out

Data structure of a file is defined as **FILE** in the library of standard I/O function definitions. Therefore, all files should be declared as type **FILE** before they are used. **FILE** is a defined data type.

When we open a file, we must specify what we want to do with the file. For example, we may write data to the file or read the already existing data.

Following is the general format for declaring and opening a file:

```
FILE    *fp;
fp = fopen("filename", "mode");
```

The first statement declares the variable **fp** as a "pointer to the data type **FILE**". As stated earlier, **FILE** is a structure that is defined in the I/O library. The second statement opens the file named *filename* and assigns an identifier to the **FILE** type pointer **fp**. This pointer which contains all the information about the file is subsequently used as a communication link between the system and the program.

The second statement also specifies the purpose of opening this file. The *mode* does this job. *Mode* can be one of the following:

> **r** open the file for reading only.
> **w** open the file for writing only.
> **a** open the file for appending (or adding) data to it.

Note that both the filename and mode are specified as strings. They should be enclosed in double quotation marks.

When trying to open a file, one of the following things may happen:

1. When the mode is 'writing', a file with the specified name is created if the file does not exist. The contents are deleted, if the file already exists.
2. When the purpose is 'appending', the file is opened with the current contents safe. A file with the specified name is created if the file does not exist.
3. If the purpose is 'reading', and if it exists, then the file is opened with the current contents safe; otherwise an error occurs.

Consider the following statements:

```
FILE  *p1, *p2;
p1  =  fopen("data", "r");
p2  =  fopen("results", "w");
```

The file **data** is opened for reading and **results** is opened for writing. In case, the **results** file already exists, its contents are deleted and the file is opened as a new file. If **data** file does not exist, an error will occur.

Many recent compilers include additional modes of operation. They include:

r+ The existing file is opened to the beginning for both reading and writing.

w+ Same as **w** except both for reading and writing.

a+ Same as **a** except both for reading and writing.

We can open and use a number of files at a time. This number however depends on the system we use.

12.3 CLOSING A FILE

A file must be closed as soon as all operations on it have been completed. This ensures that all outstanding information associated with the file is flushed out from the buffers and all links to the file are broken. It also prevents any accidental misuse of the file. In case, there is a limit to the number of files that can be kept open simultaneously, closing of unwanted files might help open the required files. Another instance where we have to close a file is when we want to reopen the same file in a different mode. The I/O library supports a function to do this for us. It takes the following form:

> **fclose**(file_pointer);

This would close the file associated with the FILE pointer **file_pointer**. Look at the following segment of a program.

```
.....
.....
FILE  *p1, *p2;
p1  =  fopen("INPUT", "w");
p2  =  fopen("OUTPUT", "r");
.....
.....
fclose(p1);
fclose(p2);
.....
```

This program opens two files and closes them after all operations on them are completed. Once a file is closed, its file pointer can be reused for another file.

As a matter of fact all files are closed automatically whenever a program terminates. However, closing a file as soon as you are done with it, is a good programming habit.

12.4 INPUT/OUTPUT OPERATIONS ON FILES

Once a file is opened, reading out of or writing to it is accomplished using the standard I/O routines that are listed in Table 12.1.

The getc and putc Functions

The simplest file I/O functions are **getc** and **putc**. These are analogous to **getchar** and **putchar** functions and handle one character at a time. Assume that a file is opened with mode **w** and file pointer **fp1**. Then, the statement

putc(c, fp1);

writes the character contained in the character variable **c** to the file associated with FILE pointer **fp1**. Similarly, **getc** is used to read a character from a file that has been opened in read mode. For example, the statement

c = getc(fp2);

would read a character from the file whose file pointer is **fp2**.

The file pointer moves by one character position for every operation of **getc** or **putc**. The **getc** will return an end-of-file marker EOF, when end of the file has been reached. Therefore, the reading should be terminated when EOF is encountered.

Example 12.1

Write a program to read data from the keyboard, write it to a file called **INPUT**, again read the same data from the **INPUT** file, and display it on the screen.

A program and the related input and output data are shown in Fig. 12.1. We enter the input data via the keyboard and the program writes it, character by character, to the file INPUT. The end of the data is indicated by entering an EOF character, which is *control-Z* in the

```
Program
/*************************************************************************/
/*                WRITING TO AND READING FROM A FILE                 */
/*************************************************************************/
#include  <stdio.h>
main( )
{
      FILE *f1;
      char  c;

      printf("Data Input\n\n");
      f1 = fopen("INPUT", "w");      /* Open the file INPUT          */
      while((c=getchar()) != EOF)/* Get a character from keyboard    */
            putc(c,f1);              /* Write a character to INPUT     */
      fclose(f1);                    /* Close the file INPUT ·         */
      printf("\nData Output\n\n");
      f1 = fopen("INPUT","r");       /* Reopen the file INPUT          */
      while((c=getc(f1)) != EOF)  /* Read a character from INPUT       */
            printf("%c",c);          /* Display a character on screen  */
      fclose(f1);                    /* Close the file INPUT           */
}
Output
Data Input

This is a program to test the file handling
features on this system^Z

Data Output

This is a program to test the file handling
features on this system
```

Fig. 12.1 *Character oriented read/write operations on a file*

reference system. (This may be *control-D* in other systems). The file INPUT is closed at this signal.

The file INPUT is reopened for reading. The program then reads its content character by character, and displays it on the screen. Reading is terminated when **getc** encounters the end-of-file mark EOF.

Testing for the end-of-file condition is important. Any attempt to read past the end of file might either cause the program to terminate with an error or result in an infinite loop situation.

The getw and putw Functions

The **getw** and **putw** are integer-oriented functions. They are similar to the **getc** and **putc** functions and are used to read and write integer values. These functions would be useful when we deal with only integer data. The general forms of **getw** and **putw** are:

putw(*integer*, *fp*);

```
getw(fp);
```

Example 12.2 illustrates the use of **putw** and **getw** functions.

Example 12.2

  A file named **DATA** contains a series of integer numbers. Code a program to read these numbers and then write all odd numbers to a file to be called **ODD** and all even numbers to a file to be called **EVEN**.

The program is shown in Fig. 12.2. It uses three files simultaneously and therefore we need to define three file pointers **f1**, **f2** and **f3**.

```
Program
/******************************************************************/
/*              HANDLING OF INTEGER DATA FILES                    */
/******************************************************************/
#include    <stdio.h>
main( )
{
    FILE   *f1, *f2, *f3;
    int    number, i;
    printf("Contents of DATA file\n\n");
    f1 = fopen("DATA", "w");   /*  Create DATA file          */
    for(i = 1; i <= 30; i++)
    {
      scanf("%d", &number);
      if(number == −1) break;
      putw(number,f1);
    }
    fclose(f1);

    f1 = fopen("DATA", "r");
    f2 = fopen("ODD", "w");
    f3 = fopen("EVEN", "w");

    while((number = getw(f1)) != EOF)/* Read from DATA file    */
    {
        if(number %2 == 0)
          putw(number, f3);                 /*  Write to EVEN file    */
        else
          putw(number, f2);                 /*  Write to ODD file     */
    }
    fclose(f1);
    fclose(f2);
    fclose(f3);

    f2 = fopen("ODD","r");
    f3 = fopen("EVEN", "r");
    printf("\n\nContents of ODD file\n\n");

    while((number = getw(f2)) != EOF)
```

```
        printf("%4d", number);
      printf("\n\nContents of EVEN file\n\n");
      while((number = getw(f3)) != EOF)
        printf("%4d", number);
      fclose(f2);
      fclose(f3);
}
```
Output
Contents of DATA file
111 222 333 444 555 666 777 888 999 000 121 232 343 454 565 −1

Contents of ODD file
  111 333 555 777 999 121 343 565
Contents of EVEN file
  222 444 666 888   0 232 454

Fig. 12.2 *Operations on integer data*

First, the file **DATA** containing integer values is created. The integer values are read from the terminal and are written to the file **DATA** with the help of the statement

putw(number, f1);

Notice that when we type −1, the reading is terminated and the file is closed. The next step is to open all the three files, **DATA** for reading, **ODD** and **EVEN** for writing. The contents of **DATA** file are read, integer by integer, by the function **getw(f1)** and written to **ODD** or **EVEN** file after an appropriate test. Note that the statement

(number = getw(f1)) != EOF

reads a value, assigns the same to **number**, and then tests for the end-of-file mark.

Finally, the program displays the contents of **ODD** and **EVEN** files. It is important to note that the files **ODD** and **EVEN** opened for writing are closed before they are reopened for reading.

The fprintf and fscanf Functions

So far, we have seen functions which can handle only one character or integer at a time. Most compilers support two other functions, namely **fprintf** and **scanf**, that can handle a group of mixed data simultaneously.

The functions **fprintf** and **fscanf** perform I/O operations that are identical to the familar **printf** and **scanf** functions, except of course that they work on files. The first argument of these functions is a file pointer which specifies the file to be used. The general form of **fprintf** is

fprintf(*fp*, "*control string*", *list*);

where *fp* is a file pointer associated with a file that has been opened for writing. The *control string* contains output specifications for the items in the *list*. The *list* may include variables, constants and strings. Example:

fprintf(f1, "%s %d %f", name, age, 7.5);

Here, **name** is an array variable of type **char** and **age** is an **int** variable.

The general format of **fscanf** is

fscanf(*fp*, "*control string*", *list*);

This statement would cause the reading of the items in the *list* from the file specified by *fp*, according to the specifications contained in the *control string*. Example:

fscanf(f2, "%s %d", item, &quantity);

Like **scanf**, **fscanf** also returns the number of items that are successfully read. When the end of file is reached, it returns the value **EOF**.

Example 12.3

Write a program to open a file named INVENTORY and store in it the following data:

Item name	Number	Price	Quantity
AAA-1	111	17.50	115
BBB-2	125	36.00	75
C-3	247	31.75	104

Extend the program to read this data from the file INVENTORY and display the inventory table with the value of each item.

The program is given in Fig. 12.3. The filename INVENTORY is supplied through the keyboard. Data is read using the function **fscanf** from the file **stdin**, which refers to the terminal and it is then written to the file that is being pointed to by the file pointer **fp**. Remember that the file pointer **fp** points to the file INVENTORY.

After closing the file INVENTORY, it is again reopened for reading. The data from the file, along with the item values are written to the file **stdout**, which refers to the screen. While reading from a file, care should be taken to use the same format specifications with which the contents have been written to the file.

```
Program
/*****************************************************************/
/*          HANDLING OF FILES WITH MIXED DATA TYPES             */
/*                    (scanf and fprintf)                       */
/*****************************************************************/
#include   <stdio.h>
main( )
{
     FILE  *fp;
     int   number, quantity, i;
     float price, value;
     char  item[10], filename[10];

     printf("Input file name\n");
     scanf("%s", filename);
```

```
                fp  =  fopen(filename, "w");
                printf("Input inventory data\n\n");
                printf("Item name  Number   Price   Quantity\n");
                for(i = 1; i <= 3; i++)
                {
                   fscanf(stdin,  "%s %d %f %d",
                                   item, &number, &price, &quantity);
                   fprintf(fp, "%s %d %.2f %d",
                                   item, number, price, quantity);
                }
                fclose(fp);
                fprintf(stdout, "\n\n");

                fp  =  fopen(filename, "r");
                printf("Item name  Number   Price   Quantity   Value\n");
                for(i = 1; i <= 3; i++)
                {
                   fscanf(fp, "%s %d %f %d",item,&number,&price,&quantity);
                   value = price * quantity;
                   fprintf(stdout, "%-8s %7d %8.2f %8d %11.2f\n",
                                   item, number, price, quantity, value);
                }
                fclose(fp);
            }
```

Output

```
Input  file name
INVENTORY
Input  inventory data

Item name  Number   Price    Quantity
AAA-1   111   17.50   115
BBB-2   125   36.00   75
C-3     247   31.75   104

Item name       Number       Price     Quantity  Value
  AAA-1          111         17.50        115     2012.50
  BBB-2          125         36.00         75     2700.00
  C-3            247         31.75        104     3302.00
```

Fig. 12.3 *Operations on mixed data types*

12.5 ERROR HANDLING DURING I/O OPERATIONS

It is possible that an error may occur during I/O operations on a file. Typical error situations include:

1. Trying to read beyond the end-of-file mark.
2. Device overflow.
3. Trying to use a file that has not been opened.
4. Trying to perform an operation on a file, when the file is opened for another type of operation.
5. Opening a file with an invalid filename.
6. Attempting to write to a write-protected file.

If we fail to check such read and write errors, a program may behave abnormally when an error occurs. An unchecked error may result in a premature termination of the program or incorrect output. Fortunately, we have two status-inquiry library functions, **feof** and **ferror** that can help us detect I/O errors in the files.

The **feof** function can be used to test for an end of file condition. It takes a **FILE** pointer as its only argument and returns a nonzero integer value if all of the data from the specified file has been read, and returns zero otherwise. If **fp** is a pointer to file that has just been opened for reading, then the statement

```
if(feof(fp) )
    printf("End of data.\n");
```

would display the message "End of data." on reaching the end of file condition.

The **ferror** function reports the status of the file indicated. It also takes a **FILE** pointer as its argument and returns a nonzero integer if an error has been detected upto that point, during processing. It returns zero otherwise. The statement

```
if(ferror(fp) != 0) .
    printf("An error has occurred.\n");
```

would print the error message, if the reading is not successful.

We know that whenever a file is opened using **fopen** function, a file pointer is returned. If the file cannot be opened for some reason, then the function returns a **null** pointer. This facility can be used to test whether a file has been opened or not. Example:

```
if(fp == NULL)
    printf("File could not be opened.\n");
```

Example 12.4

Write a program to illustrate error handling in file operations.

The program shown in Fig. 12.4 illustrates the use of the **null** pointer test and **feof** function. When we input filename as TETS, the function call

```
fopen("TETS", "r");
```

returns a **null** pointer because the file **TETS** does not exist and therefore the message "Cannot open the file" is printed out.

Similarly, the call **feof(fp2)** returns a non-zero integer when the entire data has been read, and hence the program prints the message "Ran out of data" and terminates further reading.

```
/*******************************************************************/
/*              ERROR HANDLING IN FILE OPERATIONS        */
/*******************************************************************/
#include   <stdio.h>
main( )
{
    char *filename;
```

```
        FILE   *fp1, *fp2;
        int    i, number;

        fp1 = fopen("TEST", "w");
        for(i = 10; i <= 100; i += 10)
          putw(i, fp1);

        fclose(fp1);

        printf("\nInput filename\n");

    open_file:
        scanf("%s", filename);

        if((fp2 = fopen(filename,"r")) == NULL)
        {
          printf("Cannot open the file.\n");
          printf("Type filename again.\n\n");
          goto open_file;
        }
        else

        for(i = 1; i <= 20; i++)
        { number = getw(fp2);
          if(feof(fp2))
          {
            printf("\nRan out of data. \n");
            break;
          }
          else
            printf("%d\n", number);
        }

        fclose(fp2);
}
```

Output

Input filename
TETS
Cannot open the file.
Type filename again.

TEST
10
20
30
40
50
60
70
80
90
100

Ran out of data.

Fig. 12.4 *Illustration of error handling*

12.6 RANDOM ACCESS TO FILES

So far we have discussed file functions that are useful for reading and writing data sequentially. There are occasions, however, when we are interested in accessing only a particular part of a file and not in reading the other parts. This can be achieved with the help of the functions **fseek**, **ftell**, and **rewind** available in the I/O library.

ftell takes a file pointer and returns a number of type **long**, that corresponds to the current position. This function is useful in saving the current position of a file, which can be used later in the program. It takes the following form:

$$n = ftell(fp);$$

n would give the relative offset (in bytes) of the current position. This means that n bytes have already been read (or written).

rewind takes a file pointer and resets the position to the start of the file. For example, the statement

$$rewind(fp);$$
$$n = ftell(fp);$$

would assign 0 to **n** because the file position has been set to the start of the file by **rewind**. Remember, the first byte in the file is numbered as 0, second as 1, and so on. This function helps us in reading a file more than once, without having to close and open the file. Remember that whenever a file is opened for reading or writing, a **rewind** is done implicitly.

fseek function is used to move the file position to a desired location within the file. It takes the following form:

fseek(_file ptr, offset, position_);

file ptr is a pointer to the file concerned, _offset_ is a number or variable of type **long**, and _position_ is an integer number. The _offset_ specifies the number of positions (bytes) to be moved from the location specified by _position_. The _position_ can take one of the following three values:

Value	_Meaning_
0	Beginning of file
1	Current position
2	End of file

The _offset_ may be positive, meaning move forwards, or negative, meaning move backwards. The following examples illustrate the operation of the **fseek** function:

Statement	_Meaning_
fseek(fp,0L,0);	Go to the beginning. (Similar to rewind)
fseek(fp,0L,1);	Stay at the current position. (Rarely used)
fseek(fp,0L,2);	Go to the end of the file, past the last character of the file.
fseek(fp,m,0);	Move to (m+1)th byte in the file.
fseek(fp,m,1);	Go forward by m bytes.
fseek(fp,−m,1);	Go backward by m bytes from the current position.

fseek(fp,−m,2);   Go backward by m bytes from the end.
(Positions the file to the mth character from the end.)

When the operation is successful, **fseek** returns a zero. If we attempt to move the file pointer beyond the file boundaries, an error occurs and **fseek** returns −1 (minus one). It is good practice to check whether an error has occurred or not, before proceeding further.

Example 12.5
Write a program that uses the functions **ftell** and **fseek**.

A program employing **ftell** and **fseek** functions is shown in Fig. 12.5. We have created a file **RANDOM** with the following contents:

Position ⟶ 0 1 2 25
Character stored ⟶ A B C . . . . Z

We read the file twice. First, we read the contents of every fifth position and print its value along with its position on the screen. The second time, we read the contents of the file from the end and print the same on the screen.

During the first reading, the file pointer crosses the end-of-file mark when the parameter **n** of **fseek(fp,n,0)** becomes 30. Therefore, after printing the content of position 30, the loop is terminated. (There is nothing in the position 30.)

For reading the file from the end, we use the statement

fseek(fp,−1L,2);

to position the file pointer to the last character. Since every read causes the position to move forward by one position, we have to move it back by two positions to read the next character. This is achieved by the function

fseek(fp, −2L, 1);

in the **while** statement. This statement also tests whether the file pointer has crossed the file boundary or not. The loop is terminated as soon as it crosses it.

```
Program
/*****************************************************/
/*          ILLUSTRATION OF fseek & ftell FUNCTIONS          */
/*****************************************************/
#include  <stdio.h>
main( )
{
    FILE  *fp;
    long  n;
    char  c;
    fp = fopen("RANDOM", "w");
    while((c = getchar()) != EOF)
```

```
            putc(c,fp);
        printf("No. of characters.entered = %ld\n", ftell(fp));
        fclose(fp);

        fp = fopen("RANDOM","r");
        n = 0L;

        while(feof(fp) == 0)
        {
            fseek(fp, n, 0);            /* Position to (n+1)th character    */
            printf("Position of %c is %ld\n", getc(fp), ftell(fp));
            n = n+5L;
        }
        putchar('\n');

        fseek(fp,-1L,2);                /* Position to the last character   */
        do
            {
                putchar(getc(fp));
            }
        while(!fseek(fp,-2L,1));
        fclose(fp);
}
```

Output

```
ABCDEFGHIJKLMNOPQRSTUVWXYZ^Z
No. of characters entered = 26
Position of A is 0
Position of F is 5
Position of K is 10
Position of P is 15
Position of U is 20
Position of Z is 25
Position of    is 30

ZYXWVUTSRQPONMLKJIHGFEDCBA
```

Fig. 12.5 *Illustration of **fseek** and **ftell** functions*

12.7 COMMAND LINE ARGUMENTS

What is a command line argument? It is a parameter supplied to a program when the program is invoked. This parameter may represent a filename the program should process. For example, if we want to execute a program to copy the contents of a file named **X_FILE** to another one named **Y_FILE**, then we may use a command line like

C>PROGRAM X_FILE Y_FILE

PROGRAM is the filename where the executable code of the program is stored. This eliminates the need for the program to request the user to enter the filenames during execution. How do these parameters get into the program?

We know that every C program should have one **main** function and that it marks the beginning of the program. But what we have not mentioned so far is that it can also take arguments like other functions. In fact **main** can take two arguments called **argc** and **argv** and the information contained in the command line is passed on to the program through these arguments, when **main** is called up by the system.

The variable **argc** is an *argument counter* that counts the number of arguments on the command line. The **argv** is an *argument vector* and represents an array of character pointers that point to the command line arguments. The size of this array will be equal to the value of **argc**. For instance, for the command line given above, **argc** is three and **argv** is an array of three pointers to strings as shown below:

```
argv[0] ─────────► PROGRAM
argv[1] ─────────► X_FILE
argv[2] ─────────► Y_FILE
```

In order to access the command line arguments, we must declare the **main** function and its parameters as follows:

```
main(argc, argv)
int   argc;
char  *argv[ ];
{
    .....
    .....
}
```

The first parameter in the command line is always the program name and therefore **argv[0]** always represents the program name.

Example 12.6

Write a program that will receive a filename and a line of text as command line arguments and write the text to the file.

Figure 12.6 shows the use of command line arguments. The command line is

F12_6 TEXT AAAAAA BBBBBB CCCCCC DDDDDD EEEEEE FFFFFF GGGGGG.

Each word in the command line is an argument to the **main** and therefore the total number of arguments is 9.

The argument vector **argv[1]** points to the string TEXT and therefore the statement

```
fp = fopen(argv[1], "w");
```

opens a file with the name TEXT. The **for** loop that follows immediately writes the remaining 7 arguments to the file TEXT.

Program also prints two outputs, one from the file TEXT and the other from the system memory. The *argument vector* **argv** contains the entire command line in the memory and, therefore, the statement:

```
printf("%*s\n", i*5, argv[i] );
```

prints the arguments from the memory.

Program

```
/* ********************************************************************* /
/*                    COMMAND LINE ARGUMENTS                           */
/* ********************************************************************* /
#include   <stdio.h>
main(argc, argv)                      /*      main with arguments      */
int argc;                             /*      argument count           */
char *argv[];                         /*      list of arguments        */
{
    FILE    *fp;
    int   i;
    char   word[15];

    fp  =  fopen(argv[1], "w");        /*  open file with name argv[1]  */
    printf("\nNo. of arguments in Command line = %d\n\n", argc);
    for(i = 2; i < argc; i++)
        fprintf(fp,"%s ", argv[i]);     /*  write to file argv[1]        */
    fclose(fp);
/*    Writing content of the file to screen                            */
    printf("Contents of %s file\n\n", argv[1]);
    fp  =  fopen(argv[1], "r");
    for(i = 2; i < argc; i++)
    {
        fscanf(fp,"%s", word);
        printf("%s ", word);
    }
    fclose(fp);
    printf("\n\n");
/*    Writing the arguments from memory                                */
    for(i = 0; i < argc; i++)
        printf("%*s \n", i*5,argv[i]);
}
```

Output

C>F12_6 TEXT AAAAAA BBBBBB CCCCCC DDDDDD EEEEEE FFFFFF GGGGGG

No. of arguments in Command line = 9

Contents of TEXT file

AAAAAA BBBBBB CCCCCC DDDDDD EEEEEE FFFFFF GGGGGG

```
C:\C\F12_6.EXE
  TEXT
      AAAAAA
            BBBBBB
                  CCCCCC
                        DDDDDD
                              EEEEEE
                                    FFFFFF
                                          GGGGGG
```

Fig. 12.6 *Use of command line arguments*

CASE STUDY

Appending Items to a File

A program to append additional items to the file INVENTORY and print the total contents of the file has been developed here. The program is shown in Fig. 12.7 . It uses a structure definition to describe each item and a function **append** () to add an item to the file.

On execution, the program requests for the filename to which data is to be appended. After appending the items, the position of the last character in the file is assigned to **n** and then the file is closed.

The file is reopened for reading and its contents are displayed. Note that reading and displaying are done under the control of a **while** loop. The loop tests the current file position against **n** and is terminated when they become equal.

```
Program
/************************************************************/
/*            APPENDING ITEMS TO AN EXISTING FILE          */
/************************************************************/
#include   <stdio.h>
struct invent_record
{
    char   name[10];
    int    number;
    float  price;
    int    quantity;
}
main( )
{
    struct invent_record item;
    char   filename[10];
    int    response;
    FILE   *fp;
    long   n;
    printf("Type filename:");
    scanf("%s", filename);

    fp = fopen(filename, "a+");
    do
    {
       append(&item, fp);
       printf("\nItem %s appended. \n",item.name);
       printf("\nDo you want to add another item \
(1 for YES /0 for NO)?");
       scanf("%d", &response);
    } while (response == 1);
    n = ftell(fp);                    /* Position of last character */
    fclose(fp);

    fp = fopen(filename, "r");
```

```
        while(ftell(fp) < n)
        {
            fscanf(fp,"%s %d %f %d",
                item.name, &item.number, &item.price, &item.quantity);
            fprintf(stdout,"%−8s %7d %8.2f %8d\n",
                item.name, item.number, item.price  item.quantity);
        }
        fclose(fp);
}
append(product, ptr)
struct invent_record *product;
FILE        *ptr;
{
    printf("Item name:");
    scanf("%s", product − > name);

    printf("Item number:");
    scanf("%d", &product−>number);

    printf("Item price:");
    scanf("%f", &product−>price);

    printf("Quantity:");
    scanf("%d", &product−>quantity);

    fprintf(ptr, "%s %d %.2f %d",
                product−>name,
                product−>number,
                product−>price,
                product−>quantity);
}
```

Output

Type filename:INVENTORY
Item name:XXX
Item number:444
Item price:40.50
Quantity:34

Item XXX appended.

Do you want to add another item(1 for YES /0 for NO)?1

Item name:YYY
Item number:555
Item price:50.50
Quantity:45

Item YYY appended.

Do you want to add another item(1 for YES /0 for NO)?0

AAA-1	111	17.50	115
BBB-2	125	36.00	75
C-3	247	31.75	104
XXX	444	40.50	34
YYY	555	50.50	45

Fig. 12.7 *Adding items to an existing file*

REVIEW QUESTIONS AND EXERCISES

12.1 Describe the use and limitations of the functions **getc** and **putc**.

12.2 What is the significance of EOF?

12.3 When a program is terminated, all the files used by it are automatically closed. Why is it then necessary to close a file during execution of the program?

12.4 Distinguish between the following functions:

    (a) getc and getchar.
    (b) printf and fprintf.
    (c) feof and ferror.

12.5 How does an append mode differ from a write mode?

12.6 What are the common uses of **rewind** and **ftell** functions?

12.7 Explain the general format of **fseek** function?

12.8 What is the difference between the statements **rewind(fp);** and **fseek(fp,0L,0);**?

12.9 Write a program to copy the contents of one file into another.

12.10 Two files DATA1 and DATA2 contain sorted lists of integers. Write a program to produce a third file DATA which holds a single sorted, merged list of these two lists. Use command line arguments to specify the file names.

12.11 Write a program that will generate a data file containing the list of customers and their corresponding telephone numbers. Use a structure variable to store the name and telephone of each customer. Create a data file using a sample list.

12.12 Write an interactive, menu-driven program that will access the data file created in the above problem and do one of the following tasks:

    a) Determine the telephone number of a specified customer.
    b) Determine the customer whose telephone number is specified.

DYNAMIC MEMORY ALLOCATION AND LINKED LISTS

13.1 INTRODUCTION

Most often we face situations in programming where the data is dynamic in nature. That is, the number of data items keep changing during execution of the program. For example, consider a program for processing the list of customers of a corporation. The list grows when names are added and shrinks when names are deleted. When list grows we need to allocate more memory space to the list to accomodate additional data itmes. Such situations can be handled more easily and effectively by using what is known as *dynamic data structures* in conjunction with *dynamic memory management* techniques.

Dynamic data structures provide flexibility in adding, deleting or rearranging data items at run time. Dynamic memory management techniques permit us to allocate additional memory space or to release unwanted space at run time, thus, optimizing the use of storage space. This chapter discusses the concepts of *linked lists*, one of the basic types of dynamic data structures. Before we take up linked lists, we shall briefly introduce the dynamic storage management functions that are available in C. These functions would be extensively used in processing linked lists.

13.2 DYNAMIC MEMORY ALLOCATION

C language requires the number of elements in an array to be specified at compile time. But we may not be able to do so always. Our initial judgement of size, if it is wrong, may cause failure of the program or wastage of memory space.

Many languages permit a programmer to specify an array's size at run time. Such languages have the ability to calculate and assign, during execution, the memory space required by the variables in a program. The process of allocating memory at run time is known as *dynamic memory allocation*. Although C does not inherently have this facility, there are four library routines known as "memory management functions" that can be used for allocating and freeing memory during program execution. They are listed in Table 13.1. These functions help us build complex application programs that use the available memory intelligently.

Table 13.1 Memory Allocation Functions

Function	Task
malloc	Allocates requested size of bytes and returns a pointer to the first byte of the allocated space.
calloc	Allocates space for an array of elements, initializes them to zero and then returns a pointer to the memory.
free	Frees previously allocated space.
realloc	Modifies the size of previously allocated space.

Memory Allocation Process

Before we discuss these functions, let us look at the memory allocation process associated with a C program. Figure 13.1 shows the conceptual view of storage of a C program in memory.

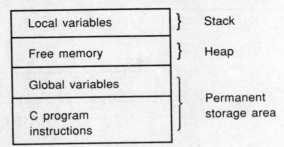

Fig.13.1 *Storage of a C program*

The program instructions and global and static variables are stored in a region known as permanent storage area and the local variables are stored in another area called *stack*. The memory space that is located between these two regions is available for dynamic allocation during execution of the program. This free memory region is called the *heap*. The size of the heap keeps changing when program is executed due to creation and death of variables that are local to functions and blocks. Therefore, it is possible to encounter memory "overflow" during dynamic allocation process. In such situations, the memory allocation functions mentioned above return a NULL pointer (when they fail to locate enough memory requested).

Allocating a Block of Memory

A block of memory may be allocated using the function **malloc**. The **malloc** function reserves a block of memory of specified size and returns a pointer of type **void**. This means that we can assign it to any type of pointer. It takes the following form:

```
ptr = (cast-type *) malloc(byte-size);
```

ptr is a pointer of type *cast-type*. The **malloc** returns a pointer (of *cast type*) to an area of memory with size *byte-size*.

Example:

$$x = (int *) malloc(100 * sizeof(int));$$

On successful execution of this statement, a memory space equivalent to "100 times the size of an **int**" bytes is reserved and the address of the first byte of the memory allocated is assigned to the pointer **x** of type of **int**

Similarly, the statement

$$cptr = (char *) malloc(10);$$

allocates 10 bytes of space for the pointer **cptr** of type **char**. This is illustrated below:

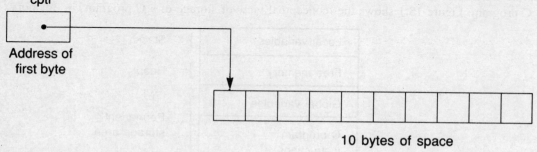

10 bytes of space

Note that the storage space allocated dynamically has no name and therefore its contents can be accessed only through a pointer.

We may also use **malloc** to allocate space for complex data types such as structures. Example:

$$st\_var = (struct\ store\ *)malloc(sizeof(struct\ store));$$

where **st_var** is a pointer of type **struct store**

Remember, the **malloc** allocates a block of contiguous bytes. The allocation can fail if the space in the heap is not sufficient to satisfy the request. If it fails, it returns a NULL. We should therefore check whether the allocation is successful before using the memory pointer. This is illustrated in the program in Fig. 13.2.

Example 13.1

Write a program that uses a table of integers whose size will be specified interactively at run time.

The program is given in Fig.13.2. It tests for availability of memory space of required size. If it is available, then the required space is allocated and the address of the first byte of the space allocated is displayed. The program also illustrates the use of pointer variable for storing and accessing the table values.

Program

```
/****************************************************************/
/*              USE OF malloc FUNCTION                          */
/****************************************************************/

#include <stdio.h>
#include <stdlib.h>
#define NULL 0

main()
{
    int  *p, *table;
    int  size;

    printf("\nWhat is the size of table ? ");
    scanf("%d", size);

    printf("\n")

    /* Memory allocation */

    if((table = (int *)malloc(size * sizeof(int))) == NULL)
      {
          printf("No space available \n");
          exit(1);
      }
    printf("\nAddress of the first byte is %u\n",table);

    /* Reading table values */

    printf("\nInput table values\n");

    for(p = table; p < table + size; p++)
      scanf("%d", p);

    /* Printing table values in reverse order */

    for(p = table + size −1; p >= table; p − −)
      printf("%d is stored at address %u \n", *p, p);
}
```

Output

What is the size of the table ? 5
Address of the first byte is 2262

Input table values
11 12 13 14 15

15 is stored at address 2270
14 is stored at address 2268
13 is stored at address 2266
12 is stored at address 2264
11 is stored at address 2262

Fig. 13.2 *Memory allocation with* **malloc**

Allocating Multiple Blocks of Memory

calloc is another memory allocation function that is normally used for requesting memory space at run time for storing derived data types such as arrays and structures. While **malloc** allocates a single block of storage space, **calloc** allocates multiple blocks of storage, each of the same size, and then sets all bytes to zero. The general form of **calloc** is:

> ptr = (*cast-type* *) **calloc** *(n,elem-size)*;

The above statement allocates contiguous space for *n* blocks, each of size *elem-size* bytes. All bytes are initialized to zero and a pointer to the first byte of the allocated region is returned. If there is not enough space, a NULL pointer is returned.

The following segment of a program allocates space for a structure variable:

```
. . . .
. . . .
struct student
{
   char      name[25];
   float     age;
   long int  id_num;
};
typedef struct student record;
record *st_ptr;
int class_size = 30;

st_ptr = (record *)calloc(class_size, sizeof(record));

. . . .
. . . .
```

record is of type **struct student** having three members: **name**, **age** and **id_num**. The **calloc** allocates memory to hold data for 30 such records. We must be sure that the requested memory has been allocated successfully before using the **st_ptr**. This may be done as follows:

```
if(st_ptr == NULL)
{
    printf("Available memory not sufficient");
    exit(1);
}
```

Releasing the Used Space

Compile-time storage of a variable is allocated and released by the system in accordance with its storage class. With the dynamic run-time allocation, it is our responsibility to release the space when it is not required. The release of storage space becomes important when the storage is limited.

When we no longer need the data we stored in a block of memory, and we do not intend to use that block for storing any other information, we may release that block of memory for future use, using the **free** function:

$$free(ptr);$$

ptr is a pointer to a memory block which has already been created by **malloc** or **calloc**. Use of an invalid pointer in the call may create problems and cause system crash. The use of **free** function has been illustrated in Example 13.2.

Altering the Size of a Block

It is likely that we discover later, the previously allocated memory is not sufficient and we need additional space for more elements. It is also possible that the memory allocated is much larger than necessary and we want to reduce it. In both the cases, we can change the memory size already allocated with the help of the function **realloc**. This process is called the *reallocation* of memory. For example, if the original allocation is done by the statement

$$ptr = \textbf{malloc}(size);$$

then reallocation of space may be done by the statement

$$ptr = \textbf{realloc}(ptr, newsize);$$

This function allocates a new memory space of size *newsize* to the pointer variable **ptr** and returns a pointer to the first byte of the new memory block. The *newsize* may be larger or smaller than the *size*. Remember, the new memory block may or may not begin at the same place as the old one. In case, it is not able to find additional space in the same region, it will create the same in an entirely new region and move the contents of the old block into the new block. The function guarantees that the old data will remain intact.

If the function is unsuccessful in locating additional space, it returns a NULL pointer and the original block is freed(lost). This implies that it is very necessary to test the success of operation before proceeding further. This is illustrated in the program of Example 13.2.

Example 13.2

Write a program to store a character string in a block of memory space created by **malloc** and then modify the same to store a larger string.

The program is shown in Fig. 13.3. The output illustrates that the original buffer size obtained is modified to contain a larger string. Note that the original contents of the buffer remains same even after modification of the original size.

```
Program

/**********************************************************************/
/*      USE OF realloc AND free FUNCTION                          */
/**********************************************************************/

#include <stdio.h>
#include <stdlib.h>
#define NULL 0
main()
{
    char  *buffer;
    /* Allocating memory */
    if((buffer = (char *)malloc(10)) == NULL)
    {
        printf("malloc failed.\n");
        exit(1);
    }
    printf("Buffer of size %d created \n",_msize(buffer));
    strcpy(buffer, "HYDERABAD");
    printf("\nBuffer contains: %s \n",buffer);
    /* Reallocation */
    if((buffer = (char *)realloc(buffer,15)) == NULL)
    {
        printf("Reallocation failed. \n");
        exit(1);
    }
    printf("\nBuffer size modified. \n");
    printf("\nBuffer still contains: %s \n",buffer);
    strcpy(buffer, "SECUNDERABAD");
    printf("\nBuffer now contains: %s \n",buffer);
```

```
            /* Freeing memory */
            free(buffer);
    }

    Output

    Buffer of size 10 created

    Buffer contains: HYDERABAD

    Buffer size modified

    Buffer still contains: HYDERABAD

    Buffer now contains: SECUNDERABAD
```

Fig. 13.3 *Reallocation and release of memory space*

13.3 CONCEPTS OF LINKED LISTS

We know that a list refers to a set of items organized sequencially. An array is an example of list. In an array, the sequential organization is provided implicitly by its index. We use the index for accessing and manipulation of array elements. One major problem with the arrays is that the size of an array must be specified precisely at the beginning. As pointed out earlier, this may be a difficult task in many practical applications.

A completely different way to represent a list is to make each item in the list part of a structure that also contains a "link" to the structure containing the next item, as whown in Fig.13.4. This type of list is called a *linked list* because it is a list whose order is given by links from one item to the next.

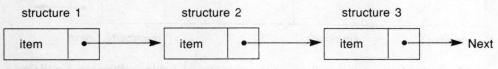

Fig.13.4 *A linked list*

Each structure of the list is called a *node* and consists of two fields, one containing the *item*, and the other containing the *address* of the next item (a pointer to the next item) in the list. A linked list is therefore a collection of structures ordered not by their physical placement in memory (like an array) but by logical links that are stored as part of the data in the structure itself. The link is in the form of a pointer to another structure of the same type. Such a structure is represented as follows:

```
            struct node
            {
                int        item;
                struct node *next;
            };
```

The first member is an integer item and the second a pointer to the next node in the list as shown below.   Remember, the **item** is an integer here only for simplicity, and could be any complex data type.

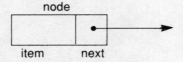

Such structures which contain a member field that point to the same structure type are called *self-refrential* structures.

A node may be represented in general form as follows:

```
struct  tag-name
{
    type member1;
    type member2;
    . . . .
    . . . .
    struct tag-name *next;
};
```

The structure may contain more than one item with different data types.   However, one of the items must be a pointer of the type **tag-name**.

Let us consider a simple example to illustrate the concept of linking. Suppose we define a structure as follows:

```
struct  link_list
{
    float  age;
    struct link_list *next;
};
```

For simplicity, let us assume that the list contains two nodes **node1** and **node2**.   They   are of type **struct link_list** and   are defined as follows:

struct link_list node1, node2;

This statement creates space for two nodes each containing two empty fields as shown
below:

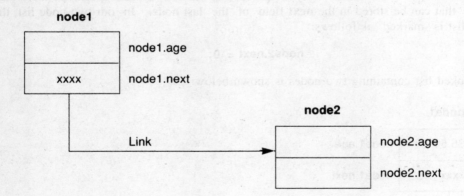

The **next** pointer of **node1** can be made to point to **node2** by the statement

node1.next = &node2;

This statement stores the address of **node2** into the field **node1.next** and thus establishes
a "link" between **node1** and **node2** as shown below:

"xxxx" is the address of **node2** where the value of the variable **node2.age** will be stored. Now
let us assign values to the field age.

node1.age = 35.50;
node2.age = 49.00;

The result is as follows:

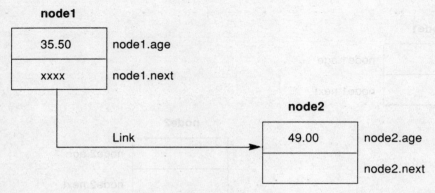

We may continue this process to create a linked list of any number of values. For example,

node2.next = &node3;

would add another link provided **node3** has been declared as a variable of type **struct link-list**.

No list goes on forever. Every list must have an end. We must therefore indicate the end of a linked list. This is necessary for processing the list. C has a special pointer value called *null* that can be stored in the **next** field of the last node. In our two-node list, the end of the list is marked as follows:

node2.next = 0;

The final linked list containing two nodes is shown below:

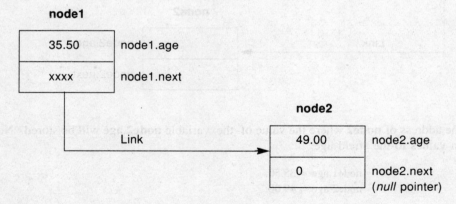

The value of the age member of **node2** can be accessed using the **next** member of **node1** as follows:

printf(" %f\n", node1.next–>age);

13.4 ADVANTAGES OF LINKED LISTS

A linked list is a *dynamic data structure*. Therefore, the primary advantage of linked lists over arrays is that linked lists can grow or shrink in size during the execution of a program. A linked list can be made just as long as required.

Another advantage is that a linked list does not waste memory space. It uses the memory that is just needed for the list at any point of time. This is because it is not necessary to specify the number of nodes to be used in the list.

The third, and the more important advantage is that the linked lists provide flexibility in allowing the items to be rearranged efficiently. It is easier to insert or delete items by rearranging the links. This is shown in Fig.13.5.

The major limitation of linked lists is that the access to any arbitrary item is little cumbersome and time consuming. Whenever we deal with a fixed length list, it would be better to use an array rather than a linked list. We must also note that a linked list will use more storage than an array with the same number of items. This is because each item has an additional link field.

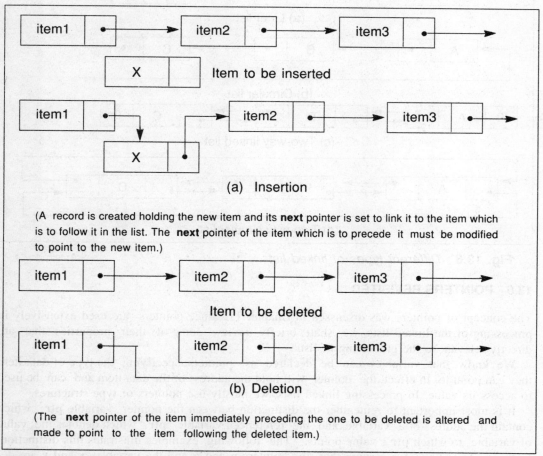

(a) Insertion

(A record is created holding the new item and its **next** pointer is set to link it to the item which is to follow it in the list. The **next** pointer of the item which is to precede it must be modified to point to the new item.)

(b) Deletion

(The **next** pointer of the item immediately preceding the one to be deleted is altered and made to point to the item following the deleted item.)

Fig. 13.5 *Insertion into and deletion from a linked list*

13.5 TYPES OF LINKED LISTS

There are different types of linked lists. The one we discussed so far is known as *linear singly linked list*. The other linked lists are:

- Circular linked lists
- Two-way or doubly linked lists
- Circular doubly linked lists

The circular linked lists have no beginning and no end. The last item points back to the first item. The doubly linked lists uses double set of pointers, one pointing to the *next* item and other pointing to the preceding item. This allows us to traverse the list in either direction. Circular doubly linked lists employs both the forward pointer and backward pointer in circlular form. Figure 13.6 illustrates various kinds of linked lists.

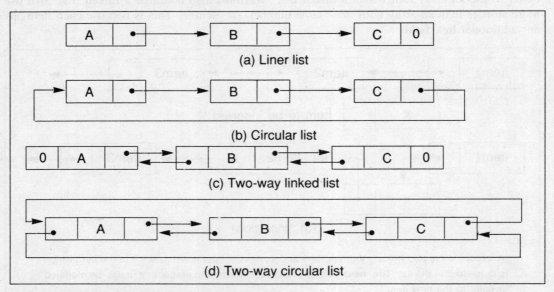

Fig. 13.6 *Different types of linked lists*

13.6 POINTERS REVISITED

The concept of pointers was discussed in Chapter 11. Since pointers are used extensively in processing of the linked lists, we shall briefly review some of their properties that are directly relevant to the processing of lists.

We know that variables can be declared as pointers, specifying the type of data item they can point to. In effect, the pointer will hold the address of the data item and can be used to access its value. In precessing linked lists, we mostly use pointers of type structures.

It is most important to remember the distinction between the pointer variable **ptr**, which contain the address of a variable, and the referenced variable ***ptr**, which denotes the value of variable to which **ptr**'s value points. The following examples illustrates this distinction. In these illustrations, we assume that the pointers **p** and **q** and the variables **x** and **y** are declared to be of same type.

(a) Initialization

p = &x;

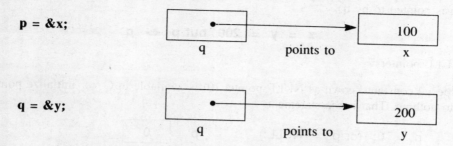

q   points to   x

q = &y;

q   points to   y

The pointer **p** contains the address of **x** and **q** contains the address of **y**.

$$^*p = 100 \quad \text{and} \quad ^*q = 200 \quad \text{and} \quad p <> q$$

(b) Assignment p = q

The assignment **p = q** assigns the address of the variable **y** to the pointer variable **p** and
therefore **p** now points to the variable **y**.

p = q;

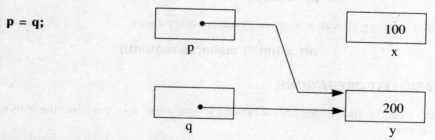

p

q

Both the pointer variables point to the same variable.

$$^*p = {}^*q = 200 \quad \text{but} \quad x <> y$$

(c) Assignment *p = *q

This assignment statement puts the value of the variable pointed to by **q** in the location of
the variable pointed to by **p**.

*p = *q;

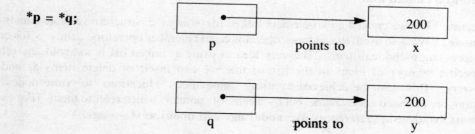

p   points to   x

q   **points to**   y

The pointer **p** still points to the same variable **x** but the old value of **x** is replaced by 200 (which is pointed to by **q**).

$$x = y = 200 \text{ but } p <> q$$

(d) NULL pointers

A special constant known as NULL pointer (0) is available in C to initialize pointers that point to nothing. That is the statements

p = 0; (or p = NULL;)   p | 0 |

q = 0; (q = NULL;)   q | 0 |

make the pointers **p** and **q** point to nothing. They can be later used to point any values.

We know that a pointer must be initialized by assigning a memory address before using it. There are two ways of assigning memory addresses to a pointer.

1. Assigning an existing variable address (static assignment)

ptr = &count;

2. Using a memory allocation funtion (dynamic assignment)

ptr = (int *) malloc(sizeof(int));

13.7 BASIC LIST OPERATIONS

We can treat a linked list as an abstract data type and perform the following basic operations:
1. Creating a list
2. Traversing the list
3. Counting the items in the list
4. Printing the list (or sublist)
5. Looking up an item for editing or printing
6. Inserting an item
7. Deleting an item
8. Concatenating two lists

Creating a Linked List

In Section 13.3 we created a two-element linked list using the structure variable names **node1** and **node2**. We also used the address operator **&** and member operators **.** and **−>** for creating and accessing individual items. The very idea of using a linked list is to avoid any reference to specific number of items in the list so that we can insert or delete items as and when necessary. This can be achieved by using "anonymous" locations to store nodes. Such locations are accessed not by name, but by means of pointers which refer to them. (For example, we must avoid using references like **node1.age** and **node1.next −> age.**)

Annonymous locations are created using pointers and dynamic memory allocation functions such as **malloc**. We use a pointer **head** to create and access anonymous nodes. Consider the following:

```
struct linked_list
{
     int  number;
     struct linked_list  *next;
};
typedef struct linked_list node;
node   *head;
head = (node *) malloc(sizeof(node));
```

The **struct** declaration merely describes the format of the nodes and does not allocate storage. Storage space for a node is created only when the function **malloc** is called in the statement

```
head = (node *) malloc(sizeof(node));
```

This statement obtains a piece of memory that is sufficient to store a node and assigns its address to the pointer variable **head**. This pointer indicates the beginning of the linked list.

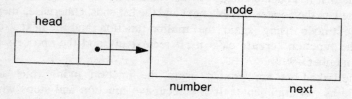

The following statements store values in the member fields:

```
head –> number  = 10;
head –> next     = NULL;
```

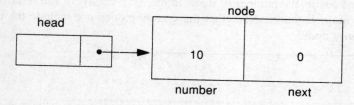

The second node can be added as follows:

```
head–>next = (node *)malloc(sizeof(node));
head–>next–>number = 20;
head–>next–>next = NULL;
```

Although this process can be continued to create any number of nodes, it becomes cumbersome and clumsy if nodes are more than two. The above process may be easily implemented using both recursion and iteration techniques. The pointer can be moved from the current node to the next node by a self-replacement statement such as

$$head = head \rightarrow next;$$

The Example 13.3 shows creation of a complete linked list and printing of its contents using recursion.

Example 13.3

Write a program to create a linear linked list interactively and print out the list and the total number of items in the list.

The program shown in Fig. 13.7 first allocates a block of memory dynamically for the first node using the statement

$$head = (node \; *)malloc(sizeof(node));$$

which returns a pointer to a structure of type **node** that has been type defined earlier. The linked list is then created by the function **create**. The function requests for the number to be placed in the current node that has been created. If the value assigned to the current node is –999, then NULL is assigned to the pointer variable **next** and the list ends. Otherwise, memory space is allocated to the next node using again the **malloc** function and the next value is placed into it. Note that the function **create** calls itself recursively and the process will continue until we enter the number –999.

The items stored in the linked list are printed using the function **print** which accept a pointer to the current node as an argument. It is a recursive function and stops when it receives a NULL pointer. Printing algorithm is as follows:

1. Start with the first node.
2. While there are valid nodes left to print
   a) print the current item and
   b) advance to next node.

Similarly, the function **count** counts the number of items in the list recursively and returns the total number of items to the **main** function. Note that the counting does not include the item – 999 (contained in the dummy node).

```
Program

/********************************************************************/
/*          CREATING A LINEAR LINKED LIST                     */
/********************************************************************/
#include <stdio.h>
#include <stdlib.h>
#define NULL 0
```

```
struct linked_list
{
    int   number;
    struct linked_list  *next;
};
typedef  struct linked_list node;  /* node type defined */

main()
{
    node  *head;
    void  create(node *p);
    int   count(node *p);
    void  print(node *p);

    head = (node *)malloc(sizeof(node));
    create(head);
    printf("\n");
    print(head);
    printf("\n");
    printf("\nNumber of items = %d \n", count(head));
}

void  create(node  *list)
{
    printf("Input a number\n");
    printf("(type -999 at end): ");
    scanf("%d", &list->number); /* create current node */

    if(list->number == -999)
    {
      list->next = NULL;
    }
    else    /* create next node */
    {
      list->next = (node *)malloc(sizeof(node));
      create(list->next);
    }
    return;
}

void print(node *list)
{
    if(list->next != NULL)
    {
    printf("%d - ->",lis ->number); /* print current item */
```

```
            if(list–>next–>next == NULL)
                printf("%d", list–>next–>number);

            print(list–>next);          /* move to next item  */
        }
    return;
}

int count(node *list)
{
    if(list–>next == NULL)
        return (0);
    else
        return(1 + count(list–>next));
}
```

Output

```
Input a number
(type –999 to end): 60
Input a number
(type –999 to end): 20
Input a number
(type –999 to end): 10
Input a number
(type –999 to end): 40
Input a number
(type –999 to end): 30
Input a number
(type –999 to end): 50
Input a number
(type –999 to end): –999


60 – –>20 – –>10 – –>40 – –>30 – –>50 – –>–999

Number of items = 6
```

Fig. 13.7 *Creating a linear linked list*

Inserting an Item

One of the advantages of linked lists is the comparative case with which new nodes can be inserted. It requires merely resetting of two pointers (rather than having to move around a list of data as would be the case with arrays).

Inserting a new item, say X, into the list has three situations:
1. Insertion at the front of the list.

2. Insertion in the middle of the list.

3. Insertion at the end of the list.

The process of insertion precedes a search for the place of insertion. The search involves in locating a node after which the new item is to be inserted. A general algorithm for insertion is as follows:

Begin

> *if* the list is empty or
> the new node comes before the head node *then*,
> insert the new node as the head node,
> *else*
> *if* the new node comes after the last node, *then*,
> insert the new node as the end node,
> *else*
> insert the new node in the body of the list.

End

Algorithm for placing the new item at the beginning of a linked list:

1. Obtain space for new node.
2. Assign data to the item field of new node.
3. Set the *next* field of the new node to point to the start of the list.
4. Change the head pointer to point to the new node.

Algorithm for inserting the new node X between two existing nodes, say, N1 and N2;

1. Set space for new node X.
2. Assign value to the item field of X
3. Set the *next* field of X to point to node N2
4. Set the *next* field of N1 to point to X

Algorithm for inserting an item at the end of the list is similar to the one for inserting in the middle, except the *next* field of the new node is set to NULL (or set to point to a dummy or sentinel node, if it exists).

Example 13.4

Write a function to insert a given item *before* a specified node known as key node.

The function **insert** shown in Fig.13.8 requests for the item to be inserted as well as the 'key node'. If the insertion happens to be at the beginning, then memory space is created for the new node, the value of new item is assigned to it and the pointer **head** is assigned to the next member. The pointer **new** which indicates the beginning of the new node is assigned to **head**. Note the following statements:

```
new->number = x;
new->next = head;
head = new;
```

```
/*******************************************************************/
/*                    FUNCTION INSERT                            */
/*******************************************************************/
node *insert(node *head)
{
  node *find(node *p, int a);
  node *new;          /* pointer to new node */
  node *n1;           /* pointer to node preceding key node */
  int  key;
  int  x;             /* new item (number) to be inserted  */

  printf("Value of new item ? ");
  scanf("%d", &x);
  printf("Value of key item ? (type –999 if last) ");
  scanf("%d", &key);

  if(head->number == key)  /* new node is first */
  {
    new = (node *) malloc(sizeof(node));
    new->number = x;
    new->next = head;
    head = new;
  }
  else        /* find key node and insert new node */
  {           /* before the key node              */
    n1 = find(head, key); /* find key node */

    if(n1 == NULL)
       printf("\n key is not found \n");
    else      /* insert new node */
    {
       new = (node *)malloc(sizeof(node));
       new->number = x;
       new->next = n1->next;
       n1->next =  new;
    }
  }
  return(head);
}
node *find(node *list, int key)
{
  if(list->next->number == key)   /* key found */
     return(list);
  else
    if(list->next->next == NULL) /* end */
      return(NULL);
    else
      find(list->next, key);
}
```

Fig. 13.8 *A function for inserting an item into a linked list*

However, if the new item is to be inserted after an existing node, then we use the function **find** recursively to locate the 'key node'. The new item is inserted before the key node using the algorithm discussed above. This is illustrated below:

Before Insertion

```
new = (node *)malloc(sizeof(node));
new->number = x ;
```

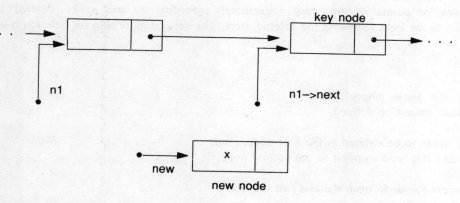

After Insertion

```
new->next = n1->next;
n1->next = new;
```

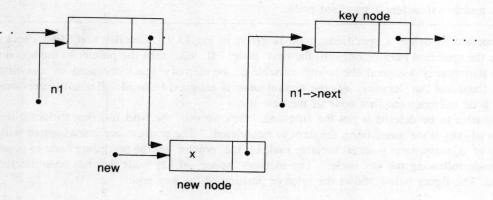

Deleting an Item

Deleting a node from the list is even easier than insertion, as only one pointer value needs to be changed. Here again we have three situations.
1. Deleting the first item
2. Deleting the last item
3. Deleting between two nodes in the middle of the list

In the first case, the head pointer is altered to point to the second item in the list. In the other two cases, the pointer of the item immediately preceding the one to be deleted is altered to point to the item following the deleted item. The general algorithm for deletion is as follows:

Begin

> *if* the list is empty , *then*,
> node cannot be deleted,
> *else*
> *if* node to be deleted is the first node, *then*,
> make the head to point to the second node,
> *else*
> delete the node from the body of the list.

End

The memory space of deleted node may be released for re-use. As in the case of insertion, the process of deletion also involves search for the item to be deleted.

Example 13.5

Write a function to delete a specified node.

A function to delete a specified node is given in Fig.13.9. The function first checks whether the specified item belongs to the first node. If yes, then the pointer to the second node is temporarily assigned the pointer variable **p**, the memory space occupied by the first node is freed and the location of the second node is assigned to **head**. Thus, the previous second node becomes the first node of the new list.

If the item to be deleted is not the first one, then we use the **find** function to locate the position of 'key node' containing the item to be deleted. The pointers are interchanged with the help of a temporary pointer variable making the pointer in the preceding node to point to the node following the key node. The memory space of key node that has been deleted is freed. The figure below shows the relative position of the key node.

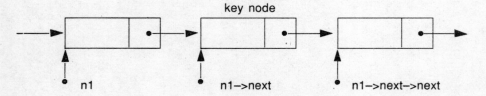

```
/*****************************************************************/
/*                 FUNCTION   DELETE                          */
/*****************************************************************/

node  *delete(node *head)
{
   node  *find(node *p, int a);
   int   key;          /*  item to be deleted */
   node  *n1;          /*  pointer to node preceding key  node */
   node  *p;           /*  temporary pointer */

   printf("\nWhat is the item (number) to be deleted? ");
   scanf("%d", &key);

   if(head->number == key)  /* first node to be deleted) */
   {
      p = head->next;     /* pointer to 2nd node in list */
      free(head);         /* release space of key node */
      head = p;           /* make head to point to 1st node*/
   }
   else                   /* find key node and delete it */
   {
      n1 = find(head, key);

      if(n1 == NULL)
         printf("\n key not found \n");
      else                /*  delete key node  */
      {
         p = n1->next->next;   /* pointer to the node
                                  following the key node */
         free(n1->next);       /* free key node */
         n1->next = p;         /* establish link */
      }
   }
   return(head);
}
              /* USE FUNCTION find() HERE */
```

Fig.13.9 *A function for deleting an item from linked list*

The execution of the following code deletes the key node.

```
p = n1->next->next;
free (n1->next);
n1->next = p;
```

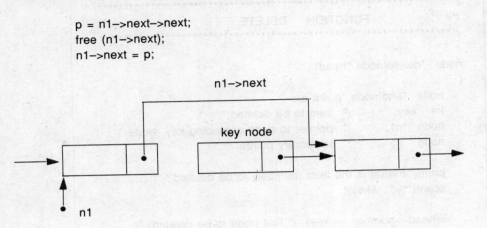

13.8 APPLICATION OF LINKED LISTS

Linked list concepts are useful to model many different abstract data types such as queues, stacks and trees.

If we restrict the process of insertions to one end of the list and deletions to the other end, then we have a model of a *queue*. That is, we can insert an item at the rear and remove an item at the front (see Fig.13.10a). This obeys the discipline of "first in, first out" (FIFO). There are many examples of queues in real-life applications.

If we restrict insertions and deletions to occur only at one end of lst, the beginning, then we model another data structure known as *stack*. Stacks are also referred to as *push-down* lists. An example of a stack is the "in" tray of a busy executive. The files pile up in the tray, and whenever the executive has time to clear the files, he takes it off from the top. That is, files are added at the top and removed from the top (see Fig.13.10b). Stacks are sometimes referred to as "last in, first out" (LIFO) structure.

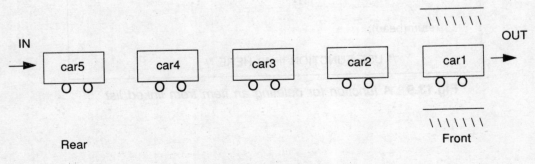

(a) Queue (Repair shop)

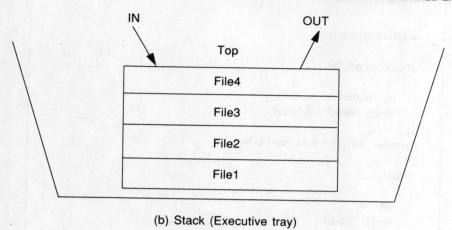

(b) Stack (Executive tray)

Fig.13.10 *Applications of linked lists*

Lists, queues and stacks are all inherently one-dimensional. A *tree* represents a two-dimensional linked list. Trees are frequently encountered in everyday life. One example is the organizational chart of a large company. Another example is the chart of sports tournaments.

CASE STUDIES

1. Insertion in a Sorted List

The task of inserting a value into the current location in a sorted linked list involves two operations:

1) Finding the node before which the new node has to be inserted. We call this node as 'Key node'.
2) Creating a new node with the value to be inserted and inserting the new node by manipulating pointers appropriately.

In order to illustrate the process of insertion, we use a sorted linked list created by the **create** function discussed in Example 13.3. Figure 13.11 shows a complete program that creates a list (using sorted input data) and then inserts a given value into the correct place using function **insert**.

```
Program

/*****************************************************************/
/*       INSERTING A NUMBER IN A SORTED LIST          */
/*****************************************************************/

#include <stdio.h>
#include <stdlib.h>
```

```
#define NULL 0

struct linked_list
{
    int   number;
    struct linked_list *next;
};
typedef  struct linked_list node;

main()
{
    int   n;
    node  *head;
    void  create(node *p);
    node  *insert(node *p, int n);
    void  print(node *p);


    head = (node *)malloc(sizeof(node));

    create(head);
    printf("\n");
    printf("Original list:  ");
    print(head);
    printf("\n\n");
    printf("Input number to be inserted: ");
    scanf("%d", &n);

    head = insert(head,n);

    printf("\n");
    printf("New list:  ");
    print(head);
}

void  create(node *list)
{
    printf("Input a number \n");
    printf("(type -999 at end):  ");
    scanf("%d", &list->number);

    if(lis->number == -999)
    {
      list->next = NULL;
    }
```

```
    else      /* create next node    */
    {
       list->next = (node *)malloc(sizeof(node));
       create(list->next);
    }
    return;
}

void print(node *list)
{
    if(list->next != NULL)
    {
     printf("%d- ->", list->number);

     if(list->next->next == NULL)
        printf("%d",list->next->number );

     print(list->next);
    }
    return;
}

node *insert(node *head,int x)
{
    node *p1,*p2,*p;
    p1 = NULL;
    p2 = head; /* p2 points to first node */

    for( ; p2->number < x ; p2 = p2->next )
    {
      p1 = p2;

      if(p2->next->next == NULL)
        {
        p2 = p2->next;   /* insertion at end */
        break;
        }
    }

    /* key node found and insert new node */

    p = (node *)malloc(sizeof (node));/* space for
                                  new node */
    p->number = x; /* place value in the new node */
```

```
        p–>next = p2; /*link new node to key node */

        if (p1 == NULL)
            head = p; /* new node becomes the first node */
        else
            p1–>next = p; /* new node inserted in middle */

        return (head);
}
```

Output

```
Input a number
(type –999 at end): 10
Input a number
(type –999 at end): 20
Input a number
(type –999 at end): 30
Input a number
(type –999 at end): 40
Input a number
(type –999 at end): –999

Original list:  10– –>20– –>30– –>40– –>–999

Input number to be inserted:  25

New list:  10– –>20– –>25– –>30– –>40– –>–999
```

Fig.13.11 *Inserting a number in a sorted linked list*

The function takes two arguments, one the value to be inserted and the other a pointer to the linked list. The function uses two pointers, **p1** and **p2** to search the list. Both the pointers are moved down the list with **p1** trailing **p2** by one node while the value **p2** points to is compared with the value to be inserted. The 'Key node' is found when the number **p2** points to is greater (or equal) to the number to be inserted.

Once the key node is found, a new node containing the number is created and inserted between the nodes pointed to by **p1** and **p2**. The figures below illustrate the entire process.

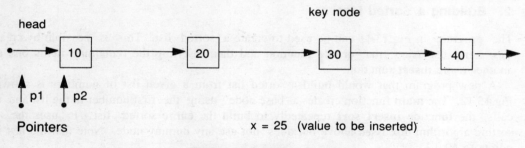

At the start of the search

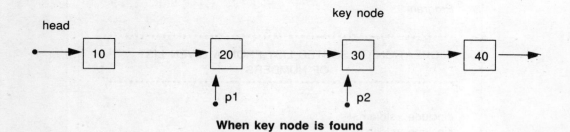

When key node is found

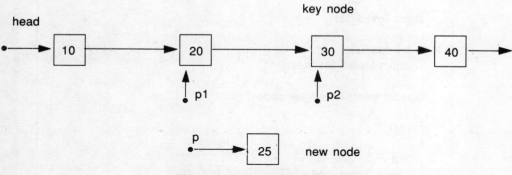

When new node is created

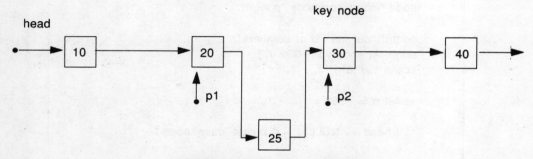

When new node is inserted

2. Building a Sorted List

The program in Fig.13.11 can be used to create a sorted list. This is possible by creating 'one item' list using the **create** function and then inserting the remaining items one after another using **insert** function.

A new program that would build a sorted list from a given list of numbers is shown in Fig.13.12. The **main** function creates a 'base node' using the first number in the list and then calls the function **insert_sort** repeatedly to build the entire sorted list. It uses the same sorting algorithm discussed above but does not use any dummy node. Note that the last item points to NULL.

```
Program

/*********************************************************************/
/*   CREATION OF SORTED LIST FROM A GIVEN LIST         */
/*                   OF NUMBERS                         */
/*********************************************************************/

#include <stdio.h>
#include <stdlib.h>
#define NULL 0

struct linked_list
{
   int number;
   struct linked_list *next;
};
typedef struct linked_list node;

main()
{
    int n;
    node *head = NULL;
    void print(node *p);
    node *insert_sort(node *p,int n);

    printf("Input the list of numbers.\n");
    printf("At end, type –999.\n");
    scanf("%d",&n);

    while( n != –999 )
    {
       if(head == NULL)      /* create 'base' node */
       {
             head = (node *)malloc(sizeof(node));
```

```
                    head->number = n;
                    head->next = NULL;
        }
        else                /* insert next item */
        {
            head = insert_sort(head,n);
        }

           scanf("%d", &n);
    }
    printf("\n");
    print(head);
    printf("\n");
}

node *insert_sort(node *list,int x)
{
    node *p1,*p2,*p;
    p1 = NULL;
    p2 = list; /* p2 points to first node */

    for( ; p2->number < x ;  p2 = p2->next )
    {
      p1 = p2;

      if( p2->next == NULL)
      {
              p2 = p2->next;         /* p2 set to NULL */
              break;          /* insert new node at end */
      }
    }

    /* key node found */
    p = (node *)malloc(sizeof(node));/*space for new node*/
    p->number = x;          /* place value in the new node */
    p->next = p2;           /* link new node to key node */

    if (p1 == NULL)
      list = p;      /* new node becomes the first node */
    else
      p1->next = p; /* new node inserted after 1st node */
    return (list);

}
```

```
void print(node *list)
{
    if(list == NULL)
      printf("NULL");
    else
    {
      printf("%d– –>",list–>number);
      print(list–>next);
    }

    return;
}
```

Output

Input the list of number.
At end, type –999.
80 70 50 40 60 –999

40– –>50– –>60– –>70– –>80– –>NULL

Input the list of number.
At end, type –999.
40 70 50 60 80 –999

40– –>50– –>60– –>70– –>80– –>NULL

Fig.13.12 *Creation of sorted list from a given list of numbers*

REVIEW QUESTIONS AND EXERCISES

13.1   What is dynamic memory allocation? How does it help in building complex programs?

13.2   What is the principal difference between the functions **malloc** and **calloc**.

13.3   Find errors, if any, in the following memory management statements:

(a)   *ptr = (int *)malloc(m, sieof(int));
(b)   table = (float *)calloc(100);
(c)   node = free(ptr);

13.4   Why a linked list is called a dynamic data structure? What are the advantages of using linked lists over arrays?

13.5   Describe different types of linked lists.

13.6   Identify errors, if any, in the following structure definition statements:

```
struct
{
        char  name[30]
        struct  *next;
};
typedef  struct  node;
```

13.7   The following code is defined in a header file *list.h*

```
typedef  struct
{
        char     name[15];
        int      age;
        float    weight;
} DATA;

struct  linked_list
{
        DATA person;
        struct  linked_list *next;
};

typedef  struct  linked_list  NODE;
typedef  NODE  *NDPTR;
```

Explain how could we use this header file for writing programs.

13.8   In Example 13.3, we have used **print()** in recursive mode. Rewrite this function using iterative technique in **for** loop.

13.9   Write a menu driven program to create a linked list of a class of students and perform the following operations:

(a) Write out the contents of the list.
(b) Edit the details of a specified student.
(c) Count the number of students above a specified age and weight.

Make use of the header file defined in Exercise 13.7.

13.10   Write recursive and nonrecursive functions for reversing the elements in a linear list. Compare the relative efficiencies of them.

13.11   Write an interactive program to create a linear linked list of customer names and their telephone numbers. The program should be menu driven and include features for adding a new customer and deleting an existing customer.

13.12   Modify the above program so that the list is always maintained in the alphabetical order of customer names.

13.13   Develop a program to combine two sorted lists to produce a third sorted list which contains one occurrence of each of the elements in the original lists.

13.14 Write a program to create a circular linked list so that the input order of data item is maintained. Add functions to carry out the following operations on circular linked list.

    (a) Count the number of nodes
    (b) Write out contents
    (c) Locate and write the contents of a given node

13.15 Write a program to construct an ordered doubly linked list and write out the contents of a specified node.

13.16 Write a function that would traverse a linear singly linked list in reverse and write out the contents in reverse order.

13.17 Given two ordered singly linked lists, write a function that will merge them into a third ordered list.

THE PREPROCESSOR

14.1 INTRODUCTION

C is a unique language in many respects. We have already seen features such as structures and pointers. Yet another unique feature of the C language is the *preprocessor*. The C preprocessor provides several tools that are unavailable in other high-level languages. The programmer can use these tools to make his program easy to read, easy to modify, portable, and more efficient.

The preprocessor, as its name implies, is a program that processes the source code before it passes through the compiler. It operates under the control of what is known as *preprocessor command lines* or *directives*. Preprocessor directives are placed in the source program before the **main** line. Before the source code passes through the compiler, it is examined by the preprocessor for any preprocessor directives. If there are any, appropriate actions (as per the directives) are taken and then the source program is handed over to the compiler.

Preprocessor directives follow special syntax rules that are different from the normal C syntax. They all begin with the symbol # in column one and do not require a semicolon at the end. We have already used the directives **#define** and **#include** to a limited extent. A set of commonly used preprocessor directives and their functions is given in Table 14.1. These directives can be divided into three categories:

1. Macro substitution directives.
2. File inclusion directives.
3. Compiler control directives.

The sections that follow describe the preprocessor directives in detail.

14.2 MACRO SUBSTITUTION

Macro substitution is a process where an identifier in a program is replaced by a predefined string composed of one or more tokens. The preprocessor accomplishes this task under the direction of **#define** statement. This statement, usually known as a *macro definition* (or simply a *macro*) takes the following general form:

> **#define** *identifier string*

Table 14.1   Preprocessor directives

Directive	Function
#define	Defines a macro substitution.
#undef	Undefines a macro.
#include	Specifies the files to be included.
#ifdef	Tests for a macro definition.
#endif	Specifies the end of #if.
#ifndef	Tests whether a macro is not defined.
#if	Tests a compile-time condition.
#else	Specifies alternatives when #if test fails.

If this statement is included in the program at the beginning, then the preprocessor replaces every occurrence of the *identifier* in the source code by the *string*. The keyword #**define** is written just as shown (starting from the first column) followed by the *identifier* and a *string*, with at least one blank space between them. Note that the definition is not terminated by a semicolon. The *string* may be any text, while the *identifier* must be a valid C name.

There are different forms of macro substitution. The most common forms are:

1. Simple macro substitution.
2. Argumented macro substitution.
3. Nested macro substitution.

Simple Macro Substitution

Simple string replacement is commonly used to define constants. Examples of definition of constants are:

```
#define    COUNT      100
#define    FALSE      0
#define    SUBJECTS   6
#define    PI         3.1415 926
#define    CAPITAL    "DELHI"
```

Notice that we have written all macros (identifiers) in capitals. It is a convention to write all macros in capitals to identify them as symbolic constants. A definition, such as

```
#define    M  5
```

will replace all occurrences of M with 5, starting from the line of definition to the end of the program. However, a macro inside a string does not get replaced. Consider the following two lines:

```
total  = M * value;
printf("M = %d\n", M);
```

These two lines would be changed during preprocessing as follows:

```
total  = 5 * value;
printf("M = %d\n", 5);
```

Notice that the string "M = %d\n" is left unchanged.

A macro definition can include more than a simple constant value. It can include expressions as well. Following are valid definitions:

```
#define    AREA      5 * 12.46
#define    SIZE      sizeof(int) * 4
#define    TWO-PI    2.0 * 3.1415596
```

Whenever we use expressions for replacement, care should be taken to prevent an unexpected order of evaluation. Consider the evaluation of the equation

ratio = D/A;

where **D** and **A** are macros defined as follows:

```
#define    D    45 − 22
#define    A    78 + 32
```

The result of the preprocessor's substitution for **D** and **A** is:

ratio = 45−22 / 78+32;

This is certainly different from the expected expression

(45−22)/(78+32)

Correct results can be obtained by using parentheses around the strings as shown below:

```
#define    D    (45−22)
#define    A    (78+32)
```

It is a wise practice to use parentheses for expressions used in macro definitions.

As mentioned earlier, the preprocessor performs a literal text substitution whenever the defined name occurs. This explains why we cannot use a semicolon to terminate the **#define** statement. This also suggests that we can use a macro to define almost anything. For example, we can use the definitions

```
#define    TEST     if(x>y)
#define    AND
#define    PRINT    printf("Very Good. \n");
```

to build a statement as follows:

TEST AND PRINT

The preprocessor would translate this line to

if(x>y) printf("Very Good.\n");

Some tokens of C syntax are confusing or are error-prone. For example, a common programming mistake is to use the token = in place of the token == in logical expressions. Similar is the case with the token **&&**. Following are a few definitions that might be useful in building error free and more readable programs:

```
#define    EQUALS       ==
#define    AND          &&
#define    OR           | |
#define    NOT_EQUAL    !=
#define    START        main( ){
```

#define	END	}
#define	MOD	%
#define	BLANK_LINE	printf("\n");
#define	INCREMENT	++

An example of the use of syntactic replacement is:

```
START
    .....
    .....
    if(total EQUALS 240 AND average EQUALS 60)
        INCREMENT count;
    .....
    .....
END
```

Macros with Arguments

The preprocessor permits us to define more complex and more useful form of replacements. It takes the form:

> #define identifier(f1, f2, ... , fn) string

Notice that there is no space between the macro *identifier* and the left parentheses. The identifiers f1, f2, ... , fn are the formal macro arguments that are analogous to the formal arguments in a function definition.

There is a basic difference between the simple replacement discussed above and the replacement of macros with arguments. Subsequent occurrence of a macro with arguments is known as a *macro call* (similar to a function call). When a macro is called, the preprocessor substitutes the *string*, replacing the formal parameters with the actual parameters. Here, the string behaves like a template.

A simple example of a macro with arguments is

> #define CUBE(x) (x*x*x)

If the following statement appears later in the program

> volume = CUBE(side);

then the preprocessor would expand this statement to:

> volume = (side * side * side);

Consider the following statement:

> volume = CUBE(a+b);

This would expand to:

> volume = (a+b * a+b * a+b);

which would obviously not produce the correct results. This is because the preprocessor performs a blind text substitution of the argument a+b in place of x. This shortcoming can be corrected by using parentheses for each occurrence of a formal argument in the *string*. Example:

#define CUBE(x) ((x) * (x) * (x))

This would result in correct expansion of **CUBE(a+b)** as shown below:

volume = ((a+b) * (a+b) * (a+b));

Remember to use parentheses for each occurrence of a formal argument, as well as the whole *string*.

Some commonly used definitions are:

#define	MAX(a,b)	(((a) > (b)) ? (a) : (b))
#define	MIN(a,b)	(((a) < (b)) ? (a) : (b))
#define	ABS(x)	(((x) > 0) ? (x) : (−(x)))
#define	STREQ(s1,s2)	(strcmp((s1), (s2)) == 0)
#define	STRGT(s1,s2)	(strcmp((s1), (s2)) > 0)

The argument supplied to a macro can be any series of characters. For example, the definition

#define PRINT(variable, format) printf("variable = %format \n",variable)

can be called-in by

PRINT(price × quantity, f);

The preprocessor will expand this as

printf("price × quantity = %f \n", price × quantity);

Note that the actual parameters are substituted for formal parameters in a macro call, although they are within a string. This definition can be used for printing integers and character strings as well.

Nesting of Macros

We can also use one macro in the definition of another macro. That is, macro definitions may be nested. For instance, consider the following macro definitions:

#define	M	5
#define	N	M+1
#define	SQUARE(x)	((x) * (x))
#define	CUBE(x)	(SQUARE(x) * (x))
#define	SIXTH(x)	(CUBE(x) * CUBE(x))

The preprocessor expands each **#define** macro, until no more macros appear in the text. For example, the last definition is first expanded into

((SQUARE(x) * (x)) * (SQUARE(x) * (x)))

Since **SQUARE(x)** is still a macro, it is further expanded into

((((x) * (x)) * (x)) * (((x) * (x)) * (x)))

which is finally evaluated as x^6.

Macros can also be used as parameters of other macros. For example, given the definitions of **M** and **N**, we can define the following macro to give the maximum of these two:

#define MAX(M,N) (((M) > (N)) ? (M) : (N))

Macro calls can be nested in much the same fashion as function calls. Example:

```
#define    HALF(x)      ( (x)/2.0)
#define    Y            HALF(HALF(x) )
```

Similarly, given the definition of MAX(a,b), we can use the following nested call to give the maximum of the three values x, y, and z:

```
MAX(x, MAX(y,z) )
```

Undefining a Macro

A defined macro can be undefined, using the statement

```
#undef identifier
```

This is useful when we want to restrict the definition only to a particular part of the program.

14.3 FILE INCLUSION

An external file containing functions or macro definitions can be included as a part of a program so that we need not rewrite those functions or macro definitions. This is achieved by the preprocessor directive

```
#include    "filename"
```

where *filename* is the name of the file containing the required definitions or functions. At this point, the preprocessor inserts the entire contents of *filename* into the source code of the program. When the *filename* is included within the double quotation marks, the search for the file is made first in the current directory and then in the standard directories.

Alternatively this directive can take the form

```
#include    <filename>
```

without double quotation marks. In this case, the file is searched only in the standard directories.

Nesting of included files is allowed. That is, an included file can include other files. However, a file cannot include itself.

If an included file is not found, an error is reported and compilation is terminated.

Let us assume that we have created the following three files:

SYNTAX.C	contains syntax definitions.
STAT.C	contains statistical functions.
TEST.C	contains test functions.

We can make use of a definition or function contained in any of these files by including them in the program as shown below:

```
#include    <stdio.h>
#include    "SYNTAX.C"
#include    "STAT.C"
```

```
#include        "TEST.C"
#define         M    100

main( )
{
    .....
    .....
    .....
}
```

14.4 COMPILER CONTROL DIRECTIVES

While developing large programs, you may face one or more of the following situations:

1. You have included a file containing some macro definitions. It is not known whether a particular macro (say, TEST) has been defined in that header file. However, you want to be certain that TEST is defined (or not defined).

2. Suppose a customer has two different types of computers and you are required to write a program that will run on both the systems. You want to use the same program, although certain lines of code must be different for each system.

3. You are developing a program (say, for sales analysis) for selling in the open market. Some customers may insist on having certain additional features. However, you would like to have a single program that would satisfy both types of customers.

4. Suppose you are in the process of testing your program, which is rather a large one. You would like to have **print** calls inserted in certain places to display intermediate results and messages in order to trace the flow of execution and errors, if any. Such statements are called 'debugging' statements. You want these statements to be a part of the program and to become 'active' only when you decide so.

One solution to these problems is to develop different programs to suit the needs of different situations. Another method is to develop a single, comprehensive program that includes all optional codes and then directs the compiler to skip over certain parts of source code when they are not required. Fortunately, the C preprocessor offers a feature known as *conditional compilation*, which can be used to 'switch' on or off a particular line or group of lines in a program.

Situation 1

This situation refers to the conditional definition of a macro. We want to ensure that the macro TEST is always defined, irrespective of whether it has been defined in the header file or not. This can be achieved as follows:

```
#include        "DEFINE.H"
#ifndef         TEST
#define         TEST    1
#endif
    .....
    .....
```

DEFINE.H is the header file that is supposed to contain the definition of **TEST** macro. The directive

        #ifndef   TEST

searches for the definition of **TEST** in the header file and *if not defined*, then all the lines between the **#ifndef** and the corresponding **#endif** directive are left 'active' in the program. That is, the preprocessor directive

        #define   TEST

is processed.

In case, the **TEST** has been defined in the header file, the **#ifndef** condition becomes *false*, therefore the directive **#define TEST** is ignored. Remember, you cannot simply write

        #define   TEST   1

because if **TEST** is already defined, an error will occur.

Similar is the case when we want the macro **TEST** never to be defined. Look at the following code:

```
.....
#ifdef      TEST
#undef      TEST
#endif
.....
.....
```

This ensures that even if **TEST** is defined in the header file, its definition is removed. Here again we cannot simply say

        #undef   TEST

because, if TEST is not defined, the directive is erroneous.

Situation 2

The main concern here is to make the program portable. This can be achieved as follows:

```
.....
.....
main( )
{
    .....
    .....
#ifdef IBM–PC
{
    .....
    .....            code for IBM_PC
    .....
}
#else {
    .....
    .....            code for HP machine
    .....
```

```
      }
      #endif
         .....
         .....
      }
```

If we want the program to run on IBM PC, we include the directive

#define   IBM–PC

in the program; otherwise we don't. Note that the compiler control directives are inside the function. Care must be taken to put the # character at column one.

The compiler compiles the code for IBM PC if **IBM–PC** is defined, or the code for the HP machine if it is not.

Situation 3

This is similar to the above situation and therefore the control directives take the following form:

```
      #ifdef  ABC
            group-A lines
      #else
            group-B lines
      #endif
```

Group-A lines are included if the customer **ABC** is defined. Otherwise, group-B lines are included.

Situation 4

Debugging and testing are done to detect errors in the program. While the compiler can detect syntactic and semantic errors, it cannot detect a faulty algorithm where the program executes, but produces wrong results.

The process of error detection and isolation begins with the testing of the program with a known set of test data. The program is divided down and **printf** statements are placed in different parts to see intermediate results. Such statements are called debugging statements and are not required once the errors are isolated and corrected. We can either delete all of them or, alternately, make them inactive using compiler control directives as shown below:

```
      .....
      .....
      #ifdef TEST
      {
            printf("Array elements \n");
            for (i = 0; i < m; i++)
              printf("x[%d] = %d\n", i, x[i]);
      }
      #endif
      .....
      .....
      #ifdef  TEST
            printf(.....);
      #endif
      .....
      .....
```

The statements between the directives **#ifdef** and **#endif** are included only if the macro **TEST** is defined. Once everything is O.K., delete or undefine the **TEST**. This makes the **#ifdef TEST** condition false and therefore all the debugging statements are left out.

The C preprocessor also supports a more general form of test condition – **#if** directive. This takes the following form:

```
#if constant expression
{
    statement-1;
    statement-2;
    .....
    .....
}
#endif
```

The *constant-expression* may be any logical expression such as

```
TEST  <=  3
(LEVEL  ==  1 || LEVEL  ==  2)
MACHINE  ==  'A'
```

If the result of the constant-expression is nonzero (true), then all the statements between the **#if** and **#endif** are included for processing; otherwise they are skipped. The names **TEST**, **LEVEL**, etc. may be defined as macros.

14.5 ANSI ADDITIONS

ANSI committee has added some more preprocessor directives to the existing list given in Table 14.1. They are:

#elif	Provides alternative test facility
#pragma	Specifies certain instructions
#error	Stops compilation when an error occurs

The ANSI standard also includes two new preprocessor operations:

#	Stringizing operator
##	Tokenpasting operator

#elif Directive

The **#elif** enables us to establish an "if..else..if.." sequence for testing multiple conditions. The general form of use of **#elif** is:

```
#if  expression 1
    statement sequence 1

#elif expression 2
    statement sequence 2

    . . . .

    . . . .

        #elif expression N
            statement sequence N
#endif
```

For example:

```
#if MACHINE == HCL
    #define FILE "hcl.h"

    #elif MACHINE == WIPRO
        #define FILE  "wipro.h"

        #elif MACHINE == DCM
            #define FILE "dcm.h"
#endif
#include FILE
```

#pragma Directive

The #pragma is an implementation oriented directive that allows us to specify various instructions to be given to the compiler. It takes the following form

```
#pragma  name
```

Where *name* is the name of the **pragma** we want. For example, under Microsoft C,

```
#pragma loop_opt(on)
```

causes loop optimization to be performed. It is ignored, if the compiler does not recognize it.

#error Directive

The **#error** directive is used to produce diagnostic messages during debugging. The general form is

```
#error   error message
```

When the **#error** directive is encountered, it displays the error message and terminates processing. Example.

```
#if !defined(FILE_G)
#error NO GRAPHICS FACILITY
#endif
```

Note that we have used a special processor operator **defined** along with **#if**. **defined** is a new addition and takes a *name* surrounded by parentheses. If a compiler does not support this, we can replace it as follows:

```
#if !defined    by    #ifndef
#if defined     by    #ifdef
```

Stringizing operator

ANSI C provides an operator # called *stringizing operator* to be used in the definition of macro functions. This operator allows a formal argument within a macro definition to be converted to a string. Consider the example below:

```
#define sum(xy) printf(#xy " = %f\n",xy)
main()
{
    . . . .
    . . . .
    sum(a+b);
    . . . .
}
```

The preprocessor will convert the line

```
sum(a+b);
```

into

```
printf("a+b" " = %f\n", a+b);
```

Which is equivalent to

```
printf("a+b = %f\n", a+b);
```

Note that the ANSI standard also stipulates that adjacent strings will be concatenated.

Token Pasting Operator

The token pasting oprator ## defined by ANSI standard enables us to combine two tokens within a macro definition to form a single token. For example:

```
#define  combine(s1,s2)  s1 ## s2
```

```
main()
{
    . . . .
    . . . .

    printf("%f", combine(total, sales));
    . . . .
}
```

The preprocessor transforms the statement

```
printf("%f", combine(total, sales));
```

into the statement

```
printf("%f", totalsales);
```

Consider another macro definition:

```
#define print(i) printf("a"#i " = %f", a##i)
```

This macro will convert the statement

```
print(5);
```

into the statement

```
printf(" a5 = %f", a5)
```

REVIEW QUESTIONS AND EXERCISES

14.1 Explain the role of the C preprocessor.

14.2 What is a macro and how is it different from a C variable name?

14.3 What precautions one should take when using macros with arguments?

14.4 What are the advantages of using macro definitions in a program?

14.5 When does a programmer use **#include** directive?

14.6 The value of a macro name cannot be changed during the running of a program. Comment?

14.7 What is conditional compilation? How does it help a programmer?

14.8 Distinguish between **#ifdef** and **#if** directives.

14.9 Comment on the following code fragment:

```
#if    0
{
    line-1;
    line-2;
    .....
    .....
    line-n;
}
#endif
```

14.10 Write a nested macro that gives the minimum of three values.

14.11 Define a macro, PRINT-VALUE which can be used to print two values of arbitrary type.

14.12 Identify errors, if any, in the following macro definitions:

    (a) `#define until(x)    while(!x)`
    (b) `#define ABS(x)    (x > 0) ? (x) : (−x)`
    (c) `#ifdef(FLAG)`
         `#undef   FLAG`
       `#endif`
    (d) `#if   n == 1 update(item)`
       `#else   print-out(item)`
       `#endif`

DEVELOPING A C PROGRAM: SOME GUIDELINES

15.1 INTRODUCTION

We have discussed so far various features of C language and are ready to write and execute programs of modest complexity. However, before attempting to develop complex programs, it is worthwhile to consider some programming techniques that would help design efficient and error-free programs.

The program development process includes three important stages, namely, program design, program coding and program testing. All the three stages contribute to the production of high-quality programs. In this chapter we shall discuss some of the techniques used for program design, coding and testing.

15.2 PROGRAM DESIGN

Program design is the foundation for a good program and is therefore an important part of the program development cycle. Before coding a program, the program should be well conceived and all aspects of the program design should be considered in detail.

Program design is basically concerned with the development of a strategy to be used in writing the program, in order to achieve the solution of a problem. This includes mapping out a solution procedure and the form the program would take. The program design involves the following stages:

1. Problem analysis.
2. Outlining the program structure.
3. Algorithm development.
4. Selection of control structures.

Problem Analysis

Before we think of a solution procedure to the problem, we must fully understand the nature of the problem and what we want the program to do. Without the comprehension and definition of the problem at hand, program design might turn into a hit-or-miss approach. We must carefully decide the following at this stage:

- What kind of data will go in,
- What kind of outputs are needed, and
- What are the constraints and conditions under which the program has to operate.

Outlining the Program Structure

Once we have decided what we want and what we have, then the next step is to decide how to do it. C as a structured language lends itself to a *top-down* approach. Top-down means decomposing of the solution procedure into tasks that form a hierarchical structure as shown in Fig. 15.1. The essence of the top-down design is to cut the whole problem into a number of independent constituent tasks, and then to cut the tasks into smaller subtasks, and so on, until they are small enough to be grasped mentally and to code easily. These tasks and subtasks can form the basis of functions in the program.

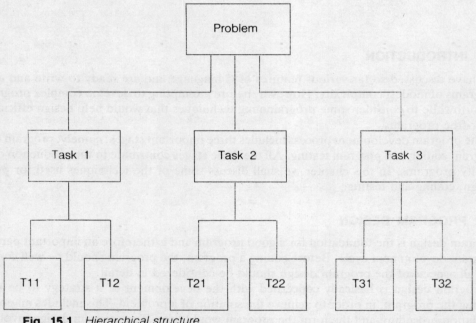

Fig. 15.1 *Hierarchical structure*

An important feature of this approach is that at each level, the details of the design of lower levels are hidden. The higher level functions are designed first, assuming certain broad tasks of the immediately lower level functions. The actual details of the lower level functions are not considered until that level is reached. Thus the design of functions proceeds from top to bottom, introducing progressively more and more refinements.

This approach will produce a readable and modular code that can be easily understood and maintained. It also helps us classify the overall functioning of the program in terms of lower-level functions.

Algorithm Development

After we have decided a solution procedure and an overall outline of the program, the next step is to work out a detailed definite, step-by-step procedure, known as *algorithm* for each function. The most common method of describing an algorithm is through the use of *flowcharts*. The other method is to write what is known as *pseudocode*. The flowchart presents the algorithm pictorially, while the pseudocode describe the solution steps in a logical order. Either method involves concepts of logic and creativity.

Since algorithm is the key factor for developing an efficient program, we should devote enough attention to this step. A problem might have many different approaches to its solution. For example, there are many sorting techniques available to sort a list. Similarly, there are many methods of finding the area under a curve. We must consider all possible approaches and select the one which is simple to follow, takes less execution time, and produces results with the required accuracy.

Control Structures

A complex solution procedure may involve a large number of control statements to direct the flow of execution. In such situations, indiscriminate use of control statements such as **goto** may lead to unreadable and uncomprehensible programs. It has been demonstrated that any algorithm can be structured, using the three basic control structures, namely, sequence structure, selection structure, and looping structure.

Sequence structure denotes the execution of statements sequentially one after another. Selection structure involves a decision, based on a condition and may have two or more branches which usually join again at a later point. **if...else** and **switch** statements in C can be used to implement a selection structure. Looping structure is used when a set of instructions is evaluated repeatedly. This structure can be implemented using **do**, **while**, or **for** statements.

A well designed program would provide the following benefits:

1. Coding is easy and error-free.
2. Testing is simple.
3. Maintenance is easy.
4. Good documentation is possible.
5. Cost estimates can be made more accurately.
6. Progress of coding may be controlled more precisely.

15.3 PROGRAM CODING

The algorithm developed in the previous section must be translated into a set of instructions that a computer can understand. The major emphasis in coding should be simplicity and clarity. A program written by one may have to be read by others later. Therefore, it should be readable and simple to understand. Complex logic and tricky coding should be avoided. The elements of coding style include internal documentation, construction of statements, generality of the program, and input/output formats.

Internal Documentation

Documentation refers to the details that describe a program. Some details may be built-in as an integral part of the program. These are known as internal documentation.

Two important aspects of internal documentation are, selection of meaningful variable names and the use of comments. Selection of meaningful names is crucial for understanding the program. For example,

area = breadth * length;

is more meaningful than

a = b * l;

Names that are likely to be confused must be avoided. The use of meaningful function names also aids in understanding and maintenance of programs.

Descriptive comments should be embedded within the body of source code to describe processing steps.

The following guidelines might help the use of comments judiciously:

1. Describe blocks of statements, rather than commenting on every line.
2. Use blank lines or indentation, so that comments are easily readable.
3. Use appropriate comments; an incorrect comment is worse than no comment at all.

Statement Construction

Although the flow of logic is decided during design, the construction of individual statements is done at the coding stage. Each statement should be simple and direct. While multiple statements per line are allowed, try to use only one statement per line with necessary indentation. Consider the following code:

```
if(quantity>0) { code = 0; quantity
= rate; } else { code = 1; sales = 0; }
```

Although it is perfectly valid, it could be reorganised as follows:

```
if(quantity>0)
{
    code = 0;
    quantity = rate;
}
else
{
    code = 1;
    sales = 0;
}
```

The general guidelines for construction of statements are:

1. Use one statement per line.
2. Use proper indentation when selection and looping structures are implemented.
3. Avoid heavy nesting of loops, preferably not more than three levels.
4. Use simple conditional tests; if necessary break complicated conditions into simple conditions.
5. Use parentheses to clarify logical and arithmetic expressions.
6. Use spaces, wherever possible, to improve readability.

Input/Output Formats

Input/output formats should be simple and acceptable to users. A number of guidelines should be considered during coding.

1. Keep formats simple.
2. Use end-of-file indicators, rather than the user requiring to specify the number of items.
3. Label all interactive input requests.
4. Label all output reports.
5. Use output messages when the output contains some peculiar results.

Generality of Programs

Care should be taken to minimize the dependence of a program on a particular set of data, or on a particular value of a parameter. Example:

```
for(sum  =  0, i  =  1; i  <=  10; i++)
         sum  =  sum+i;
```

This loop adds numbers 1, 2, ...,10. This can be made more general as follows:

```
sum  =  0;
for(i  =  m; i  <=  n; i  =  i+step);
         sum  =  sum + i;
```

The initial value **m**, the final value **n**, and the increment size **step** can be specified interactively during program execution. When m=2, n=100, and step = 2, the loop adds all even numbers upto, and including 100.

15.4 COMMON PROGRAMMING ERRORS

By now you must be aware that C has certain features that are easily amenable to bugs. Added to this, it does not check and report all kinds of run-time errors. It is therefore advisable to keep track of such errors and to see that these known errors are not present in the program. This section examines some of the more common mistakes that a less experienced C programmer could make.

Missing Semicolons

Every C statement must end with a semicolon. A missing semicolon may cause considerable confusion to the compiler and result in 'misleading' error messages. Consider the following statements:

```
a  =  x+y
b  =  m/n;
```

The compiler will treat the second line as a part of the first one and treat yb as a variable name. You may therefore get an "undefined name" error message in the second line. Note that both the message and location are incorrect. In such situations where there are no errors in a reported line, we should check the preceding line for a missing semicolon.

There may be an instance when a missing semicolon might cause the compiler to go 'crazy' and to produce a series of error messages. If they are found to be dubious errors, check for a missing semicolon in the beginning of the error list.

Misuse of Semicolon

Another common mistake is to put a semicolon in a wrong place. Consider the following code:

```
for(i = 1; i <= 10; i++);
    sum = sum + i;
```

This code is supposed to sum all the integers from 1 to 10. But what actually happens is that only the 'exit' value of i is added to the **sum**. Other examples of such mistake are:

```
1. while(x < MAX);
   {
       ...
       ...
   }
2. if(T >= 200);
   grade = 'A';
```

A simple semicolon represents a null statement and therefore it is syntactically valid. The compiler does not produce any error message. Remember, this kind of errors are worse than syntax errors.

Use of = instead of ==

It is quite possible to forget the use of double equal signs when we perform a relational test. Example:

```
if(code = 1)
    count++;
```

It is a syntactically valid statement. The variable **code** is assigned 1 and then, because **code = 1** is true, the **count** is incremented. In fact, the above statement does not perform any relational test on **code**. Irrespective of the previous value of **code**, **count++**; is always executed.

Similar mistakes can occur in other control statements, such as **for** and **while**. Such a mistake in the loop control statements might cause infinite loops.

Missing Braces

It is common to forget a closing brace when coding a deeply nested loop. It will be usually detected by the compiler because the number of opening braces should match with the closing ones. However, if we put a matching brace in a wrong place, the compiler won't notice the mistake and the program will produce unexpected results.

Another serious problem with the braces is, not using them when multiple statements are to be grouped together. For instance, consider the following statements:

```
for(i = 1; i <= 10; i++)
    sum1 = sum1 + i;
    sum2 = sum2 + i*i;
printf("%d %d\n", sum1, sum2);
```

This code is intended to compute **sum1**, **sum2** for i varying from 1 to 10, in steps of 1 and then to print their values. But, actually the **for** loop treats only the first statement, namely,

```
            sum1 = sum1 + i;
```

as its body and therefore the statement

```
            sum2 = sum2 + i*i;
```

is evaluated only once when the loop is exited. The correct way to code this segment is to place braces as follows:

```
for(i = 1; i <= 10; i++)
{
    sum1 = sum1 + i;
    sum2 = sum2 + i*i;
}
printf("%d %d\n", sum1, sum2);
```

In case, only one brace is supplied, the behaviour of the compiler becomes unpredictable.

Missing Quotes

Every string must be enclosed in double quotes, while a single character constant in single quotes. If we miss them out, the string (or the character) will be interpreted as a variable name. Examples:

```
    if(response == YES)      /* YES is a string            */
        grade = A;           /* A is a character constant */
```

Here YES and A are treated as variables and therefore, a message "undefined names" may occur.

Misusing Quotes

It is likely that we use single quotes whenever we handle single characters. Care should be exercised to see that the associated variables are declared properly. For example, the statement

```
    city = 'M';
```

would be invalid if **city** has been declared as a **char** variable with dimension (i.e., pointer to **char**).

Improper Comment Characters

Every comment should start with a /* and end with a */. Anything between them is ignored by the compiler. If we miss out the closing */, then the compiler searches for a closing */ further down in the program, treating all the lines as comments. In case, it fails to find a closing */, we may get an error message. Consider the following lines:

```
    .....
    /*      comment line 1
    statement1;
    statement2;

    /*      comment line 2 */
    statement3;
    .....
```

Since the closing */ is missing in the comment line 1, all the statements that follow, until the closing comment */ in comment line 2 are ignored.

We should remember that C does not support nested comments. Assume that we want to comment out the following segment:

```
.....
x = a−b;
y = c−d;
/* compute ratio */
ratio = x/y;
.....
.....
```

We may be tempted to add comment characters as follows:

```
        .....
/*  x = a−b;
    y = c−d;
    /* compute ratio */
    ratio = x/y; */
    .....
    .....
```

This is incorrect. The first opening comment matches with the first closing comment and therefore the lines between these two are ignored. The statement

ratio = x/y;

is not commented out. The correct way to comment out this segment is as shown below.

```
        .....
/*  x = a−b;
    y = c−d; */
/*  compute ratio  */
/*  ratio = x/y; */
    .....
```

Undeclared Variables

C requires every variable to be declared for its type, before it is used. During the development of a large program, it is quite possible to use a variable to hold intermediate results and to forget to declare it.

Forgetting the Precedence of Operators

Expressions are evaluated according to the precedence of operators. It is common among beginners to forget this. Consider the statement

if(value = product( ) >= 100)
        tax = 0.05 * value;

The call **product( )** returns the product of two numbers, which is compared to 100. If it is equal to or greater than 100, the relational test is true, and a 1 is assigned to **value**; otherwise a 0 is assigned. In either case, the only values **value** can take on are 1 or 0. This certainly is not what the programmer wanted.

The statement was actually expected to assign the value returned by **product( )** to **value** and then compare **value** with 100. If **value** was equal to or greater than 100, tax should have been computed, using the statement

tax = 0.05 * value;

The error is due to the higher precedence of the relational operator compared to the assignment operator. We can force the assignment to occur first by using parentheses as follows:

if((value = product( )) >= 100)
tax = 0.05 * value;

Similarly, the logical operators **&&** and ‖ have lower precedence than arithmetic and relational operators and among these two, **&&** has higher precedence than ‖. Try, if there is any difference between the following statements:

1. if(p > 50 ‖ c > 50 && m > 60 && T > 180)
   x = 1;
2. if((p > 50 ‖ c > 50) && m > 60 && T > 180)
   x = 1;
3. if((p > 50 ‖ c > 50 && m > 60) && T > 180)
   x = 1;

Ignoring the Order of Evaluation of Increment/Decrement Operators

We often use increment or decrement operators in loops. Example:

```
.....
i = 0;
while( (c = getchar( ) ) != '\n')
{
    string[i++] = c;
}
string[i-1] = '\n';
```

The statement **string[i++] = c;** is equivalent to:

```
string[i] = c;
i = i+1;
```

This is not the same as the statement **string[++i] = c;** which is equivalent to

```
i = i+1;
string[i] = c;
```

Forgetting to Declare Function Parameters

Remember to declare all function parameters in the function header.

Mismatching of Actual and Formal Parameter Types in Function Calls

When a function with parameters is called, we should ensure that the type of values passed, match with the type expected by the called function. Otherwise, erroneous results may occur. If necessary, we may use the *type cast* operator to change the type locally. Example:

$$y = \cos(\ (\textbf{double})x);$$

Nondeclaration of Functions

Every function that is called should be declared in the calling function for the type of value it returns. Consider the following program:

```
main( )
{
    float  a = 12.75;
    float  b = 7.36;
    printf("%f\n", division(a,b) );
}
double division(x,y)
float x, y;
{
    return(x/y);
}
```

The function returns a **double** type value but this fact is not known to the calling function and therefore it expects to receive an **int** type value. The program produces either meaningless results or error message such as "redefinition".

The function **division** is like any other variable for the **main** and therefore it should be declared as **double** in the **main**.

Now, let us assume that the function **division** is coded as follows:

```
division(x,y)
float x,y;
{
   return(x/y);
}
```

Although the values **x** and **y** are floats and the result of **x/y** is also float, the function returns only integer value because no type specifier is given in the function definition. This is wrong too. The function header should include the type specifier to force the function to return a particular type of value.

Missing & Operator in scanf Parameters

All non-pointer variables in a **scanf** call should be preceded by an **&** operator. If the variable **code** is declared as an integer, then the statement

```
scanf("%d", code);
```

is wrong. The correct one is

```
scanf("%d", &code);
```

Remember, the compiler will not detect this error and you may get a crazy output.

Crossing the Bounds of an Array

All C indices start from 0. A common mistake is to start the index from 1. For example, the segment

```
int  x[10], sum, i;
sum = 0;
for(i = 1; i <= 10; i++)
    sum = sum + x[i];
```

would not find the correct sum of the elements of array **x**. The **for** loop expressions should be corrected as follows:

```
for(i = 0; i < 10; i++)
```

Forgetting a Space for Null Character in a String

All character arrays are terminated with a null character and therefore their size should be declared to hold one character more than the actual string size.

Using Uninitialized Pointers

An uninitialized pointer points to garbage. The following program is wrong.

```
main( )
{
    int a, *ptr;
    a = 25;
    *ptr = a+5;
    .....
}
```

The pointer **ptr** has not been initialized.

Missing Indirection and Address Operators

Another common error is to forget to use the operators * and & in certain places. Consider the following program:

```
main( )
{
    int  m, *p1;
    m = 5;
    p1 = m;
    printf("%d\n", *p1);
}
```

This will print some unknown value because the pointer assignment

```
p1 = m;
```

is wrong. It should be:

```
p1 = &m;
```

Consider the following expression:

```
y = p1 + 10;
```

Perhaps, **y** was expected to be assigned the value at location **p1** plus 10. But it does not happen. **y** will contain some unknown address value. The above expression should be rewritten as

```
y = *p1 + 10;
```

Missing Parentheses in Pointer Expressions

The following two statements are not the same:

$$x = *p1 + 1;$$
$$x = *(p1 + 1);$$

The first statement would assign the value at location **p1** plus 1 to **x** while the second would assign the value at location **p1+1**.

Omitting Parentheses around Arguments in Macro Definitions

This would cause incorrect evaluation of expressions when the macro definition is substituted. Example:

$$\#\textbf{define} \quad f(x) \quad x * x + 1$$

The call

$$y = f(a+b);$$

will be evaluated as

$$y = a+b * a+b+1;$$

which is wrong.

Some other mistakes that we commonly make are:

- Wrong indexing of loops.
- Wrong termination of loops.
- Unending loops.
- Use of incorrect relational test.
- Failure to consider all possible conditions of a variable.
- Trying to divide by zero.
- Mismatching of data specifications and variables in **scanf** and **printf** statements.
- Forgetting truncation and rounding off errors.

15.5 PROGRAM TESTING AND DEBUGGING

Testing and debugging refer to the tasks of detecting and removing errors in a program, so that the program produces the desired results on all occasions. Every programmer should be aware of the fact that rarely does a program run perfectly the first time. No matter how thoroughly the design is carried out, and no matter how much care is taken in coding, one can never say that the program would be 100 per cent error-free. It is therefore necessary to make efforts to detect, isolate and correct any errors that are likely to be present in the program.

Types of Errors

We have discussed a number of common errors. There might be many other errors, some obvious and others not so obvious. All these errors can be classified under four types, namely, syntax errors, run-time errors, logical errors, and latent errors.

Syntax errors: Any violation of rules of the language results in syntax errors. The compiler can detect and isolate such errors. When syntax errors are present, the compilation fails and is terminated after listing the errors and the line numbers in the source program, where the errors have occurred. Remember, in some cases, the line number may not exactly indicate the place of the error. In other cases, one syntax error may result in a long list of errors. Correction of one or two errors at the beginning of the program may eliminate the entire list.

Run-time errors: Errors such as a mismatch of data types or referencing an out-of-range array element go undetected by the compiler. A program with these mistakes will run, but produce erroneous results and therefore the name run-time errors. Isolating a run-time error is usually a difficult task.

Logical errors: As the name implies, these errors are related to the logic of the program execution. Such actions as taking a wrong path, failure to consider a particular condition, and incorrect order of evaluation of statements belong to this category. Logical errors do not show up as compiler-generated error messages. Rather, they cause incorrect results. These errors are primarily due to a poor understanding of the problem, incorrect translation of the algorithm into the program and a lack of clarity of hierarchy of operators. Consider the following statement:

if(x == y)
printf("They are equal \n");

When **x** and **y** are float type values, they rarely become equal, due to truncation errors. The **printf** call may not be executed at all. A test like **while(x != y)** might create an infinite loop.

Latent errors: It is a 'hidden' error that shows up only when a particular set of data is used. For example, consider the following statement:

ratio = (x+y) / (p−q);

An error occurs only when p and q are equal. An error of this kind can be detected only by using all possible combinations of test data.

Program Testing

Testing is the process of reviewing and executing a program with the intent of detecting errors, which may belong to any of the four kinds discussed above. We know that while the compiler can detect syntactic and semantic errors, it cannot detect run-time and logical errors that show up during the execution of the program. Testing, therefore, should include necessary steps to detect all possible errors in the program. It is, however, important to remember that it is impractical to find all errors. Testing process may include the following two stages:

1. Human testing.
2. Computer-based testing.

Human testing is an effective error-detection process and is done before the computer-based testing begins. Human testing methods include code inspection by the programmer, code inspection by a test group, and a review by a peer group. The test is carried out statement by statement and is analyzed with respect to a checklist of common programming errors. In addition to finding the errors, the programming style and choice of algorithm are also reviewed.

Computer-based testing involves two stages, namely, compiler testing and run-time testing. Compiler testing is the simplest of the two and detects yet undiscovered syntax errors. The program executes when the compiler detects no more errors. Should it mean that the program is correct? Will it produce the expected results? The answer is negative. The program may still contain run-time and logic errors.

Run-time errors may produce run-time error messages such as "null pointer assignment" and "stack overflow". When the program is free from all such errors, it produces output which might or might not be correct. Now comes the crucial test, the test for the *expected output*. The goal is to ensure that the program produces expected results under all conditions of input data.

Test for correct output is done using *test data* with known results for the purpose of comparison. The most important consideration here is the design or invention of effective test data. A useful criteria for test data is that all the various conditions and paths that the processing may take during execution must be tested.

Program testing can be done either at module (function) level or at program level. Module level test, often known as *unit test*, is conducted on each of the modules to uncover errors within the boundary of the module. Unit testing becomes simple when a module is designed to perform only one function.

Once all modules are unit tested, they should be *integrated together* to perform the desired function(s). There are likely to be interfacing problems, such as data mismatch between the modules. An *integration test* is performed to discover errors associated with interfacing.

Program Debugging

Debugging is the process of isolating and correcting the errors. One simple method of debugging is to place print statements throughout the program to display the values of variables. It displays the dynamics of a program and allows us to examine and compare the information at various points. Once the location of an error is identified and the error corrected, the debugging statements may be removed. We can use the conditional compilation statements discussed in Chapter 14 to switch on or off the debugging statements.

Another approach is to use the process of *deduction*. The location of an error is arrived at using the process of elimination and refinement. This is done using a list of possible causes of the error.

The third error-locating method is to *backtrack* the incorrect results through the logic of the program until the mistake is located. That is, beginning at the place where the symptom has been uncovered, the program is traced backward until the error is located.

15.6 PROGRAM EFFICIENCY

Two critical resources of a computer system are **execution time** and **memory**. The efficiency of a program is measured in terms of these two resources. Efficiency can be improved with good design and coding practices.

Execution Time

The execution time is directly tied to the efficiency of the algorithm selected. However, certain coding techniques can considerably improve the execution efficiency. The following are some of the techniques which could be applied while coding the program.

1. Select the fastest algorithm possible.
2. Simplify arithmetic and logical expressions.
3. Use fast arithmetic operations, whenever possible.
4. Carefully evaluate loops to avoid any unnecessary calculations within the loops.
5. If possible, avoid the use of multi-dimensional arrays.
6. Use pointers for handling arrays and strings.

However, remember the following, while attempting to improve efficiency.

1. Analyse the algorithm and various parts of the program before attempting any efficiency changes.
2. Make it work before making it faster.
3. Keep it right while trying to make it faster.
4. Do not sacrifice clarity for efficiency.

Memory Requirement

Memory restrictions in the microcomputer environment is a real concern to the programmer. It is therefore desirable to take all necessary steps to compress memory requirements.

1. Keep the program simple. This is the key to memory efficiency.
2. Use an algorithm that is simple and requires less steps.
3. Declare arrays and strings with correct sizes.
4. When possible, limit the use of multi-dimensional arrays.
5. Try to evaluate and incorporate memory compression features available with the language.

REVIEW QUESTIONS AND EXERCISES

15.1 Discuss the various aspects of program design.

15.2 How does program design relate to program efficiency?

15.3 Readability is more important than efficiency. Comment.

15.4 Distinguish between the following:

(a) Syntactic errors and semantic errors.
(b) Run-time errors and logical errors.
(c) Run-time errors and latent errors.
(d) Debugging and testing.
(e) Compiler testing and run-time testing.

15.5 A program has been compiled and linked successfully. When you run this program you face one or more of the following situations.

(a) Program is executed but no output.
(b) It produces incorrect answers.
(c) It does not stop running.

What are the possible causes in each case and what steps would you take to correct them?

15.6 List five common programming mistakes. Write a small program containing these errors and try to locate them with the help of computer.

15.7 In a program, two values are compared for convergence, using the statement

$$\text{if(} (x-y) < 0.00001) \ .....$$

Does the statement contain any error? If yes, explain the error.

15.8 A program contains the following **if** statements:

```
.....
.....
if(x > 1 && y == 0) p = p/x;
if(x == 5 || p > 2) p = p+2;
.....
.....
```

Draw a flowchart to illustrate various logic paths for this segment of the program and list test data cases that could be used to test the execution of every path shown.

15.9 Given below is a function to compute the yth power of an integer x.

```
power(x,y)
int x, y;
{
    int p;
    p = y;
    while(y > 0)
        x *= y--;
    return(x);
}
```

This function contains some bugs. Write a test procedure to locate the errors with the help of a computer.

15.10 A program reads three values from the terminal, representing the lengths of three sides of a box namely length, width, and height and prints a message stating whether the box is a cube, rectangle, or semi-rectangle. Prepare sets of data that you feel would adequately test this program.

APPENDIX-I
BIT-LEVEL PROGRAMMING

1. INTRODUCTION

One of the unique features of C language as compared to other high-level languages is that it allows direct manipulation of individual bits within a word. Bit-level manipulations are used in setting a particular bit or group of bits to 1 or 0. They are also used to perform certain numerical computations faster. As pointed out in Chapter 3, C supports the following operators:

1. Bitwise logical operators
2. Bitwise shift operators
3. One's complement operator

All these operators work only on integer type operands.

2. BITWISE LOGICAL OPERATORS

There are three logical bitwise operators. They are:

● *Bitwise* AND (&)
● *Bitwise* OR (|)
● *Bitwise exclusive* OR (^)

These are binary operators and require two integer-type operands. These operators work on their operands bit by bit starting from the least significant (i.e. the rightmost) bit, setting each bit in the result as shown in Table 1.

Table 1 Result of Logical Bitwise Operations

op1	op2	op1 & op2	op1 | op2	op1 ^ op2
1	1	1	1	0
1	0	0	1	1
0	1	0	1	1
0	0	0	0	0

Bitwise AND

The bitwise AND operator is represented by a single ampersand (&) and is surrounded on both sides by integer expressions. The result of ANDing operation is 1 if both the bits have a value of 1; otherwise it is 0. Let us consider two variables **x** and **y** whose values are 13 and 25. The binary representation of these two variables are

$$x - - -> \quad 0000\ 0000\ 0000\ 1101$$
$$y - - -> \quad 0000\ 0000\ 0001\ 1001$$

If we execute statement

$$z = x\ \&\ y\ ;$$

then the result would be:

$$z - - -> \quad 0000\ 0000\ 0000\ 1001$$

Although the resulting bit pattern represents the decimal number 9, there is no apparent connection between the decimal values of these three variables.

Bitwise ANDing is often used to test whether a particular bit is 1 or 0. For example, the following program tests whether the fourth bit of the variable **flag** is 1 or 0.

```
#define  TEST  8 /* represents 00.......01000 */
main()
{
        int  flag;
        . . . .
        . . . .

        if((flag & TEST) != 0)  /* test 4th bit */
        {
           printf(" Fourth bit is set \n");
        }
        . . . .
        . . . .
}
```

Note that the bitwise logical operators have lower precedence than the relational operators and therefore additional parantheses are necessary as shown above.

The following program tests whether a given number is odd or even.

```
main()
{
        int  test = 1;
        int  number;

        printf("Input a number \n");
        scanf("%d", &number);

        while(number != -1)
```

```
                    {
                        if(number & test)
                            printf("Number is odd\n\n");
                        else
                            printf("Number is even\n\n");

                        printf("Input a number \n");
                        scanf("%d", &number);
                    }
            }
```

Output

```
Input a number
20
Number is even

Input a number
9
Number is odd

Input a number
-1
```

Bitwise OR

The bitwise OR is represented by the symbol | (vertical bar) and is surrounded by two integer operands. The result of OR operation is 1 if *at least* one of the bits has a value of 1; otherwise it is zero. Consider the variables **x** and **y** discussed above.

```
x - - ->        0000 0000 0000 1101
y - - ->        0000 0000 0001 1001
          _____

x|y - - ->      0000 0000 0001 1101
          _____
```

The bitwise inclusion OR operation is often used to set a particular bit to 1 in a flag. Example:

```
            #define SET 8

            main()
            {
                int  flag;
                . . . .
                . . . .

                flag = flag | SET;

                if(( flag & SET) != 0)
```

```
            {
                printf("flag is set \n");
            }
            . . . .
            . . . .
        }
```

The statement

flag = flag | SET;

causes the fourth bit of **flag** to set 1 if it is 0 and does not change it if it is already 1.

Bitwise Exclusive OR

The bitwise *exclusive* OR is represented by the symbol ^. The result of exclusive OR is 1 if *only one* of the bits is 1; otherwise it is 0. Consider again the same variables **x** and **y** discussed above.

x – – –>	0000 0000 0000 1101
y – – –>	0000 0000 0001 1001
x^y – – –>	0000 0000 0001 0100

3. BITWISE SHIFT OPERATORS

The shift operators are used to move bit patterns either to the left or to the right. The shift operators are represented by the symbols << and >> and are used in the following form:

Left shift :   *op* **<<** *n*

Right shift: *op* **>>** *n*

op is the integer expression that is to be shifted and *n* is the number of bit positions to be shifted.

The left-shift operation causes all the bits in the operand *op* to be shifted to the left by *n* positions. The leftmost *n* bits in the original bit pattern will be lost and the rightmost *n* bit positions that are vacated will be filled with 0s.

Similarly, the right-shift operation causes all the bits in the operand *op* to be shifted to the right by *n* positions. The rightmost *n* bits will be lost . The leftmost *n* bit positions that are vacated will be filled with zero, if the *op* is an *unsigned integer*. If the variable to be shifted is **signed**, then the operation is machine dependent.

Both the operands *op* and *n* can be constants or variables. There are two restrictions on the value of *n*. It may not be negative and it may not exceed the number of bits used to represent the left operand *op*.

Let us suppose **x** is an unsigned integer whose bit pattern is

0100 1001 1100 1011

then,

vacated
positions

x << 3 =   0100 1110 0101 1̄0̄0̄0̄

x >> 3 =   0̲0̲0̲0̲ 1001 0011 1001
          vacated
          positions

Shift operators are often used for multiplication and division by powers of two.

Consider the following statement:

$$x = y << 1;$$

This statement shifts one bit to the left in y and then the result is assigned to x. The decimal value of x will be the value of y multiplied by 2. Similarly, the statement

$$x = y >> 1;$$

shifts y one bit to the right and assigns the result to x. In this case, the value of x will be the value of y divided by 2.

The shift operators, when combined with the logical bitwise operators, are useful for extracting data from an integer field that holds multiple pieces of information. This process is known as *masking*. Masking is discussed in Section 5.

4. BITWISE COMPLEMENT OPERATORS

The complement operator ~ (also called the one's complement operator) is an unary operator and inverts all the bits represented by its operand. That is, 0s become 1s and 1s become zero. Example:

x   = 1001 0110 1100 1011
~x = 0110 1001 0011 0100

This operator is often combined with the bitwise AND operator to turn off a particular bit. For example, the statements

x = 8;   /* 0000 0000 0000 1000 */
flag = flag & ~x;

would turn off the fourth bit in the variable **flag**.

5. MASKING

Masking refers to the process of extracting desired bits from (or transforming desired bits in) a variable by using logical bitwise operation. The operand (a constant or variable) that is used to perform masking is called the *mask*. Examples:

```
y = x & mask;
y = x | mask;
```

Masking is used in many different ways.

- To decide bit pattern of an integer variable.
- To.copy a portion of a given bit pattern to a new variable, while the remainder of the new variable is filled with 0s (using bitwise AND).
- To copy a portion of a given bit pattern to a new variable, while the remainder of the new variable is filled with 1s (using bitwise OR).
- To copy a portion of a given bit pattern to a new variable, while the remainder of the original bit pattern is inverted within the new variable (using bitwise *exclusive* OR).

The following function uses a mask to display the bit pattern of a variable.

```
void bit_pattern(int u)
{
        int   i, x, word;
        unsigned mask;

        mask = 1;
        word = 8 * sizeof(int);
        mask =   mask << (word − 1);
                  /* shift 1 to the leftmost position */

        for(i = 1; i<= word; i++)
        {
            x = (u & mask) ? 1 : 0;  /* identify the bit */
            printf("%d", x);  /* print bit value */
            mask >>= 1;  /* shift mask by 1 position to right */
        }
}
```

APPENDIX-II
ASCII VALUES OF CHARACTERS

ASCII Value	Character	ASCII Value	Character	ASCII Value	Character	ASCII Value	Character
000	NUL	032	blank	064	@	096	`
001	SOH	033	!	065	A	097	a
002	STX	034	"	066	B	098	b
003	ETX	035	#	067	C	099	c
004	EOT	036	$	068	D	100	d
005	ENQ	037	%	069	E	101	e
006	ACK	038	&	070	F	102	f
007	BEL	039	'	071	G	103	g
008	BS	040	(	072	H	104	h
009	HT	041	)	073	I	105	i
010	LF	042	*	074	J	106	j
011	VT	043	+	075	K	107	k
012	FF	044	,	076	L	108	l
013	CR	045	−	077	M	109	m
014	SO	046	.	078	N	110	n
015	SI	047	/	079	O	111	o
016	DLE	048	0	080	P	112	p
017	DC1	049	1	081	Q	113	q
018	DC2	050	2	082	R	114	r
019	DC3	051	3	083	S	115	s
020	DC4	052	4	084	T	116	t
021	NAK	053	5	085	U	117	u
022	SYN	054	6	086	V	118	v
023	ETB	055	7	087	W	119	w
024	CAN	056	8	088	X	120	x
025	EM	057	9	089	Y	121	y
026	SUB	058	:	090	Z	122	z
027	ESC	059	;	091	[	123	{
028	FS	060	<	092	\	124		
029	GS	061	=	093	]	125	}
030	RS	062	>	094	↑	126	~
031	US	063	?	095	-	127	DEL

Note:The first 32 characters and the last character are control characters; they cannot be printed.

APPENDIX-III
ANSI C LIBRARY FUNCTIONS

The C language is accompanied by a number of library functions that perform various tasks. The ANSI committee has standardized header files which contain these functions. What follows is a list of commonly used functions and the header files where they are defined. For a more complete list, the reader should refer to the manual of the version of C that is being used.

The header files that are included in this Appendix are:

<ctype.h>	Character testing and conversion functions
<math.h>	Mathematical functions
<stdio.h>	Standard I/O library functions
<stdlib.h>	Utility functions such as string conversion routines, memory allocation routines, random number generator, etc.
<string.h>	String manipulation functions
<time.h>	Time manipulation functions

Note: The following function parameters are used:

c   -   character type argument
d   -   double precision argument
f   -   file argument
i   -   integer argument
l   -   long integer argument
p   -   pointer argument
s   -   string argument
u   -   unsigned integer argument
An asterisk (*) denotes a pointer

Function	Data type returned	Task
<ctype.h>		
isalnum(c)	int	Determine if argument is alphanumberic. Return nonzero value if true; 0 otherwise.
isalpha(c)	int	Determine if argument is alphabetic. Return nonzero value if true; 0 otherwise.
isascii(c)	int	Determine if argument is an ASCII character. Return nonzero value if true; 0 otherwise.
iscntrl(c)	int	Determine if argument is an ASCII control character. Return nonzero value if true; 0 otherwise.
isdigit(c)	int	Determine if argument is a decimal digit. Return nonzero value if true; 0 otherwise.
isgraph(c)	int	Determine if argument is a graphic printing ASCII character. Return nonzero value if true; 0 otherwise.
islower(c)	int	Determine if argument is lowercase. Return nonzero value if true; 0 otherwise.
isodigit(c)	int	Determine if argument is an octal digit. Return nonzero value if true; 0 otherwise.
isprint(c)	int	Determine if argument is a printing ASCII character. Return nonzero value if true; 0 otherwise.
ispunct(c)	int	Determine if argument is a punctuation character. Return nonzero value if true; 0 otherwise.
isspace(c)	int	Determine if argument is a whitespace character. Return nonzero value if true; 0 otherwise.
isupper(c)	int	Determine if argument is uppercase. Return nonzero value if true; 0 otherwise.
isxdigit(c)	int	Determine if argument is a hexadecimal digit. Return nonzero value if true; 0 otherwise.
toascii(c)	int	Convert value of argument to ASCII.
tolower(c)	int	Convert letter to lowercase.
toupper(c)	int	Convert letter to uppercase.
<math.h>		
acos(d)	double	Return the arc cosine of d.
asin(d)	double	Return the arc sine of d.
atan(d)	double	Return the arc tangent of d.
atan2(d1,d2)	double	Return the arc tangent of d1/d2.
ceil(d)	double	Return a value rounded up to the next higher integer.
cos(d)	double	Return the cosine of d.
cosh(d)	double	Return the hyperbolic cosine of d.
exp(d)	double	Raise e to the power d.
fabs(d)	double	Return the absolute value of d.
floor(d)	double	Return a value rounded down to the next lower integer.

fmod(d1,d2)	double	Return the remainder of d1/d2 (with same sign as d1).
labs(l)	long int	Return the absolute value of l.
log(d)	double	Return the natural logarithm of d.
log10(d)	double	Return the logarithm (base 10) of d.
pow(d1,d2)	double	Return d1 raised to the d2 power.
sin(d)	double	Return the sine of d.
sinh(d)	double	Return the hyperbolic sine of d.
sqrt(d)	double	Return the square root of d.
tan(d)	double	Return the tangent of d.
tanh(d)	double	Return the hyperbolic tangent of d.

<stdio.h>

fclose(f)	int	Close file f. Return 0 if file is successfully closed.
feof(f)	int	Determine if an end-of-file condition has been reached. If so, return a nonzero value; otherwise, return 0.
fgetc(f)	int	Enter a single character form file f.
fgets(s, i, f)	char*	Enter string s, containing i characters, from file f.
fopen(s1,s2)	file*	Open a file named s1 of type s2. Return a pointer to the file.
fprintf(f,...)	int	Send data items to file f.
fputc(c,f)	int	Send a single character to file f.
fputs(s,f)	int	Send string s to file f.
fread(s,i1,i2,f)	int	Enter i2 data items, each of size i1 bytes, from file f to string s.
fscanf(f,...)	int	Enter data items from file f
fseek(f,l,i)	int	Move the pointer for file f a distance l bytes from location i.
ftell(f)	long int	Return the current pointer position within file f.
fwrite(s,i1,i2,f)	int	Send i2 data items, each of size i1 bytes from string s to file f.
getc(f)	int	Enter a single character from file f.
getchar(void)	int	Enter a single character from the standard input device.
gets(s)	char*	Enter string s from the standard input device.
printf(...)	int	Send data items to the standard output device.
putc(c,f)	int	Send a single character to file f.
putchar(c)	int	Send a single character to the standard output device.
puts(s)	int	Send string s to the standard output device.
rewind(f)	void	Move the pointer to the beginning of file f.
scanf(...)	int	Enter data items from the standard input device.

<stdlib.h>

abs(i)	int	Return the absolute value of i.
atof(s)	double	Convert string s to a adouble-precision quantity.
atoi(s)	int	Convert string s to an integer
atol(s)	long	Convert string s to a long integer.
calloc(u1,u2)	void*	Allocate memory for an array having u1 elements, each of length u2 bytes. Return a pointer to the beginning of the allocated space.
exit(u)	void	Close all files and buffers, and terminate the program. (Value of u is assigned by the function, to indicate termination status.)

free(p)	void	Free a block of allocated memory whose beginning is indicated by p.
malloc(u)	void*	Allocate u bytes of memory. Return a pointer to the beginning of the allocated space.
rand(void)	int	Return a random positive integer.
realloc(p, u)	void*	Allocate u bytes of new memory to the pointer variable p. Return a pointer to the beginning of the new memory space.
srand(u)	void	Initialize the random number generator.
system(s)	int	Pass command string s to the operating system. Return 0 if the command is successfully executed; otherwise, return a nonzero value typically −1.

<string.h>

strcmp(s1,s2)	int	Compare two strings lexicographically. Return a negative value if s1<s2; 0 if s1 and s2 are identical; and a positive value if s1>s2.
strcmpi(s1, s2)	int	Compare two strings lexicographically, without regard to case. Return a negative value if s1<s2; 0 if s1 and s2 are identical; and a value if s1 > s2.
strcpy(s1, s2)	char*	Copy string s2 to string s1.
strlen(s)	int	Return the number of characters in string s.
strset(s, c)	char*	Set all characters within s to c(excluding the terminating null character \0).

<time.h>

difftime(l1,l2)	double	Return the time difference l1 ~ l2, Where l1 and l2 represent elapsed times beyond a designated base time(see the time function).
time(p)	long int	Return the number of seconds elapsed beyond a designated base time.

BIBLIOGRAPHY

Barkakati, N., *Microsoft C Bible*, SAMS, 1990.

Barker, L., *C Tools for Scientists and Engineers*, McGraw-Hill, 1989.

Berry, R. E. and Meekings, B.A.E., *A Book on C*, Macmillan, 1987.

Hancock, L. and Krieger, M., *The C Primer*, McGraw-Hill, 1987.

Hunt, W. J., *The C Toolbox*, Addison-Wesley, 1985.

Hunter, B. H., *Understanding C*, Sybex, 1985.

Kernighan, B. W. and Ritchie, D. M., *The C Programming Language*, Prentice-Hall, 1977.

Kochan, S. G., *Programming in C*, Hyden, 1983.

Miller, L. H. and Quilici, E. A., *C Programming Language: An Applied Perspective*, John Wiley & Sons, 1987.

Purdum, J. J., *C Programming Guide*, Que Corporation, 1985.

Radcliffe, R. A., *Encyclopaedia C*, Sybex, 1990.

Schildt, H., *C Made Easy*, Osborne McGraw-Hill, 1987.

Schildt, H., *Advanced C*, Osborne McGraw-Hill, 1988.

Tim Grady, M., *Turbo C! Programming Principles and Practices*, McGraw-Hill, 1989.

WSI Staff, *C User's Handbook*, Addison-Wesely, 1984.

Wortman, L.A., and Sidebottom, T.O., *The C Programming Tutor*, Prentice-Hall, 1984.

INDEX